Democracy and Authoritarianism in the Postcommunist World

Edited by

VALERIE BUNCE
Cornell University

MICHAEL McFAUL
Stanford University

KATHRYN STONER-WEISS
Stanford University

CAMBRIDGE
UNIVERSITY PRESS

CAMBRIDGE UNIVERSITY PRESS
Cambridge, New York, Melbourne, Madrid, Cape Town, Singapore,
São Paulo, Delhi, Dubai, Tokyo

Cambridge University Press
32 Avenue of the Americas, New York, NY 10013-2473, USA

www.cambridge.org
Information on this title: www.cambridge.org/9780521133081

First published 2010

Printed in the United States of America

A catalog record for this publication is available from the British Library.

Library of Congress Cataloging in Publication data

Democracy and authoritarianism in the postcommunist world / edited by
Valerie Bunce, Michael McFaul, Kathryn Stoner-Weiss.
    p.   cm.
Includes bibliographical references and index.
ISBN 978-0-521-11598-8 (hardback) – ISBN 978-0-521-13308-1 (pbk.)
    1. Former communist countries – Politics and government.   2. Democracy –
Former communist countries.   3. Authoritarianism – Former communist
countries.   I. Bunce, Valerie, 1949–   II. McFaul, Michael, 1963–
III. Stoner-Weiss, Kathryn, 1965–   IV. Title
JN96.A58D423   2010
320.9171′7 – dc22   2009019255

ISBN   978-0-521-11598-8 Hardback
ISBN   978-0-521-13308-1 Paperback

Contents

Prologue

Waves and Troughs of Democracy and Dictatorship

Valerie Bunce, Michael McFaul,
and Kathryn Stoner-Weiss

DIVERSITY AND TYPICALITY

The experiences of postcommunist Europe and Eurasia over the past two decades contain important lessons about democratization – not just the rise, development, and cross-national spread of democratic orders, but also, just as importantly, the limits of democratic change, the sources of democratic breakdown, and the resilience of authoritarianism. This region is ideal for enriching our understanding of both regime stability and change because it provides the ingredients we need to assess hypotheses and draw generalizations. Thus, although this region shares the important commonality of a communist past, it is also composed, at the same time, of an unusually diverse set of countries, and the differences among them relate precisely to the areas that have figured prominently in debates about the rise and sustainability of democracy. For example, the twenty-nine states that compose this region include both old and new states (with the newest recruits being Montenegro in 2007 and Kosovo in 2008); culturally heterogeneous *and* homogeneous societies; states with stable borders and states whose borders have been contested since the transition began; national economies that fall into all four categories of development used by the World Bank (low-income, lower-middle-income, upper-middle-income, and high-income states); and both economic and political regime types that run the gamut from "fully free" to "not free" (to use the designations, respectively, of the *Wall Street Journal* and Freedom House).

At the same time, the postcommunist experience has been typical in many ways of other parts of the world, such as East Asia, Southeast Asia, and Sub-Saharan Africa, where regimes have also been in flux over the past twenty years. One similarity is the wavelike character of democratic change in the region – that is, the tendency of democratic transitions to occur in similar ways while clustering across time and space.[1] Another is that the democratic project has shared the stage often, but not always, with a neoliberal economic project. Although analysts disagree about whether these two ventures are mutually supportive or antagonistic, they nonetheless argue in unison that the double transition generates powerful interactive effects.

Finally, the outcome of the fall of authoritarianism has been very similar in all of these regions. The general rule has not been the rise of democracy, but, rather, the formation of regimes that are located in the middle of a continuum anchored by democracy at one pole and dictatorship at the other. Whether termed competitive or semiauthoritarian regimes, illiberal or electoral democracies, or hybrid or mixed regimes, these melded political orders feature a distinctive profile – in the postcommunist region as elsewhere.[2] They are unusually prone to regime shifts over time, and they are far more likely than other regimes to be failed states.[3]

The purpose of this volume is to take intellectual advantage of the diversity yet typicality of this part of the world to draw some key lessons about the rise, development, and breakdown of *both* democracy and dictatorship. We approach these issues by analyzing three waves of democratic change in the region. The first wave is the one that is the most familiar to our readers: the rapid rise of democratic regimes from 1989 to 1992 from the ashes of communism and communist states. Although this wave of democracy missed most countries in the region, it did not constitute the end of the democratization story. Beginning in the mid-1990s, two more waves of democratic change began. One was associated with accession to the European Union (which finally took place in 2004 and 2007), and the other with the electoral defeat of dictators (the key dates of which are 1996 to 2005).

Although these three waves took place in different countries and involved different strategies, they shared nonetheless several overarching commonalities.

[1] See, for example, Mark Beissinger, *Nationalist Mobilization and the Collapse of the Soviet State* (New York: Cambridge University Press, 2002); Valerie Bunce and Sharon Wolchik, "International Diffusion and Postcommunist Electoral Revolutions." *Communist and Postcommunist Studies,* 39 (September 2006), pp. 283–304; Zachary Elkins and Beth Simmons, "On Waves, Clusters, and Diffusion: A Conceptual Framework." *Annals of the American Academy of Political and Social Science,* No. 598 (2005); Daniel Brinks and Michael Coppedge, "Diffusion Is No Illusion: Neighbor Emulation in the Third Wave." *Comparative Political Studies,* 39, No. 4 (May 2006), pp. 463–89.

[2] Steven Levitsky and Lucan Way, "The Rise of Competitive Authoritarianism." *Journal of Democracy,* 13, No. 2 (April 2002), pp. 51–72; Steven Levitsky and Lucan Way, *Competitive Authoritarianism: The Origins and Evolution of Hybrid Regimes in the Post–Cold War Era.* Unpublished book manuscript; Larry Diamond, "Hybrid Regimes." *Journal of Democracy,* 13, No. 2 (April 2002), pp. 3–20; Marina Ottaway, *Democracy Challenged: The Rise of Semi-Authoritarianism* (Washington, DC: Carnegie Endowment, 2003).

[3] Marc Howard and Philip Roessler, "Measuring and Analyzing Post-Cold War Political Regimes." Paper presented at the Conference on Democratization by Elections, University of Florida, Gainesville, November 30–December 2, 2007; David L. Epstein, Robert Bates, Jack Goldstone, Ida Kristensen, and Sharyn O'Halloran, "Democratic Transitions." *American Journal of Political Science,* 50, No. 3 (July 2006), pp. 551–69.

International factors played a role in all three waves, as did citizens demanding political change. Further, if each of these waves produced some democratic success stories, each one was also associated with some failures. Each wave revealed not just victorious democrats but also highly resourceful authoritarians. Indeed, the two developments, as we will discover, were closely tied to one another.

ORGANIZATION OF THE BOOK

The volume is divided into four parts. The purpose of Part I and the chapters by Michael McFaul and by Valerie Bunce and Sharon Wolchik is to set the stage for the rest of the book in two ways. One is to highlight through comparison the key characteristics of the events of 1989, that is, the fall of communism and communist states and the Cold War international order. The other is to introduce three lines of argument that will appear repeatedly in the chapters that follow: that is, the importance for democratic change of international support, mobilized democrats, and peaceful approaches to regime transition.

In Part II, Alina Mungiu-Pippidi and Milada Anna Vachudova analyze a second wave of democratic change by focusing on interactions between international influences on democratization and domestic struggles for democracy in a group of regimes located in East Central and Southeastern Europe that failed to leap to democracy in the first wave. What these two chapters suggest is that the regional context of democratization is critical. Developments outside the state can go very far to undermine or support both authoritarian and democratic regimes.

In Part III, Tsveta Petrova, Valerie Bunce, Sharon Wolchik, Cory Welt, and Michael McFaul analyze the third wave of postcommunist democratization by focusing on pivotal elections that led to the defeat of dictators and the empowerment of more liberal political leaders. Like the first wave, both popular protests against authoritarian leaders and the cross-national diffusion of challenges to authoritarian rule played key roles. Also striking is a similarity that spans all three waves: the power of transnational coalitions bringing together local democrats and international allies.

In Part IV, however, Lucan Way, Kathryn Stoner-Weiss, Vitali Silitski, and Scott Radnitz all confront directly the other side of our diffusion story, that is, continuing democratic struggles after electoral breakthroughs and the politics of countries where authoritarian leaders succeeded in resisting electoral challenges to their rule. Indeed, just as even the third wave missed some countries in the postcommunist region, so some mixed regimes in the region became more authoritarian over time. Moreover, the international position of states, democratic threats in the neighborhood, and variations in institutions among mixed regimes had the effect in some cases of giving authoritarian leaders both the incentive and the capacity to block threats to their tenure and to the systems they constructed.

DRAWING LESSONS

What lessons about the rise and sustainability of democracy and dictatorship can we draw from our three waves? We would highlight six sets of lessons in particular. One is that, although students of democratization are correct that democracy tends to spread within regions in a wavelike manner, the devil of diffusion is in the details. Thus, we would add several points to these discussions: Diffusion can occur in multiple waves that are both separate from one another and related, with the latter reflecting in part the incomplete character of each wave and a recycling of earlier strategies used to promote democracy. These strategies, however, change both within and across waves, and seemingly similar cases of the diffusion of democracy can mask substantially different dynamics – for example, the considerable power of demonstration effects in the first wave and the role of transnational democracy-promotion networks in the third wave.

We also found support for the argument that mixed regimes are both very common and relatively unstable. It is striking, for example, that each wave was most successful where authoritarianism had been compromised. Here we refer, for example, to the importance of civil society development during communism for the first wave and during postcommunism for the second and third waves. At the same time, legacies of weak civil societies can serve as strong impediments to democratic change – as can well-institutionalized authoritarian orders and vigilant authoritarian leaders. Indeed, mixed regimes with such profiles usually become more authoritarian over time.

A third lesson is that the international system plays a critical role in democratization. However, its role is highly variable – not just in form but also in consequences. The international system can play a permissive role, as well as a very active role, in democratization, and it can support or block democratic change. Thus, powerful states in the international system – whether the Soviet Union during the first wave or the United States during the third wave – can withdraw support from authoritarian regimes, thereby opening up possibilities for regime change and even methods by which authoritarianism is challenged. At the same time, powerful states and ensembles of states, such as the European Union, can encourage democratic change through such mechanisms as supporting transnational networks that invest in democratic development, providing incentives and resources to strengthen local coalitions supporting democratic development, and investing in such building blocks of democracy as free and fair elections and civil society. However, we must also note that the international system, often in alliance with local coalitions, can insulate authoritarian rulers from democratic pressures in the neighborhood. In this sense, the importance of the international system is that it can instigate (with local allies) preemptive strikes against both democracy and dictatorship.

Fourth, the struggle for democracy is the struggle not just of activists and their international partners but also of everyday citizens. If dictatorships often derive their powers from demobilization of publics, then democratization usually involves their remobilization. What is striking in our comparison of these three waves, for example, is not just the power of publics in these processes, but also the *positive* impact of significant citizen mobilization on the defeat of dictators and the shift in domestic politics in a decidedly more democratic direction. Here, we can point to the striking contrast between Serbia in 2000 and Russia under Putin.

Fifth, to quote Thomas Friedman (who was in turn paraphrasing Donald Rumsfeld, when he was Secretary of Defense): "You go to democracy with the country you have, not the country you wish you had."[4] Although necessary for democratic development, the defeat of authoritarians – whether in the streets, at the ballot box, or through political and economic assistance provided by the European Union – is only the beginning of the democratic story. Even in this instance, the important factors seem to be both international support for democratic development and an active citizenry demanding democracy, with collaboration between the two ideals.

Finally and more generally, we are unlikely to understand democratization without understanding both mixed regimes and full-scale dictatorships. Just as the study of recent transitions to democracy has often been too preoccupied with new democracies, so the analysis of the diffusion of democracy has tended to overlook large gaps in the places democracy has traveled. The fact is that regime stability and change is a story that involves analyzing both the proponents and the enemies of democracy, and, therefore, all the political possibilities, while also recognizing the variability of these possibilities over time, as well as across countries. Indeed, it was precisely the variability of regime stories in the postcommunist region and elsewhere that prompted us to put together the chapters that compose this volume.

[4] Thomas Friedman, "The Country We've Got." *New York Times* (January 6, 2005), p. A27.

PART I

WAVES OF REGIME CHANGE: FROM DICTATORSHIP
TO DEMOCRACY ... AND BACK?

I

The Missing Variable

The "International System" as the Link between Third and Fourth Wave Models of Democratization

Michael McFaul
Stanford University

The *first* transitions from communist rule in Eastern Europe and Eurasia at the end of the 1980s and the beginning of the 1990s did not resemble many of the transitions from authoritarian rule in the previous two decades.[1] Why? Some have suggested that countries in the communist world shared distinguishing historical legacies or particular institutional configurations that made them different from countries in Latin America and Southern Europe, which had path-dependent consequences for the kind of transition they experienced.[2] These differences are most certainly a major part of the explanation. However, this chapter argues that the configuration of the international system also played a causal role. The bipolar system of the Cold War constrained the kinds of transitions possible, both in the "East" and in the "West." By 1989, this international system was in transition to a new global order anchored by one hegemon, the United States. This new system allowed a wider range of transitions than were possible in the previous era. The international system is the missing independent variable that helps unify theories about the third wave and the fourth wave, and moves us closer to a general theory of democratization.

To demonstrate the causal influence of the international system on regime transitions, the essay proceeds as follows. Section I outlines the basic elements of the third wave literature and then contrasts this paradigm with the basic elements of the fourth wave model. Section II outlines how the Cold War bipolar international system defined one set of conditions permitting regime

---

[1] Here, I emphasize the word *first* because some countries, such Serbia, Ukraine, and Georgia, have undergone more than one "transition" or "democratic breakthrough." Likewise, one could argue that other countries in the region, such as Belarus and Russia, have undergone two "transitions" in the last twenty years, one that produced a more democratic regime, and another that produced a more autocratic regime.

[2] See Valerie Bunce, "Comparative Democratization: Big and Bounded Generalizations." *Comparative Political Studies*, 33, Nos. 6–7 (August–September 2000), pp. 703–34. See also Grzegorz Ekiert, *The State Against Society. Political Crises and Their Aftermath in East Central Europe* (Princeton, NJ: Princeton University Press, 1996).

change around the world. Section III outlines how the post–Cold War unipolar international system defined a different set of conditions permitting regime change. Section IV examines the American influence on regime change within the Soviet Union. Section V concludes.

I. COMPARING THE THIRD WAVE AND THE FOURTH WAVE

The Third Wave of Democratization

There is no single theory of democratization. There also is no unified theory of third wave democratization, defined here as the wave of transitions from autocracy in the capitalist world that began with Portugal in 1974. Most of the major theorists examining these transitions at the time explicitly rejected the idea that there could be a unified theory. Moreover, because these transitions were either just starting or still in motion when this literature was produced, analysts tended to emphasize contingency and uncertainty, concepts antithetical to the development of general theories or predictions.

And yet a paradigm or analytical model did emerge from this literature. First and foremost, the third wave literature rejected structural causes of democratization and instead focused on actors. They contended that individuals make history, not innate structural forces. Socioeconomic, cultural, and historical structures shaped and constrained the menus of choices available to individuals, but ultimately these innate forces have causal significance only if translated into human action.[3] Cultural and modernization theories may provide important generalizations over time – in the long run Lipset is always right[4] – but they are inappropriate for explaining variation over a short period of time.[5] Therefore, just as there are no uniform causes of democratization, there are also no necessary preconditions for, or determinants of, democracy.[6]

[3] Peter Ordeshook, "The Emerging Discipline of Political Economy." In *Perspectives on Positive Political Economy*, James Alt and Kenneth Shepsle, eds., p. 13 (Cambridge: Cambridge University Press, 1990); Timur Kuran, "Surprise in the East European Revolutions." In *Liberalization and Democratization: Change in the Soviet Union and Eastern Europe*, Nancy Bermeo, ed., p. 22 (Baltimore: Johns Hopkins University Press, 1991).

[4] Seymour Martin Lipset, "Some Social Requisites of Democracy: Economic Development and Political Legitimacy." *American Political Science Review*, 53 (March 1959): pp. 69–105, esp. p. 75.

[5] Even if only temporary, the interregnums that interrupt the evolutionary march of economic and political modernization can be quite consequential for world history. On the fascist interlude in Germany, see Sheri Berman, "Modernization in Historical Perspective: The Case of Imperial Germany." *World Politics*, 53, No. 3 (April 2001), pp. 431–62. Economic growth and then democracy also are not inevitable; countries on the path can diverge and take decades or centuries to get back on, as the trajectories of North American versus South America over the last hundred years suggest. See Douglass C. North, William Summerhill, and Barry R. Weingast, "Order, Disorder, and Economic Change: Latin America vs. North America." In *Governing for Prosperity*, Bruce Bueno de Mesquita and Hilton Root, eds., pp. 17–58 (New Haven, CT: Yale University Press, 2000).

[6] Terry Lynn Karl, "Dilemmas of Democratization in Latin America." *Comparative Politics*, 23, No. 1 (October 1990), p. 2.

Second, the principal theoretical contribution from the literature on third wave democratization concerns the causal role assigned to the mode of transition in determining successful and unsuccessful transitions to democracy. The theory is based on temporal path dependence. Choices made at certain critical junctures influence the course of regime formation. The model identifies four choice-making actors in the transition drama: soft-liners and hard-liners within the ruling elite of the *ancien régime* emerge, as do moderates and radicals among the challengers to the *ancien régime*. The cause of the split within the *ancien régime* varies, but the appearance of such a split really starts the process of regime change, even when democratization is halted before a new polity emerges.

In some cases, moderates from the old order dominate the transition process and dictate the new rules of the game for a democratic polity. This mode of imposed transition occurred at earlier times in Europe and Asia but was not prevalent in the third wave in Latin America. During the third wave, a democratic outcome was most likely when soft-liners and moderates chose to negotiate, that is, to enter into pacts that navigated the transition from dictatorship to democracy.[7] Conversely, if the transition was not accomplished through pacts, it was more likely to fail. As defined by O'Donnell and Schmitter, pacts are interim arrangements between a "select set of actors" that seek to "(1) limit the agenda of policy choice, (2) share proportionally in the distribution of benefits, and (3) restrict the participation of outsiders in decision-making."[8] All three components are critical for success.

Agreements that limit agendas reduce uncertainty about actors' ultimate intentions. A pact "lessens the fears of moderates that they will be overwhelmed by a triumphant, radical, majority which will implement drastic changes."[9] If property rights, the territorial integrity of the state, or international alliances are threatened by a revolutionary force from below, then the leaders of the *ancien régime* will roll back democratic gains.[10] During the wave of transitions to democracy in Latin America and Southern Europe in the 1970s and 1980s, the simultaneous negotiation of political and economic institutions rarely occurred. As O'Donnell and Schmitter concluded, "all previously known transitions to political democracy have observed one fundamental restriction: it is forbidden to take, or even to checkmate, the king of one of the players. In other words,

---

[7] Terry Lynn Karl, "Petroleum and Political Pacts: The Transition to Democracy in Venezuela." *Latin American Research Review*, 22 (1987), pp. 63–94, and "Dilemmas of Democratization in Latin America"; and O'Donnell and Schmitter, *Tentative Conclusions*, Chap. 4. A pact is not a necessary condition for a successful democratic transition, but certainly enhances the probability of success. See Terry Lynn Karl and Philippe Schmitter, "Democratization around the Globe: Opportunities and Risks." In *World Security*, Michael Klare and Daniel Thomas, eds., pp. 43–62 (New York: St. Martin's Press, 1994).

[8] O'Donnell and Schmitter, *Tentative Conclusions*, p. 41.

[9] Daniel Friedman, "Bringing Society Back into Democratic Transition Theory after 1989: Pact Making and Regime Collapse." *East European Politics and Societies*, 7, No. 3 (Fall 1993), p. 484.

[10] O'Donnell and Schmitter, *Tentative Conclusions*, p. 27.

during the transition, the property rights of the bourgeoisie are inviolable."[11] More generally, negotiations over contested issues, in which the stakes are indivisible or the outcomes irreversible, are more likely to generate irreconcilable preferences among actors than issues with divisible stakes and reversible outcomes.[12] Consequently, keeping such issues off the table was considered an important component of successful transitions. Limits on the agenda in question usually took place through the negotiation of pacts.

Further, sharing in the benefits of change provides both sides with positive-sum outcomes. Tradeoffs – which may even include institutionalizing non-democratic practices – are critical to making pacts work.[13] As Daniel Friedman writes, "Negotiated transitions increase democratic stability by encouraging important interests to compromise on such basic issues as to whether new democratic institutions should be parliamentary or presidential, when to schedule the first free elections, and whether to grant clemency to human rights abusers or attempt to 'even the score.' Without compromises on such fundamental issues, powerful interest groups can have less incentive to cooperate with the new democratic regime."[14]

Finally, these theorists have placed special emphasis on limiting the role of radicals in the negotiation process. Transitions based on pacts are elite affairs; mobilized masses are considered dangerous.[15] The Jacobins must be sidelined to attain success.[16] If the masses are part of the equation, then revolution, not democracy, results.[17] As Karl posits, "no stable political democracy has resulted from regime transitions in which mass actors have gained control even momentarily over traditional ruling classes."[18] Huntington agrees:

Democratic regimes that last seldom if ever have been instituted by popular action. Almost always, democracy has come as much from the top down as from the bottom up; it is as likely to be the product of oligarchy as of protest against oligarchy. The passionate dissidents from authoritarian rule and the crusaders for democratic principles, the Tom

---

[11] O'Donnell and Schmitter, *Tentative Conclusions*, p. 69. See also Adam Przeworski, "Problems in the Study of Transition to Democracy." In *Transitions from Authoritarian Rule: Comparative Perspectives*, Vol. 3, Guillermo O'Donnell, Philippe Schmitter, and Lawrence Whitehead, eds., p. 63 (Baltimore, MD: Johns Hopkins University Press, 1986).

[12] Elizabeth Jean Wood, *Forging Democracy from Below*, pp. 78–110 (Cambridge: Cambridge University Press, 2000); and Bunce, "Comparative Democratization."

[13] Karl, (Dilemmas of Democratization) has called these "birth defects."

[14] Daniel Friedman, "Bringing Society Back," p. 483.

[15] For an excellent and skeptical review of this argument, see Nancy Bermeo, "Myths of Moderation: Confrontation and Conflict During the Democratic Transitions." *Comparative Politics*, 29, No. 3 (April 1997), pp. 305–22.

[16] Giuseppe Di Palma, *To Craft Democracies: An Essay on Democratic Transitions* (Berkeley: University of California Press, 1990).

[17] Important exceptions are Bermeo, "Myths of Moderation"; Barrington Moore, *Social Origins of Dictatorship and Democracy: Lord and Peasant in the Making of the Modern World* (Boston: Beacon Press, 1966); and Ruth Collier, *Paths towards Democracy: The Working Class and Elites in Western Europe and Southern America* (Cambridge: Cambridge University Press, 1999).

[18] Terry Karl, "Dilemmas of Democratization in Latin America." *Comparative Politics*, 23 (October 1990), p. 8.

Paines of this world, do not create democratic institutions; that requires James Madison. Those institutions come into existence through negotiations and compromises among political elites calculating their own interests and desires.[19]

In transitions from authoritarian rule in capitalist countries, trade unions, the left, and radicals in general must not play a major role in the transition process, and can only play a limited role in the new political system that eventually emerges.[20] As O'Donnell and Schmitter warn, "Put in a nutshell, parties of the Right-Center and Right must be 'helped' to do well, and parties of the Left-Center and Left should not win by an overwhelming majority."[21] Elites guarantee such outcomes through the manipulation of electoral laws or other institutional tools.

But what causes pacts between moderate elites to materialize in the first place? Though often not explicitly stated, analysts of the third wave answer this question by examining the balance of power between the challenged and challengers. When the distribution of power is relatively equal, negotiated transitions are most likely. In summing up the results of their multivolume study, O'Donnell and Schmitter asserted, "political democracy is produced by stalemate and dissensus rather than by prior unity and consensus."[22] Roeder has made the same claim in his analysis of postcommunist transitions: "The more heterogeneous in objectives and the more evenly balanced in relative leverage are the participants in the bargaining process of constitutional design, the more likely is the outcome to be a democratic constitution."[23] When both sides realize that they cannot prevail unilaterally, they agree to seek win–win solutions for everyone. Democratization requires a stalemate – "a prolonged and inconclusive struggle."[24]

[19] Samuel Huntington, "Will More Countries Become Democratic?" *Political Science Quarterly*, 99, No. 2 (Summer 1984), p. 6.
[20] Myron Weiner, "Empirical Democratic Theory." In *Competitive Elections in Developing Countries*, Myron Weiner and Ergun Ozbudin, eds., p. 26 (Durham: Duke University Press, 1987). See also Przeworski, "Problems in the Study of Transition to Democracy"; and J. Samuel Valenzuela, "Labor Movements in Transitions to Democracy." *Comparative Politics*, 21, No. 3 (July 1989), pp. 405–26. Even a study devoted to the role of the workers in democratization underscores the dangers of too mobilized a society. See Dietrich Rueschemeyer, Evelyne Huber Stephens, and John D. Stephens, *Capitalist Development and Democratic Change*, p. 271 (Chicago: University of Chicago Press, 1992).
[21] O'Donnell and Schmitter, *Transitions from Authoritarian Rule*, p. 62.
[22] Ibid., p. 72.
[23] Phillip Roeder, "Transitions from Communism: State-Centered Approaches." In *Can Democracy Take Root in Post-Soviet Russia?* Harry Eckstein, Frederic Fleron, Erik Hoffman, and William Reisinger, eds., p. 209 (Lantham, MD: Roman and Littlefield, 1998).
[24] Dankwart Rustow, "Transition to Democracy: Toward a Dynamic Model." *Comparative Politics*, 2 (1970), p. 352. For an application to the Russian case in which he discusses "the (possible) virtues of deadlock," see Steven Fish, "Russia's Crisis and the Crisis of Russology." In *Reexamining the Soviet Experience*, David Holloway and Norman Naimark, eds., especially pp. 158–61 (Boulder, CO: Westview Press, 1996) Kenneth Waltz's celebration of bipolarity as a guarantor of peace is the rough equivalent in the subfield of international relations. See Waltz, *Theory of International Politics* (New York: McGraw-Hill, 1979).

Przeworski has extended this argument to posit that *uncertain* balances of power are most likely to lead to the most democratic arrangements; "If everyone is behind the Rawlsian veil, that is, if they know little about their political strength under the eventual democratic institutions, all opt for a maximizing solution: institutions that introduce checks and balances and maximize the political influence of minorities, or, equivalently, make policy highly insensitive to fluctuations in public opinion."[25] Uncertainty enhances the probability of compromise, and relatively equal distributions of power create uncertainty.

This approach emphasizes the process itself, rather than the individual actors, as the primary casual variable producing successful transitions.[26] When the process is more important than the individuals or their ideas, it becomes possible to produce "democracy without democrats." As Roeder argues, "democracy emerges not because it is the object of the politicians' collective ambition but because it is a practical compromise among politicians blocked from achieving their particular objectives."[27] The dynamics of the strategic situation, not the actual actors or their preferences, produce or fail to produce democracy. As Dan Levine excellently summed up, "democracies emerge out of mutual fear among opponents rather than as the deliberate outcome of concerted commitments to make democratic political arrangements work."[28] Moderate, evolutionary processes are considered good for democratic emergence; radical, revolutionary processes are considered bad. Cooperative bargains produce democratic institutions; noncooperative processes do not.[29] Similarly, Przeworski concludes, "Democracy cannot be dictated; it emerges from bargaining."[30]

Such processes work best when they are protracted, slow, and deliberate. Drawing on earlier experiences of democratization, Eckstein has asserted that postcommunist "democratization should proceed gradually, incrementally, and by the use of syncretic devices.... Social transformations is only likely to be accomplished, and to be accomplished without destructive disorders, if it is spaced out over a good deal of time, if it is approached incrementally (i.e. sequentially), and if it builds syncretically upon the existing order rather than trying to eradicate it."[31] Advocates of this theoretical approach assert that "conservative transitions are more durable" than radical transformations.[32]

---

[25] Adam Przeworski, *Democracy and the Market: Political and Economic Reforms in Eastern Europe and Latin America*, p. 87 (Cambridge: Cambridge University Press, 1991).

[26] Roeder, "Transitions from Communism," fn. 23, p. 207.

[27] Ibid., p. 208.

[28] Daniel Levine, "Paradigm Lost: Dependence to Democracy." *World Politics*, 40 (April 1988), p. 379.

[29] See Hardin's review and then rejection of this approach in Russell Hardin, *Liberalism, Constitutionalism, and Democracy* (Oxford: Oxford University Press, 1999).

[30] Przeworski, *Democracy and the Market*, fn. 25, p. 90.

[31] Harry Ekstein, "Lessons for the 'Third Wave.'" In Eckstein et al., *Can Democracy Take Root in Post-Soviet Russia?* p. 264.

[32] Levine, "Paradigm Lost," fn. 28, p. 392.

This set of arguments has a close affinity with positivist accounts of institutionalism that have emerged from cooperative game theory. The crafting of new democratic institutions is framed as a positive-sum game in which both sides may not obtain their most preferred outcome, but settle for second-best outcomes that nonetheless represent an improvement over the status quo.[33] Uncertainty during the crafting of rules plays a positive role in producing efficient and/or liberal institutions.[34] These approaches to institutional emergence also emphasize the importance of shared distributions that result from the new institutional arrangements. Above all else, the transition to democracy is a bargain from which everyone gains. In the metaphorical frame of a prisoner's dilemma, it is settling for the payoffs of cooperation, rather than gambling to obtain the higher gains from confrontation.

The "Fourth Wave"

Actor-centric, cooperative approaches to democratization offer a useful starting point for explaining postcommunist regime transformations. This framework rightly focuses on actors, rather than structures, and offers an explanation for both democracy and dictatorship.[35] Many of the actors in the region even claimed that they were attempting to navigate a transition from communism to democracy; the literature on transitions to democracy, therefore, offered appropriate metaphors and analogies to compare to these postcommunist transitions.

When the third wave hypotheses are applied to the postcommunist world, some stand the test of time and new cases. Rustow's observations about preconditions seem relevant to the postcommunist transitions. Though consensus about borders was not necessary to begin political liberalization processes, and some transitions have continued along a democratic trajectory without firmly resolving borders issues, the resolution of major sovereignty contests was a precondition for new regime emergence in most of the region. Most importantly, three multiethnic states had to collapse before democratic or autocratic regimes could consolidate. Twenty-two of the twenty-seven states in the postcommunist world did not exist before communism's collapse. Rather than an extension of the third wave of democratization that, as noted earlier, first started in Portugal, this explosion of new states is more analogous to the wave of decolonization and regime emergence after World War II throughout the British, French, and Portuguese empires. And as in this earlier wave of state

---

[33] Di Palma, *To Craft Democracies,* fn. 16; Rustow, *Transitions to Democracy,* fn. 24, p. 357.

[34] Writers from the positivist tradition in institutional analysis make a similar argument regarding the positive relationship between ex ante uncertainty and the emergence of efficient institutions. See Geoffrey Brennan and James Buchanan, *The Reason of Rules,* p. 30 (Cambridge: Cambridge University Press, 1985); and George Tsebelis, *Nested Games: Rational Choice in Comparative Politics,* p. 118 (Berkeley: University of California Press, 1990).

[35] This said, most work in this tradition has focused on successful democratic transitions, and not on failed cases. Edited volumes on democratization rarely incorporate cases such as Angola, Saudi Arabia, or Uzbekistan.

emergence, the delineation of borders may have been a necessary, but certainly not a sufficient, condition for democratization. Most of the new postcolonial states that formed after World War II claimed to be transitioning to democracy, but only a few successfully consolidated democratic systems. In Africa and Asia, disputes about the borders of the states were a major impediment to democratic consolidation. Similarly, in the postcommunist world, the emergence of democracy has been the exception, not the rule, and border disputes figure prominently in several (though not all) stalled transitions.

After Rustow's observation, further application of the transitions metaphor begins to distort rather than illuminate.[36] The central cause of political liberalization in the postcommunist world was not elite division. In most cases, as discussed in greater detail below, and to some degree by Bunce and Wolchik in the next chapter in this volume, it was the initiative of reforms by an outside agent – Mikhail Gorbachev. Even within the Soviet Union, Gorbachev did not emerge as leader as the result of elite divisions. On the contrary, he was the consensus candidate to assume dictatorial power as the General Secretary of the Communist Party of the Soviet Union in 1985. For the first two years after becoming General Secretary, he consolidated political power to a greater extent than any Soviet leader since Stalin. It was his reforms that later spawned elite divisions as a response.[37] Explaining the original causes of liberalization, however, has never been a robust part of any transition theory and therefore does not deserve extensive scrutiny here.[38]

Explaining outcomes of transitions (rather than the causes of transitional moments themselves) has been the central project of transitology and positivist institutionalism. Upon closer examination, however, these analytical frames seem inappropriate to explaining postcommunist regime change. Most importantly, the preponderance of dictatorships in the postcommunist world and the lack of democracies raise real questions about why postcommunist transitions should be subsumed within the third wave at all. In the long run, all countries may be in transition to democracy.[39] In the short run, however, the differences between the third wave and the postcommunist fourth wave should be recognized and explained. Besides a somewhat loose temporal relationship,

[36] Bunce, "Comparative Democratization: Lessons from Russia and the Postcommunist World," In *After the Collapse of Communism: Comparative Lessons of Transition*, Michael McFaul and Kathryn Stoner-Weiss, eds., pp. 207–31 (Cambridge: Cambridge University Press, 2004).

[37] Michael McFaul, *Russia's Unfinished Revolution: Political Change from Gorbachev to Putin* (Ithaca: Cornell University Press, 2001).

[38] One could make the same claim about theories of revolution, especially those that introduce actors into the equation – for instance, Timur Kuran's "Now Out of Never." *World Politics*, 44, No. 1 (October 1991), pp. 7–48, which offers a compelling account of a revolutionary process without ever explicating how the process got underway in the first place. Likewise, Tilly has distinguished between revolutionary situations and revolutionary outcomes as two independent outcomes that may have different causal variables producing them. Such distinctions allow research programs that focus on the latter while treating the former as a constant or an exogenous shock.

[39] Francis Fukuyama, *The End of History and the Last Man* (New York: Avon Books, 1992).

Portugal's coup in 1974 and the Soviet collapse in 1991 have little in common.[40] By framing the question in terms of democratization, the study of transitions in the postcommunist world becomes a search for negative variables – what factors *prevented* democracy from emerging – which may not generate an effective research agenda for understanding these regime changes.[41]

Yet, even if one accepts that the postcommunist transitions are a subset of the more general phenomena of democratization – that is, both successful and failed cases of democratization – the dynamics of transition in the fourth wave have many characteristics that are different from, if not diametrically opposed to, the third wave transitions. Most importantly, regime change in the postcommunist world only rarely resulted from negotiations between old elites and societal challengers. Confrontation was much more prevalent. The rules of the game in the new regime were dictated by the most powerful – whether old elites or anti-regime social movements. Pacts, or the conditions that make them, appear to be unimportant in determining the success or failure of democratic emergence in the postcommunist world.

In the third wave literature, pacts were assumed to limit the scope of change, and particularly to prevent a renegotiation of the economic institutions governing property rights. In looking at the postcommunist transitions, therefore, third-wave analysts presupposed that economic and political reform could not be undertaken simultaneously.[42] The danger of multiple agendas of change, frequently trumpeted in the earlier literature on democratization, has not seen clear empirical confirmation in the postcommunist world. Because communism bundled the political and the economic, and the challenge to communism occurred so rapidly, sequencing proved impossible and simultaneity was unavoidable. Generally, the reorganization of economic institutions did not undermine democratic transitions.[43] On the contrary, those countries that moved the fastest regarding economic transformation also have achieved the greatest success in consolidating democratic institutions.[44] Countries that

---

[40] On the comparison, see Valerie Bunce, "Regional Differences in Democratization: The East versus the South." *Post-Soviet Affairs*, 14, No. 3 (1998), pp. 187–211; Valerie Bunce, "Should Transitologists Be Grounded?" *Slavic Review*, 54, No. 1 (1995), pp. 111–27; Philippe Schmitter with Terry Karl, "The Conceptual Travels of Transitologists and Consolidologists: How Far East Should They Go?" *Slavic Review*, 53, No. 1 (Spring 1994), pp. 173–85.

[41] For most elites in the region, "state-building" – not regime making, be it democracy or dictatorship – is the central enterprise under way.

[42] Przeworski, *Democracy and the Market*.

[43] For a study confirming the dangers of simultaneity for democratic emergence, see Michael McFaul, *Russia's Unfinished Revolution: Political Change from Gorbachev to Putin* (Ithaca: Cornell University Press, 2001).

[44] Joel S. Hellman, "Winners Take All: The Politics of Partial Reform in Postcommunist Transitions." *World Politics*, 50 (January 1998), pp. 203–34; Valerie Bunce, "The Political Economy of Postsocialism." *Slavic Review*, 58 (Winter 1999), pp. 756–93; Anders Åslund, *Building Capitalism: The Transformation of the Former Soviet Bloc* (Cambridge University Press, 2002), Chap. 9. If the correlation between democracy and economic reform is positive, one cannot argue that economic reform caused democracy. Economic reform cannot be used as a predictor

attempted to keep economic issues off the agenda or slowed the process of transformation, such as Belarus, have achieved the least progress in democratic consolidation, as noted in the chapter by Silitski later in this volume.[45]

Moreover, the most important condition for a successful pact – a stalemated balance of power – also does not figure prominently as a causal variable for producing postcommunist democracies. In countries where pacts were important to starting a transition process, such as Poland and Hungary, pacts did not result from protracted stalemates between relatively equal powers, did not unravel quickly once the transitions gained momentum, and did not lock permanent compromises into place. In the fourth wave, the mode of transition that most frequently produced democracy was an imbalance of power in favor of the democratic challengers.

The kinds of actors involved in making democracy in the fourth wave were also different from those postulated in the third wave. In some cases, similar players in the *ancien régime* – soft-liners and hard-liners – could be identified in these successful communist transitions to democracy, though the divide played a much less significant role. Instead, the degree of cooperation and mobilization within society was more salient. In some cases, such as Poland, Czechoslovakia, Georgia, and to a lesser extent Russia and eventually Ukraine, mass movements played a much more prominent role in bringing about regime change. Evidently, then, the mass actors so damaging to democratization in third wave analyses were instrumental to fourth wave successes. Revolutionary movements from below – not elites from above – toppled communist regimes and created new democratic institutions. The role of unity versus division among these actors also looks rather different when the two waves are compared. Consensus among these *ancien régime* challengers, not dissensus, aided the cause of democratic transition.[46]

Finally, because this different kind of actor – societal actors with power – were involved in the process, they often employed confrontational and uncooperative tactics to achieve democratic goals. Third wave literature does not

---

of successful democratic reform, because the two processes began simultaneously. In many of the countries that have experienced successful economic reform, the initial consequence of the reform package was economic downturn, not growth. Surveys suggest that these downturns did not make people more positive about democracy. Tracing the causal relationship between successful privatization and democracy has not been done, either deductively or empirically. Rather, what appears to occur in these "successful" countries is the reinforcement of democracy by successful economic growth. The original cause of a successful transition to democracy must come from somewhere else.

[45] Przeworski's *Democracy and the Market* predicted the exact opposite.

[46] At first cut, the argument of this chapter may sound similar to that of Burton, Gunther, and Higley, who argue compellingly that elite consensus produces successful democratic transitions. As conceptualized in this chapter, however, this consensus need not emerge only among elites to be important. Communist elites, after all, did not agree on democracy until they were forced to do so. Michael Burton, Richard Gunther, and John Higley, "The Elite Variable in Democratic Transitions and Breakdowns." *American Sociological Review*, 54 (February 1989), pp. 17–32.

highlight this dynamic. When events such as elections or street demonstrations proved that the balance of power was in their favor, societal actors imposed their will on antidemocratic elites.[47] Bargaining was neither essential nor conducive to democratic emergence. Alternatively, one can think of these transitions as situations in which the old communists "acquiesced" to the new democratic rules of the game. They acquiesced largely because they had no real choice, no power to resist.[48] These were revolutionary transformations of the political system, not moderate evolutions from one system to the next.

This discussion of the fourth wave so far has addressed only successful cases of democratic transition. The cases of unsuccessful transition – that is, the transition from communist autocracy to capitalist autocracy – also were confrontational processes not based on pacts, but with a different set of actors holding all the power. As with the first path, the stronger side dictated the rules of the game to the weaker side. Only, in this situation, the stronger embraced autocratic ideas and preserved or reconstituted authoritarian institutions. As with the first path, and in stark contrast to situations in which the distribution of power was relatively equal, these transitions imposed from above reached a new equilibrium point rather quickly. In most cases, the resulting regimes are just as consolidated as the liberal democracies.

In a third situation, when the distribution of power is more equally divided, the range of outcomes is wide: transitions based on pacts leading to partial democracy, or protracted and often violent confrontations leading to either partial democracy or partial dictatorship. The logic of the pact-based transitions that resulted from a relatively equal distribution of power between the old and the new – that is, the third wave model – can be identified in at least one postcommunist transition: Moldova. But other countries, such as Russia and Tajikistan, with similar power distributions did not produce pacts or liberal democracies. Instead, in these countries and several others, both sides fought to impose their wills until one side won. The result of this mode of transition was partial, unconsolidated democracy at best; civil war at worst. Significantly, no stalemated transition in the postcommunist world produced liberal democracy in the first years after the collapse of communism.

That conflict can result from equal distributions of power should not be surprising. Analysts of the third wave overlooked failures and focused only on successful cases of democracy that emerged from stalemate. If all countries

---

[47] Of course, establishing an independent measure of the balance of power is critical to avoiding a tautological argument. Following Bunce and Fish, I use the results of the first postcommunist elections as an important measure, but then supplement this data point with elections just prior to collapse and definitive examples of popular mobilization. In particular, the March 1990 elections to the Supreme Soviets of the fifteen republics in the Soviet Union will be used to provide a balance-of-power measure (with variation) for these cases at the same time in history.

[48] On why acquiescence is more important for constitutions, whereas agreement is more important for contracts, see Russell Hardin, "Why a Constitution?" In *The Federalist Papers and the New Institutionalism*, Bernard Grofman and Donald Wittman, eds., pp. 100–20 (New York: Agathon Press, 1989).

undergoing stalemated transitions are brought into the analysis, then the causal influence of the mode of transition becomes less clear however. Angola, for instance, experienced a stalemated transition between competing powers after decolonization, but a pact-based transition to democracy did not result. Rather, the country was in stalemate for decades.

Why, in the fourth wave (and elsewhere), have relatively equal distributions of power between democrats and autocrats not always compelled both sides to negotiate a pact? The reason is that equal distributions can tempt both sides into believing that they can prevail over their opponents. Equal power distribution fuels uncertainty about the distribution, whereas asymmetric distributions are much easier to identify. If both sides perceive that they have a chance of prevailing through the use of force, they may be tempted to fight.

The logic of this dynamic becomes clearer if an ideal case is constructed. In a world of complete information, perfect knowledge about the distribution of power could predict all outcomes. If the losers of a battle (in the boardroom or on the battlefield) knew that they were going to lose beforehand, they would not incur the costs of the fight.[49] Complete information about power would produce efficient solutions to conflicts. In the real world, however, information about power is always incomplete. The greater the uncertainty about the distribution of power, the more difficult it is for actors to make strategic calculations. In such situations, actors may to opt to hedge their bets about the uncertain future by agreeing to new rules that constrain all. However, uncertainty about the future may also tempt actors to go for broke because they think they have some chance of winning. Ambiguous calculations about power constitute a major cause of conflict. As Geoffrey Blaney concluded in his analysis of the precipitants of armed conflict, "War usually begins when two nations disagree on their relative strength and wars usually cease when the fighting nationals agree on their relative strength."[50]

The same could be said about confrontation and reconciliation between competing forces within a domestic polity, especially during periods of revolutionary change when domestic anarchy begins to approximate the anarchy in the international system posited by international relations theories.

What is especially striking about this type of trajectory is the protracted nature of the transition. In many countries that experienced this mode of transition, the outcome of regime change is still uncertain. Nor can the final outcomes be predicted for countries exhibiting such a configuration of political forces.

In all three modes of transition in the fourth wave, the phenomenon resembles to varying degrees noncooperative strategic situations that produce

---

[49] For elaboration on this point, see James Fearon, "Rationalist Explanations for War." *International Organization*, 49, No. 3 (Summer 1995), pp. 379–414. Geoffrey Blaney makes a related observation in *The Causes of War* (New York: The Free Press, 1973), p. 26.

[50] Blaney, *The Causes of War*, p. 246. See also R. Harrison Wagner, "Peace, War, and the Balance of Power." *American Political Science Review*, 88, No. 3 (September 1994), pp. 596–7.

distributional institutions. The process is the opposite of "democracy-without-democrats." Non-negotiated transitions are more prone to produce institutions, which skew the distributional benefits in favor of those dictating the rules. The logic is simple: If actors agree to a set of rules during a pact-making period, they share the distribution of benefits of the pact in a manner acceptable to all signatories. Actors agree to commit to a pact because they believe they will be better off in agreeing to the pact than in not agreeing.[51]

The logic of these arguments about the fourth wave bears a strong resemblance to realist accounts of institutional design.[52] The crafting of new institutions – democratic or otherwise – is framed as a zero-sum game, in which one side in the contest obtains its most preferred outcome, and the other side must settle for second- and third-best outcomes. In transitions to democracy, the losers usually obtain second-best outcomes; that is, they too make relative gains over the status quo ante. In transitions to dictatorship, the losers' gains are much less substantial. This approach to institutional emergence emphasizes the importance of skewed distributions that result from the new institutional arrangements. Above all, the transition is not a bargain, but a confrontation, with winners and losers. This is the most common procedure by which institutions, especially political institutions, emerge.[53] Though the social contract metaphor is often employed to describe constitutional emergence and stability, institutional arrangements that maximize everyone's utility are rare in the political world.

The Missing Variable Uniting Third and Fourth Wave Theories: The International System

The sketches above of the third wave model and the fourth wave model are oversimplified and unduly dichotomous. For instance, without question, some third wave transitions included mass movements and economic reform agendas, whereas some fourth wave transitions included elements of pacts. At the same time, the differences between the two theories describing/explaining the

---

[51] Aside from this general proposition, we still have very poorly developed ideas about what factors make pacts credible commitments. On this point, see Barry Weingast, "The Political Foundations of Democracy and the Rule of Law." *American Political Science Review*, 91, No. 2 (June 1997), pp. 245–63.

[52] Jack Knight, *Institutions and Social Conflict* (Cambridge: Cambridge University Press, 1992); Tsebelis, *Nested Games*; Stephen Krasner, "Global Communications and National Power: Life on the Pareto Frontier." *World Politics*, 43 (1991), pp. 336–66; and Lloyd Gruber, *Ruling the World: Power Politics and the Rise of Supranational Institutions* (Princeton, NJ: Princeton University Press, 2000).

[53] Political institutions are particularly prone to inefficiency and distributive functions. In recognizing this fundamental distinction between economic and political institutions, Terry Moe has questioned the theoretical utility of comparing the two. See Moe, "The Politics of Structural Choice: Toward a Theory of Public Bureaucracy." In *Organization Theory: From Chester Barnard to the Present and Beyond*, Oliver Williamson, ed., pp. 116–53 (Oxford: Oxford University Press, 1990).

two sets of cases are more striking than their similarities. Robust general theories, however, should not be limited by geography or time. The quest for a general theory of democratization must seek to identify new or hidden variables that, if introduced into the analysis, would help to explain both third and fourth wave transitions (or the lack thereof). One such variable is the international system. This variable changed from a bipolar, ideologically divided system in the third wave to a unipolar, ideologically united system during the fourth wave. This change had profound causal consequences for the modes of transition permissible in the third versus fourth wave, consequences that have been underappreciated by scholars of democratization.

In his seminal article published nearly thirty years ago, "Second Image Reversed," Peter Gourevitch outlined a set of arguments as to why and how to study the international causes of domestic outcomes. This framework had a profound effect on several literatures, but only caused a minor ripple in the study of regime change.[54] The third wave transitologists gave only passing attention to the international dimensions of democratization. Laurence Whitehead did write an important chapter on the international aspects of democratization in the fourth volume of the four-volume study on transitions from autocratic rule edited by O'Donnell, Schmitter, and Whitehead. Yet, in one of the introductory essays in their collective project, Schmitter wrote that one "of the firmest conclusions that emerged . . . was that transitions from authoritarian rule and immediate prospects for political democracy were largely to be explained in terms of national forces and calculations. External actors tended to play an indirect and usually marginal role. . . . "[55]

Scholars writing about democratization after the end of the Cold War have devoted more attention to international factors. Yet those who focus on international dimensions of democratization focus predominantly on democratic consolidation, not democratic transition. And in these analyses, it is not the structure of the international system as a whole that is the focus of inquiry, but rather international institutions that offer incentives for states to deepen democracy.[56] There is also a growing literature on the role of individual states

---

[54] See John Owen, "The Foreign Imposition of Domestic Institutions." *International Organization*, 56, No. 2 (Spring 2002), pp. 375–410; Jon C. Pevehouse, "Democracy from the Outside-In? International Organizations and Democratization." *International Organization*, 65, No. 3 (Summer 2002), pp. 515–49; and Laurence Whitehead, "International Aspects of Democratization." In *Transitions from Authoritarian Rule: Comparative Perspectives*, Guillermo O'Donnell, Philippe C. Schmitter, and Laurence Whitehead, eds., pp. 3–46 (Baltimore: Johns Hopkins University Press, 1986).

[55] Schmitter, "An Introduction to Southern European Transitions." In O'Donnell, Schmitter, and Whitehead, eds., p. 5 *Transitions from Authoritarian Rule: Southern Europe*.

[56] Peceny, Vacudova, Senem Aydin, and Fuat Keyman, *European Integration and the Transformation of Turkish Democracy*, EU–Turkey Working Papers, No. 2 (August 2004); Richard Youngs, *The European Union and the Promotion of Democracy: Europe's Mediterranean and Asian Policies* (Oxford: Oxford University Press, 2002); Paul Kubicek, ed., *The European Union and Democratization* (London: Routledge, 2003); Frank Schimmelfennig and Ulrich Sedelmeier, eds., *The Europeanization of Central and Eastern Europe* (Ithaca: Cornell

and NGOs (nongovernmental organizations) in promoting democracy, but again the focus is predominantly on democratic consolidation (or the lack thereof), and not transition or regime change.[57] Still, as one study recently concluded, "The international dimension of democracy promotion nonetheless remains at best understudied and poorly understood.... "[58] Moreover, this literature has also remained largely descriptive, with few testable hypotheses or aggregating theoretical statements. And even with the development of this new and growing literature on international sources of democracy, its impact on "transitologists" or comparativists studying democratization or regime change has been rather minimal. The massive new literature on postcommunist transitions has devoted only a fraction of its attention to international factors.[59] To date, no one has tried to compare the international effects on democratization in the third wave of transitions systematically with the international effects on democratization in the fourth wave.

II. THE BIPOLAR INTERNATIONAL SYSTEM AND THE THIRD WAVE

Bipolarity defined the international system that structured politics between the end of World War II and the end of the Cold War. But the two superpowers that anchored this system – the United States and the Soviet Union – were not just the countries with the greatest military and economic power in the world. These two states also anchored two world systems (as the Soviets used to call them), with states and economies organized in fundamentally different ways. The capitalist world system was composed of states whose economies had some elements of markets and private property. Within the bloc, the polities were organized very differently – some democracies, some autocracies, and some colonies. Yet even the autocracies were set up in ways that looked qualitatively different from the one-party totalitarian regimes in the communist world. In the communist world, there was also variation in the composition of both the economy and the polity. Poland had some private property and some markets not controlled by the state; the Soviet Union had very few. Likewise, the

University Press, 2005); Michael Emerson, ed., *Democratization in the European Neighbourhood* (Washington, DC: Brookings Institution Press, 2005); and Geoffrey Pridham, *Designing Democracy: EU Enlargement and Regime Change in Post-Communist Europe* (Basingstoke, UK: Palgrave Macmillan, 2005).

[57] Thomas Carothers, *Aiding Democracy Abroad: The Learning Curve* (Washington, DC: Carnegie Endowment for International Peace, 1999); Larry Diamond, *Promoting Democracy in the 1990s: Actors and Instruments, Issues and Imperatives* (New York: Carnegie Corporation of New York, 1995); and Peter Burnell, "Democracy Assistance: The State of the Art." In *Democracy Assistance: International Cooperation for Democratization*, Peter Burnell, ed., pp. 339–62 (London: Frank Cass, 2000).

[58] Peter Schraeder, "The State of the Art in International Democracy Promotion: Results of a Joint European–North American Research Network." *Democratization*, 10, No. 2 (Summer 2003), pp. 21–44, esp. 22.

[59] Michael McFaul, "The Fourth Wave of Democracy and Dictatorship: Noncooperative Transitions in the Postcommunist World." *World Politics*, 54, No. 2 (January 2002), pp. 212–44.

Hungarian regime was much less totalitarian than the Romanian regime. Compared to the world capitalist system, however, countries in the communist bloc shared certain distinctive features, including one-party regimes and command economies in which the state owned (most) property, managed transactions, and set prices. Both world systems also had international institutions such as NATO, the IMF, and the World Bank in the West and the Warsaw Pact and COMECON in the East, which preserved the cohesion of each system while also helping insulate each system from the other.

Given the antagonistic, antithetical natures of these two systems, competition between them was not limited simply to balancing between the two superpowers and other significant powers in the international system. Instead, the ideological dimension, or the competing models for organizing the polity and economy, extended the zero-sum competition between "capitalism" and "communism" to encompass the entire world.[60] Leaders in Washington and Moscow both held the view that victory for the enemy, even in a peripheral country such as Vietnam or Mozambique, could trigger a domino effect on other countries within their blocs. Given the rigidity of division in Europe, the arena of competition between the capitalist and communist systems shifted to the periphery of the international system.

Regime Change within the Capitalist World

This unique international system had a particular limiting effect on democratic regime change, as well as other types of regime change. As the anchor of the world capitalist system (or what others would call the "free world," even though many countries within this world were governed by dictatorships), the United States's central foreign policy objective was to contain communism. This grand strategy transformed the United States from a weak supporter of democratic regime change and national self-determination to a strong supporter of the status quo within its bloc. To be sure, American leaders did support decolonization and transitions from authoritarian rule during the Cold War. But the parameters of the possible modes of transition were severely constricted.

Most importantly, American power, along with local elites, limited the agenda of change during transitional moments in autocracies within the capitalist world system. In particular, it was the United States – not only local actors – that ensured that "during the transition, the property rights of the bourgeoisie [were] inviolable."[61]

---

[60] Fred Halliday, "The Sixth Great Power: On the Study of Revolution in the International System." *Review of International Studies*, 16 (1990), pp. 217–19.

[61] O'Donnell and Schmitter, *Tentative Conclusions*, p. 69. See also Adam Przeworski, "Problems in the Study of Transition to Democracy." In *Transitions from Authoritarian Rule: Comparative Perspectives*, Vol. 3, Guillermo O'Donnell, Philippe Schmitter, and Lawrence Whitehead, eds., p. 63 (Baltimore, MD: Johns Hopkins University Press, 1986).

This defining feature of successful democratic transition came directly from the international system. When American officials perceived that this precondition for transition was being violated, they often tried to intervene – either directly or through proxies – to stop or roll back the transition process.[62] American officials impeded simultaneous transformation of political and economic institutions in the capitalist world. Redefining the borders of the state was strongly discouraged and security institutions were also inviolable. Any challenge to alliance relationships or bilateral security agreements with the United States immediately triggered deep involvement of Washington officials in a regime transition process.[63]

Within the world capitalist system, the United States also played a central role in limiting the kinds of actors allowed to participate in transitional negotiations. Mass actors scared Washington officials, as did socialists, because they were perceived to (and sometimes did) have links to the Soviet Union and the communist world movement. The United States developed close relationships with right-of-center elites in Western Europe, Africa, Latin America, and Africa to shift the local balance of power in favor of so-called "anti-communist forces." All successful transitions from autocracy to democracy during the Cold War, therefore, either were imposed by these pro-American elites or were pact-based transitions that did not involve actors interested in more radical transformation of economic institutions, and rarely involved mass mobilization from below.

The peaceful and evolutionary nature of democratic transitions in the world capitalist system was also the direct consequence of American hegemony. Washington associated violent, revolutionary change with the Soviet Union. Movements that espoused these tactics, such as the national liberation movements in southern Africa, were quickly cast as antidemocratic, anticapitalist, and anti-Western. This approach often became a self-fulfilling prophecy, because these groups turned to the communist world when they did not receive assistance from the West.[64]

Some countries in the capitalist world system did experience regime change that broke free from these internationally defined constraints. However, none of these regime transitions produced democracy, though all of the new regimes became enemies of the United States.

Regime Change within the Communist World

Limits on internal change were even more severe within the communist world. In addition to not tolerating the transformation of economic institutions, Soviet

---

[62] Richard Barnett, *Intervention and Revolution: American Confrontation with Insurgent Movements around the World* (New York: New American Library/World, 1968).

[63] David Adesnik and Michael McFaul, "Engaging Autocratic Allies to Promote Democracy." *The Washington Quarterly* (Spring 2006), pp. 7–26.

[64] Michael McFaul, "Southern African Liberation and Great Power Intervention: Towards a Theory of Revolution in an International Context." Unpublished Ph.D. dissertation, 1991.

officials also tried to block even incremental changes of political institutions. In other words, transitions of any type were simply thwarted, either through changing the balance of power in favor of ruling communist elites in Eastern Europe, or when that failed, through direct military intervention.

Because transitions of any sort were discouraged, Soviet officials usually worked to limit the emergence of both soft-liners within the *ancien régime* and moderate forces within the society, that is, the kinds of actors that helped to produce democratic transitions in the world capitalist system. After Stalin's death in 1953 and Khrushchev's deliberate efforts to thaw communism, soft-liners within communist Eastern Europe did take advantage of the apparent new policy from Moscow to press for incremental changes in the rules of the game for governing their countries. In all cases, however – East Germany in 1953, Poland in 1956, and Hungary in 1956 – the reform trajectory went beyond what Moscow had intended, a situation that triggered internal crackdowns in East Germany and Poland and Soviet military intervention in Hungary. Twelve years later, in 1968, the same occurred in Czechoslovakia. Soviet power simply did not allow regime change in the Soviet bloc.

The Solidarity movement in Poland in 1980–81 represented a new "mode of transition" in the communist world, as impetus for change came from a mass-based societal movement outside of the regime. The scale and success of Solidarity created real dilemmas for Soviet officials and their allies in Warsaw, because a Soviet military intervention against a movement ten million strong would be much more costly and destabilizing than previous Soviet invasions in Hungary in 1956 or Czechoslovakia in 1968. The specter of repression hung in the air throughout Solidarity's ascendancy. Solidarity leaders deliberately tried to limit the scope of their agenda of change; the term "self-limiting revolution" was coined to signal their understanding of the parameters of the possible.[65] Eventually, however, even a self-limiting revolution could not be tolerated; in December 1981, General Jaruzelski declared martial law, arrested Solidarity leaders, and squashed this attempted transition.

The structure of this international system also played a major role in organizing the "ideologies of opposition" among social movements seeking regime change around the world. Albeit with lots of variation and nuance, those pursuing regime change in the world capitalist system gravitated toward communist ideologies, driven by the logic that "the enemy of my enemy is my friend." Those pursuing regime change in the world communist system gravitated toward capitalist and democratic ideologies, driven by similar logic. This polarization produced some peculiar paradoxes. For instance, the trade union movements in Poland and South Africa in the 1980s had many similar demands and were composed of similar kinds of activists. But because Solidarity opposed the communist regime in Poland, it gravitated toward procapitalist, prodemocratic ideas (at least before the transition), whereas COSATU in South

[65] Jadwiga Staniszkis, *Poland's Self-Limiting Revolution* (Princeton, NJ: Princeton University Press, 1984).

Africa – being in opposition to a regime allied with the West – gravitated toward prosocialist ideas (again, at least before the transition).

Iran in 1953, Hungary in 1956, Chile in 1973, and Poland in 1980 (which occurred after the third wave had begun in 1974) are rarely treated in the democratization literature as cases of attempted transition. Yet, had these failed cases of transition been included in the analysis, the overwhelming role of the bipolar international system in shaping regime change outcomes would have been more apparent.

III. THE UNIPOLAR INTERNATIONAL SYSTEM AND THE FOURTH WAVE

The bipolar international system described above disappeared at the end of the 1980s. In its place emerged a unipolar system anchored by the United States.[66] This new international system, at least in its first decade of existence, also contained a great deal of consensus about how economies and polities should be organized and how states should interact with each other.[67] Market capitalism became the only legitimate form of economic organization. Democracy became the most legitimate form of political organization. New variants of autocracy have emerged in several states that emerged from the USSR's dissolution, whereas autocrats still calling their regimes communist remain in China, Cuba, and Vietnam. Yet, in all of these dictatorships, those in power no longer champion a form of government *alternative* to democracy. Rather, they claim either that their regimes are already democratic even if they are not (Russia) or that they are moving their countries step by step toward democracy (China).[68] For the vast majority of the world, democracy is either the practice or the stated goal. Pockets of illiberal creeds, racist norms, patrimonial rituals, and antidemocratic ideologies exist throughout the world, but only bin Ladenism and its variants constitute a serious *transnational* alternative to liberal

---

[66] William Wohlforth, "The Stability of a Unipolar World." *International Security*, 24, No. 1 (Summer 1999), pp. 5–41. Some, though, think that this system will not last long. See Immanuel Wallerstein, "The Eagle has Crash Landed." *Foreign Policy*, 131 (July–August 2002), pp. 60–9; and Charles Kupchan, *The End of the American Era: U.S. Foreign Policy and the Geopolitics of the Twenty-First Century* (New York: Knopf, 2002).

[67] Fukuyama, *The End of History*. This is not the only international system, however, that has exhibited a high level of agreement about international and domestic norms. For instance, the period in European history immediately preceding the French Revolution offers a case of high homogeneity concerning principles of international relations, in sharp contrast to the U.S.–Soviet relationship from 1947 to 1990. See Richard Rosecrance, *Action and Reaction in World Politics: International Systems in Perspective*, Chap. 2, pp. 17–30 (Boston: Little, Brown, 1963). The European Concert is also frequently cited as a more homogeneous world, if not a return to the pre-1789 system. See, for instance, Edward Gulik, *Europe's Classical Balance of Power* (Ithaca: Cornell University Press, 1955); Henry Kissinger, *A World Restored* (Boston: Houghton Mifflin, 1957).

[68] In his visit to the United States in April 2006, the Chinese leader Hu Jintao used the phrase "democratic management," whereas Putin's public relations specialists coined the term "managed democracy" and then "sovereign democracy."

democracy. This alternative has neither mass appeal nor a powerful state or set of states behind it.[69]

For regime change around the world, but especially in the postcommunist world, this new international system had profound consequences for the mode of transition. First, when the Soviet Union disappeared both as a state and as a great power, there was no longer an external actor capable of skewing the balance of power in favor of the ruling regimes within Eastern Europe or in the newly independent states to emerge from the Soviet Union. When this exogenous supplier of power for the status quo weakened and then vanished, the distribution of power between supporters of democratic change and supporters of a new kind of autocracy became the central, if not only, determinant of regime change outcomes in the Eurasian communist world.[70] Whether democracy emerged or not, however, was a function of the local balance of power at the time of transition, and not the result of American or European attempts to reconfigure the internal balances of power in the former communist world.[71] Incentives to join Western multilateral institutions such as NATO or the European Union only have a causal effect on the period *after* transition, or in other words, during the consolidation phase, as detailed in the chapters by Vachudova, Mungiu-Pippidi, and Petrova later in this volume. Stalemated, relatively equal balances of power between the old regime and societal challengers did not produce democratic transitions. Without the specter of Soviet intervention, democracy emerged in those countries where the internal distribution of power strongly favored the challengers to the *ancien régime*, making

---

[69] Bin Laden and the more serious thinkers who preceded him (if bin Laden is the Lenin of this antisystematic movement, Qutb is the Marx) have developed a comprehensive set of beliefs that claim to explain everything in the world. According to their worldview, the central drama in international affairs is not a conflict between states, but a normative, Manichean struggle between the forces of good and evil. This ideological movement not only rejects democracy as the best system of government, but also offers an alternative values-based polity, which, they submit, is both better than any Western model and also essential for living a proper Muslim life. After decades of decline, bin Ladenism and its ideological soul mates gained new vibrancy after September 11 and the American-led invasion of Iraq. Yet this ideological alternative is hardly a worldwide challenger to democracy as the most valued political system in the world. Adherents to bin Ladenism have not (yet) seized control of a major state. The Taliban regime in Afghanistan is now gone. The ideological energy of the Islamic Republic of Iran is also extinguished, even if the mullahs' dictatorship lingers on. And even in Iran, officials from the government claim to be practicing democracy, or more minimally, introducing changes to make the regime more democratic.

[70] Some communist regimes, such as Yugoslavia, China, or Vietnam, did not rely on Soviet support and therefore endured because of domestic distributions of powers well before Soviet decline. However, some peripheral communist regimes, such as Mozambique, Angola, and Cuba, did rely on Soviet support and therefore experienced different kinds of regime change trajectories in the new international system. Some, such as the regime in Mozambique, collapsed, whereas others, such as Fidel Castro's dictatorship, had enough domestic power to survive without Moscow's support.

[71] On the limited role of the United States in changing the internal balance of power in favor of democrats, see Steven Levitsky and Lucan Way, "International Linkage and Democratization." *Journal of Democracy*, 16, No. 3 (2005), pp. 20–34.

diffusion of protest possible, as explained in Chapter 2 by Valerie Bunce and Sharon Wolchik. This mode of transition – very different from the mode of transition in the third wave democracies – was a direct result of changes in the external environment.

Second and related, the unipolar international system no longer placed strict limits on the kinds of actors that could participate in transition processes. In the third wave, "no stable political democracy has resulted from regime transitions in which mass actors have gained control even momentarily over traditional ruling classes"[72] because the United States or Soviet Union would intervene to shore up these ruling classes when challenged by mass actors. When mass actors began to assert themselves in the transition process in places such as Poland, East Germany, and Czechoslovakia in 1989, the world's last standing hegemon did little to discourage them. On the contrary, prior to this transition moment, American governments and nongovernmental organizations actively sought to strengthen these mass-based actors. For instance, "In the end," according to Arch Puddington, "the AFL-CIO was responsible for channeling over $4 million to Solidarity" in Poland during the 1980s.[73]

Third, this new hegemon – the United States – also did not see the need to press for pacts, negotiation, and evolutionary change in the communist world. In its own neighborhood, the United States abhorred rapid, violent regime change, because it was unpredictable and usually empowered anti-American forces. Americans did not have such fears about opposition forces in communist Europe or in the former Soviet Union, because these radicals were also pro-American. President George H. W. Bush did fear state dissolution in the Soviet Union after witnessing the violent collapse of Yugoslavia. But the United States never pressed opposition movements to negotiate with elites from the old order. And when opposition movements violated pacts, as in Poland after the first election, Americans only applauded. The earlier priority placed on cooperation and negotiation as the method for transitions weakened.

Fourth, the new international system allowed the agenda of change on the table during transition to widen – first to include full-scale political change, but also to include fundamental reorganization of economic institutions and even a redrawing of state borders. During the Cold War, the Soviet Union allowed no agenda of change at all. With the Soviet Union gone, the United States actively expanded the agenda of change to include economic institutions, even though some transitologists were writing about the deleterious consequences of simultaneous change of political and economic institutions.[74] As the anchor of the international system, the United States did not actively promote the expansion of the agenda of change during transitions to include the redrawing

[72] Terry Karl, "Dilemmas of Democratization in Latin America." *Comparative Politics*, 23 (October 1990), p. 8.

[73] Arch Puddington, *Lane Kirkland: Champion of American Labor* (New York: Wiley, 2005), p. 189.

[74] Przeworski, *Democracy and the Market*.

of state borders, except in the case of German unification. On the contrary, President George H. W. Bush actively tried to keep this issue off the agenda during the transition period in the Soviet Union. As he stated in his famous "Chicken Kiev" speech in the summer of 1991, "freedom is not the same as independence. Americans will not support those who seek independence in order to replace a far-off tyranny with a local despotism. They will not aid those who promote a suicidal nationalism based on ethnic hatred."[75] When several republics of the Soviet Union declared their independence, including the Russian Federation, the United States did not formally recognize any of these aspiring states.[76] Yet the United States also did not support those who tried to impede state disintegration (in contrast, for instance, to American support for the Nigerian federal government when it launched a brutal war against the Ibos in 1967 to prevent the breakup of the Nigerian state). The United States only welcomed new states into the international community once local independent movements' leaders had created irreversible facts on the ground securing statehood.

Fifth, the unipolar international system became more permissive regarding regime change at the end of the 1980s and early 1990s because the number of legitimate regime alternatives had narrowed to one – democracy. Earlier in the century, both superpowers feared that a process of political liberalization might lead unintentionally to regime change of the "wrong" kind. American leadership's worries about such outcomes diminished in the 1990s, when Soviet leaders simply did not exist to resist the kinds of regime outcomes that occurred in places such as Poland, Hungary, and the Czech Republic. Fifteen years later, American officials would begin to worry again about the kind of regimes that might emerge from transitions in the Middle East. Likewise, a new autocratic regime in Moscow under Vladimir Putin wielded Russian power yet again to support antidemocratic regimes and political groups throughout the former Soviet space.[77] But for the first transitions in the fourth wave, the emergence of antidemocratic, anti-Western regimes was not a major concern.[78]

The unipolar international system had its most profound effects on transitions in the former communist world, but not only in this region. In South Africa, mass actors and even radical mass actors such as the South African Communist Party (SACP) played a central role in the successful transition to

75 George Bush, "Remarks to the Supreme Soviet of the Ukrainian Soviet Socialist Republic, Kiev, Ukraine, August 1, 1991." In U.S. Department of State Dispatch, August 12, 1991, pp. 596–8.
76 James Goldgeier and Michael McFaul, *Power and Purpose*, Chap. 2, pp. 18–40 (Washington, DC: Brookings Institution Press, 2003).
77 Michael Allen and Carl Gershman, "The Assault on Democracy Assistance." *Journal of Democracy* (April 2006); Ivan Krastev, "Russia's Post-Orange Empire." OpenDemocracy.net, available at http://www.opendemocracy.net/democracy-europe_constitution/postorange_2947.jsp; accessed October 20, 2005.
78 The specter of a fascist regime did emerge in the early 1990s in Russia, but never crystallized. See Michael McFaul, "Thwarting the Specter of Russian Fascism." *Demokratizatsiya*, 1, No. 2 (Winter 1993), pp. 1–19.

democracy in this hitherto polarized society. It is difficult to imagine that the United States would have withdrawn support from the apartheid regime and acquiesced to the African National Congress (ANC) or SACP during the heyday of Soviet expansion into Africa in the 1970s.[79] Even in the recent transitions from autocratic rule that have empowered terrorist organizations, such as the election in the Palestinian Authority that brought Hamas to power, it is hard to imagine the United States acquiescing to such an outcome if Hamas enjoyed a direct alliance with a major anti-American revisionist superpower in the international system. American nervous acceptance of the rise of Islamic parties through electoral processes in Egypt and Morocco is also a consequence, in part, of a new international system still dominated by the United States. During the Cold War, a victory for an anti-American political group in a country as remote as Angola was interpreted in Washington as another data point in calculating the "correlation of forces" between capitalism and communism.

In this new international system, victories for anti-American political movements in peripheral countries are still a concern for Washington leaders, but are less worrisome because there is no menacing ideologically motivated hegemon to support these newly victorious forces. Western leaders are more willing to coopt these challengers to the status quo through the democratic process than they were willing to try to coopt communist challengers when they threatened to assume power in peripheral countries during the Cold War.

Finally, beyond the scope of this chapter, but taken up in Part II of this volume, the effects of this new international system were greatest regarding democratic consolidation.[80] Most strikingly, as already mentioned, European Union conditionality played a central role in pulling new, fragile democracies in Europe toward liberal democracy.[81] Other international institutions, such as the OAS and NATO, also have played positive, democracy-enhancing roles in their regions.

IV. AMERICAN INFLUENCE ON THE SOVIET "TRANSITION"

Conceptually, of course, it is rather awkward to discuss a change in the value of the independent variable labeled "international system" in this essay when the change in the value of this variable was brought about by a regime change in one of the countries being discussed – the Soviet Union. It is perhaps more accurate to cast this international unipolar system as a causal structural variable influencing the fourth wave transitions only after the Soviet/Russian transition had unfolded far enough so that the system had only one power, not two. Pinpointing precisely when this occurred is difficult, especially because the

---

[79] This said, George Shultz did agree to meet with ANC officials in 1986, well before the Soviet Union had shown signs of weakness. (Author's conversations with Shultz, October 2005.)

[80] Levitsky and Way, "International Linkage and Democratization."

[81] Milada Vachudova, *Europe Undivided: Democracy, Leverage and Integration after Communism* (New York: Oxford University Press, 2005).

ideational shift from two competing systems to one occurred much earlier than the change in the power shift from bipolarity to unipolarity. In 1989, the Soviet Union had the military resources to *try* to roll back the regime change underway in Poland (though whether such actions would have been successful is another matter). But when it became clear that the roundtable negotiations underway in Poland that year might lead to a fundamental reorganization of the political institutions governing Poland, Soviet leader Mikhail Gorbachev made the decision not to intervene. It was not power but preferences, informed by a new set of ideas about how to organize states internally and how to organize interaction between states, that shaped Soviet actions at the time. Obviously, this Soviet signal of acceptance of regime change in other parts of the communist world had a profound effect on democratization throughout the region. Soviet "new thinking" was a necessary condition for regime change in the region. In fact, it may not be an overstatement that the entire process of democratization in the western part of the communist world and autocratization in the eastern part of the communist world started in Moscow, not Warsaw or Prague.[82]

This interpretation of external sources of domestic change in the fourth wave cries out for an answer to the question of what role external forces played in the Soviet/Russian transition itself. The withdrawal of Soviet support for communist regimes in the Warsaw Pact was an obvious external trigger for regime change in these countries, but Soviet weakness obviously cannot have been the *external* cause for Soviet/Russian regime change. A comprehensive discussion of all external factors on Soviet/Russian political change is beyond the scope of this essay, but several brief points must be made.

First, compared to transitions in smaller countries in both the third and fourth waves, the regime change that started from Moscow was more insulated from international forces. Generally, the larger the country, the less impact the outside world has on the development of revolutionary situations and revolutionary outcomes.[83] In contrast to East Central Europe, Russia's enormity and longer experiences with autocracy made the collapse of old institutions and the rise of new institutions more of a domestic affair.

Second, Soviet relative weakness compared to American strength did not compel regime change. Some, for instance, have suggested that the American military buildup and the initiation of the Strategic Defense Initiative (SDI) in the 1980s forced Soviet leaders to increase military spending, which in turn bankrupted the Soviet economy. The evidence for this hypothesis, however, is extremely thin.[84] Soviet military spending did not rise in proportion to American military spending during the first term of the Reagan administration. Nor

[82] Of course, this is a contentious assertion, but not outlandishly contentious. For an alternative view, see Daniel Thomas, *The Helsinki Effect: International Norms, Human Rights and the Demise of Communism* (Princeton, NJ: Princeton University Press, 2001).

[83] This is the argument in McFaul, "Southern African Liberation and Great Power Intervention."

[84] Matthew Evangelista, *Unarmed Forces: The Transitional Movement to End the Cold War* (Ithaca: Cornell University Press, 1999).

was the Soviet reaction to SDI fear or capitulation, but rather emulation. For good technological reasons (which still hold true twenty years later), Soviet leaders were also confident that they could overwhelm any new antiballistic defense system with new offensive weapons. Some have also posited that imperial overreach throughout the world, exacerbated by American support for anticommunist guerilla movements in Nicaragua, Angola, Cambodia, and Afghanistan, brought down the Soviet system. Although Soviet foreign policy elites most certainly rethought the benefits of propping up these satellites, the economic and military costs of these adventures, including even the Afghan war, were not sufficient to cripple the Soviet economy.[85] Nor, more generally, was the Soviet economy on the verge of collapse when Gorbachev began to implement economic and political changes.[86] The Soviet command economy could have survived for decades, especially with recent spikes in energy prices, before collapsing from Western pressure.

Third, direct American engagement of moderate reformers within the old regime, including first and foremost Mikhail Gorbachev, was real.[87] Improved Soviet–American relations created a permissive environment for internal change within the Soviet Union. Likewise, American NGOs did provide a modicum of technical and financial assistance to democratic opposition groups in Russian society during the period of transition.[88] Direct American efforts to shape the transition, however, were very limited. The one major intervention by the United States in the Gorbachev era regarding these fundamental debates was George Bush's infamous speech in Kiev, Ukraine in June 1991, mentioned above, in which he urged caution and patience regarding the redrawing of the borders of the Soviet Union, an intervention that obviously had little impact on the outcome of this debate.

Ultimately, the Soviet transition began because Soviet leader Mikhail Gorbachev decided to begin it. It was his preference for change, not innate forces from inside or out, that started the process of regime change in the Soviet Union and then Russia.[89] Without question, the West helped shape Gorbachev's preferences for change. He was well aware that the standard of living in his country was well below that of Europe and he wanted to close the gap.[90] In other words, the West and the United States in particular provided examples of a more prosperous and efficient economy. It was the pull of this Western example, not the threat of American military power, that shaped Gorbachev's

---

[85] On rethinking, see Sarah Mendelson, *Changing Course: Ideas, Politics, and the Soviet Withdrawal from Afghanistan* (Princeton, NJ: Princeton University Press, 1998).

[86] Alexander Dallin, "Causes of the Collapse of the USSR." *Post-Soviet Affairs* No. 4 (1992), pp. 279–302.

[87] Shultz; Gorbachev.

[88] For details, see Goldgeier and McFaul, *Power and Purpose*.

[89] The totalitarian structure of the Soviet regime meant that change had to begin with the General Secretary. For elaboration, see McFaul, *Russia's Unfinished Revolution*, Chap. 2.

[90] Mikhail Gorbachev, *Memoirs*, based on translation by Georges Peronansky and Tatjana Varsavsky (New York: Doubleday, 1996).

particular response to the economic and moral malaise that he perceived in the Soviet Union when he took power.[91] The democratic principles of the American system also played an inspirational role for Soviet dissidents and influenced the thinking of important reformers in Gorbachev's Politburo, such as Aleksandr Yakovlev.[92] Once he initiated the process of reform, however, the West did not play a direct causal role in influencing outcomes regarding the major debates about institutional change underway at the time. Gorbachev eventually lost control of the process, but when he did, the United States and other Western countries played only a marginal role in steering the chaotic transformation.

Later in the Soviet/Russian transition, external actors helped to shape the ideas and tactics of the opposition (in the language of third wave transitologists, the moderates from civil society) involved in the Soviet and Russian drama. For instance, Yeltsin and his allies adopted more radically pro-Western positions during their struggle against Gorbachev to help win recognition from the West. They also refrained from using violence to overthrow the Soviet regime and resisted punishing Gorbachev after they seized power (a popular figure in the West at the time) in part to win favor in the West.[93] After victory and the thwarting of the coup attempt in August 1991, Russian institutional designers mimicked Western institutional arrangements, in part as a strategy for obtaining Western financial assistance. International intervention in Russian domestic debates about the design of new institutions was much more aggressive after the Soviet collapse, especially regarding the design of economic institutions. At the same time, Western governmental leaders mostly refrained from trying to influence domestic debates about political institutions. Strikingly, neither the United States nor any European power punished the Yeltsin administration for dissolving the Congress of People's Deputies in 1993 or invading Chechnya in 1994, the two most egregious violations of democratic principles of this transition period. The Clinton administration helped to bolster Yeltsin's reelection efforts in 1996 by providing a timely new IMF package three months before the election. Privately, the Clinton administration did send signals about the negative consequences of postponing the 1996 elections. Yet these interventions only influenced Russian politics on the margins. In the two biggest battles regarding the design of political institutions, which culminated in

[91] Gorbachev or another leader in his place could have selected an alternative strategy for responding to this same situation. Instead of emulating the West or reaching out to the West, the Soviet leader could have responded instead with more restrictive economic policies at home or more imperial, diversionary policies abroad. See Daniel Deudney and John Ikenberry, "The International Sources of Soviet Change." *International Security*, 16, No. 3 (Winter 1991–2), pp. 74–118.

[92] Yakovlev studied as an exchange student in the United States and then spent a decade living in Canada as the Soviet ambassador. See Leon Aron, "The 'Mystery' of the Soviet Collapse." *Journal of Democracy*, 16, No. 2 (2006), pp. 21–35.

[93] See Michael McFaul, "The Sovereignty Script: Red Book for Russian Revolutionaries." In *Problematic Sovereignty*, Stephen Krasner, ed., pp. 194–223 (New York: Columbia University Press, 2001).

armed conflict in 1991 and again in 1993, external actors played almost no role at all.[94]

Western NGOs also spent much greater resources after the Soviet collapse in an effort to consolidate Russian democracy, but these efforts focused on consolidation not regime change.[95] Moreover, because Russia's regime has become more autocratic in recent years, especially under Vladimir Putin's presidency from 2000–2008, these efforts appeared to have produced little impact.[96]

V. CONCLUSION

When examined from a comparative perspective, the third wave transitions look different from the fourth wave transitions. Through this same comparative lens, the explanation for these differences seems related to historical and cultural differences, including the experience with democracy in an earlier period or divergent starting points (i.e., communist dictatorship compared to noncommunist dictatorship). Yet domestic-level explanations of the differences between third wave and fourth wave theories of democratization (or the lack thereof) are not sufficient. A missing and changing variable – the international system – must be brought into the analysis if we are ever to have a unified theory of democratization.

[94] For elaboration, see Goldgeier and McFaul, *Power and Purpose.*
[95] Thomas Carothers, *Aiding Democracy Abroad: The Learning Curve* (Washington, DC: Carnegie Endowment for International Peace, 1999); Larry Diamond, *Promoting Democracy in the 1990s: Actors and Instruments, Issues and Imperatives* (New York: Carnegie Corporation of New York, 1995); Michael Pinto-Duschinsky, "The Rise of 'Political Aid.'" In *Consolidating the Third Wave Democracies: Regional Challenges*, Larry Diamond, Marc Plattner, Yun-han Chu, and Hung-mao Tien, eds., pp. 295–324 (Baltimore: Johns Hopkins University Press, 1997).
[96] Goldgeier and McFaul, *Power and Purpose.*

2

A Regional Tradition

The Diffusion of Democratic Change under Communism and Postcommunism

Valerie Bunce
Cornell University

Sharon Wolchik
George Washington University

The large-scale involvement of citizens in political life, images of town squares packed with people, along with occasions of euphoria, brought back memories of November, 1989, when the communist regime in Czechoslovakia collapsed.

Martin Butora on the 1998 Slovak election[1]

DEMOCRATIZATION AND DIFFUSION[2]

In a recent statistical analysis of the global spread of democratic governance, Daniel Brinks and Michael Coppedge argue that a major characteristic of the Third Wave has been the intraregional diffusion of transitions from dictatorship to democracy.[3] Thus, even when other influential factors are taken into account, democratization in one state seems to increase the probability of democratization in adjacent states. It is the clustering of democratic change in both temporal and geographical terms since the mid-1970s, therefore, that provides strong evidence for Brinks and Coppedge of cross-national diffusion dynamics at work.

---

[1] Martin Butora, "OK98: A Campaign of Slovak NGOs for Free and Fair Elections." In *Reclaiming Democracy: Civil Society and Electoral Change in Central and Eastern Europe*, Joerg Forbrig and Pavol Demes, eds., pp. 21–52 (Washington, DC: German Marshall Fund, 2007b).

[2] We are thankful to the International Center for Non-Violent Conflict, the Smith Richardson Foundation, the Einaudi Center for International Studies, and the Institute for the Social Sciences at Cornell University for their support of this project. In addition, we thank Vlad Micic, Sara Rzyeva, Nancy Meyers, and Melissa Aten for their research assistance and Holly Case, Padraic Kenney, Mike McFaul, and Kathryn Stoner-Weiss for their comments on earlier drafts of this chapter.

[3] Daniel Brinks and Michael Coppedge, "Diffusion Is No Illusion: Neighbor Emulation in the Third Wave of Democracy." *Comparative Political Studies*, 39, No. 7 (September 2006), pp. 1–23; also see Samuel Huntington, *The Third Wave: Democratization in the Late Twentieth Century* (Norman, OK: University of Oklahoma Press, 1991).

This is an important finding. However, like many diffusion studies, this one suffers from a "high altitude problem."[4] Because the authors are relatively removed from what is happening on the ground, they leave a number of important questions about the diffusion of democracy unanswered. First, it is not clear in their study what exactly is being diffused – the idea of democracy, the precedent of removing authoritarian leaders from office, a set of common strategies for challenging authoritarian rule, or a similar ensemble of new political institutions. Second, this study is silent on the question of how the diffusion of democracy actually works, that is, how democratic changes are transferred from one place to another. Finally, Brinks and Coppedge have little to say about the details of diffusion – for example, why some countries lead the way in the spread of democracy; why some countries follow in their footsteps; and why diffusion is finite in its geographical reach.

EXPLAINING WAVES OF DEMOCRATIC CHANGE UNDER COMMUNISM AND POSTCOMMUNISM

The purpose of this chapter is to bring some comparative evidence to bear on these important issues related to the cross-national diffusion of democracy. We focus on one aspect of democratic development: major challenges to authoritarian rule mounted by political oppositions and everyday citizens. As a number of recent studies have suggested and as most of the chapters in this volume support, although far from guaranteeing the rise and consolidation of democracy, mobilizations "from below" against authoritarian governance have usually functioned as both a first and necessary step in the transition from dictatorship to democracy.[5] An equally important consideration is that protests against authoritarian politics have shown themselves to be quite amenable at certain times to diffusion across national boundaries – the revolutions of 1848 being a case in point.[6]

The mobilizations of interest in this chapter, not surprisingly as a result of the focus of this volume, have taken place in postcommunist Europe and Eurasia.

---

[4] Wade Jacoby, "Inspiration, Coalition and Substitution: External Influences on Postcommunist Transformations." *World Politics*, 58, No. 4 (July 2006), pp. 623–51.

[5] See, for example, Valerie Bunce, "Comparative Democratization: Big and Bounded Generalizations." *Comparative Political Studies*, 33, Nos. 6–7 (August–September 2000), pp. 703–34; Valerie Bunce, "Rethinking Recent Democratization: Lessons from the Postcommunist Experience." *World Politics*, 55 (January 2003), pp. 167–92; Peter Ackerman and Adrian Karatnycky, *How Freedom Is Won: From Civic Resistance to Durable Democracy* (New York: Freedom House, 2005); Axel Hadenius and Jan Teorell, "Pathways from Authoritarianism." *Journal of Democracy*, 18, No. 1 (January, 2007), pp. 143–56; Peter Ackerman and Jack Duvall, *A Force More Powerful: A Century of Nonviolent Conflict* (New York: Palgrave, 2000); Kurt Schock, "Nonviolent Action and Its Misconceptions: Insights for Social Scientists," *PS*, 36, No. 4 (October 2003), pp. 705–12; Kurt Schock, *Unarmed Insurrections: People Power Movements in Nondemocracies* (Minneapolis: University of Minnesota Press, 2005).

[6] See John Markoff, *Waves of Democracy: Social Movements and Political Change. Sociology for a New Century* (Thousand Oaks, CA: Pine Forge Press, 1996).

However, in contrast to most diffusion studies, which limit their attention to a single round of change, we compare *two* waves of challenges to dictatorial rule in this region.[7] The first and more widely studied spread of mass mobilizations against authoritarianism took place from 1987 to 1990, when citizens across the region took to the streets to challenge the right and capacity of communist parties to rule them. These protests had dramatic consequences – no less than the end of the communist experiment, the Cold War international order, and three long-established states in the region, the Soviet Union, Czechoslovakia, and Yugoslavia.

The second wave of mobilizations against dictators took place under post-communism, not communism. Thus, from 1996 to 2005, mass publics, once again in collaboration with opposition groups, reentered the political arena in large numbers to defeat dictators in many states in the region where the 1989 protests had not played a significant role or where they had failed to translate into the formation of fully democratic and capitalist orders.[8] In this round, the regime context was different from the first wave in two respects: one was that the communist version of authoritarianism had been replaced by other types of regimes, and the other was that the regime sites for mobilizations against authoritarian leaders were far from uniform, ranging from the relatively democratic polity of Bulgaria to the relatively authoritarian regime in Serbia. Citizen mobilization in the second wave also took somewhat different forms – instead of mass protests in the streets, which was characteristic of the first wave, the focus of activity in the second round involved in all cases voting for

[7] But see Markoff, *Waves of Democracy*; Sidney Tarrow, *The New Transnational Activism* (Cambridge: Cambridge University Press, 2005); Sidney Tarrow and D. della Porta, "Globalization, Complex Internationalism and Transnational Contention." In *Transnational Protest and Global Activism*, Donatella della Porta and S. Tarrow, eds., pp. 227–46 (Lanham, MD: Rowman and Littlefield, 2005).

[8] See, for example, the chapters in this volume by Petrova, McFaul, Welt, and Radnitz, and also see Valerie Bunce and Sharon Wolchik, "Favorable Conditions and Electoral Revolutions." *Journal of Democracy*, 17 (2006), pp. 7–18; Valerie Bunce and Sharon Wolchik, "International Diffusion and Postcommunist Electoral Revolutions." *Communist and Postcommunist Studies*, 39, No. 3 (September 2006), pp. 283–304; Valerie Bunce and Sharon Wolchik, "Democratizing Elections in the Postcommunist World: Definitions, Dynamics and Diffusion." *St. Antony's International Review*, 2, No. 2 (February 2007), pp. 64–89; Valerie Bunce and Sharon Wolchik, "Youth and Postcommunist Electoral Revolutions: Never Trust Anyone Over 300?" In *Reclaiming Democracy: Civil Society and Electoral Change in Central and Eastern Europe*, Joerg Forbrig and Pavol Demes, eds., pp. 191–204 (Washington, DC: German Marshall Fund, 2007); Valerie Bunce and Sharon Wolchik, *American Democracy Promotion and Electoral Change in Postcommunist Europe and Eurasia* (2008); Valerie Bunce and Sharon Wolchik, "Getting Real about Real Causes: A Reply to Lucan Way." *Journal of Democracy*, 20 (2009), pp. 69–73; Valerie Bunce, "Global Patterns and Postcommunist Dynamics." *Orbis* 50, No. 4 (2006), pp. 601–20; Larissa Kurekova, "Electoral Revolutions and Their Socio-economic Impact: Bulgaria and Slovakia in Comparative Perspective." Master's thesis, Central European University, Budapest, 2006; Michael McFaul, "Transitions from Postcommunism." *Journal of Democracy* 16, No. 3 (2005), Joerg and Pavol Demes, eds., *Reclaiming Democracy: Civil Society and Electoral Change in Central and Eastern Europe* (Washington, DC: German Marshall Fund, 2007).

the liberal opposition in competitive or semicompetitive elections, and, in the more authoritarian contexts of Serbia, Georgia, Ukraine, and Kyrgyzstan, carrying out protests after the election to force a transfer of political power from authoritarians, who lost the election, to the victorious democratic opposition.

A comparison of these two waves of democratic change has the methodological advantages of providing a large number of cases of mobilization against authoritarian rule and holding constant the region, a communist past, and by all counts a diffusion dynamic, yet at the same time varying the regime context and the methods used to challenge authoritarian rule.[9] This comparison also allows us to accomplish three related objectives. One follows from what has already been argued: to fill in some of the gaps in our understanding of how democracy diffuses within regions. Another is to recognize, as this volume does, that democratization is far from a one-shot deal and to compare, as a result, successive attempts within the same region to break with authoritarian rule. Finally, these two waves provide an excellent opportunity to explore systematically the causal dynamic of central interest in this book: that is, how international influences and the activities of everyday citizens and opposition groups interact with each other to shape regime developments.

Our analysis begins by defining diffusion and outlining some of its core properties. We then provide a summary of the two rounds of popular confrontations with authoritarian rule, providing somewhat more detail with respect to the more recent and less fully studied electoral challenges to authoritarian politics (from 1996 to 2005). In the final part of this chapter, we return to the questions posed earlier about leaders and followers in diffusion dynamics; the changing nature of the challenges to authoritarian rule as they radiate outward from the original sites where they took place; the uneven geography of diffusion; and the underlying mechanisms that transferred mobilizations in one country to other locations in the region. As we will discover, each of the two waves followed a pattern typical of diffusion dynamics – for example, the importance of simultaneous expansion of domestic and international opportunities for democratic change; cross-national variations in the willingness and capacity of domestic (and often international) actors to exploit these opportunities; and the roles of demonstration effects, similar local conditions, and transnational networks in transferring specific approaches to ending authoritarian rule from one country to others. Although similar in many respects, however, the two waves did diverge from one another. If the international system permitted diffusion in the first wave, its role in the second is more accurately summarized as active promotion. Second, although similarities in local conditions were paramount

---

[9] On the diffusion interpretation, see Nils R. Muiznieks, "The Influence of the Baltic Popular Movements on the Process of Soviet Disintegration." *Europe–Asia Studies*, 47, No. 1 (1995), pp. 3–25; Stanley Vardys, "Polish Echoes in the Baltics." *Problems of Communism*, 32 (July–August 1983), pp. 21–34; Archie Brown, "Transnational Influences in the Transition from Communism." *Post-Soviet Affairs*, 16 (2000); Bunce and Wolchik, "International Diffusion and Postcommunist Electoral Revolutions." *American Democracy Promotion.*

in the spread of political protests in 1989, transnational networks loomed much larger in facilitating the geographical reach of electoral challenges to authoritarian rule.

DEFINING DIFFUSION

Diffusion is a process in which new ideas, institutions, policies, models, or repertoires of behavior spread from their point of origin to new sites – for example, from one enterprise, governing unit, or nongovernmental organization to others.[10] Diffusion, therefore, implies a coincidence of time and geography with respect to similar new ways of doing things. When applied to the issues of interest here, diffusion refers to a significant shift in mass political behavior – that is, mobilization against authoritarian regimes in the streets and during elections – in one country that then moves to neighboring countries.

In our view, diffusion always involves a conscious decision by local actors, sometimes in collaboration with international allies, to copy innovations introduced by actors in other contexts – a decision that flows from their values and interests and that takes into account expanded opportunities, incentives, and capacity for change. How this process plays out, however, varies. One dynamic is what have been termed demonstration effects. This pattern occurs when a new development in one setting alters the calculus of actors in other settings – by redefining what is possible,[11] by alerting actors in other settings to a highly attractive course of action, and, as a result, by tilting the ratio of benefits versus risks attached to innovation in the decided favor of the former. Central to this scenario is the appeal of importing change from abroad because of dress rehearsals that establish positive precedents.

A second model of transmission is more structural, emphasizing similar cross-national conditions, including similar profiles of local problems and assets. Here, actors are prone to import a change when they see it as applicable and achievable in their own circumstances. The key issue in this scenario is a close cross-national fit – at least in the eyes of would-be importers – and the

---

[10] See, for example, Ackerman and Duvall, *A Force More Powerful*; Barbara Wehnert, "Diffusion and Development of Democracy, 1800–1999." *American Sociological Review*, 70, No. 1 (February 2005), pp. 53–81; Chang Kil Lee and David Strang, "The International Diffusion of Public Sector Downsizing." *International Organization*, 60, No. 4 (Fall 2005), pp. 883–909; Mark Beissinger, *Nationalist Mobilization and the Collapse of the Soviet State* (Cambridge: Cambridge University Press, 2002); Brinks and Coppedge, "Diffusion Is No Illusion"; Markoff, *Waves of Democracy*; Tarrow, *The New Transnational Activism*; Tarrow and della Porta, "Globalization, Complex Internationalism and Transnational Contention"; Johanna Bockman and Gil Eyal, "Eastern Europe as a Laboratory for Economic Knowledge: The Transnational Roots of Neoliberalism." *American Journal of Sociology*, 108, No. 1 (September 2002), pp. 310–52; Bunce and Wolchik, "International Diffusion and Postcommunist Electoral Revolutions," "Democratizing Elections in the Postcommunist World."

[11] As astutely observed by Adam Przeworski in an analysis of Solidarity; see Adam Przeworski, "The Man of Iron and the Men of Power in Poland." *Political Science*, 15 (Winter 1982), pp. 15–31.

intersection, given structural similarities and (we would emphasize) the reading by both exporters and importers of these similarities, of two conditions: the relevance of the innovation and positive assessments of its benefits.

Finally and less often noted: diffusion can take place because there are expanding collaborative networks that support change and that fan out from the original point of innovation. In this dynamic, two types of diffusion are at work and interact: the movement of the innovation itself and the movement of a complex array of actors supporting that innovation.[12]

Let us now step back from these definitions and transmission scenarios and provide both complications and refinements. First, most diffusion processes seem to combine at least the first two scenarios and sometimes the third as well.[13] Thus, innovations in one country often move elsewhere, because they are facilitated by structural similarities, and they are seen to be relevant and beneficial, as well as relatively easy to implement, by constituencies in another country – often in the same region. Such a combination is particularly important for the movement of highly controversial innovations, that is, changes that represent not just a considerable departure from past practices, but also a fundamental reordering of existing political, social, and economic hierarchies. Large-scale confrontations with authoritarian regimes are an obvious example.

For these very reasons, both the introduction of innovations, such as collective challenges to authoritarianism, and their spread across national boundaries are usually the work of both structural factors conducive to change – for instance, shifts in international politics that leave regimes more isolated and regimes that become more vulnerable as a result of economic difficulties and declining public support – and agency effects – for example, new strategies adopted by both challengers to the status quo and its resolute defenders.[14] This is one reason that it is a mistake to assume (as is common in retrospective studies of major political events, such as revolutions) that dramatic shifts in politics are somehow inevitable because of, say, regime decline, and that it is also a mistake to attribute major changes to very recent developments (which was the approach adopted in the earliest studies of the Third Wave of democratization). Just as "inevitable" changes are usually the product of long struggles that combine with actors willing and able to exploit short-term shifts

---

[12] See, especially, Bookman and Eyal, "Eastern Europe as a Laboratory for Economic Knowledge"; Jacoby, "Inspiration, Coalition, and Substitution"; Muiznieks, "The Influence of the Baltic Popular Movements"; and especially Tarrow, *The New Transnational Activism* and Tarrow and della Porta, "Globalization, Complex Internationalism and Transnational Contention" on both "rooted cosmopolitans" and the critical role of trust.

[13] See, especially, Jacoby, "Inspiration, Coalition, and Substitution"; Beissinger, *Nationalist Mobilization*.

[14] See Bunce and Wolchik, *American Democracy Promotion*; but see Lucan Way, "The Real Causes of the Color Revolutions." *Journal of Democracy*, 19, No. 3 (July 2008), pp. 55–69; Lucan Way, "Authoritarian State-Building and the Sources of Regime Competitiveness in the Fourth Wave: The Cases of Belarus, Moldova, Russia and Ukraine." *World Politics*, 57 (January 2005), pp. 231–61; Lucan Way, "Ukraine's Orange Revolution: Kuchma's Failed Authoritarianism." *Journal of Democracy*, 16 (April 2005), pp. 131–45.

in opportunities and capacities for change, so a preoccupation with proximate causality runs the risks of mislabeling effects as causes; overlooking the long-term accumulation of learning on the part of both the regime and its opponents; and exaggerating the power of new ideas, international actors (who are often portrayed as "dictating" change), and "sudden" events that transform local circumstances.[15]

Moreover, innovations themselves are usually the product of diffusion processes. In the social world, there are precious few examples of pure originality. Instead, many innovations are the product of mini innovations in the past, and they are often the successors to partial, instructive, and earlier dry runs. For example, just as the 1989 protests were strongly influenced by earlier rounds of protest in the region, beginning in 1953 in Czechoslovakia and East Germany, so the electoral model of democratization – or elaborate and well-planned attempts by liberal oppositions to use competitive elections in semiauthoritarian regimes to defeat dictators in a variety of postcommunist regimes from 1996 to 2005 – built upon the experience of earlier electoral efforts in these countries, including recent victories by opposition parties in local political contests. Moreover, the lineage of the model goes back to the Philippines in 1986, when Ferdinand Marcos was running for reelection, and the 1988 Pinochet referendum in Chile. These challenges to authoritarianism in Latin America and Southeast Asia had several consequences that proved to be critical for the subsequent rise and success of the electoral model in the postcommunist region. For example, they contributed to a major shift in American foreign policy from support of dictators to support of democrats. At the same time, some American policy makers involved in these earlier confrontations with authoritarian rulers became engaged many years later in the efforts to support free and fair elections in Serbia and the defeat of Milošević in 2000.[16]

We can now close this discussion of diffusion with a final generalization drawn from the literature on this subject that will prove useful for the discussion that follows. The cross-national spread of innovation follows a relatively predictable pattern. Just as innovations change as they move from their origins

---

[15] Bookman and Eyal, "Eastern Europe as a Laboratory for Economic Knowledge"; Herbert Kitschelt, "Accounting for Postcommunist Regime Diversity: What Counts as a Good Cause?" In *Capitalism and Democracy in Central and Eastern Europe: Assessing the Legacy of Communist Rule*, Grzegorz Ekiert and Stephen Hanson, eds., pp. 613–34 (Cambridge: Cambridge University Press, 2003).

[16] We are thankful to Ambassador Robert Gelbard, Daniel Serwer, and Jim O'Brien, in particular, for providing insights into these dynamics. However, it is important to recognize, at the same time, that precedents can be abused by policy makers eager to rationalize their actions and careless about whether analogies are appropriate. For example, 1989 in East Central Europe seems to have informed discussions in the Bush administration about what would happen following American interventions in Iraq. That Poland was culturally homogeneous, that the Polish opposition had worked long and hard to develop its political skills and reach, and that Poland was located in a region ripe for change in part because of colonial rule were all differences that the Bush administration failed to recognize.

to new areas,[17] so they tend to appear first in optimal settings and then move to places less supportive of change. As diffusion progresses, therefore, the lure and logic of demonstration effects can easily outrun local capacity; adopters, eager to import, are prone to underestimate the difficulties involved; and defenders of the status quo are alerted to possible threats and prepare accordingly. Although change can be contagious, then, the contagion is uneven.

WAVE ONE: THE COLLAPSE OF COMMUNISM

There is a sizeable literature on the events of 1987–90. Our summary, as a result, will just touch on the main elements of this diffusion process.[18] The mass protests that eventually led to the disintegration of communism and communist states began in fact in two places: in the Soviet Union in 1987, with the rise of popular fronts in support of perestroika in Russia and the Baltic states, and in Slovenia, with the rise of a student movement that, by entering the forbidden zone of military affairs, took on both the Yugoslav state and the regime.[19] Protests then broke out in Poland in the fall of 1988 (much to the consternation of Lech Walesa, who was losing control over his movement) and culminated in an unprecedented roundtable between the opposition and the Party in the early months of 1989 that focused on ending the political stalemate in Poland, in place since martial law was declared in 1981, through the creation of a transitional regime that added some competitive political features to authoritarian rule in Poland. However, semicompetitive elections in June 1989 led by August of that year to an unthinkable development: the formation of an opposition-led government that then laid the groundwork for a rapid transition to democracy.

The Polish precedent, coupled with the considerable loosening of strictures on political change in Eastern Europe as a result of the Gorbachev reforms, was powerful enough to lead in the late summer of 1989 to a roundtable in Hungary, which was different in important respects from its Polish counterpart – for example, it was not televised; it featured a more complex and focused set of working groups; and it involved more detailed planning for a democratic future, including fully competitive elections in the following year. In the fall

---

[17] See Bunce and Wolchik in this volume.

[18] See, for example, Valerie Bunce, *Subversive Institutions: The Design and the Destruction of Socialism and the State* (New York: Cambridge University Press, 1999); John Glenn, III, *Framing Democracy: Civil Society and Civic Movements in Eastern Europe* (Stanford: Stanford University Press, 2000); Christian Joppke, *East German Dissidents and the Revolution of 1989: Social Movement in a Leninist Regime* (New York: New York University Press, 1995); Gale Stokes, *The Walls Came Tumbling Down: The Collapse of Communism in Eastern Europe* (Oxford: Oxford University Press, 1993); Brown, "Transnational Influences in the Transition from Communism"; Beissinger, *Nationalist Mobilization*.

[19] Tomaz Mastnak, "From Social Movements to National Sovereignty," in *Independent Slovenia: Origins, Movements, Prospects*, Jill Benderly and Evan Kraft, eds., pp. 93–112 (New York: St. Martin's, 1994).

of 1989, massive protests then broke out in East Germany, which were then followed by similar developments in Czechoslovakia – with participants in the latter speaking directly of demonstration effects and similarities in domestic conditions. Protests, albeit smaller and with less direct translation into democratic politics, then followed in Bulgaria, Romania, and Albania. In the course of these developments, moreover, protests within the Soviet Union continued and spread, as they did within Yugoslavia, where the Slovenian developments influenced, by all accounts, subsequent mass mobilization in both Croatia and Serbia. Indeed, even the Hungarians, scarred by 1956, eventually carried out demonstrations of their own on Republic Day – though these protests came later and grew out of renewed debates about what happened during the Hungarian Revolution.

MASS MOBILIZATION AND ELECTORAL REVOLUTIONS

Let us now turn to the second wave of citizen confrontations with authoritarian rule – from 1996 to 2005.[20] In this round, the form of protests changed to some degree (moving from entirely street-based activity to electoral activity that was combined, in many cases, with street demonstrations). The regime context also changed from communism to regimes that either fell short of being full democracies (as with Bulgaria, Romania, and Slovakia) or were somewhat or very authoritarian (with the clearest contrast that between Georgia and Croatia in the last years of dictatorial rule, on the one hand, and Serbia, on the other). These distinctions aside, however, the issue on the table was the same, whether in Bulgaria in 1996–7 or Ukraine in 2004: popular challenges to authoritarian rule. Moreover, in most cases (but see Radnitz on Kyrgyzstan in this volume),[21] the pivotal elections featured an upsurge in the turnout of voters supporting change – and in Croatia, Slovakia, and Ukraine, an overall increase in turnout, especially in comparison with declining turnout across earlier elections over the course of the postcommunist era. For example, in the 1998 Slovak elections, turnout increased nine percent over that in the 1994 elections, and in the 2000 Croatian elections, six percent over the 1997 presidential elections and eight percent over the 1995 parliamentary elections. In discussing this wave, we will provide greater detail, largely because these events have been less fully explored by scholars interested in comparisons among them or in the role of diffusion.[22]

As we noted above, it is always hard to date exactly when a process of diffusion actually begins. In the cases of interest here, we would argue that

---

[20] For a more detailed analysis, see Bunce and Wolchik, *American Democracy Promotion.*

[21] Here, we draw upon the data collected by the Swedish-based International Institute for Democracy and Electoral Assistance, available at http://www.idea.int/vt/survey/voter_turnout2.cfm; accessed September 21, 2007.

[22] But see Bunce and Wolchik, "Getting Real about Real Causes"; Way, "The Real Causes of the Color Revolutions"; Michael McFaul, "Transitions from Postcommunism"; Joerg Forbrig and Pavol Demes, eds., *Reclaiming Democracy: Civil Society and Electoral Change in Central and Eastern Europe* (Washington, DC: German Marshall Fund, 2007).

the emergence of the model of democratizing elections began with four inter-connected political struggles in Serbia, Bulgaria, Romania, and Slovakia from 1996 to 1998 – countries that provided a regional hothouse for political change, because of the combination of democratic deficits, active and interactive oppo-sitions, and shared borders. From 1996 to 1997 there were massive three-month-long protests in Serbia – protests that were motivated by Milošević's attempt to deny the opposition its significant victories in many of the local elec-tions that took place in 1996.[23] These protests, as in the cases that followed in their footsteps, built on previous rounds of political protest – in the Serbian case going back to the early 1980s and in Romania, Bulgaria, and Slovakia to 1989 (and even during the communist period, as in Slovakia from 1967 to 1968 and the miners' strikes in Romania during the 1980s). As Jim O'Brien, who served as the Washington-based coordinator of American assistance to Serbian opposition groups from 1999 to 2000, put it: "We built on the plumb-ing of the past."[24] Although the Serbian protests failed in the short term, they contributed in important ways to the election-based protests in the fall of 2000 that we explore in a later chapter in this volume.[25]

The second set of struggles took place in Romania, where the liberal oppo-sition finally came together and ran a sophisticated political campaign that succeeded in 1996 in replacing the former communist incumbent president (who came back to power in 2000) with a candidate with far stronger lib-eral credentials and commitments.[26] The third set of struggles took place in Bulgaria at roughly the same time.[27] In Bulgaria, Serbian protests next door were influential in particular in bringing labor and other groups out into the streets. Although lagged in their response and to some degree shamed by the spontaneity of their own citizenry, Bulgarian intellectuals and leaders of the opposition finally recognized, especially given the poor performance of the incumbent regime, that such protests could lead to a new election and pave the way for the Union of Democratic Forces (which, prior to this time, would be better characterized as a fractious ensemble) to take power (which they did in 1997). Although the cohesion of the Bulgarian liberal opposition proved to be temporary and their effectiveness limited (as in the Romanian story as well), their victory (again as in Romania) served as a decisive political

[23] Mladen Lazić and Liljana Nikolić, *Protest in Belgrade: Winter of Discontent* (Budapest: Central European University Press, 1999); Dusan Pavlovic, *Akteri I modeli: Ogledi o politici u Srbiji pod Milosevic* (Belgrade: B92, 2005); Robert Thomas, *The Politics of Serbia in the 1990s* (New York: Columbia University Press, 1999).

[24] Interview, November 16, 2006, Washington, DC.

[25] And see Milan Stoyan Protich, *Izneverena revolutiutsija* (Belgrade: Chigoya, 2005); Florian Bieber, "The Serbian Transition and Civil Society: Roots of the Delayed Transition in Serbia." *International Journal of Politics, Culture and Society*, 17 (Fall 2003), pp. 73–90; Ognjen Pribicevic, "Serbia After Milosevic." *Southeast Europe and Black Sea Studies*, 4, No. 1 (January, 2004), pp. 107–18.

[26] See Bunce and Wolchik, *American Democracy Promotion*, Chap. 5.

[27] See Petrova in this volume.

turning point – as indicated, for example, by the consistent improvements in Freedom House scores following these pivotal elections in both countries.[28]

The same generalization applies to the fourth participant in the story of the spread of the electoral model of democratization: Slovakia.[29] As we discuss in our other chapter in this volume, it was there that all the components of the electoral model of defeating authoritarian leaders came together, with a variety of players, such as leaders of the Slovak, Bulgarian, and Romanian oppositions, the American ambassadors to Slovakia and the Czech Republic, "graduates" of the Romanian and Bulgarian turnarounds, and representatives of organizations such as the International Republican Institute, the National Democratic Institute, Freedom House, and the National Endowment for Democracy, combining forces to create the OK98 campaign that led to the defeat of Vladimír Mečiar in the 1998 Slovakian parliamentary elections. This model, which can be termed the innovation that diffused throughout the region, included such components as the formation of a cohesive opposition; pressures on election commissions to improve their procedures and render them more transparent; ambitious campaigns to register voters, advertise the costs of the incumbent regime, and get out the vote; and the deployment of both domestic and international election monitoring, as well as exit polls, to provide quick feedback on turnout during election day, to catalog election-day abuses by the regime, and to provide evidence of actual voter preferences.[30]

Fully articulated and successful when implemented in Slovakia in 1998, the electoral model was then applied in a number of competitive authoritarian regimes.[31] Its first stop in the diffusion process was in Croatia in 2000, where the death of the long-serving dictator, Franjo Tudjman, in 1999 had weakened the governing party and provided an opportunity for the opposition to win power. In this case, as in Bulgaria and Romania, the election was for the Presidency, and as in these cases as well as in Slovakia, the electoral outcome produced a smooth transition. The Croatian opposition also benefited (as would Serbia later in the same year) from assistance provided by the Slovakian opposition and the electoral playbook it devised in collaboration with regional and Western actors, along with some earlier successes in local

---

[28] Lucia Kurekova, "Electoral Revolutions and Their Socio-economic Impact (Bulgaria and Slovakia in Comparative Perspective," MA thesis, Department of International Relations and European Studies, Central European University, 2006; Venelin Ganev, *Preying on the State: State Transformation in Postcommunist Bulgaria (1989–1997)* (Ithaca: Cornell University Press, 2007).

[29] See Bunce and Wolchik, *American Democracy Promotion*, Chap. 5.

[30] And for other consequences, see Susan Hyde, "Can International Election Observers Deter Electoral Fraud? Evidence from a Natural Experiment." Unpublished manuscript, Department of Political Science, Yale University, June 26, 2006.

[31] See Levitsky and Way in this volume, and Steven Levitsky and Lucan Way, "The Rise of Competitive Authoritarianism." *Journal of Democracy*, 13, No. 2 (2002), pp. 51–65; Larry Diamond, "Thinking about Hybrid Regimes." *Journal of Democracy*, 13, No. 2 (2002), pp. 21–35; Andreas Schedler, ed., *Electoral Authoritarianism: The Dynamics of Unfree Competition* (Boulder, CO: Lynne Rienner, 2006).

elections and earlier actions by the hardline regime to prevent the translation of voter preferences into representative governments. As in Slovakia, and in contrast to the situation in Bulgaria and Romania after these pivotal elections, the electoral revolution had dramatic effects on democratization in Croatia. A political corner was turned.

Later in 2000, the electoral revolution moved to Serbia.[32] Although the implementation of the electoral model was as careful and thoroughgoing as it had been in Slovakia and Croatia, there were, nonetheless, some differences that distinguish Serbia from these other cases. One was that the struggle against Milošević was severely constrained by the increasingly heavy authoritarian hand of the regime. Thus, for example, there were no external election monitors in Serbia in the fall 2000 elections and the media were closely controlled by Milošević. However, there was one similarity to Slovakia: the key role played by young people and their organizations, such as Otpor in Serbia.

The Serbian presidential election of 2000 was a turning point for elections as democratizing agents, because the incumbent regime had been in power much longer and was far more authoritarian than the earlier sites for such revolutions, and because these very characteristics meant that the regime refused to vacate office, once the election and the tabulations of the vote, both fraudulent and accurate, had concluded. This led to massive political protests that succeeded in taking control over the capital and forcing Milošević to resign. Although the result, as in Croatia, was a regime change and not just a change in government, the Serbian opposition has continued to be plagued by severe divisions that were exacerbated by the continuing border problems represented by Kosovo and Montenegro (with the first on its way to statehood and the second, following the summer 2006 referendum, already there); growing pressures for expanded autonomy in Vojvodina; and pressures on the part of the international community to move quickly in cooperating with the demands of the Hague War Crimes Tribunal.[33] The assassination of Đinđić in 2003 – the most effective and certainly charismatic leader of the Serbian opposition – did not help matters.[34]

The Georgian opposition then followed suit in the 2003 parliamentary elections – though this produced, it is important to recognize, a coup d'état by the opposition, because the long-serving President, Eduard Shevardnadze, left office without having been in fact up for reelection.[35] In Georgia, the political context was less constraining than in Serbia, especially given the lackluster

---

[32] See Bunce and Wolchik in this volume for details with respect to the Serbian dynamics; also see Bunce and Wolchik, *American Democracy Promotion*, Chap. 6; Protich, *Izneverena revoliutsija*.

[33] See Bieber, "The Serbian Transition and Civil Society."

[34] And see Eric Miller, "Georgia's New Start." *Problems of Communism*, 51, No. 2 (April 2004), pp. 12–21, and the nuanced appraisal by Sonja Licht, "Serbia between Autocratic and Democratic Transition: A Case Study." Paper presented at the Project on Democratic Transitions, Seminar II: Lessons Learned and Testing Tsheir Applicability, Foreign Policy Research Institute, Philadelphia, February 22–4, 2007.

[35] See Cory Welt in this volume; Bunce and Wolchik, *American Democracy Promotion*, Chap. 8.

campaign by Shevardnadze's allies, the defection of so many key players from the ruling group to the opposition (such as Mikheil Saakashvili, the current president), the relative openness of the Georgian media, the formation of a youth group in support of political change (Kmara) that worked closely with the Georgian opposition around Saakashvili, and the presence of a significant number of local and international election monitors.[36] As in the other cases, moreover, it was clear that the Georgian opposition modeled its campaign on the previous electoral breakthroughs in the region and benefited as well from various kinds of support from the Open Society Foundation and various American groups.[37]

The next successful democratizing election occurred in Ukraine a year later.[38] As in the Georgian case, a single charismatic politician – in this case, Viktor Yushchenko – played a critical role. As in both the Georgian and Serbian cases, the successful political breakthrough exploited the record of a leadership that had grown increasingly corrupt, careless, and violent; benefited from defections from the ruling circles; built upon earlier rounds of protests and recent successes in local elections; and reached out to diverse groups, with young people playing nearly as important a role as in Serbia with Otpor. Moreover, as in Serbia and Georgia, political protests after the election (which were as large as those in Serbia and longer lasting) were again necessary to force the authoritarian challenger to admit defeat. More distinctive to the Ukrainian case, however, was the breakdown of central control over the media during the campaign and especially during the protests, and the remarkable role of the Supreme Court, which came down in support of the opposition's argument that the elections had been fraudulent and had to be repeated. As in Serbia, moreover, the unity of the opposition was short-lived, a factor that has blocked a consistent movement toward the creation of a stable and fully democratic polity.[39]

---

[36] Zurab Karumidze and James V. Wertsch, eds., *Enough! The Rose Revolution in the Republic of Georgia 2003* (New York: Nova Science Publishers, 2005).

[37] Jaba Devdariani, "The Impact of International Assistance," available at www.idea.int/publications/goegia/upload/Book-08_src.pdf; accessed November 21, 2005; A. Cooley and J. Ron, "The NGO Scramble: Organizational Insecurity and the Political Economy of Transnational Action." *International Security*, 27 (Summer 2002), pp. 5–39.

[38] See, in particular, McFaul in this volume and Taras Kuzio, "From Kuchma to Yushchenko: Orange Revolution in Ukraine." *Problems of Postcommunism*, 52 (March–April 2005), pp. 29–44; Paul Kubicek, "The European Union and Democratization in Ukraine." *Communist and Post-communist Studies*, 38 (2005), pp. 269–92; Way, "Authoritarian State-Building," "Ukraine's Orange Revolution"; Anders Åslund and Michael McFaul, eds., *Revolution in Orange: The Origins of the Ukrainian Democratic Breakthrough* (Washington, DC: Carnegie Endowment, 2006); Andrew Wilson, *Virtual Politics: Faking Democracy in the Post-Soviet World* (New Haven, CT: Yale University Press, 2005).

[39] But see McFaul in this volume; Way, "Ukraine's Orange Revolution"; Mykola Riabchuk, "Applying Lessons from Early Postcommunist Transitions." Paper presented at the Project on Democratic Transitions, Seminar II: Lessons Learned and Testing Their Applicability, Foreign Policy Research Institute, Philadelphia, February 22–4, 2007.

Significant electoral challenges to authoritarian incumbents, coupled with mass demonstrations challenging the official electoral results, also took place in a number of other countries in the region, including Kyrgyzstan in 2005, where President Askar Akaev panicked in the face of protests following the parliamentary election and left office (see Radnitz in the volume) and in a series of presidential and parliamentary elections that took place in Armenia, Azerbaijan, and Belarus from 2001 to 2008, where the common result was that authoritarian incumbents or their anointed successors remained in power in the face of popular protests over electoral fraud.[40] What made these cases of election-based protests against authoritarian rule similar to one another, but different from the earlier challenges to authoritarian leaders, was two factors. First, the collaborative networks that brought together graduates of earlier and successful electoral confrontations with dictators, Western democracy promoters, and local opposition groups and that played such a pivotal role in breaking with authoritarian rule in Slovakia, Croatia, Serbia, Georgia, and Ukraine from 1998 to 2004 were far less present and influential in Armenia, Azerbaijan, and Belarus. Second, the electoral model was not fully deployed in these three countries. This was in part because of a thinning out of transnational networks, but also because of preemptive strikes on the part of authoritarian rulers (who were watching electoral change in the neighborhood with interest equal to that of the opposition) and failures on the part of oppositions, given their own limitations and those imposed by the regime, to construct sufficiently large coalitions and mount sufficiently ambitious political campaigns and electoral monitoring programs.[41]

DIFFUSION OF MOBILIZATION: GENERAL PATTERNS

We can now step back from the details of these two waves of popular mobilization against authoritarianism and apply the arguments presented in our earlier discussion of diffusion dynamics. We begin at the most general level. Each round of collective action aimed against dictators featured a roughly similar repertoire of innovative behaviors that were adopted in lagged fashion by key actors in a number of countries in the region. What we find, in short, is a diffusion-like dynamic. Moreover, each wave was foreshadowed by a clear

---

[40] See Valerie Bunce and Sharon Wolchik, "Defeating Dictators: Electoral Change and Stability in Competitive Authoritarian Regimes." *World Politics*, 62 (January 2010), forthcoming; Valerieerie Bunce and Sharon Wolchik, "Azerbaijan's 2005 Parliamentary Elections: A Failed Attempt at Transition." Paper prepared for the CDDRL Workshop on External Influences on Democratic Transitions, Stanford University, October 25, 2008; Valerie Bunce and Sharon Wolchik, "Opposition versus Dictators: Explaining Divergent Election Outcomes in Post-communist Europe and Eurasia." In *Democratization by Elections* Staffan Lindberg, ed. (Johns Hopkins University Press, forthcoming); Anar M. Valiyev, "Parliamentary Elections in Azerbaijan: A Failed Revolution." *Problems of Postcommunism*, 53, No. 3 (May–June 2006), pp. 17–35; and Silitsky in this volume.
[41] See Bunce and Wolchik, *American Democracy Promotion*, Chap. 11 for more details.

expansion in international opportunities for democratic change – opportunities that were exploited, albeit to varying degrees, by local democratic activists and everyday citizens. Here we refer, for example, to the role of the Helsinki Process and the Gorbachev reforms in the first wave, and in the second the rise, beginning in the early 1990s, of an international democracy promotion community that provided important assistance to democratic activists in the postcommunist region.[42] Just as important for both rounds was a transnational factor: the development of regionally based opposition networks that collaborated closely with one another in support of a showdown with incumbent authoritarian regimes.[43] Just as these networks benefited primarily from what could be termed a more "permissive" international environment in the second round, so in the second wave international actors played a more active role – by supporting the development of civil society, open media, and free and fair elections; encouraging the unity of the opposition; encouraging ties between the opposition and civil society groups; providing training and support with respect to campaign techniques; and offering strong and very public criticisms of authoritarian incumbents when they attempted to steal elections.

Finally, our overview of the two waves provides strong support for the importance of both structural mechanisms in diffusion dynamics, such as the obvious institutional similarities among regimes during the communist period and similarities after communism in the combination of democratic deficits, yet electoral competition, and an actor-rich process that involved, most importantly, local actors, but also their regional and Western allies, and that was

---

[42] See McFaul and Vachudova in this volume; Milada Vachudova, *Europe Undivided: Democracy, Leverage and Integration after Communism* (Oxford: Oxford University Press, 2005); Daniel Thomas, *The Helsinki Effect: International Norms, Human Rights, and the Demise of Communism* (Princeton, NJ: Princeton University Press, 2001); Steven F. Finkel, Anibal Perez-Linan, Mitchell A. Seligson, and Dinorah Azpuru, *Effects of US Foreign Assistance on Democracy Building: Results of a Cross-National Quantitative Study.* Final Report, Version No. 34, USAID (January 12, 2006). Available at http://www.usaid.gov/our_work/democracy_and_governance/publications/pdfs/; accessed February 15, impact_of_democracy_assistance.pdf; accessed February 17, 2006; Bunce and Wolchik, "International Diffusion and Postcommunist Electoral Revolutions"; Thomas Carothers, *Critical Missions: Essays on Democracy Promotion* (Washington, DC: Carnegie Endowment, 2004); Sarah Elizabeth Mendelson and John K. Glenn, *The Power and Limits of NGOs: A Critical Look at Building Democracy in Eastern Europe and Eurasia* (New York: Columbia University Press, 2002).

[43] See, for example, Bunce and Wolchik, "Favorable Conditions and Electoral Revolutions," "International Diffusion and Postcommunist Electoral Revolutions." "Democratizing Elections in the Postcommunist World," "Youth and Postcommunist Electoral Revolutions." For the earlier round, 1986 appears to have been a turning point in building cross-national ties, particularly among oppositions in Eastern Europe, but also between these oppositions and various Western groups. As a small sample, see, for example, "Budapest Forum as Seen by Prague," Radio Free Europe, CZSL SR0001, January 7, 1986; "Polish Solidarity Contacts Charter 77," Radio Free Europe, CZSL SR/0012, September 5, 1986; "Eastern European Dissidents Appeal on Hungarian Revolution Anniversary," RAD BR 0151, October 28, 1986; and "Eastern European Dissidents Join Western Groups in Addressing Vienna Conference," RAD BR0164, November 14, 1986.

responsible for exploiting domestic and international opportunities for demo-cratic change by defining strategies, applying them, and transferring them to new locales. Moreover, as noted in the discussion of the two waves, we also see changes in the innovation itself as it moved from the point of origin to other contexts, and the declining effectiveness of the model as it proceeded from more to less supportive local settings.

Here, two sets of examples are instructive. Just as the protests in Bulgaria at the end of 1989 – in contrast to the earlier protests against communism in Czechoslovakia – were carried out by a less experienced and smaller opposition and were more successfully countered by a better-prepared and more ensconced communist party, with the result that the breakage with communist party rule was less clear-cut, so in the second wave the electoral challenges to authoritarian rule in Slovakia in 1998 were more successful in consolidating democratic change than the challenges to Milošević that took place two years later in Serbia. In the latter context, the regime was far more authoritarian; popular protests had been added to the electoral model of democratic change; and these protests served as an indicator of how difficult subsequent democratic development would be after the 2000 election.

BEGINNING THE DIFFUSION DYNAMIC

Let us now turn to some more specific questions, all of which are central to the understanding of how diffusion actually works. First, why were particular models of citizen challenges to authoritarianism selected – that is, the focus in the first wave on popular protests and in a few cases roundtables, and the focus in the second wave on elections, sometimes combined with popular protests? The simple answer is that these models of change were selected because of historical experiences and the forms of opposition activity imposed by the nature of the regime itself. To elaborate: in the first wave, the focus on politi-cal protests reflected the constraints in state socialist regimes on how citizens can register their preferences and their dissatisfaction, along with a time-tested dynamic in the Soviet bloc during the communist era, wherein divisions within the Soviet leadership or a decisive shift by them in a reformist direction had the predictable effects of weakening Central and Eastern European parties and thereby creating opportunities for citizen mobilization. Also critical was the accumulation of experiences with protest, aided by regimes that, because of their centralization of politics and their control over the economy, unwittingly forged optimal conditions for concerted actions on the part of the public. State socialist regimes, for example, identified a common enemy for their cit-izens, and they introduced major and sudden shifts in policy that affected citizens in similar ways at virtually the same moment.[44] Moreover, although elections under communism could serve indirectly as instruments of policy

---

[44] See, for example, Bunce, *Subversive Institutions*.

accountability, they were too controlled and too ritualized to be used as referenda on communist party rule.[45]

The selection of electoral confrontations in the second round also spoke to a number of influences. They included successful application of the electoral model in other parts of the world (which American democracy promoters, at least, recognized); the close tie in the popular mind between democracy and competitive elections; the expectations for democratic possibilities unleashed by the fall of communism, yet the continuing power of the communists in these hybrid regimes; and striking similarities between the rigged electoral rituals of the past and the partially rigged character of elections after communism. Here, we can cite a succinct and telling observation made by Robert Gelbard, who was involved in the discussions in the National Security Council during the Chilean Referendum in 1988 and in American support for the Serbian opposition from 1999 to 2000: "If leaders use the forms of democracy, publics come to expect the substance."[46]

However, perhaps the most important influence was that elections were widely recognized by local and international democracy activists as an *ideal* mechanism for challenging the regime. All the regimes where electoral revolutions took place allowed oppositions to participate, although with varying constraints. Moreover, elections are understood by citizens as verdicts on the regime's right to rule. Finally, elections have visible results that speak to power, rights, and policies, and they have the advantage for both oppositions and citizens of being associated with specific activities that are bounded in time and that have scheduled and visible consequences. It is also far harder for regimes to justify the use of force against their citizenries during elections than at other times.[47]

The differences in the particular strategies selected for regime confrontation across the two waves, however, should not blind us to several commonalities. One is that the electoral model was in fact often combined with popular protests – either before the election, as in Bulgaria, or after the election, as in Serbia, Georgia, Ukraine, and Kyrgyzstan. Another similarity is that we see in both rounds a "selection moment" that reflects a sudden decline in the costs of mobilization and a rise in expected payoffs. In the case of the successful electoral breakthroughs, there was both significant support for democratic change provided by the United States and, to a lesser extent, the European Union – not just long-term investments in civil society and fair elections, for example, but also clear signaling of dissatisfaction with both the incumbent regime and its conduct of the election (though this was less apparent in the Bulgarian and

---

[45] Victor Zaslavsky and Robert Brym, "The Functions of Elections in the USSR." *Soviet Studies*, 30, No. 3 (July 1978), pp. 362–71.

[46] Interview in Ithaca, New York, March 1, 2007; also see Schedler, ed., *Electoral Authoritarianism*.

[47] Karen Dawisha and Stephen Deets, "Political Learning in Postcommunist Elections." *East European Politics and Societies*, 20, No. 4 (2006), pp. 1–38.

Romanian cases) – and increasingly visible evidence testifying to the vulnerability of the regime and its rejection of political niceties and the democratic rules of the game.

In the first round, evidence of growth in regime vulnerability was also important, as was the clear message that the Soviets were unwilling to use force against protesters within the Soviet Union (though there were some exceptions) and certainly in Central and Eastern Europe. However, like American assistance in the second wave, this version of international change was not a purely short-term development. In fact, long before Gorbachev, we find a clear decline over time in the Soviet use of force against Soviet allies in Central and Eastern Europe – a pattern that reflected in part Soviet concerns about the longer-term costs of such actions and in part variations in the forms of local resistance to Soviet intervention. Thus, the Soviet invasion of Hungary in 1956 involved a large number of deaths; the Soviet invasion of Czechoslovakia in 1968 was far less bloody; and declaration of martial law, rather than armed intervention, in 1981 was the Soviet strategy of choice in Poland in reaction to the rise of Solidarity a year earlier. In addition, there is some evidence that there were in fact significant divisions within the Politburo regarding the invasion of Czechoslovakia in 1968 – divisions that grew out of the fears of the Ukrainian members at the time that Slovak nationalist protests might diffuse to the Ukraine.[48] This pattern also explains why the violent transitions in Central and Eastern Europe when communism fell took place in the states that had distanced themselves most from the Soviet bloc – Romania, Yugoslavia, and Albania – and that did not have Soviet troops stationed within their borders. In these three countries, command and control resided in the local party, not in Moscow, and it was the local party (or, more specifically in the Yugoslav case, Serbia) that deployed force to protect its privileges.

This observation leads to a second insight about the beginning of the two waves and the sources of innovations in the key countries. In both rounds of mass mobilization, the "lead" states in this diffusion story fit the profile of contexts that exhibited, by regional comparative standards of the time, the optimal conditions for antiregime mobilization. This was because expanded opportunities for democratic change (or what social movement theorists term a change in the political opportunity structure)[49] were joined with two other factors that were much more in evidence in some countries than in others. One was regime vulnerability, which grew out of a variety of conditions, ranging from mounting economic difficulties and recent changes in political leadership to a history of antiregime protests and lack of legitimacy from the beginning for rule by the communists, whether local communists or those in Moscow. The other was the availability of substantial resources for popular mobilization

---

[48] Grey Hodnett and Peter Potichnyj, *The Ukraine and the Czechoslovak Crisis* (Canberra: Department of Political Science/Research School of Social Sciences/Australian National University, 1970).

[49] See Tarrow, *The New Transnational Activism*.

against the regime. Here, the key indicators included the existence of popular grievances, an established tradition of protest, the rise of more liberalized politics during the communist era, and religious and ethnic homogeneity.

Poland in 1988–9 provides the closest fit to this profile, and Poland became, not surprisingly, a leader in the fall of communism. However, other "early risers"[50] in the collapse of communism share many of the same characteristics. For example, Armenia, Lithuania, and Slovenia were unusually homogeneous republics; the three Central and Eastern European leaders of 1989 (Poland, Hungary, and Yugoslavia) were distinctive in combining serious economic crises with comparatively liberal politics; and a history of protests during communism was common to Armenia, Georgia, Poland, Hungary, the Czech Republic, and Slovakia.

In similar vein, the rise of the electoral model in Serbia (1996–7), Romania, Bulgaria, and Slovakia is far from surprising. In Serbia, the key issue was the long-term ripening of the opposition. Also critical in all these countries was their close proximity to one another and a domestic context (except in Serbia) that permitted significant room for democratic maneuver. Moreover, as already noted, the Romanian and especially the Bulgarian and Serbian economies were in terrible shape (as is typical of postcommunist regimes that straddled democracy and dictatorship);[51] the incumbent regimes were extremely unpopular and also corrupt and incompetent; and American democracy promoters, like the EU, had made democratic change in Bulgaria, Romania, and Slovakia a very high priority (as they were to do a few years later in Serbia, when the Dayton-related pressure for tolerating the Milošević regime had dissipated).

DIFFUSION MECHANISMS

This leads to another question of interest in this chapter: how and why the mobilization models traveled across national boundaries. Both waves of popular challenges to authoritarian rule reflected in fact the impact of all three diffusion models outlined earlier; that is, demonstration effects, similar conditions, and the spread of transnational networks. However, as the domestic and international regime contexts were very different in the two waves, the weights of these three drivers of diffusion were different as well.

Demonstration effects, which were unusually important in the first wave, can be seen most clearly in the changing calculus of opposition leaders and citizens. It was not just that they were aware of successful confrontations in the neighborhood; it was also that these precedents pointed to far lower costs attached to change than they had come to expect. The role of the Soviet leadership in the events of 1987–90 is a case in point. It was not simply that Gorbachev encouraged the rise of popular fronts in support of perestroika; supported the Polish

---

[50] To borrow from Beissinger, *Nationalist Mobilization*.

[51] As is typical of postcommunist regimes that straddled democracy and dictatorship, see Bunce, *Subversive Institutions*.

roundtable and even favorable stories of Lech Walesa in Soviet newspapers; chided the hard-line East German and Romanian regimes (which often censored his speeches), while refusing to back up their demand that the Hungarian government should prevent defection of East German tourists to the West; and stood aside while massive protests broke out in East Germany, Czechoslovakia, and other countries. It was also that in the early part of the wave regimes did not use force to defend themselves – in part because control over force resided in Moscow. Thus, the early mobilizations against communism were both successful and seemingly low-cost – which, especially given unusually similar domestic regimes and the common effect of a more permissive environment for political change, encouraged emulation.

For some of the same reasons, demonstration effects were also critical in the spread of electoral challenges to authoritarian rule. Although we should not minimize the hard work and risk involved in these struggles, the electoral precedent sets of Romania, Bulgaria, and Slovakia from 1996 to 1998 were quite attractive for several reasons. One was that these electoral confrontations in the neighborhood had been both successful and relatively cost-free. The other was that competitive elections had become a staple of political life in the postcommunist world. As a result, focusing on elections was seen as an efficient and effective way to get rid of incumbents and, not incidentally, as a winning strategy for opposition leaders to finally succeed in their goal of capturing political power.

SIMILAR CONDITIONS

This leads to a second mechanism in play in both waves. As implied in the discussion thus far, a critical factor was also the existence, at least in the minds of opposition leaders viewing their victorious counterparts, of similarities in problems, opportunities, and goals. These similarities, however, were easier to draw in the first than in the second wave.

A number of analysts have commented on the ways in which the structure of domestic communist regimes, the Soviet bloc, and even the ethnofederal Yugoslav, Soviet, and Czechoslovak states was ideally suited for the transmission of political and economic change, whether supportive of Soviet and local party control or threatening to both. The case for structural isomorphism and the ways in which this eventually undermined the centers in these three constellations – that is, the Soviet Union in the bloc, communist parties in individual countries, and the center as opposed to the republics in the ethnofederations – has been made in detail elsewhere.[52] However, it is important to recognize the *attitudinal* side to this story. These similarities were widely recognized, not just by Soviet leaders intent on homogenization and domination and Soviet generals afraid that one leak could bring the entire ship down, but also by

---

[52] Bunce, *Subversive Institutions*.

oppositions and citizens.[53] This is one major reason that, despite political constraints, the oppositions in Poland, Hungary, and the Czech lands began to pool ideas and resources in the second half of the 1980s; to issue common manifestos; and to publicize in various ways their support for oppositions in more repressive contexts, such as Romania, Bulgaria, East Germany, and Russia. Thus, although oppositions were diverse in size, strategies, and goals, they nonetheless assumed that their struggle against authoritarianism was a common struggle.[54]

The multiplication of states and types of regimes that took place in the region from 1989 to 1992, in contrast, erected boundaries among regimes in the postcommunist period that, in theory at least, should have considerably weakened the regional impulse for cross-national diffusion of political change. However, there were nonetheless some factors that rendered these new boundaries more porous than they might have seemed from a purely structural perspective. One was widespread awareness on the part of oppositions and citizens throughout the region, as a result of the political and economic performance of Poland, Hungary, the Czech Republic, and Slovenia in the 1990s, that there was an optimal approach to transition, and that it consisted of a sharp political (including electoral) break with the authoritarian past followed by a rapid transition to democracy and capitalism.[55] At the same time, to downplay the potential for diffusion on the basis of growing dissimilarities after communism is to ignore the existence of many parallels among the regimes that served as the sites of democratic change through application of the electoral model.

Just as these countries shared a communist past, with its similar ledger of obstacles to transition, so they shared a similar postcommunist profile. This profile included in most cases a recent transition to independent statehood; earlier rounds of political protests, both accompanying state disintegration and more recently focusing on such issues as corruption and threats to democracy; former communists in power who used familiar and similar ploys to maintain their political positions; and heterogeneous populations that, although often providing a pretext for authoritarian leaders to maintain power by accentuating cultural and ethnic differences, also made consolidation of authoritarianism difficult as a result of the politicization of difference. With the exceptions of Bulgaria and Slovakia, moreover, the regimes that experienced these pivotal elections tended to be hybrids of democracy and dictatorship that featured regular elections, limited opportunities for political competition, and some

---

[53] A. Mlynar, *Nightfrost in Prague: The End of Humane Socialism* (New York: Karz Publishers, 1980).

[54] See Joppke, *East German Dissidents and the Revolution of 1989*; Padraic Kenney, *Carnival of Revolution: Central Europe, 1989* (Princeton, NJ: Princeton University Press, 2002); Alan Renwick, "Anti-political or Just Anti-communist? Varieties of Dissidence in East-Central Europe and Their Implications for the Development of Political Society." *East European Politics and Society*, v20 (Spring 2006), pp. 286–318.

[55] Valerie Bunce, "East European Democratization: Global Patterns and Postcommunist Dynamics." *Orbis*, 50 (Fall 2006), pp. 3–23.

civil liberties and political rights, but also (in every case) fragmented liberal oppositions and corrupt authoritarian incumbents. Moreover, most of them suffered from serious economic problems – though this was less true of Slovakia and Croatia.

COLLABORATIVE NETWORKS

The third mechanism by which innovations move from place to place is transnational collaborative networks that fan out from the original site of the innovation and that carry the new model with them. It is easy to forget that the history of communism was not just the history of the spread of a regime type and its eventual decline; it was also a history of the spread first of networks that supported the diffusion of communism and then of another set of networks that poked holes in its legitimacy and that were eventually responsible for ending its political hegemony. In the course of this chapter, we have already said a great deal about these networks under communism and postcommunism. However, it is important to recognize that these networks featured different structures in the two waves and played a far more important role in the cross-national diffusion of electoral confrontations with authoritarian rule.

During communism, the networks were primarily contained within the region, though the Helsinki Process and periodic linkages with various Western European groups did occur.[56] However, these ties with groups outside the region were difficult to forge, given the closed borders of most of these countries and ideological tensions between a Western left focused on issues of peace and divided over the Soviet experiment and the politics of dissent in the communist region, which was less taken with the overarching importance of peace and certainly not divided over the meaning of the Soviet experiment.[57] Moreover, cross-national linkages among dissident communities within the region were hard to assemble and solidify, both because of border control and because dissident cultures varied from place to place. As a result, it was primarily in the 1980s that dissidents from various countries in the region began to make common cause.

The transnational networks that arose in support of the electoral model of democratization, by contrast, brought together an unusually complex array of players, including local and regional dissidents, a range of nongovernmental organizations, private players, such as the Open Society and its founder

---

[56] See, for instance, Sharon Wolchik, "The PCI, Leninism, and Democratic Politics in Italy." In *Marxism in the Contemporary World,* Charles F. Elliott and Carl A. Linden, eds., pp. 145–73 (Boulder, CO: Westview Press, 1980); Thomas, *The Helsinki Effect;* Gillian Wylie, "Social Movements and International Change: The Case of Détente 'From Below.'" *International Journal of Peace Studies,* 4, No. 2 (July 1999), pp. 28–42; Matthew Evangelista, *Unarmed Forces: The Transnational Movement to End the Cold War* (Ithaca: Cornell University Press, 1999); Kenney, *Carnival of Revolution.*

[57] Kenney, *Carnival of Revolution;* Joppke, *East German Dissidents and the Revolution of 1989;* Wylie, "Social Movements and International Change."

George Soros, the Mott Foundations, and Rockefeller Brothers, and democracy promoters from both Europe and the United States (such as United States Agency for International Development, or USAID, and their funded projects and groups, such as Freedom House, the International Republican Institute, and the National Democratic Institute, along with the German Marshall Fund of the United States, and the International Foundation for Electoral Systems, or IFES).[58] Although authoritarian leaders tried to prevent these networks from ending their rule, especially in the more authoritarian contexts of Serbia, Georgia, Ukraine, and Kyrgyzstan, and although they were especially successful in this endeavor in Armenia, Azerbaijan, Belarus, Kazakhstan, Russia, and Uzbekistan, for the successful electoral challenges to authoritarian rule, at least, there were far fewer barriers to the expansion and geographical extension of transnational networks supporting the defeat of dictators after communism than during it. Moreover, the West, in direct contrast to the situation for much of the communist era, had shifted in the decided direction of full support for democracy abroad – especially, it is important to recognize, in the postcommunist region (although even there, concerns about oil and gas, as well as security, sometimes trumped this priority).[59]

Two other factors were critical. One was the rapid proliferation of nongovernmental communities in postcommunist countries, beginning in the late 1980s – a proliferation that served as a focus both for Western assistance and for opposition activities. At the same time, the electoral model itself facilitated transnational organization. Political protests do not always invite support, even from purportedly committed democrats, but free and fair elections do. And electoral assistance, it can be argued, is far less complex to administer and far easier to frame as legitimate activity to leaders in target states than, say, external support for mass demonstrations against the government.

We have addressed elsewhere the role of the United States in electoral revolutions and the role as well of regional networks bringing together graduates of these electoral revolutions with local oppositions and nongovernmental organizations.[60] Suffice it to note here that the electoral challenges to authoritarianism depended upon a convergence among American verbal and financial support of free and fair elections; committed and energetic regional exporters armed with valuable lessons about strategies; and vibrant local oppositions and NGO communities. Although it is fair to argue that the first wave of mobilization from 1987 to 1990 was assisted by transnational networks, the second wave of electoral revolutions was *fueled* by such networks.

[58] See Bunce and Wolchik, *American Democracy Promotion*; Carothers, *Critical Missions*.

[59] However, even there, concerns about oil and gas, as well as security, sometimes trumped this priority.

[60] Bunce and Wolchik, "Favorable Conditions and Electoral Revolutions," "International Diffusion and Postcommunist Electoral Revolutions." "Democratizing Elections in the Postcommunist World," "Youth and Postcommunist Electoral Revolutions."

This comparison of the drivers behind the two waves of mobilizations against authoritarianism carries several key lessons for diffusion and the role of domestic and international factors in regime change. One is that perceptions – and not just objective conditions – matter. As our interviews with participants in both waves indicated, the assumption by opposition groups of similar political contexts and opportunities played a key role in the cross-national spread of challenges to authoritarian rule. Another is that the spread of subversive innovations has stiff requirements. Similar conditions, demonstration effects, or transnational networks are not sufficient in themselves to transfer highly controversial innovations from one country to others. Finally, the weight of our three mechanisms nonetheless varied across the two waves, given changes in both domestic and international regime contexts.

THE UNEVEN CHARACTER OF DIFFUSION

This leads to the final issue of interest in this chapter – the finite reach of diffusion. In both waves, some countries participated in the process, but others did not, and diffusion itself came to a close. Why did this happen? We would argue that similar factors came into play, whether we look at the first or the second wave, the uneven spread of challenges to authoritarian rule across time and space within each wave, or the fact that both waves of democratic change ended. First, as we argued earlier, the diffusion of controversial innovations, in particular, moves from more to less optimal circumstances – which is one reason that some countries emerge as leaders in this difficult process and others as followers. Thus, from a purely structural standpoint, some regimes are more vulnerable than others, given differences in, say, economic performance, the size and experience of the opposition and civil society organizations, and the political capacity of authoritarians to build durable coalitions and institutionalize their rule.[61] Not all hybrid or authoritarian regimes, in short, are equally good candidates for major and successful challenges to their continuation in power.

At the same time, agency effects play a key role as well. As the wave progresses and as a result of variations in, say, the electoral calendar in the second wave, authoritarians, especially if they are vigilant, have more and more opportunities to learn from the experiences of their neighbors. Thus, they are able, because of the luxury of being "structural laggards," to fashion strategies that protect their rule – for example, courting the police and security forces; increasing their control over public spaces, the media, civil society organizations, and electoral procedures; harassing, dividing, and demobilizing the opposition; cracking down on allies who might consider defecting; and even

---

[61] See, especially, Bunce and Wolchik, *American Democracy Promotion*, Chap. 2; Way, "Ukraine's Orange Revolution," "The Real Causes"; Valerie Bunce and Sharon Wolchik, "Getting Real about Real Causes"; and Stoner-Weiss and Way in this volume.

using the economy to court citizens in general and difficult groups, such as students, in particular.[62] At the same time, because these actions make mobilization more difficult and because oppositions often assume in the light of the run of electoral victories in the neighborhood that successful challenges to authoritarian rule are not hard to orchestrate, challenges to authoritarian rule that take place later in the wave tend to be far less planned and elaborate and, therefore, weaker in their impact than mobilizations that occur earlier in the wave. For instance, just as the protests in Armenia in 2008 were much smaller than in Serbia in 2000, Georgia in 2003, and Ukraine in 2004, so the Armenian opposition, like the oppositions in Belarus in 2006, Azerbaijan in 2005, and Russia in 2008, although forging greater unity than in the past, nonetheless fell considerably short of forming the broad electoral coalitions that were victorious in Serbia, Georgia, and Ukraine. Also striking is the fact that electoral mobilizations failed to unseat dictators when the elections lacked the full-scale deployment of external and/or internal election monitors – a failure that prevented democratic oppositions in Armenia, Azerbaijan, and Belarus from being able to document for all citizens to see, once the votes were tabulated, a clear contrast between the "real" election results and the ones announced by the regime.

Yet another constraint on the ability of each of these waves to blanket the region as a whole was the accumulation over the course of the wave of less and less attractive political outcomes associated with mobilizations against authoritarianism. For example, just as authoritarian leaders in both Armenia and Azerbaijan have been very quick to legitimate their rule and cast serious doubt on the wisdom of mounting popular protests against them by highlighting (and

---

[62] As Nazarbayev did on the eve of the 2005 elections in Kazakhstan; as Yel'tsin did in 1996; and as Putin and Medvedev did as well in the 2007 to 2008 parliamentary and presidential elections in Russia. See Randall Stone, *Lending Credibility: The International Monetary Fund and the Postcommunist Transition*, pp. 116–168 (Princeton, NJ: Princeton University Press, 2002); and Sophia Koshkovsky, "Kremlin Secures Price Controls on Food Items before Elections." *New York Times* (October 25, 2007), p. A7; Leonard Benardo and Aryeh Neier, "Russia: The Persecution of Civil Society." *New York Review of Books*, 53, No. 7 (April 27, 2006), pp. 35–7; C.J. Chivers, "Kremlin Puts Foreign Private Organizations on Notice." *New York Times* (October 20, 2006), p. A8; Daniel Kimmage, "Analysis: Nipping Oranges and Roses in the Bud – Post-Soviet Elites against Revolution." *RFERL* (January 21, 2005); M. Steven Fish, *Democracy Derailed in Russia. The Failure of Open Politics* (Cambridge: Cambridge University Press, 2005); Pierre Hassner, "Russia's Transition to Autocracy." *Journal of Democracy*, 19, No. 2 (2008), pp. 5–15; Michael McFaul and Kathryn Stoner-Weiss, "The Myth of the Authoritarian Model: How Putin's Crackdown Holds Russia Back." *Foreign Affairs*, 87 (January–February 2008); Fred Weier, "'Color Revolutions' Wane: Russia Asserts Its Influence ahead of Elections in Belarus and Ukraine." *Christian Science Monitor* (May 7, 2006); National Endowment for Democracy, "The Backlash Against Democracy Assistance: A Report Prepared by the National Endowment for Democracy for Senator Richard G. Lugar, Chairman, Committee on Foreign Relations," U.S. Senate (June 8, 2006); Regine A. Spector and Andrej Krickovic, "The Anti-revolutionary Toolkit." Unpublished manuscript, Department of Political Science and Institute for International Studies, University of California, Berkeley, March 7, 2007; Bunce and Wolchik, *American Democracy Promotion*.

usually exaggerating) the chaos next door as a result of the Georgian electoral breakthrough in 2003, so Lukashenka in Belarus and Putin/Medvedev in Russia have done the same with respect to developments in Ukraine after the victory of Yushchenko in 2004. Put succinctly: nothing supports the continuation of authoritarian rule like nearby examples of the costs involved in challenging such rule.

In the second wave, moreover, two additional constraints on collective action against regimes presented themselves as the wave of electoral confrontations with authoritarian leaders moved from the Balkans to the post-Soviet space. One was, as already noted, a fraying of the transnational network as it spread to locales further and further removed from Central and Southeastern Europe, where it had originated and where it had benefited from shared borders, established contacts among oppositions, and the accumulation among American democracy promoters in particular of rich experiences drawn from multiple postings in the states of Eastern and Central Europe. The other was a change in American policies regarding democracy promotion. Energy politics, strategic geopolitical location, and the victory of Hamas in Palestine in 2006 together reduced the priority the United States attached to, say, the defeat of dictators in Azerbaijan, Armenia, Russia, and Kazakhstan.

CONCLUSIONS

The purpose of this chapter has been to explore the intraregional diffusion of democracy by analyzing two waves of mobilization against authoritarian rule: the challenges to communist rule from 1987 to 1990, when popular protests sometimes combined with elite agreements served as the major venue, and the electoral defeats of authoritarian leaders from 1996 to 2005. As we discovered, although there were differences in political contexts and the instruments used, the diffusion process itself was remarkably similar. Challenges to authoritarian rule moved from more to less optimal circumstances, with this pattern explaining in turn the limits to diffusion and its uneven geography of diffusion; the form of these challenges shifted in response to changing international and domestic regime contexts; and demonstration effects, similar conditions, and transnational networks served as key (but variable) drivers in the spread of popular challenges to authoritarian governance.

We can now step back from these conclusions and highlight several implications. One is that some regions of the world, such as the postcommunist area, are unusually prone to diffusion dynamics – a pattern that in the region of interest in this chapter goes back in fact to the revolutions of 1848.[63] We would suggest that this regional tradition speaks to a history of shifting political borders in this region, on the one hand, and, on the other, to the powerful effects on oppositions and their political repertoires of the shared experiences

---

[63] Zvi Gitelman, *The Diffusion of Innovation from Eastern Europe to the Soviet Union* (Beverly Hills, CA: Sage Publications, 1974).

with communism. Another implication is that diffusion is always a matter of both structure and agency. Although structural conditions can support political change at home and encourage its cross-national transfer, it is the purposive actions of individuals that are responsible for seizing opportunities, fashioning effective strategies, bringing down authoritarians, and sharing experiences with neighbors. Finally, if democracy itself is always an unfinished project, subject to revision, expansion, and contraction, so struggles against authoritarian rule are necessarily ongoing enterprises as well. They are struggles, moreover, that, although changing in form and location over time, nonetheless profit from domestic experiences and opportunities and from international assistance and precedents.

PART II

ENCOURAGING DEMOCRACY: THE ROLE OF THE EUROPEAN UNION

3

When Europeanization Meets Transformation

Lessons from the Unfinished Eastern European Revolutions

Alina Mungiu-Pippidi
Hertie School of Governance, Berlin

I. INTRODUCTION: UNDERSTANDING THE GRAVITY MODEL

One of the main theses of this book is that the international system plays a critical role in democratization, although a highly variable one. Undeniably, foreign influence was a powerful factor in the democratic transformation of Eastern Europe, from Gorbachev's decision that Eastern Europe needed to liberalize its Communist regimes to NATO bombing Milošević out of Serbian voters' favor and the European Union's commitment to include Romania and Bulgaria. There is no need for sophisticated analyses here: a simple counterfactual shows that if Communism as a global order had not broken down in Eastern Europe, the designated heir of Nicolae Ceauşescu, his son Nicu, would in all likelihood govern present day Romania, just as the son of Assad governs Syria and Kim Il Jong rules North Korea, following in his father's footsteps.

It is the "how" more than the "if" that is the focus of the present chapter, which concerns Europe's power to initiate and stimulate transformative processes in neighbor and/or accession countries. In comparison to the rest of the world, transitions with a European Union (EU) accession perspective have proved best so far: they seem to lead to democracy and prosperity faster and with smaller uncertainties and risks.[1] This is the most robust illustration of the democratization mechanism known as the "gravity model," "according to which fast and deep democratization is explained to a significant degree by the proximity and possibility of anchorage and integration with a major world centre of democracy."[2] The evidence is not so linear, however, if we compare Eastern European countries. The Western Balkans have experienced difficult transitions, and their European inclusion was still more of a promise than a

[1] See Jeffrey Kopstein and David Reilly. "Geographic Diffusion and the Transformation of the Post-Communist World." *World Politics*, 53, No. 1 (2000), pp. 1–37.
[2] M. Emerson and G. Noutcheva. "Europeanization as a Gravity Model of Democratisation," Working Document 214 (Brussels: Center for Policy Studies, November 2004). Available online at http://shop.ceps.eu/BookDetail.php?item_id=1175.

reality by 2008. The new EU member countries, particularly (but not only) Romania and Bulgaria, experienced some backsliding on various democratic indicators, particularly on the rule of law and the freedom of the media, immediately *after* their EU accession.[3] If Estonia turned out a success and Macedonia a failure at the end of the day, was it the EU that made the difference? And why exactly did the pull of Europe work in one case and not the other? Although the argument for European proximity as a factor that makes democratization possible is perfectly sound, the argument that European *enlargement* explains successful transitions faces a problem of circularity. To be invited to join, a country has to be "ready" – in other words, to have already succeeded in its transition or to be far along the road to success. Slovenia, Estonia, and the so-called Visegrád countries had achieved the essentials of their successful transitions prior to any serious discussion of EU accession. Their Freedom House scores indicated the status of consolidated democracies only two to three years after the 1989–91 revolutions and independence. Problematic countries are not even considered for EU accession – either they are excluded or they exclude themselves. Discerning between postcommunist countries on the basis of EU accession and nonaccession therefore does not tell us much about the EU's smart power, because the fundamental difference between these cases existed prior to accession, and should therefore be explained by other factors. Also, for theoretical as well as policy purposes, we need to understand the mechanism that makes the EU's smart power work.[4] Would Macedonia have ended up as successful as Estonia if only the EU had acted toward the former as it has toward the latter? If EU accession is the powerful transformative agent that some scholars believe it to be, Western Balkan countries will eventually solve their problems simply by having an enlargement perspective. But if it is only an enabler, we cannot expect the enlargement to succeed everywhere similarly, particularly as the difficult countries are left behind and accumulate. Solving difficult transitional and developmental problems will then require transformation, not Europeanization, strategies. The two processes differ substantially: transformation is about *building* states, economic systems, and the rule of law. Europeanization is about *integrating* already functioning systems of this kind and rendering them compatible with the European model.

I want to argue that the EU's smart power is an extremely complex process, and according to domestic and/or European circumstances, one or the other of its mechanisms is activated. But because the mechanisms are not all equally effective, we cannot expect smart power to work similarly everywhere,

---

[3] See Freedom House *Nations in Transit* reports 2007, 2008. Available online at www .freedomhouse.org.

[4] The EU enlargement commissioner Oli Rehn, addressing an Oxford audience, defined "smart power" as a combination of hard and soft power, the use of "the whole spectrum of our policy instruments and economic resources." See Olli Rehn, 'Europe's Smart Power in Its Region and the World.' Speech at the European Studies Centre, St. Antony's College, University of Oxford, 1 May 2008. Available online at http://www.sant.ox.ac.uk/seesox/pdf/rehn_speech2008.pdf.

particularly because countries with difficult transitions are left behind and accumulate over time. To prove my point, I will focus on difficult Eastern European transitions and compare them with other transitions that were made under relatively similar circumstances in terms of European proximity. The interesting pool of countries for my research questions is the Southeastern European (SEE) countries, namely Romania, Albania, Bulgaria, and the former Yugoslavia. Although, in contrast to Georgia or Ukraine, the European vocation of these countries is beyond dispute, these transitions offer a particularly challenging mix of democratization and state- and nation-building. What is the specific nature of these transitions and what impact has Europe had so far?

A considerable body of literature is dedicated to studying the effectiveness of the strategies and instruments that the EU uses to promote Europeanization. Some studies primarily look at factors (at the level of the EU) that account for the effectiveness of conditionality.[5] Others explicitly contrast the relative effectiveness of conditionality and alternative strategies,[6] or focus on the domestic level, trying to discern the factors that mediate the EU's influence,[7] or simply consider alternative Europeanization mechanisms.[8] My contribution focuses on the specific EU input into difficult and unfinished transformations, particularly in the crucial areas of state- and nation-building. I seek to assess the impact of EU influence before, during, and after the EU accession and to understand the mechanisms explaining the change – or lack of it.

This chapter is organized in four parts. In the first, I simply outline my research question. In the second, I propose a model of the Southeastern European transition, contrasting it with the Central European one. In the third, I review the evidence on the EU's impact in the crucial areas for this particular transition model: nation- and state-building. In the fourth, I conclude by proposing a more developmental approach to understanding when and how EU smart power works. I argue that when Europeanization meets transformation, as in the cases that I discuss in this chapter, the Europeanization

---

[5] See, for example, H. Grabbe. *The EU's Transformative Power. Europeanization through Conditionality in Central and Eastern Europe* (New York: Palgrave Macmillan, 2006); G. Pridham. "Designing Democracy: EU Enlargement and Regime Change in Post-Communist Europe." *Journal of Common Market Studies* 45, No. 2 (2005): 524–5; M. A. Vachudov'a. *Europe Undivided: Democracy, Leverage and Integration After Communism* (Oxford / New York: Oxford University Press, 2005).

[6] J. G. Kelley. *Ethnic Politics in Europe: The Power of Norms and Incentives* (Princeton, NJ: Princeton University Press, 2004); Paul J. Kubicek, "International Norms, the European Union, and Democratization: Tentative Theory and Evidence." in *The European Union and Democratization*, Paul J. Kubicek, ed., pp. 1–29 (London: Routledge, 2003).

[7] F. Schimmelfennig and U. Sedelmeier, "Conclusions: The Impact of the EU on the Accession Countries," in *The Europeanization of Central and Eastern Europe*, F. Schimmelfennig and U. Sedelmeier (eds.), pp. 210–228 (Ithaca: Cornell University Press, 2005).

[8] For example, Wade Jacoby, *The Enlargement of the European Union and NATO: Ordering from the Menu in Central Europe* (Cambridge, UK/New York: Cambridge University Press, 2004).

theory coined in Western Europe is insufficient to explain the outcomes. It needs to be complemented with classic democratization and political development theory.

II. DEMOCRATIZATION WITHOUT DECOMMUNIZATION: A TRANSITION MODEL

In 2008, the Balkan region presented various stages of democratic accomplishment and development. Slovenia, which has the highest income per capita of all former communist countries, became an EU member in 2004. Romania and Bulgaria (the Eastern Balkan countries) joined in 2007. Serbia–Montenegro has been pursuing a democratic path since the fall of its wartime dictator Slobodan Milošević, despite periodic scares of returns by nationalists; in the spring of 2006 it split peacefully into two separate countries, each hoping to join the EU as well. Croatia and Macedonia have signed Stabilization and Accession Treaties (SAP), a preliminary step to joining the European Union; the former has concluded negotiations in a relatively short time, whereas the latter was still struggling to start them by the end of 2008. Albania signed a SAP in 2006 and became a NATO member in 2008. More difficult situations are faced by countries with serious state-building problems – such as Bosnia and the former Yugoslav province of Kosovo, which were still international protectorates at the end of 2008, despite being formally independent.

Overall, however, the success of the region is limited. Freedom House *Nations in Transit* democracy scores continue to be far worse for Balkan countries, even for Romania and Bulgaria, than for Central Europe. Much of the disparity is due especially to their history in the early 1990s, and they do score better than the former Soviet Union (FSU) countries. Additionally, Balkan countries form an essential intermediary group between Central Europe and the FSU, justifying their treatment as a common region by previous scholars.[9]

By 1989, the year of great change in East Central Europe, three distinct Communist systems operated in the region with differing implications for postcommunist reform: essentially Stalinist, totalitarian regimes in Romania and Albania; an orthodox Communist regime in the Soviet-bloc state Bulgaria; and a reformed Communist system in Yugoslavia that had incorporated some liberal elements and that shared a number of features with the Central European states. For this reason, and also because of devolutionist pressures from its constituent republics, Yugoslavia was the most open to Central European influences. The Yugoslav transition, however, was marked by the breakup of the federation, which took a path completely different from the rest. The first free elections of the region were less decisively favorable to challengers of Communist regimes than in Central Europe; on the contrary, Communist leaders managed to manipulate elections to their advantage. The electoral

[9] G. Pridham and T. Gallagher, *Experimenting with Democracy: Regime Change in the Balkans* (London: Routledge, 2000).

landscape immediately after 1990 was similar in the Balkans, characterized by anticommunist cities (particularly the capital) and a conservative country-side where voters preferred a slower reform path. Early surveys such as Times Mirror Gallup 1991 showed that totalitarianism had a favorable legacy in public opinion. Majorities still endorsed the one-party system that year in both Romania and Bulgaria, and although people did not want to revert to Communism, some – peasants especially – were in favor of a moderate authoritarian regime and considered the replacement of the leaders Ceauşescu and Jivkov to represent change enough.

Despite their different outcomes, the transitions of the Eastern and Western Balkans shared many similarities, even if we consider the exceptional breakup of the former Yugoslavia, the only federation of the region. Croatia and Slovenia are the furthest from the pattern and cluster better with Central European countries, mostly because their transformations to a Western model were initiated long before the total collapse of communism. Slovenia's economic integration with Carinthia, the neighboring Austrian region, had started in the 1960s and was very advanced by 1989. The rest of the Balkan countries shared common transition patterns, consisting of:

1. Societal demands for liberalization only *after* communism was already breaking up in Central Europe, and explicitly emulating Central European examples.

2. Huge popular mobilization with street rallies to compensate for the absence of any organized opposition groups, leading to anarchical transitions, often fought in the streets. Romania and Albania are the best examples.

3. Attempts to manage pluralism and democratic processes by established Communist elites who controlled most of the transition. For instance, President Ion Iliescu of Romania asked the coal miners to crush the students' opposition to him.

4. The specific combination of national communisms (unlike the Baltic states) and a multiethnic structure (unlike Central Europe, except Slovakia), leading to major problems of nation- and state-building during transition, without the additional benefit of national liberation supporting democratization.

5. Consequently, Communist Party manipulation of nationalism to defend its political monopoly. Milošević was the central figure, although former Communists in Romania, Bulgaria, and Macedonia resorted to similar mechanisms to ensure their survival in power, particularly in the first part of the transition.

6. Important "state capture" by communist elites and criminal networks.

To be sure, these SEE transitions followed similar patterns not just because these countries imitated one another, but also because of the many similarities between their societies. Yugoslavia's particular brand of communism, combined with devolutionist pressures from its constituent republics, gave

Yugoslavia the most autonomous society and made it the most open to Central European influences. The other countries had few isolated dissidents and monolithic Communist parties – both crucial differences from Central Europe with its liberal, internally plural Communist parties and large dissident groups.

Unlike Central Europe, where martial law was needed in Poland to keep things frozen, the degree of control of society by Communist parties was very high in the Balkans by 1989. Challenger elites were practically nonexistent, again in contrast to Central Europe, with the partial exception of Yugoslavia. What did exist, however, were the widespread perception that communism was a total failure as a regime and an urgent desire to be reformed by copying a Western model. Once it became clear from Central European examples that repression was no longer working, oppositions began to emerge. At first, their manifestation was anarchical because the political police – which were far more effective and aggressive than in Central Europe – prevented any form of organization. Yet this grassroots opposition stemmed from communism's total lack of legitimacy at the time of its demise. This explains why these oppositions included many groups besides intellectuals: workers, minorities, taxi drivers, Communist party members, and a constellation of other social groups.

The SEE transformations are therefore part of the larger wave of change in the region, explicitly initiated with the wish to catch up with the transformations and the "return to Europe" of Central Europe. Unlike the Central European postcommunists, who had to dig deep for the skills to reinvent themselves as successful democratic politicians, the Balkan Communist leaders who saw communism falling apart in Central Europe understood that stopping the process was impossible, and tried instead to manage it by becoming the first democrats. The rest of the transition depended on how able the civil society and the opposition were to create a strong alternative to such opportunistic and skillful leaders as Milošević and Iliescu; this alternative needed to be strong enough both to win elections and to prevent them from being stolen. The entire democratic transition process benefited from lessons learned from neighbors, and took advantage of the cross-border regional momentum to boost a movement within its own nations.

The crucial difference between SEE and Central and Eastern Europe (CEE) is to be found in this *control of the early transition by the Communist power establishment*, which set a path for the rest of the transition. Whereas in Central Europe anticommunists won by a landslide, in SEE Communists managed to control the change and initiate a process of "democratization without decommunization."[10] This meant advancing on the path of political pluralism while protecting the Communist power establishment in nearly every field, most notably the judiciary, bureaucracy, and secret services. These early

---

[10] Vachudova calls these regimes "illiberal democracies." See Milada Anna Vachudova, *Europe Undivided: Democracy, Leverage and Integration After Communism* (Oxford: Oxford University Press, 2005).

leaders favored veritable *predatory elites*[11] with a political project of extraction (taking advantage of privatization and using administrative resources for their own benefit), resorting in high elite corruption. This is an important feature of Balkan transitions, as well as those in the FSU, although the phenomenon did exist to a smaller extent in Central Europe as well. The repressive agencies from communist times were also recycled and put to more profitable use. Agents of the communist secret service made themselves very busy in Albania, Serbia, and Romania during these transitions, and it was often difficult to distinguish a spontaneous riot from a planned diversion. Former communist power establishments were stronger and more dedicated to protecting their advantage in the Balkans than in Central Europe, because communist leaders in Central Europe felt they had less to fear because the worst of communism could be blamed on the Soviets. In all the countries in the Balkans, due to the absence of the Soviet Union from the immediate picture, national networks of power developed, linking secret services with the army, party figures, opinion leaders, and managers of state companies.

These formerly communist networks worked hard to maintain their influence and convert it into wealth, even if that meant sacrificing the Communist party itself, as in Romania, and creating an opportunistic one (the National Salvation Front, which later changed its name four times to keep up with the times). An example of this can be seen in the corruption and organized crime that the European Union was still monitoring in Romania and Bulgaria after their 2007 accession; these negative characteristics were actually due to the entrenchment of interest networks in their political and business life – a sign of their unfinished revolutions. Romania's post-1989 President Ion Iliescu managed to stay in power for ten years (with an interruption between 1996 and 2000), whereas Slobodan Milošević ruled until 2000 and left only due to a popular urban riot. Bulgaria had the most balanced transition, with milder communists and a stronger opposition. Yet, even there, the former regime managed to control essential institutions, such as the courts. Higher courts staffed with communist establishment magistrates in all these countries fought hard to preserve the old patterns of power and influence. The main stake of the transition, therefore, was competition for the control of the transformation (accepted as unavoidable by all sides), and the elites of the former regime had far more resources for this goal than the unorganized street movements opposing them. It was only because of this inequality of resources that former regime elites finally agreed to give up their monopoly on power. They expected that by doing so they would win the first free elections, stop the challenge from the streets, and gain some international legitimacy. And this is precisely how it worked in the first part of the transitions.

---

[11] The term was coined by historian Barrington Moore to describe a group of people who in the process of generating wealth for themselves generate large-scale poverty for their society. See Barrington Moore, Jr., *Injustice: The Social Bases of Obedience and Revolt* (White Plains, NY: M. E. Sharpe, 1978).

Due to the complicated state- and nation-building problems of their societies (mainly due to federalism and important ethnic minorities), Balkan Communist parties also discovered an alternative ideology to preserve their clout: *national communism*. Nationalism and socialism combined proved to have a stronger appeal than socialism alone, providing former communist elites with a remarkable tool of survival. To reinforce their mass appeal, the communist successors in Serbia and Romania turned to more and more nationalistic strategies, which proved to be to their electoral advantage. They also repeatedly allied themselves with chauvinistic right-wing parties, showing how little international public opinion mattered in the early nineties to the former communist leaders in these countries. The combination of a unitary state, proportional representation, and cooperation among democrats across ethnic lines was nevertheless enough to keep the ethnic conflict in a peaceful framework in Romania and Bulgaria. The reverse proved true for the former federal Socialist Republic of Yugoslavia. The only Central European state with problems similar to those of the Balkans was Slovakia. With its important Hungarian minority, Slovakia had a trajectory similar to those of Romania and Bulgaria, being for the first part of the transition a laggard in both democracy and EU integration.

In the end, the behavior of postcommunist parties in transition (in the Balkans, authoritarian and nationalistic; in Central Europe, compromising and ready to transform) is far more important in explaining the performance of these emerging democracies than the behavior of the anticommunists – roughly similar everywhere, despite important differences in strength and numbers. The *policy distance* between incumbent and challenger political elites was smaller from the onset in Central Europe than in Romania, Bulgaria, or the Commonwealth of Independent States.

The successful transitions of Central Europe are explained by the consensus, between postcommunists and anticommunists, from the onset of the transition in 1989 that there needed to be a different regime. This developed mostly because the communist parties in Central Europe had already exhausted the possibilities of reforming the socialist economy by 1989. In countries where the communist parties had not yet exhausted these possibilities, such as in Serbia and Romania, they tried a compromise "third-way" approach in the first years of the transition and ultimately failed, leaving their economies in far worse shape than when they started. However, in the second part of the transition, policy distance decreased considerably between the postcommunists and challengers in Romania and Bulgaria, very much like Central Europe. The main contributor to this development was European integration, which came quite late in the picture.

The legacies of the early transitions of Southeastern Europe therefore were the entrenched communist structures (for instance, in the secret services), the states captured by opportunistic elites originating in the old regime, and the old ethnic conflicts revived and made worse by democratization. These legacies, combined with failed economic transitions and the additional burden of the war in former Yugoslavia and the embargo imposed on the Milošević regime,

TABLE 3.1. *Steps to EU Accession*

Step	Visegrád Group (Hungary, Czechoslovakia, Poland)	Bulgaria and Romania
Association agreements signed	1991	1993
Membership applications by	1994	1995
Invitation to start negotiations	1997 (Slovakia in 1999)	1999
Year treaty signed	2003	2005
Accession year	2004	2007

further crippled the regional economies. In 1996, Bulgaria experienced a currency crash; in 1999, Romania underwent a severe recession and a new violent descent of the miners on the capital; and the Kosovo war brought fresh disaster to former Yugoslavia. When in December 1999 at the Helsinki summit the EU invited Romania and Bulgaria to join, it was not to reward the success of their transitions, but to offer the two anticommunist governments in place a means of stabilizing their countries while Serbia and Albania slid into anarchy, and spillover from Kosovo threatened Macedonia.

III. EUROPE'S IMPACT ON NATION AND STATE BUILDING

The Visegrád countries had seen very successful economic transitions and were consolidated democracies by the time they received invitations to start negotiations with the EU. But the SEE countries, as well as Slovakia and Lithuania, were still struggling in their transitions by the Helsinki summit. They were behind economically, as well as politically, even if by 1999 they had all experienced at least one democratic swing. Romania and Bulgaria tried to keep up with their former Warsaw pact fellows, applying first to sign association economic agreements, then for EU membership (see Table 3.1). The Baltic states also tried to catch up with the most advanced Central European countries, leaving only the distressed states of the former Yugoslavia behind. For these applicants with unfinished transitions, Europeanization meant speeding up the building of market institutions, administrative capacity, and the rule of law altogether. On the EU side as well, the formal integration process from the Austrian and Swedish accessions needed to be complemented by a huge assistance effort to help these countries accomplish their transformations successfully. Thus Europeanization met transformation and another vast front was opened on the side of EU accession. The problem became even more complicated after the EU made the promise to enlarge to the Western Balkans at the Thessaloniki summit in the hope that this pledge would stabilize the region, as those countries were clearly unable to solve their problems by themselves.

The countries in ECE (European Community) had been part of the same system for many years. Comparisons across these countries and some degree of competition between them were very strong during transition and EU accession.

The demonstration effect present during early transition continued; Eastern Europeans wanted to be like their Western counterparts – free and prosperous. Throughout the decades of "return to Europe," followed by the more formal EU accession process, public support for EU integration was very high in ECE, except for Serbia–Montenegro, where the West came to be perceived as the enemy after the two Yugoslav wars. This crucial variable explains the conversion of postcommunist elites, who became opportunistic pro-Europeans and adopted accession policies. The Eastern Balkan publics wanted to join Europe, in particular, due to increasing poverty and the stark contrast between their economic performance and that of the Central European countries. The laggard status that Eastern Balkan countries experienced throughout most of the transition was bitterly resented and attracted constant media criticism of domestic governments. Romania and Bulgaria attracted little foreign direct investment in the nineties due to the mismanagement of their early transitions. Europe was therefore needed as much for its money as for regime legitimacy and security. After securing domestic domination (in business as well as the judicial system and politics), communist successor parties in Romania, Bulgaria, and Albania made European accession their next important objective. But the advance toward Europe was done together with the former power establishment, not against it, or it would not have been possible at all. Democratization without decommunization was followed by a similar Europeanization. The elite conversion to Europe took place in a spectacular way; but it remains to be seen if it was a real conversion, or just an opportunistic one.

In the early SEE transitions, the international factor manifested itself mostly through the vanishing of the Soviet enforcement of Communism and the learning of revolutionary practices across borders. It was on a parallel issue, the conflict in the former Yugoslavia, that most of the international influence was exercised, leading to the creation of two international protectorates, Bosnia and Kosovo. Historians remember, however, more the absence of timely management of the Yugoslav conflict on the part of the international community in general, and Europe in particular, rather than their influence. The EU, together with the OSCE and other international actors, needed some years to become proactive in the region and to deploy some effort to ensure that ethnic wars on the model of that in the former Yugoslavia did not occur in the other countries of SEE. Europe's most cherished intervention was in brokering the Ohrid agreement in Macedonia in 2001. How sustainable this power-sharing arrangement actually is remains a matter of debate.

While Yugoslavia was breaking up, the remaining countries of the Eastern bloc were slowly socialized by the international community, instituting policies of better treatment of their ethnic minorities. This led to the adoption of best practice European and international laws on the matter in all accession countries, in most cases before the invitation to join the EU. The Council of Europe was the main actor in the first part of the transition, pushing the issue to Eastern European countries with the help of Western ambassadors, very much as in interwar times. Of EU institutions, the European Parliament was the most active in this direction. Other international actors, such as NATO (with its preconditions for joining), also played an important role.

In June 1993, the EU Copenhagen Council (which enacted the "Copenhagen accession criteria") borrowed from the existing OSCE norms for democratic states guaranteeing human rights and protecting minorities. The EU did not evaluate the candidates' aptitude to fulfill the democracy, market economy, and *acquis* criteria until July 1997, when the European Commission issued its opinion on each country's application for membership. By then, all countries from the region had officially submitted membership applications, and in the first assessment, the Commission acknowledged that their minority issues were not an impediment to joining. Although monitoring of the treatment of minorities was constant during accession and the EU supported various reform bills, the only moment when it had to display strong conditionality was when Vladimír Mečiar's party threatened to return to government when it came in first in the 2002 Slovak elections. As Mečiar had insufficient votes to form a government, pressure from the EU and NATO isolated Mečiar and stimulated the creation of a countercoalition. This remains, to date, the strongest intervention by the EU in the domestic affairs of a candidate country. No new EU member country has any specification in its accession treaty related to minorities.

The result of this EU approach to the minority issue is that all successful EU new members to date are unitary states that treat their minorities fairly, but did not make any concessions to them in the area of "collective rights." Citizenship is defined firmly on an individual, not a collective basis in all these countries, despite the existence of counterdesigns from some minorities during the accession process. Although the EU brokered a power-sharing arrangement in Macedonia and subscribed to the Dayton agreement, those countries remain the most problematic cases where EU accession is concerned, and EU officials themselves acknowledge that the Dayton constitution is a major obstacle to Bosnia's EU accession.

The most successful solution to the ethnic problems emerged in Romania, Bulgaria, and Slovakia, three ECE countries with important minorities that had experienced conflict and nationalism to a considerable degree by the beginning of their transitions. Starting in the late nineties, however, they registered a very positive evolution: ethnic minorities have become associated with government as nearly permanent members, coupled with the left and the right in turn, with little or no popular opposition to this development. By 2005, when Romania and Bulgaria signed their respective EU accession treaties, and Slovakia had already been a member for more than a year, minorities in these three countries had managed to get important positions at all levels of government, despite the absence of explicit demands of the EU in this regard. Compared to the early nineties, minorities' parties gained significantly in terms of appointed political positions in the central government and administration, and their elected offices have grown to a proportion superior to their demographic share. This development was largely due to domestic and organic developments, although enabled by the framework of EU accession. Due mostly to the structure of constituencies and the voting systems, at some point anticommunists in all three countries needed the support of minority parties to form governments (prior to receiving the Helsinki invitation). When socialists eventually returned to government, they also needed these minority voters to get a majority of seats. Also, they saw the additional value in preserving cross-ethnic alliances to show that they had abandoned their earlier nationalistic ways and thus to appease eventual EU fears regarding their sincerity on minority treatment.

The choice of power sharing among ethnic parties over any other possible constitutional arrangement (for instance, granting special status to minority-inhabited regions or ethnofederalism) and the success of these ethnic parties in becoming nearly permanent and unquestioned features of the political systems in their respective countries (with significant reduction of nationalism in public opinion) resulted from a combination of domestic factors and the EU context. The fact that the Baltic republics did not follow suit for years and resisted similar EU pressure for any power sharing with their Russian minorities shows that the effect of EU conditionality did not lead directly to developments on ethnic minority rights in Romania and Bulgaria. The presence of the EU, in all of its forms, conditionality and funds, seems to have had more of a mediating effect rather than a direct one. It is more of a catalytic effect than anything else. Catalysts are chemical substances (such as enzymes in living cells) that decisively facilitate reactions between other chemical substances without themselves being directly consumed in the process. This seems to have been largely the case for the influence that the EU had on the status of minorities and on minority–majority relations in these three ECE countries. The European environment empowered the politicians who were moderate and in favor of cooperation across ethnic lines both on the majority and on the minority sides. It thus contributed, to an extent that is hard to determine, to the emergence of an organically grown, power-sharing arrangement negotiated step by step, which has proved sustainable through several electoral cycles. This *enabling* quality of the EU, which led to the empowerment of political and societal groups that could benefit from Europeanization, has been discussed frequently in the literature and appears as the most salient factor in the field of nation-building.[12]

After elite conversion and nation-building, state-building was the third crucial area of EU influence, due to the specificities of SEE transitions that I have discussed in Section II of this chapter. Corruption has also been a problem in Central Europe, but due to the early rise of alternative elites to power and to superior development, corruption did not involve the systemic, state-capturing character seen in the Balkans. Although the new member states have undergone important reforms to reorganize their governments after

---

[12] See also on this M. Keating, J. Loughlin, and K. Deschouwer, *Culture, Institutions and Economic Development. A Study of Eight European Regions* (Aldershot: Edward Elgar, 2003); also Heather Grabbe, "How Does Europeanization Affect CEE Governance? Conditionality, Diffusion and Diversity." *Journal of European Public Policy*, 8 (2001), p 6; and Schimmelfennig and Sedelmeier, 2005, note 3.

Communism,[13] this was largely an unfinished job by the beginning of EU negotiations. The ship built at sea retained important elements of the old ship, particularly in the Eastern Balkans. During negotiations with the EU, reforms of the judiciary, administration, policymaking structures, and civil service were important issues. Despite EU not having an *acquis per se* in these areas, the European Commission, with the help of other international organizations, invested considerable amounts of assistance, monitoring, and coaching. Conditionality was also strong, particularly for the laggards, and a safeguard mechanism was created for the three postaccession years in case the new member countries did not meet their commitments.

Despite all this, reports by Freedom House in *Nations in Transit* (*NIT*) indicate no statistically significant progress over years of negotiation in the key areas of governance and rule of law. The lack of significant evolution is also reflected in the aggregated governance indicators of the World Bank, based on far more sources than *NIT*. A comparison of scores from 2000 to 2004 shows only minor, statistically insignificant changes, even for Estonia, which seems to have progressed the most. Slovakia recorded the largest progress in the overall Freedom House *NIT* democracy scores, and the Czech Republic displayed the biggest regress. The lack of sufficient progress is particularly problematic for Bulgaria and Romania, which were trailing behind from the start. Other governance scores also show insignificant progress, such as the Heritage Foundation's reports on property rights. Despite half of the new EU member countries scoring poorly on the latter, by accession year 2004 the Heritage scores showed no improvement compared to 2000. No governance indicators that we can find show significant progress on state building during the EU accession, and the evolution of democracy scores in general remains mixed, with some countries progressing, but others, which had been best practice examples during transition, sliding back. In the same interval, however, *NIT* scores record significant progress in Albania and Serbia, which were not subjected to such strong conditionality as EU candidate countries (see Table 3.2).

What can explain this situation? To be certain, at the level of input indicators, there are plenty of signs of Europeanization.[14] The rate of transposition of EU legislation into domestic one is very high for new member countries. But at the level of implementation and impact we do not find much evidence of real evolution toward European standards in the key governance areas. One simple answer would be that it is still too early to see any evolution, and the good governance policies will work if given more time. It seems that it is not too early, however, for some countries to display *negative* evolution of some practices. Practically the next day after accession, when conditionality

[13] See K. H. Goetz, and H. Z. Margetts, "The Solitary Centre: The Core Executive in Central and Eastern Europe." *Governance*, 12, No. 4 (1999), 425–53.

[14] See H. Grabbe, *The EU's Transformative Power: Europeanization through Conditionality in Central and Eastern Europe* (New York: Palgrave Macmillan, 2006).

TABLE 3.2. *Governance Progress during Negotiations with the EU*

Countries	NIT Score 1999–2000	NIT Score 2004–2005	Downgrades 1999–2007	General Change 1999–2004	Governance Progress	Rule of Law Progress
Albania	4.75	4.04	0	0.71	a	0.75
Bulgaria	3.58	3.18	1	0.40	0.25	0.25
Czech Republic	2.08	2.33	2	–0.25	–0.25	–1.00
Estonia	2.25	1.92	1	0.32	0	0.50
Hungary	1.88	1.96	3	–0.08	–0.75	0
Latvia	2.29	2.17	0	0.12	0.25	0
Lithuania	2.29	2.13	1	0.16	0	0.25
Poland	1.58	1.75	5	–0.17	–0.25	0
Romania	3.54	3.89	3	–0.35	0.25	0.25
Serbia	5.67	3.75	1	1.92	1.50	0.75
Slovakia	2.71	2.08	1	0.64	0.75	0.50
Slovenia	1.88	1.75	0	0.13	0.50	–0.25
Average change in EUAC by category			1.7	0.092	–0.08	0.05

Note: The scores range from 1 to 7, with 1 the best performance and 7 the worst. The original performance of the countries in the aggregated democracy score is in the column 1 and the performance in the year of signing the accession treaty is in column 2. Column 4 shows the general evolution in this interval, whereas columns 6 and 7 show evolution in the subscores of governance and judicial reform (changed to plus to facilitate reading). Column 4 measures the number of downgrades to a country by Freedom House in the interval 1999–2007, in other words, the number of times when the yearly score was worse to demonstrate a negative development in the country. For Serbia the year 1999 is the aggregated score of Yugoslavia (including Montenegro). The interval measured for Serbia and Albania is 1999–2004 and their scores are not included in the regional averages.

Source: Freedom House *Nations in Transit.* Available at http://www.freedomhouse.org/nit/.

disappeared, politicians tried to close down some of the most reputed anti-corruption agencies that the EU had inspired and sponsored. Latvia, Slovenia, and Romania are notorious cases. There were also steps back on procurement legislation, on control of public broadcasting, and on politicization of the administration, which had never fully gone away before returning in force. But even during negotiations, when conditionality was strong, the reform pace slowed down compared to previous times, mainly because elites already considered the prize won. Also, besides this domestic factor, the nature of the process of accession itself did not help much. With its stress on the adoption of official institutions meant to integrate a country into the European Union, the enlargement process is very formal in nature.[15] The massive top-down legislation that was imported thus only touches the surface of the governance process at the domestic level; it cannot induce substantial changes in existing patterns of behavior if it is not supported by respective bottom-up developments.[16]

For the postcommunist candidate countries, conditionality was the key mechanism that the EU relied upon: a mixture of conditional positive incentives (ultimately EU membership) and negative incentives (delaying negotiation closure, accession date, withholding of EU funds). These countries did not negotiate as previous EU entrants had done: they had to take in the EU *acquis* in full. Conditionality is supposed to be smart power. It offers an incentive to shape behavior. But it may well be that a general incentive (EU integration) is insufficient to motivate all the social groups that need to change their behavior. The fundamental alteration of rules of the game for politicians, bureaucrats, and magistrates in the SEE countries, for instance, presumes that they stand to win more than lose from the change. In other words, for such a process to be successful, it has to incentivize key groups and not just rely on the presumption that what is good for the country is also good for them. Supportive constituencies of EU accession are not the same as key groups that support reforms. Those directly concerned, from bureaucrats to magistrates, displayed considerably less enthusiasm than the general public or democracy-minded NGOs. A review of every significant area in the field of governance reforms shows that motivating agents to change their behavior was extremely difficult. Incentives for local elites in the accession process often seem to have been wrong, confusing, or absent, leading to an overall effort shaped very much like an old Communist plan.

First, the negotiations themselves developed some wrong incentives. The detailed requirements of the Commission during negotiations and the related conditionality created a relationship where the EC became the sole principal (instead of domestic publics or their representatives) and the government its agent. Reforms were not driven by impact evaluations, but by the need to satisfy

---

[15] See also on this J. K. Glenn, "From Nation-States to Member States: Accession Negotiations as an Instrument of Europeanization." *Comparative European Politics*, 2, No. 1 (2004), 3–28.
[16] See G. Atanasova, "Governance through Conditionality." Paper prepared for delivery at the 2004 Annual Meeting of the American Political Science Association, 2 September, 2004.

the pressing bureaucratic *reporting needs* for the EC regular monitoring reports. One-off special efforts to reach certain EU targets and islands of excellence in administrative units able to attain deadlines were the prevailing approaches, instead of sound, system-building administrative reform. As the EC went quite far in suggesting concrete means to achieve targets (such as the creation of new government bodies) and governments needed positive ratings for their efforts to keep up the pace of the accession process, a "prescription-based" perverse incentive mechanism was created. Countries came to be evaluated not by the effectiveness of reforms or even their real change potential, but by the number of "prescription pills" taken. A "patient" (assisted country) was rated higher the more advice it accepted, with little or no checking of "symptoms." Predictably, reforms driven by such purely bureaucratic incentives were not very effective or sustainable.

Second, confusing or conflicting incentives also developed frequently, for instance, in regional policy. Opinions of the EC in 1997 identified weak regional administrative capacity for the first time as a key problem for enlargement. It appears that from very early stages, competing views developed within the Commission over whether Chapter Twenty-One of the *acquis* entailed a model of regionalization and how it should be implemented by the CEECs[17] (Central and East European Countries). The issue was political as well as technical. All countries involved were unitary states, many of them with historical ethnic minorities. Was regionalization to be political or statistical? Originally the EC argued that countries must reconfigure their administrative regional organizations to increase absorption capacity. Some of these countries had already embarked on serious decentralization, but they all had their own historical territorial divisions, and the passage from their old structures to completely new ones was bound to be complicated. The argument that regions or meso-governments would also increase accountability and participation was not grounded in evidence. Between 2000 and 2004, Romania's governing party, the SDP, used infrastructure funds to lure more than 50 percent of Romania's directly elected mayors to switch to the SDP (thus completely vitiating results of local elections) precisely during the negotiation years, and the EC barely made mention of this in its regular report. What drove regionalization was the EC technocrats' presumption that the effective absorption of regional funds was facilitated by a given structure, on the basis of their previous experience in other countries. After some ECE countries managed to implement such reforms (for instance, Poland), the realization of the high costs and uncertain benefits, combined with the incentive to spend the funds by an approaching deadline, led the EC to abandon this policy. So by early 2001 the Commission began to proactively stress a clear preference for the *centralized* management of

[17] On structural funds see J. Hughes, G. Sasse, and C. Gordon, *Europeanization and Regionalization in the EU's Enlargement to Central and Eastern Europe: The Myth of Conditionality*, (New York: Palgrave Macmillan, 2004).

structural funds in the candidate countries, realizing that capacity was superior at that level.[18]

The area of civil service reform is also illustrative in this respect. Despite overall compliance with EU requirements, most reviews found that the reforms failed to make substantial progress on Europeanization.[19] Recorded instances of progress seem to be related to local circumstances and not specific assistance efforts.[20] The attempt to build civil service management systems failed, and politicization endured.[21] As the latter was perceived as the key problem of administrative performance, the EU sponsored legislation that granted tenure to all civil servants, thus removing a crucial incentive for linking career to performance without, however, eliminating any incentive for politicization, as formal requirements to the contrary proved easy to bypass. Rigid labor codes inherited from communism prevented further attempts to design performance-oriented civil service systems.

Third and last, in the crucial area of the rule of law, incentives for radical change were altogether missing. During accession years, European and American donors together pushed for an independent judiciary, considered a key to good performance of the judicial system. By the time accession started, many ECE countries had already granted tenure to all judges. Problems such as corruption of magistrates and dominance of Communist-era judges in the judiciary persisted. Some countries had tried to solve the problem of independence by entrusting the powers of control to self-governing judiciaries, through the establishment of independent bodies and Judicial Councils, a model encouraged by EC for the accession laggards.[22] But disillusionment came fast, as the new Judicial Councils were not subject to conditionality (as governments were), either directly or indirectly. They did not have constituencies to respond to for

[18] See J. Hughes, G. Sasse, and C. Gordon, "EU Enlargement and Power Asymmetries: Conditionality and the Commission's Role in Regionalisation in Central and Eastern Europe," Working Paper (London: London School of Economics and Political Science, 2003). Available online at http://www.lse.ac.uk/collections/europeanInstitute/articles/hughesj2.pdf; also L. Vass, "Regional Reform in Hungary: Does EU Enlargement Matter?" In *Driven to Change: The European Union's Enlargement Viewed from the East*, A. L. Dimitrova, ed., pp. 131–44 (Manchester/New York: Manchester University Press, 2004)

[19] See A. Dimitrova, "Enlargement, Institution-Building and the EU's Administrative Capacity Requirement." *West European Politics* 25, No. 4 (2002), 171–90.

[20] See T. Verheijen, *Administrative Capacity in the New Member States: The Limits of Innovation?* World Bank Report 36930-GLB (Washington, DC: World Bank, 2006). Available online at http://siteresources.worldbank.org/INTECA/Resources/EU8_AdminCapacity_Dec06.pdf.

[21] See J.-H. Meyer-Sahling, "Civil Service Reform in Post-Communist Europe: The Bumpy Road to Depoliticisation." *West European Politics*, 27, No. 1 (2004), 77–103; also J.-H. Meyer-Sahling, "The Institutionalization of Political Discretion in Post-Communist Civil Service Systems: The Case of Hungary." *Public Administration*, 84, No. 3 (2006), 693–715.

[22] For a larger argument on this see D. Smilov, "EU Enlargement and the Constitutional Principle of Judicial Independence." in *Spreading Democracy and the Rule of Law? The Impact of EU Enlargement on the Rule of Law, Democracy and Constitutionalism in Post-Communist Legal Orders*, W. Sadurski, A. Czarnota, and M. Krygier, eds., pp. 313–34 (Netherlands: Springer, 2005).

an eventual delay in EU accession, as governments did. Their constituents were the magistrates, who were no longer accountable to anybody. Their pay was increased to stimulate performance and curb corruption, but attempts to set up any serious checks on their performance did not succeed. Magistrates had been promoters of reform as long their independence from political intervention was at stake: once they became completely independent their *esprit de corps* flourished and no incentives were left for them to pursue self-improvement.

Incentives were also missing in the field of anticorruption, another area stressed by the EC. Corruption in postcommunist societies is systemic and goes beyond simple bribery. It can best be defined as the discretionary distribution of public services by the state to the benefit of particular groups or individuals. This touched nearly everything at the beginning of transition, when everything was state property, and gradually diminished as privatization progressed and market institutions consolidated. Inequality before the law remains, however, a crucial component of postcommunist corruption, and the distribution of public funds (including the remarkable new resources of EU money) persists in being anything but random, even after accession.

Passing special legislation to favor certain economic interests was another frequent occurrence during the transition years and continued during accession. The EC, following the OECD's SIGMA advice, pressed for the creation of policy management units within governments to take charge of planning and impact evaluation of new legislation, in the hope that this would bring a more objective and transparent basis to policy formulation. Reviewers found, however, that most decision making continued to go through informal channels such as ministers' cabinets, frequently bypassing the management unit.[23] When more grassroots anticorruption eventually developed in Slovakia, Bulgaria, or Romania in the form of civil society coalitions, the EU was not among its main sponsors. It continued to invest in incremental (though costly) capacity building, corruption awareness campaigns (despite evidence that awareness was very high), and adoption of more anticorruption legislation to be passed to provide guarantees that new member countries would be able to implement EU *acquis*. And so, immediately after accession, the whole front of EU-sponsored anticorruption institutions came under assault from politicians. A motion against Romanian Justice Minister Monica Macovei, a favorite reformer with the EU Commission, had been prepared by a group of MPs weeks in advance, but was presented only after the accession date. The accusing text read like the list of bills passed in the previous two years at the request of the EU. The Slovenian Commission for Prevention of Corruption, an EU-inspired body, entrusted with control of conflicts of interests of elected politicians, was saved by the Constitutional Court, as MPs after accession promptly voted for its closing. In Latvia, a success story for anticorruption in the accession years, the public had to rally to defend the anticorruption agency boss from being fired by the Prime

[23] Interview with SIGMA consultant, 2005.

Minister in 2007, but could not protect him when he was ousted by Latvian lawmakers with 52 votes in favor to 40 against in June 2008. In Bulgaria, the Minister of Internal Affairs had to resign under EU pressure in spring 2008 after a meeting with the head of organized crime: he claimed he was meeting that person in order to meet the EU's demands that at least one of the many mob-style execution cases end up with an official charge against someone. Serious evidence of fraud with EU funds made the European Commission act against Bulgaria, slashing some of its EU funds due in 2008. Obviously, Bulgaria's EU accession had not solved its corruption problem, but rather nourished it with fresh funding.

IV. CONCLUSION: DECONSTRUCTING "SMART" POWER

Such evidence casts doubt on both the power and the sustainability of over-ambitious conditionality-driven reforms in the absence of a domestic reform dynamic. By and large, reforms stopped in the unfinished revolutions of these countries. In the judiciary and administration, many old-timers still held important positions of influence, so they could block or sabotage the reforms. Governance reforms seem to have gone against the vested interests of the power establishment in many new EU member countries, particularly in Southeastern Europe. With the benefit of hindsight, Europeanization of political elites was taken for granted by the EU. After accession, when the EU lost most of its levers, all those opportunistic Europeanizers returned to their previous profitable practices, such as clientele-based distribution of spending budgets, control of public media, and immunity from corruption accusations. The situation varies across countries[24] and is worst in Romania and Bulgaria, but symptoms exist in other new EU member countries as well. They are proportional to the degree of a country's transformation – or lack of it.

One critical problem with studies looking at the impact of the EU on other countries (and this work is no exception) is that of isolating its influence from the rest of the factors at work. In the classic democratic transition, which I call early transition in this chapter (until the first democratic government swing), it is easier to differentiate the influence of various factors because change is still very restricted, when not altogether obstructed by repression or closed borders. In the more advanced phases of transformation, the picture is far more complex. When Europeanization starts, it is far from being the only game in town. *Transformation* continues in some areas (for instance, the rule of law), proving a lengthy process in many countries, especially those that had a late start in their democratization process. The speed and depth of this transformation is

---

[24] See A. Mungiu-Pippidi, "EU Accession Is No End of History." *Journal of Democracy*, 18, No. 4 (2007), pp. 8–16.

largely dependent on the type of Communism that a country experienced.[25] However, we can presume, in Tocquevillian terms, that the main motor for transformation remains revolutionary in essence, and it tends to run as long as new emerging elites have not successfully displaced the communist ones from the main positions of influence.[26] The politicization of administration in nearly all the countries should not be seen as clientelism alone (though it does generate some) but rather as a symptom of unfinished revolutions. Alongside these two processes, East European countries also embark on various ideologically driven reforms with little or no connection to EU integration: they reform their welfare or tax systems, for instance, sometimes taking paths quite divergent from the main EU practice (such as the adoption of flat tax systems). Transformation in this sense corresponds to the classic development process that Gabriel Almond described for preindustrial nations, a process of system building, ranging from the rule of law to a performing economy.[27] Reform corresponds to the policy process of postindustrial nations that he describes, consisting more in the fine tuning of policies or the maintenance of systems already created, driven by either ideology or a need to adjust to a changing environment. Finally, Europeanization is a completely new addition: it includes special policies of integration and harmonization on the EU model, a characteristic of East Central European transformations. Transformation, reform, and Europeanization thus come together or conflict in the formulation of public policy in new Europe, a fact that makes reliance only on the Europeanization theory developed for the western EU sometimes problematic.[28]

The second problem arising from studies of the EU as a transformative agent is the limitations imposed by methodology. Many studies look at the formal transposition of *acquis*, following a model from developed Europe that takes implementation for granted. The most interesting ones try to take domestic and EU factors into account at the same time, but it is very difficult to extend such a comprehensive approach beyond a restricted policy area. The mechanisms of influence described for Europe therefore come from quite different methodologies and are generally more process-oriented than impact-oriented, making a synthesis very difficult.

To integrate these mechanisms described by Europeanization theory (such as conditionality, socialization, and emulation) with the transition mechanisms from democratization theory, I propose to divide the Europeanization of

---

[25] J. Linz, and A. Stepan, *Problems of Democratic Transition and Consolidation: Southern Europe, South America and Post-Communist Europe*, (Baltimore: Johns Hopkins University Press, 1996).

[26] Alexis de Tocqueville's *Memoirs* open with this remarkable definition of "revolution," as watching the 1848 events unfolding he sees them only as the last episode of the 1789 revolution.

[27] See G. A. Almond, *Comparative Politics Today: A World View* (Boston: Little Brown, 1974), pp. 14–41.

[28] See Ulrich Sedelmeier, "Europeanisation in New Member and Candidate States." *Living Reviews in European Governance*, 1 (2006). Available online at http://www.livingreviews.org/lreg-2006-3.

TABLE 3.3. *Historical Processes of European Integration of ECE*

Process	Return to Europe	Relate to Europe	Report to Europe
Mechanism	Revolution Emulation Socialization	Diffusion Socialization	Conditionality Socialization
Driver of Process	Domestic, Mostly East	Domestic, Mostly West	EU (Mostly European Commission)
Level of Process	Governmental and Societal	Mostly Societal	Intergovernmental Governmental

Eastern Europe into three broad historical processes, each operating through one or more mechanisms (see Table 3.3). The first process is what scholars have called *return to Europe*. The crucial idea guiding the anticommunist resistance and then the subsequent transition to capitalism and democracy in Central Europe was the concept of a common European identity, which should lead in the end to the reunification of the continent into one political construction. Centered on identity, rather than ideology, the idea evolved in the hands of very talented East European intellectuals such as Milan Kundera to reach the proportions of a social representation, one widely held by citizens of the region and leaders alike. To become European again meant simply to *emulate* the ways of Western Europe, seen not as the embodiment of an alternative ideology, but as a given of European identity. The step forward became, in this rhetoric of return, a step back. Long before accession was on the table, a considerable amount of Western imitation guided Central European transformations. This was an organic grassroots mechanism grounded in both Western and Eastern Europe and as such it was tremendously effective. Freedom House scores show that most progress in new Central European member countries in nearly all chapters was made long before these countries were invited to join and EU conditionality existed for them. Southeast Europeans then tried to emulate the Central Europeans in order not to be left behind; historically, however, they missed most of this process. Regimes in Bulgaria, Romania, and Albania were still frozen by the time when even communists in Central Europe (but also Yugoslavia) were trying to reform their regimes by copying the European concept of a social market economy.

The second important Europeanization process is related to EU accession, but still collateral. I would call this mechanism *relating to Europe*. Its trigger is the (economic) association agreement with the EU, but in some countries it starts even before that. Hungarian governments privatized their economy fast by selling it mostly to Western (notably European) companies. Similarly, Scandinavians bought the banks of the Baltic states, greatly helping the economic transformation there, and the Carinthian Austrians invested in neighboring Slovenia, guided by a feeling of belonging there due to precommunist ties, at least as much as by the prospect of sheer profit. Austrian banks such as Reiffeisen returned to an area that had belonged traditionally to Austrian–Hungarian banks, planting cash machines from Albania to the Crimea. There was also a policy component in addition to the grassroots business one. A special institution, the European Bank for Reconstruction and Development, was created to lead the way in investing in these recently opened economies. Even the originally less open economies of Romania, Bulgaria, and Croatia, which attracted only 4 billion euros in FDI by 2002, went up to 16 billion euros by 2006 due to their EU accession. This attracted European investors, who then largely financed the economic recovery of these countries. By the end of this period, EU investors had a serious stake in the Eastern economies, which now related to their own again after decades of forced interruption by communism. The countries that did best on EU accession were those that related most to the EU's economies. The lesson was learned in belated accession countries. By 2006, the Adrian Nastase government in Romania, following years of discrimination against foreign investors, was offering public contracts at prices above market to favorite EU companies such as da Vinci or EADS to help unblock the country's negotiations with the EU.

The third process is formal accession itself, the most frequently studied, but probably the least influential in determining a successful integration in the absence of the other two processes. I would call it *report to Europe*. Conditionality pushed the *acquis* in a record time to new member countries. But if the resulting transposition rates were high, the consequent Europeanization seems to have been rather superficial and problems postponed rather than solved. Negotiations carry all the stigma of planning, always the worst development assistance mechanism possible. If Europeanization is reduced to negotiations and conditionality is its sole mechanism, it cannot solve difficult transformations.

Smart power resulted, historically, from a combination of these three processes, and is made formidable by the coming together of these various drivers of Europeanization. What makes it "smart" is the incentive-driven part. The formal accession perspective triggers or helps mechanisms 1 and 2. The planned integration works far less well. The EU manages to be influential only when it creates incentives for key groups, from investors to magistrates. If such incentives do not materialize, and domestic actors of change are not activated, conditionality itself produces only limited and unsustainable effects.

The third process is quite similar across accession countries: what made the difference between successful and unsuccessful cases was the first two processes, which are closely tied to the historical transition a country experienced and its historical situation more generally. Estonia is close on all counts to neighboring Finland, whose electronic government greatly inspired its own reforms, making it the most successful case of state building from the whole lot without any direct EU intervention. Ukraine does not relate so closely to any country in Europe, with the partial exception of Poland. There was far less relation to Romania and Bulgaria to help their accession (though France helped

Romania due to their historical ties), less even than for belated Croatia, which is about to become an EU member despite the fact that violent organized crime is still a serious problem. But Croatia relates extremely well to Europe: from German universities that organize summer schools in Dubrovnik to Brussels Eurocrats who buy real estate in its islands. Can Turkey and Macedonia's accessions, to give just two examples of countries still struggling with development, be solved by the third mechanism, the only one really existing for them? No: they are set up for failure. Unless leaders of these countries, together with their few allies in the EU, discover how to put in motion their full European return and relate mechanisms, they will still be planning their development and Europeanization for another twenty years – and failing.

4

Democratization in Postcommunist Europe

Illiberal Regimes and the Leverage of the European Union

Milada Anna Vachudova
Department of Political Science
University of North Carolina at Chapel Hill

The European Union may well be presiding over the most successful democracy-promotion program ever implemented by an international actor. All of the states that have become credible future EU members over the last decade are making progress toward liberal democracy and more transparent market economies. The puzzle is one of causation: Does the EU only accept liberal democracies? Or does the *condition* of being a credible future EU member create incentives for political actors to make their political agendas compatible with liberal democracy and the state's bid for EU membership?

The convergence that we see toward liberal democracy today is all the more puzzling given the divergence in regimes in the region some fifteen years ago. In some postcommunist states, democratically elected governments began laying the foundations of liberal democracy and implementing comprehensive economic reforms immediately after the collapse of the communist regime. By liberal democracy, I mean a political system where state institutions and democratically elected rulers respect juridical limits on their powers and political liberties. They uphold the rule of law, a separation of powers, and boundaries between the state and the economy. They also uphold basic liberties, such as speech, assembly, religion, and property. Important for our cases, they do not violate the limits on their powers or the political liberties of citizens in order to suppress rival political parties or groups.

In other postcommunist states, however, one faction monopolized power and created the conditions of illiberal democracy for their own political and economic gain. In illiberal democracies, important requirements of EU membership were at loggerheads with the sources of the political power of ruling elites. Progress toward membership in the EU was slow or absent. Even as the EU began to implement the conditionality of the preaccession process, it had little success in changing domestic policies in illiberal democracies: governments turned their backs on the benefits of EU membership to protect their power and rent-seeking opportunities.

The condition of being a credible future EU member impacted domestic politics in illiberal democracies in a number of ways that are more complicated and intriguing than simple conditionality. I argue in this chapter that over time the EU's leverage strengthened the hand of liberal forces against illiberal ones: not in a duel where good vanquished evil, but in an iterated electoral game where sooner or later most political actors – especially political parties – saw the benefits of moving their own agenda toward compatibility with the state's bid for EU membership. As postcommunist politics has demonstrated over and over again, with a little fine tuning most political actors – however dispirited, discredited, or despised – can find their way back into the political game and indeed back into office. Only in the run up to joining the EU, there is a twist: the EU's leverage helps set the parameters and write the rules of the game.

How does EU leverage translate into domestic political change in illiberal democracies? I have identified four mechanisms, two that operate before and two that operate after what I call "watershed elections." These are the elections in which illiberal elites that have monopolized power since the end of communism lose power decisively, and are forced to leave office.

Before watershed elections, moving toward European integration and away from international isolation serves as a *focal point for cooperation* among opposition parties and groups that have in most cases been highly fragmented and querulous. The second mechanism is *adapting*: the prospect of joining the EU creates incentives for opposition politicians to adapt their political and economic agendas to come closer to satisfying the expectations of the EU and other international organizations such as the Organization for Security and Cooperation in Europe (OSCE), the Council of Europe, and the International Criminal Tribunal for the Former Yugoslavia (ICTY).

After watershed elections, straightforward *conditionality* is at play: moving forward in the EU's preaccession process and receiving various intermediate rewards are tied to adopting laws and implementing reforms. Second, the process itself serves as a *credible commitment to reform*. Reversing direction becomes very costly for any future government. As candidates move forward in the process, governments are locked into a predictable course of policy making that serves as an important signal to internal and external economic actors. Through the preaccession process, the EU bundles together the influence of many international organizations and other international actors and sustains this influence over time.

The five cases that I explore – with the corresponding watershed election years in parentheses – are Romania (1996), Bulgaria (1997), Slovakia (1998), Croatia (2000), and Serbia–Montenegro (2000).[1] I am not arguing that the wish

---

[1] It is debatable whether the 2000 elections in Bosnia–Herzegovina count as full watershed elections, because the nationalists stayed out of power only briefly. The 2006 elections may have come closer, but the 2008 elections were a step backward. Serbia–Montenegro did have decisive watershed elections in 2000, but political parties have adapted to the Western liberal democratic and economic agenda only slowly. It is significant that Bosnia–Herzegovina and Serbia are the states where fundamental questions of statehood remain unsettled or unresolved.

to join the European Union influenced how voters cast their ballots in these elections: in all five cases, voters had more immediate reasons to vote against the incumbents.[2] Instead, EU leverage contributed to a redirection of domestic politics that occurred in two steps: First, the EU and other international actors helped shape the agendas of the opposition parties that were waiting in the wings to win these elections. Second, once in power, these parties set in motion a reform process that has sometimes slowed down, but that has never derailed, thanks to the strictures of the EU's preaccession process, and this despite subsequent political turnovers and even the return of the formerly illiberal parties to power. As the reform momentum becomes locked in, it triggers – in most cases – another wave of *adapting* as many of the formerly illiberal parties adjust their political agendas to be compatible with liberal democracy and comprehensive economic reform. For the country's future democratic trajectory, this second wave of *adapting* is the most significant aspect of political change. I also explore briefly why *adapting* has not worked in the case of Bosnia–Herzegovina.

Scholars have only begun to explain the substantial variation in the policies and the institutions adopted by the so-called early reformers, but the question of why postcommunist governments with liberal preferences adopted generally liberal policies is ultimately not that puzzling. For my cases, I have therefore selected those countries that were dominated by illiberal rulers for a substantial period of time after 1989, but that eventually changed course toward liberal democracy. In the cases of Serbia and Bosnia–Herzegovina, the mechanisms that I identify have functioned weakly, and the status of Bosnia–Herzegovina as an international protectorate split in two by the Dayton Agreement means that they have functioned differently. And although all six countries have made progress, exploring the variation in the speed and content of that progress helps illuminate the domestic conditions that determine how well external incentives can help overcome illiberal rule.

This chapter is organized into five parts. The first part will show the divergence in political and economic trajectories among postcommunist states after 1989 and the signs of convergence among credible future EU members over the last decade. The second part will explore the theories that help us understand the influence of international actors on democratization in general, and the impact of the EU on candidate states in particular. The third part will explain the mechanisms of *focal point for cooperation* and *adapting*. The fourth part will explain the mechanisms of *conditionality* and *credible commitment to reform*. The fifth part will explore alternative mechanisms that could drive political change, looking at the recent cases of "democratic breakthroughs" in postcommunist states that are not in the EU membership queue.

---

[2] For the argument that the prospect of EU membership does impact how voters cast their ballots, see Joshua A. Tucker, Alexander C. Pacek, and Adam J. Berinsky, "Transitional Winners and Losers: Attitudes toward EU Membership in Post-Communist Countries." *American Journal of Political Science*, 46, No. 3 (2002), pp. 557–71.

DIVERGENCE AND CONVERGENCE IN THE POSTCOMMUNIST WORLD

The collapse of communism between 1989 and 1991 throughout the region, accompanied by the end of the Soviet Union, was a critical juncture for the political development of all East European states. For many, it was also a period that set in motion forces seeking national independence: the "communist" region went from nine states in 1989[3] to twenty-seven in 1995. By 1995 the spectrum of political outcomes among these twenty-seven states ranged from liberal democracy to rigid authoritarianism.[4] It was not surprising that states emerging newly independent from the Soviet Union after over seven decades of Soviet communism would initially follow trajectories different from those of states in East Central and Southeastern Europe. But the variation among the states of East Central and Southeastern Europe was also striking, ranging from liberal democracy in Poland and Hungary to authoritarianism and war in the disintegrating Yugoslavia.[5]

A decade later, do we see a convergence toward liberal democracy among the subset of postcommunist states that are credible future members of the EU? By plotting the scores that these states have received from Freedom House and the European Bank for Reconstruction and Development, respectively, we can see such a convergence. Figure 4.1 shows that in 1997 the six states in this study were receiving low scores for both political freedom and economic liberalization, putting them far behind East Central Europe's early reformers and in close proximity to states such as Kyrgyzstan and Ukraine. Figure 4.2 shows that in 2003 all but Bosnia–Herzegovina had pulled away from the post-Soviet states on their political freedom scores.[6] In comparison to 1997, Bulgaria, Romania,

---

[3] The Soviet Union, Poland, Hungary, Czechoslovakia, Bulgaria, Romania, East Germany, Albania, and Yugoslavia. For the 27 postcommunist states on the European continent (without the "east" of unified Germany), see Figure 4.1.

[4] For a careful analysis of divergence among postcommunist states, see David Cameron, "The Quality of Democracy in Post-communist Europe." Paper presented at the Annual Meeting of the American Political Science Association, Washington, DC, 2005.

[5] For a more comprehensive treatment of political outcomes in the CEE states, see Valerie Bunce, "The Political Economy of Postsocialism." *Slavic Review*, 58, No. 4 (1999), pp. 756–93; Grzegorz Ekiert and Stephen E. Hanson, eds., *Capitalism and Democracy in Central and Eastern Europe: Assessing the Legacy of Communist Rule* (Cambridge: Cambridge University Press, 2003); Jacques Rupnik, "The Post-communist Divide." *Journal of Democracy*, 10, No. 1 (1999), pp. 57–62; and Milada Anna Vachudova, *Europe Undivided: Democracy, Leverage and Integration after Communism* (Oxford: Oxford University Press, 2005).

[6] Excluding the Western Balkan states from the group of EU candidates, David Cameron finds that between 1991 and 2001 the ten EU candidates extended rights and liberties so that they were comparable to those in many EU member states. But the other postcommunist states actually experienced a *decrease* in the average score; in the latter group, rights and liberties were, on average, *less* extensive and secure in 2001 than they had been in 1991. David Cameron, "Post-communist Democracy: The Impact of the European Union," *Post-Soviet Affairs*, 23(3), pp. 185–217.

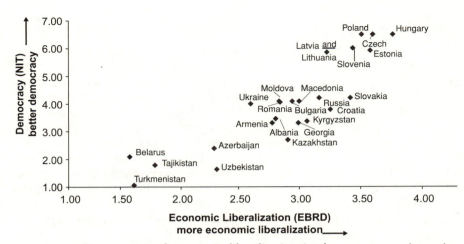

FIGURE 4.1. Democracy and economic liberalization in the postcommunist region in 1997. The democracy scale runs from the lowest score (=1) to the highest score (=7). The economic liberalization scale runs from the lowest score (=1) to the highest score (=4.3). *Sources:* European Bank for Reconstruction and Development, 1 *Transition Report 1997* (London: European Bank for Reconstruction and Development, 1997); Freedom House, "Table 2: Nations in Transit Scores 1997 to 2003." In *Nations in Transit 2003* (New York: Freedom House, 2003). Available at <http://www.freedomhouse.org/research/nitransit/2003/index.htm>. Accessed 13 March 2007.]

Croatia, and most dramatically Slovakia had made substantial progress in catching up with the early reformers with political and economic reform.

We can also point to a variety of other measures that indicate progress and convergence after 1995. Elections are free and fair and, except perhaps in Serbia, all of the mainstream parties are committed to the democratic rules of the game. Ethnic minorities are in a better position in Romania, Slovakia, and Croatia, with no signs of reversal. Croatia, Serbia, and Montenegro have established democracies that function quite well, given that these states have only recently emerged from authoritarianism and war that implicated all three polities in state-sponsored genocide. Governments are now cooperating extensively with the ICTY, and full cooperation from Belgrade seems to be only a matter of time. All of the formerly illiberal democracies have made progress toward the next milestone of EU membership – from a catapult into membership on the part of Slovakia to the signing, finally, of an association agreement between the EU and Serbia. There are still a myriad problems with the quality of democracy in absolute terms in all of these states, but the relative progress of each state since 1995 is indisputable.

It is more difficult to make the case, however, that Bosnia–Herzegovina is overcoming the ethnic political divisions reified by the Dayton Agreement in order to create a sufficiently functional central state that can prepare for EU

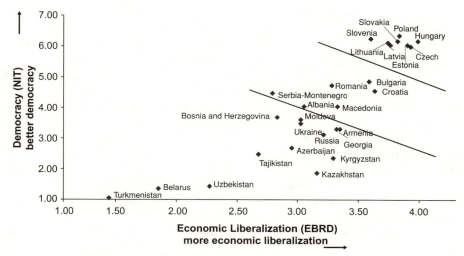

FIGURE 4.2. Democracy and economic liberalization in the postcommunist region in 2003. The democracy scale runs from the lowest score (=1) to the highest score (=7). The economic liberalization scale runs from the lowest score (=1) to the highest score (=4.3). *Sources:* European Bank for Reconstruction and Development, *Transition Report 2003* (London: European Bank for Reconstruction and Development, 2003); Freedom House, "Table 2: Nations in Transit Scores 1997 to 2003." In *Nations in Transit 2003* (New York: Freedom House, 2003). Available at <http://www.freedomhouse.org/research/nitransit/2003/index.htm>. Accessed 13 March 2007.

membership. It is also more difficult to make the case that several Western Balkan states – Albania, Bosnia–Herzegovina, Macedonia, Serbia, and Montenegro – are converging with the frontrunners on the measures of economic liberalization and economic institutional change alone. Indeed, as Figure 4.2 shows, they fit quite comfortably in the second group of slow-paced reformers. Only Croatia shows signs of rapid economic progress. This is the finding of George Georgiadis after analysis of the aggregate transition scores for economic institutional change across the twenty-seven cases from 1991 to 2002. He argues that it is the ten candidates for EU membership that form a group within which countries are converging economically, with Croatia knocking at the door.[7] There are good reasons, however, that we may expect that progress in the EU's preaccession process, tied to greater access to the EU market and more foreign investment, will eventually help bring economic liberalization and institutional improvements even in the other Western Balkan states.

---

[7] George Georgiadis, *Adapting by Expectation: Early EU Polices in the CEE Region and the Consolidation of the Two "Orbits" of Post-communist Economic Transformation.* Working Paper No. 05–02 (Weatherhead Center for International Affairs, Harvard University, 2005).

One of the most difficult issues in studying democratization is untangling political change from economic upswings and downturns, and from changes in the way that ruling elites administer the economy. In the postcommunist region, fifteen years of data reveal that greater political freedom, more economic liberalization, and better economic performance have all gone hand in hand. Figures 4.1 and 4.2 show a correlation between a country's political freedom rating and its implementation of economic reform. That is, the higher a country is rated for the quality of its democracy, the more progress it has generally made in market reform. Similar patterns emerge using different indices for economic reform, such as those of the World Bank, against the Freedom House democratization index.[8] There is also a correlation between the completeness of economic reforms and the level of aggregate social welfare ten years after the transition began. That is, those countries that put in place the most rapid and complete economic reforms recovered most quickly, registered the highest levels of economic growth, and generated the least increase in income disparities.[9] All of this is important because it shows that there is relatively little tension between the democratic and economic reforms that are requirements of EU membership, and in particular that economic liberalization does not come at the cost of the well-being of the general population. In Latin American states, for example, the relationship between democratization and market liberalization that we see in Figures 4.1 and 4.2 would look quite different.[10]

INTERNATIONAL ACTORS AND DEMOCRATIZATION

The impact of international actors on democratization, and on domestic political change more generally, is now one of the most exciting areas of study in comparative politics.[11] This is something of a departure from past scholarship.

---

[8] Using a World Bank/EBRD Structural Reform index against Freedom House data, others have averaged the scores received for each year between 1990 and 2000 for a similar result. See Chap. 9 in Thomas Oatley, *International Political Economy: Interests and Institutions in the Global Economy*, pp. 379–92 (New York: Pearson Longman, 2004), at p. 386; and Anders Åslund, *Building Capitalism: The Transformation of the Former Soviet Bloc*, p. 362 (Cambridge: Cambridge University Press, 2002). See also European Bank for Reconstruction and Development, *Transition Report* (London: EBRD, 2000).

[9] World Bank, *The First Ten Years: Analysis and Lessons for Eastern Europe and the Former Soviet Union* (Washington, DC: World Bank, 2002), pp. 16, 73–4, 107.

[10] Among other factors, the structural changes that these states experienced under communism, including high levels of literacy and low levels of income inequality, made labor forces relatively well prepared to adjust to and profit from market liberalization and the proximity of the wealthy EU market. It is also likely for some countries that the EU's insistence that economic liberalization be accompanied by institutional change helped create a better functioning market economy. See Valerie Bunce, "Rethinking Recent Democratization, Lessons from the Post-communist Experience." *World Politics*, 55, No. 2 (2003), pp. 167–92; and Philip G. Roeder, "The Revolution of 1989: Postcommunism and the Social Sciences." *Slavic Review*, 58, No. 4 (1999), pp. 743–55.

[11] Philippe C. Schmitter, "The Influence of the International Context Upon the Choice of National Institutions and Policies in Neo-Democracies." In *The International Dimensions of*

In the literature on democratization in Latin America, the Caribbean, Asia, or Africa, the impact of external actors on democratic consolidation has usually been considered harmful or at best indifferent. The exception is democratization on the European continent, where the prospect of joining the EU is credited with supporting transition and consolidation in Portugal, Spain, and Greece as well as in the postcommunist states that are nearby.[12]

The democratization of communist states seemed in many ways incomparable to democratization in other parts of the world, owing to the uniqueness of communism's impact on the polity, economy, and society.[13] However, the behavior of ruling elites when seizing and holding power in that gray zone between liberal democracy and outright authoritarianism – be it called illiberal democracy, electoral democracy, hybrid democracy, or competitive authoritarianism – is in many respects similar across countries and regions. This chapter contributes to the recent comparative politics literature on the origin, the dynamics, and the demise of such democratic hybrids.[14] It demonstrates how the EU has played an important role in loosening the grip of elites that seek to perpetuate illiberal democracy. And in contrast to democracy promotion efforts by other international actors, it explains how the EU has had a sustained impact on the quality of the democratization and economic reform efforts that have followed regime change.[15]

In the study of EU enlargement to include postcommunist states, there is broad agreement that the EU's preaccession process has brought potent if uneven conditionality and socialization to bear on domestic politics in the

Democratization: Europe and the Americas, Expanded Edition, Laurence Whitehead, ed., pp. 26–54 (Oxford: Oxford University Press, 2001). See also Laurence Whitehead, "Three International Dimensions of Democratization." In *International Dimensions*, Laurence Whitehead, ed., pp. 3–25, and the other contributions to this volume. See also Geoffrey Pridham, Eric Herring, and George Sanford, eds., *Building Democracy? The International Dimension of Democratization in Eastern Europe* (London: Leicester University Press, 1997).

[12] Geoffrey Pridham, ed., *Encouraging Democracy: The International Context of Regime Transition in Southern Europe* (Leicester: Leicester University Press, 1991); and Laurence Whitehead, "Democracy by Convergence: Southern Europe." in *International Dimensions*, Laurence Whitehead, ed., pp. 261–84. See also Daniel Ziblatt and Nick Biziouras, "The State and the Shadow of the European Union: Party Politics and the Politicization of the State in Southern and Eastern Europe." Paper presented at the European Union Studies Association Ninth Biennial Conference, Austin, TX, 2005.

[13] Valerie Bunce, "Should Transitologists Be Grounded?" *Slavic Review*, 54, No. 1 (1995), pp. 111–27; in debate with Philippe C. Schmitter and Terry Lynn Karl, "The Conceptual Travels of Transitologists and Consolidologists: How Far to the East Should They Attempt to Go." *Slavic Review*, 53, No. 1 (1995), pp. 173–85.

[14] Terry Lynn Karl, "The Hybrid Regimes of Central America." *Journal of Democracy*, 6, No. 3 (1995), pp. 72–87; Fareed Zakaria, "The Rise of Illiberal Democracy." *Foreign Affairs*, 76, No. 6 (1997), pp. 22–43; Larry Diamond, "Thinking about Hybrid Regimes." *Journal of Democracy*, 13, No. 2 (2002), pp. 21–35; and Steven Levitsky and Lucan Way, "The Rise of Competitive Authoritarianism." *Journal of Democracy*, 13, No. 2 (2002), pp. 51–65.

[15] For variation in Western influence on competitive authoritarian regimes in different regions of the world, see Steven Levitsky and Lucan Way, "Linkage versus Leverage: Rethinking the International Dimension of Regime Change." *Comparative Politics*, 38, No. 4 (2006), pp. 379–400.

candidate states. Most studies focus on how the institutions and the content of domestic policy making have been influenced by EU conditionality during the negotiations for membership.[16] But those states where illiberal democracy took hold and economic reforms were neglected had a long way to go in their relationship with the EU before they could begin negotiations, or even obtain candidate status.[17] Although neglecting the impact of EU conditionality on specific policy areas[18] and state institutions, in this chapter I seek to shed light on the mechanisms by which EU leverage undermined illiberal regimes, and then locked in progress toward liberal democracy and economic liberalization after these regimes were ousted.

Here it is important to take a step back and look at the nature of the relationship between the EU and its democratizing postcommunist neighbors. Despite fears of diminished national sovereignty and increased economic vulnerability, EU membership rapidly emerged as a matter of national interest after 1989 in many of the early reformers because it offered substantial geopolitical, sociocultural, and, most important, economic benefits. But between 1989 and 1994, the EU and other international actors had little impact on the course of political change: they reinforced liberal strategies of reform in some states, but failed to avert, end, or significantly diminish rent-seeking strategies for winning and exercising power in others. The turning point occurred in 1995 as the EU made it clear that for those states recognized as credible future EU members, compliance with EU requirements would be rewarded by EU membership – and that the voluntary decision to apply for EU membership would subject a candidate to a battery of unilateral monitoring and reporting.

The EU's leverage was animated by the fact that the substantial benefits of EU membership – and the costs of exclusion – create incentives for states to satisfy the entry requirements. Following this logic alone, we may conclude that the benefits of EU membership for postcommunist states must be immense: At no time in history have sovereign states voluntarily agreed to meet such vast domestic requirements and then subjected themselves to such intrusive

---

[16] Heather Grabbe, "How Does Europeanisation Affect CEE Governance? Conditionality, Diffusion and Diversity." *Journal of European Public Policy*, 8, No. 4 (2001), pp. 1013–31; and Beate Sissenich, "State Building by a Nonstate." Ph.D. dissertation, Cornell University, Ithaca, NY, 2003. See also the contributions to Frank Schimmelfennig and Ulrich Sedelmeier, eds., *The Europeanization of Central and Eastern Europe* (Ithaca: Cornell University Press, 2005).

[17] For the groundbreaking study on how the EU and other international actors used conditionality and socialization to change the treatment of ethnic minorities, see Judith Kelley, *Ethnic Politics in Europe: The Power of Norms and Incentives* (Princeton, NJ: Princeton University Press, 2004).

[18] See Rachel Epstein, "Cultivating Consensus and Creating Conflict: International Institutions and the (De)politicization of Economic Policy in Post-communist Europe." *Comparative Political Studies*, 39, No. 8 (2006), pp. 1019–42. Wade Jacoby, *The Enlargement of the European Union and NATO: Ordering from the Menu in Central Europe* (Cambridge: Cambridge University Press, 2004); and Liliana B. Andonova, *Transnational Politics of the Environment. The EU and Environmental Policy in Central and Eastern Europe* (Cambridge: MIT Press, 2003).

verification procedures to enter an international organization. A steady flow of aid, expertise, trade, and foreign direct investment is diverted away from states that fail to enter the queue to join an enlarging EU along with their neighbors toward those that succeed. The costs of exclusion can weigh heavily on relatively rich states as well as poor ones. Walter Mattli has shown that economic integration can cause three kinds of negative externalities for states left outside: trade diversion, investment diversion, and aid diversion. These costs help explain the applications of rich West European states as well as relatively backward states from postcommunist Europe for EU membership.[19]

The *potential* political will to satisfy the EU's entry requirements set the stage for the effectiveness of conditionality within the EU's preaccession process. As I will show in the next two sections, this process has mediated the costs and benefits of satisfying EU membership criteria in such a way as to make compliance attractive – and noncompliance visible and costly. In addition to the benefits and the requirements of membership, there are three characteristics of the preaccession process – of the way that the EU applies political and economic conditionality – that have made the EU's leverage effective. They are asymmetric interdependence, enforcement, and meritocracy.[20] These characteristics amplify the incentives to comply with the EU's membership requirements because they make the EU's threat of exclusion, as well as its promises of membership, more credible. Power in this interdependent relationship flows from asymmetry, and the ECE states have much more to gain from the relationship than the EU.[21] Such patterns of asymmetrical interdependence have determined relations between the EU and candidate states in the past – and also among EU member states during major treaty negotiations.[22] Meanwhile, the monitoring of the progress of candidates in satisfying EU requirements through annual reports and through chapter-by-chapter negotiations on the *acquis communautaire* have built an imperfect but high level of enforcement into the preaccession process.

Although asymmetric interdependence and enforcement both give credibility to the EU's threats of exclusion, meritocracy gives credibility to its promises of eventual membership. So far the EU has adopted a roughly merit-based approach: an applicant's place in the membership queue has corresponded to the progress it has made toward fulfilling the EU's requirements. The European Commission's evaluations and the European Council's decisions about the status of candidates or protocandidates have been accepted as reflecting

---

[19] Walter Mattli, *The Logic of Regional Integration, Europe and Beyond* (New York: Cambridge University Press, 1999).

[20] For a fuller discussion, see Vachudova, *Europe Undivided*, Chap. 5.

[21] Robert O. Keohane and Joseph S. Nye, *Power and Interdependence* (Boston: Little Brown, 1977).

[22] Andrew Moravcsik, "Negotiating the Single European Act: National Interests and Conventional Statecraft in the European Community." *International Organization*, 45, No. 1 (1991), pp. 19–56; and Andrew Moravcsik, *The Choice for Europe: Social Purpose and State Power from Messina to Maastricht* (Ithaca: Cornell University Press, 1998), Chap. 1.

accurately the state of compliance.[23] In the run-up to the 2004 enlargement, with certain exceptions, the right balance was struck: candidates were neither too confident (thanks to asymmetric interdependence), nor too disingenuous (thanks to enforcement), nor did they despair that the system was stacked against them (thanks to meritocracy). In subsequent years, however, the system has worked less well: Bulgaria and Romania are widely seen to have been admitted prematurely, with insufficient enforcement in areas such as the rule of law and public administration reform. The decision on Turkey's eventual accession, moreover, is now widely recognized as a matter of EU domestic politics and not of merit.

The very extensive requirements of EU membership are mostly a product of the very high levels of integration among EU member states. For the rest, they were not designed to coax and cajole every conceivably "European" state into making itself desirable. In the middle of the 1990s, the emphasis was rather on keeping unqualified states outside of the EU. By the late 1990s, however, enlargement and foreign policy had become closely intertwined, as it became clear that the EU's leverage on aspiring members was the most powerful and successful aspect of the EU's emerging foreign policy. Recognizing this, EU leaders made the prospect of EU membership the cornerstone of the EU's foreign policy toward the Western Balkans in the EU-led Stability Pact for Southeastern Europe in 1999. It was in this region, after all, that the EU's credibility as a foreign policy actor was most clearly at stake. The Stability Pact opened the EU's official membership queue in 1999 to eighteen candidates and protocandidates.[24]

For the illiberal democracies in the EU's membership queue, the EU's approach gradually became one of explicit democracy promotion – this was weakest in the cases of Romania and Bulgaria, and most overt in Serbia–Montenegro and of course Bosnia–Herzegovina. What turned out to be important was that the meritocracy principle was extended across time in one country as well as across countries. In other words, however dismal a country's past record of respecting democratic standards and human rights, it could "rehabilitate" itself by implementing the necessary reforms under a future government. Serbia–Montenegro became a credible future member of the EU in 1999, and as such had a clear and relatively certain track toward membership despite

---

[23] This was put to the test in 2005 by the European Council's decision to put on hold the start of negotiations with Croatia because of the government's failure to cooperate fully with the ICTY in delivering an indicted war criminal, General Ante Gotovina, to the Hague. Despite protests that the state administration had been cooperating, the Croatian government responded with a number of initiatives to improve compliance, reforming the military, the police, and the judiciary.

[24] Poland, Hungary, Slovenia, Slovakia, the Czech Republic, Estonia, Latvia, Lithuania, Cyprus, and Malta joined the EU in May 2004, leaving Bulgaria, Romania, Turkey, Croatia, Macedonia, Albania, Serbia–Montenegro, and Bosnia–Herzegovina at various points in the membership queue.

the fact that the regime of Slobodan Milošević was still firmly in place. In Slovakia, commenting on the intransigence of the regime of Vladimír Mečiar, the EU Commissioner for External Relations, Hans Van den Broek, explained in the spring of 1998 that "The question is not whether Slovakia will enter the EU, but when this will take place. The answer is in the hands of the Slovak government."[25]

REGIME CHANGE IN ILLIBERAL DEMOCRACIES

There is substantial evidence that the quality of political competition determined the early trajectories of postcommunist states. I argue that under conditions of limited political competition, rent-seeking elites could win and hold power by further suppressing rival groups, promising slow economic reform, and exploiting ethnic nationalism – all the while extracting significant rents from slow economic reform.[26] Several other scholars have offered compatible explanations for the variation in political outcomes that we observe after 1989. These include the configuration of domestic elites at the moment of regime change;[27] the outcome of the first democratic elections;[28] and the character of political competition in the new polity.[29] There is a separate though related debate about additional domestic factors that brought to power the regimes that presided over the ethnic cleansing and war that accompanied the disintegration of Yugoslavia.[30] The mechanisms that I highlight in this article all work to improve the quality or character of political competition by breaking the concentration of power in the hands of illiberal elites, and eventually changing the positions of major, formerly illiberal political parties.

In the relationship between the EU and all credible future members, we can expect compliance with EU requirements when ruling elites consider that a closer relationship with the EU will bolster their popularity, and when the EU's conditions for moving forward are compatible with the ways that they win and

---

[25] "Hans Van den Broek: Slovensko má svoj osud vo vlastných rukách." *SME* (18 June 1998).

[26] Vachudova, *Europe Undivided*, Chaps. 1–2.

[27] Michael McFaul, "The Fourth Wave of Democracy *and* Dictatorship: Noncooperative Transitions in the Post-communist World." *World Politics*, 54, No. 2 (2002), pp. 212–44.

[28] M. Steven Fish, "The Determinants of Economic Reform in the Post-communist World." *East European Politics and Societies*, 12, No. 1 (1998), pp. 31–78.

[29] Conor O'Dwyer, "Runaway State Building: How Political Parties Shape States in Postcommunist Europe." *World Politics*, 56, No. 4 (2004), pp. 520–53; Mitchell Orenstein, *Out of the Red* (Ann Arbor, MI: University of Michigan Press, 2001); and Anna Grzymała-Busse, "Political Competition and the Politicization of the State in East Central Europe." *Comparative Political Studies*, 36, No. 10 (2003), pp. 1123–47.

[30] See Valerie Bunce, *Subversive Institutions, The Design and the Destruction of Socialism and the State* (Cambridge: Cambridge University Press, 1999); and Ellen Comisso, "Is Breaking Up Hard to Do? Security, Nationalism and the Emergence of Sovereign States in the Balkans." Paper presented at the Annual Convention of the American Political Science Association, Washington, DC, 2005.

hold power at home.[31] For illiberal regimes, satisfying the requirements of EU membership was far too costly, as these were in direct conflict with the interests of their domestic power bases. The EU's leverage was only marginally effective in moderating the domestic policies of illiberal governments directly, though the EU and other international actors may have frightened some regimes away from further antidemocratic excesses. And here analysis of the involvement of a myriad international actors in the wars in the former Yugoslavia must stand alone.

I argue that the relationship between the EU and credible future members helped change the domestic balance of power in illiberal states against rent-seeking elites, undermining the strength of their domestic power bases. The key was the impact of the EU's active leverage on opposition political parties and other groups in societies. These domestic actors served as interlocutors between the EU and the citizens, and they were the only realistic vehicle for rapid change given the intransigence of the ruling political parties. It was the interplay of domestic opposition actors and the EU's leverage (and not external pressure alone) that helped bring about political change. Ultimately EU leverage helped create what the illiberal democracies were missing at the moment of transition: a more coherent and moderate opposition, and an open and pluralistic political arena.

Focal Points of Cooperation

Ending exclusion from Europe and securing EU membership became a *focal point for cooperation* among very different opposition political parties and civic groups. In Romania, Slovakia, Croatia, and Serbia, small parties and factions of the center left and center right competed and feuded with one another, substantially weakening the power of moderate voices in parliament through wasted votes and infighting. Liberal, pro-Western actors in these countries had little or no history of cooperation in an opposition movement against communism to help establish habits of compromise and organizational strength. Meanwhile, the ruling political parties worked hard to undermine and divide the opposition parties by manipulating the electoral law, labeling critics of government policy as unpatriotic, and also engaging in physical harassment in all of the cases except Bulgaria. Although their differences on matters of social and economic policy spanned the entire moderate (and sometimes immoderate) political spectrum, electoral defeats and harassment by the regime showed that the opposition forces would have to band together in order to unseat the ruling elites. Some Western actors took a very direct role in trying to unite the feuding opposition parties in Slovakia, Croatia, and Serbia and the nonnationalist parties in Bosnia–Herzegovina around a European agenda.

---

[31] Kelley, *Ethnic Politics in Europe*; and Vachudova, *Europe Undivided*. For the related external incentives model, see the contributions to Schimmelfennig and Sedelmeier, eds., *The Europeanization of Central and Eastern Europe*.

Reproaching the ruling elites for forsaking the country's place in Europe – and promising to move the country decisively toward Europe – formed part of the opposition agenda upon which all parties and other opposition groups could agree. In some cases, this was very concrete: In Slovakia, the opposition parties agreed to satisfy all EU requirements in an attempt to rejoin the first group of countries joining the EU. In Serbia, the forces opposing the Milošević regime all agreed on ending Serbia's exclusion from Europe – but they were far from agreeing on cooperation with the ICTY, or understanding the scope of the compliance that would be demanded of them on the road to the EU.[32]

Why would opposition forces in these illiberal democracies need European integration as a focal point for their cooperation? After all, they could unite simply in opposition to the illiberal regime. However, international actors including the EU signaled that only certain groupings of opposition elites would be acceptable partners for the return to Europe, ending the practice of some opposition elites of episodic cooperation with the illiberal rulers and preventing the defection of others. The goal of rejoining Europe is important for another reason: it lays out some map for what will happen after regime change, whether or not the parameters of this effort are well understood.

Adapting

Western actors offered information to opposition political elites that were *adapting* to a political and economic agenda compatible with liberal democracy and comprehensive market reform. Parties of the center right and center left had been neither strong nor unified in these countries after 1989, nor had they necessarily been "moderate" or "liberal." Over time, many opposition politicians have substantially shifted their positions on ethnic minority rights and on economic reform to make their parties fit the increasingly attractive pro-EU space in the political spectrum. What motivated individual political elites was in each case a different mixture of political calculation, on the one hand, and a desire to learn about and promote European norms and values, on the other. But in most cases the steady defection of politicians from the ruling parties suggested that these individuals considered the political prospects of the opposition parties more attractive than the short-term gains of remaining part of the ruling clique.[33]

Western representatives of international institutions, governments, and non-governmental organizations (NGOs) were on hand with information for opposition politicians and local civil society leaders on the substance of a liberal democratic agenda, placing particular emphasis on political accountability, on

---

[32] See the translated issues of the first EU-focused publication in Belgrade, *Evropski Forum*, with articles and editorials by Serbian and Montenegrin politicians. Available in translation on my website.

[33] Pavol Demeš, leader of the Third Sector, interview in Bratislava, 1998 and 2005. Interviews with former opposition members in Zagreb, Belgrade, and Sarajevo in 2004 and 2005.

fostering an open pluralistic political arena, and on rights for ethnic minorities within this arena, ideally decoupling questions of ethnicity from those of citizenship. Many different Western organizations and governments were involved in supporting opposition groups with financial assistance and interacting with opposition elites through countless meetings, workshops, and conferences in national capitals and abroad.[34] Local opposition elites often moved directly from Western-funded NGOs or academic institutions into politics. EU leverage, in concert with the influence of other international actors, strengthened pro-EU civic groups and shaped how opposition parties portrayed themselves in the election campaign, which parties they chose to cooperate with before and after the elections, and how they governed once in power.

Scholars studying the incidence and success of democratization have turned in recent years to the role of NGOs and civic groups in mobilizing the population against undemocratic leaders.[35] In many cases international actors have been linked to civic mobilization, for example, through funding for NGOs, election monitoring, and advising. Grzegorz Ekiert and Jan Kubik note the "virtuous circle" between Polish domestic organizations and their Western partners, which provided support critical to establishing a strong civil society in Poland in the early 1990s. The most support was channeled to the three states that needed it least – Poland, Hungary, and the Czech Republic – at the expense of "deepening vicious circles" elsewhere.[36] But by the late 1990s, Western funding for and attention to NGOs in other postcommunist countries had increased substantially.[37] A virtuous circle emerged most clearly in Slovakia. Local NGOs played a special role, compensating for the weakness of opposition parties with extensive surveillance and criticism of the illiberal government, and eventually creating the momentum for cooperation among the opposition parties. Since then, the Slovak model for turning civil society against illiberal rulers has been exported by Slovak NGOs to Croatia and Serbia with Western assistance.

Another factor that paved the way for local politicians *adapting* to an EU-compatible agenda was that the EU enlargement process helped break

---

[34] The organizations included the British Council, the British Know How Fund, the Charles Mott Foundation, the EastWest Institute, the Foundation for a Civil Society, the International Republican Institute, the Konrad Adenauer Foundation, and the National Democratic Institute.

[35] Pavol Demeš and Joerg Forbrig eds., *Reclaiming Democracy: Civil Society and Electoral Change in Central and Eastern Europe.* Washington, DC: German Marshall Fund, 2007.

[36] Grzegorz Ekiert and Jan Kubik, "Civil Society From Abroad: The Role of Foreign Assistance in the Democratization of Poland." Working Paper No. 00–01, 48–49, Weatherhead Center for International Affairs, Harvard University, 2000.

[37] Robert Benjamin, National Democratic Institute, interview in Washington, DC, 2003. For the debate, Sarah E. Mendelson and John K. Glenn, eds., *The Power and Limits of NGOs: A Critical Look at Building Democracy in Eastern Europe and Eurasia* (New York: Columbia University Press, 2002); and Marina Ottaway and Thomas Carothers, eds., *Funding Virtue: Civil Society Aid and Democracy Promotion* (New York: Carnegie Endowment for International Peace, 2000).

the information monopoly of the illiberal regime. Evaluations of a country's progress within the EU's preaccession process provided a powerful alternative source of information on the political and economic performance of the government. Although the Commission does not have an information strategy as such, it does make an effort to explain fully and publicly its assessments of the states involved in the preaccession process.[38] As the enlargement project has continued, EU leaders have became more willing to take decisive stands on issues of domestic politics in the candidate countries, leading to very specific demarches against the Mečiar government in Slovakia and outright coaching of the opposition elites in Serbia.

The EU's vocal criticism – echoed by a growing number of local civil society groups and opposition parties – gradually helped reveal that illiberal ruling parties were not, despite their claims, leading the countries to prosperity and to Europe. This criticism undermined the political strategies of ethnic nationalism and economic corruption used by rent-seeking elites and suggested alternative strategies that were compellingly usable for opposition elites. It countered two messages: that ethnic nationalism was about protecting the nation, and that slow reform was about protecting the average citizen. The role of the EU in changing the information environment echoes Jack Snyder's argument that "the influence of the international community may be essential to help break up information monopolies, especially in states with very weak journalistic traditions and a weak civil society."[39]

STAYING THE COURSE AFTER WATERSHED ELECTIONS

Illiberal regimes lost elections in Romania in 1996, in Bulgaria in 1997, in Slovakia in 1998, in Croatia in 2000, and in Serbia–Montenegro in 2000. The two most compelling reasons for these defeats were the peril of monopoly,[40] and the toll of economic deterioration or crisis. The peril of monopoly is analogous to the problem encountered by the communist regimes: as the only actor with any political power before 1989, the communist party could reasonably be blamed for everything that went wrong. The new governments in all five cases moved rapidly to implement political and economic reforms and move the country forward in the EU's preaccession process.

Once a state becomes enmeshed in the EU's preaccession process, the high costs of pulling out of this process have motivated even previously illiberal ruling parties to adopt political strategies that are compatible with qualifying

---

[38] Pierre Mirel, interview in Brussels, 2003. Interviews with other Commission officials in Brussels, 2005.

[39] Jack Snyder, *From Voting to Violence: Democratization and Nationalist Conflict*, p. 355 (New York: Norton, 2000).

[40] I am indebted to Valerie Bunce for this concept.

for EU membership. After the watershed elections, we see little backsliding as successive governments make progress on political and economic reform. They may move forward quickly (Slovakia) or very slowly (Serbia), but there have been no sharp reversals of policy, despite electoral turnover. After the assassination of Prime Minister Zoran Đinđić in March 2003, Serbia–Montenegro suffered a severe slowdown in reform, but by 2004, reform had accelerated and moving up in the EU's preaccession process was fixed again as the goal. A similar slowdown in reform occurred in Serbia 2007, but was again followed by renewed momentum in 2008.

Sooner or later, more open political competition in combination with the costs of being excluded from Europe has driven most political parties in the candidate states toward a consensus on qualifying for EU membership. This can be understood as the second phase of *adapting*: now it is the formerly illiberal rulers who adapt their political agendas to EU membership. Political parties learn that they can adapt their agendas to the expectations of the EU and other international actors – and, in some cases, get back in the political game very quickly. The most dramatic turnarounds were by the PSDR in Romania and the HDZ in Croatia.[41] Upon winning reelection in 2000 and 2004, respectively, both parties continued to satisfy EU requirements – and on some measures did a better job than their predecessors.

Besides the Radicals and perhaps the Socialists in Serbia, there are virtually no parties left in any countries in the EU queue that openly oppose qualifying for membership and that might win elections or take part in a governing coalition. In the toughest cases, particularly Serbia, the adaptation of formerly illiberal elites has been more of a trickle than a flood, but even members of Milošević's Socialist party are seeking to become informed about the EU; the reform wing of the party is happy to adopt EU membership as a forward-looking economic program.[42] Still, it is easy to see why *adapting* has not worked across the board in Serbia: Serbia's unresolved national and territorial issues – especially Kosovo – provided an appealing and ongoing platform for Serbia's nationalist parties (why change?). But it is political party elites in Bosnia–Herzegovina that challenge more profoundly the *adapting* mechanism: Although leaders of all three constituent nations speak in favor of European integration, they are unwilling to make the constitutional compromises that would allow the state to adopt and implement EU rules. The domestic power of the ruling politicians – especially those elected in 2008 – is based squarely on ethnic identity, ethnic rivalry, and ethnic clientelism, making the EU's leverage much less effective. To put it another way, Bosnia–Herzegovina may still be waiting for true watershed elections for a long time.

---

[41] On the turnaround of PSD leader Ion Iliescu, see the interviews by Vladimir Tismaneanu in *The Great Shock at the End of a Short Century: On Communism, Post-communism and Democracy* (Boulder, CO: East European Monographs, distributed by New York: Columbia University Press, 2006).
[42] Official, interview in Belgrade, 2004.

Conditionality

Conditionality has played a key role in ensuring the implementation of political and economic reforms by the governments that succeeded the illiberal rulers in power. The character of the EU's preaccession process required implementation: in order to deliver on promises to improve the country's standing, opposition politicians had to follow through with extensive reforms once in office. Opposition politicians knew that their preelection rhetoric would be judged against their postelection actions in the EU's monitoring reports. The tasks at hand and the payoffs for these politicians have varied enormously. In 1998, Slovak party leaders worked to correct the political transgressions of the previous regime and catch up with ECE frontrunners in the negotiations in order to join the EU in the first wave in 2004. In 2000, Serbian party leaders began cooperation with the ICTY and attempting basic economic reforms in order to end Serbia's isolation and acute economic backwardness, and in hopes of signing an association agreement with the EU.

The EU's leverage compels *all* governments to tackle certain politically difficult and inconvenient reforms, such as creating an independent civil service, reforming the judiciary, or accelerating bank privatization, and to stick to them over time. Ultimately the preaccession process is centered on a strategy of gatekeeping: if a candidate does not comply, it can be held back from the next stage in the process. For the first eight postcommunist candidates, the main stages were as follows: (1) beginning screening; (2) opening negotiations after satisfying the Copenhagen Criteria; (3) closing particular chapters in the negotiations; and (4) completing the negotiations. A candidate could move up thanks to accelerated reform, or slip back as a sanction for unfulfilled promises to implement reform – though toward the end of the process the decision to admit eight postcommunist states all at once in 2004 was a political one. For Bulgaria and Romania, a fifth step has been added consisting of a final evaluation of their administrative capabilities with the possibility of postponing accession by one year.

For the Western Balkan states, several stages have been added at the front end of the process: (1) a feasibility study for opening negotiations on an association agreement, called the Stabilization and Association Agreement (SAA); (2) negotiating the SAA; and (3) signing the SAA.[43] For Slovakia, the challenge was getting the green light to begin negotiations with the EU. For Bulgaria and Romania, it was the implementation of the reforms demanded by the EU for membership that was the greatest hurdle, because of corruption and weak state capacity. For Croatia, economic reforms are well under way, but cooperation with the ICTY and reform of state institutions connected to the secret services and the military prevented the start of negotiations for membership.

---

[43] This is not without precedent: in the early 1990s, the EU did attach conditions to signing an association agreement, then called a Europe Agreement, with the first round of postcommunist applicants, though it did not do much to enforce them.

Serbia–Montenegro shares all of Croatia's problems, and the economy and general state capacity are very weak, although the territorial definition of the state remained unresolved for so long. But in the spring of 2005 the Commission assessed Serbia–Montenegro's progress positively in its feasibility study, and negotiations on an SAA started in late 2005 – and the agreement was finally signed in April 2008 (in an overt move on the part of the EU to bolster European forces in the upcoming May elections). What is important here is that once illiberal rulers are forced to exit power, EU conditionality kicks in and promotes progress regardless of how far behind a country finds itself on the road to joining the EU.

Credible Commitment to Reform

Economic actors have had every reason after 1989 to question how far post-communist states would go in implementing liberalizing reforms. Indeed, many have stopped at some kind of partial economic reform that privileges insiders and fosters corruption. How can postcommunist governments signal that they are serious about reform?[44] Equally important to the conditionality mechanism in motivating reform is the fact that the EU preaccession process serves as a commitment device. For domestic and foreign economic actors, especially investors, progress in the EU's preaccession process serves as a credible commitment to ongoing and predictable economic reforms and also to certain ongoing political reforms, especially pertaining to state regulation of the economy. Most simply, as Peter Hall and Rosemary Taylor argue, "institutions affect action by structuring expectations about what others will do;" for economic actors, the preaccession process created expectations that comprehensive economic reforms would proceed apace.[45] Elsewhere governments also become members of regional organizations in order to signal their commitment to ongoing reform by tying the hands of the country's current and future governments through the rules of the organization.[46]

Once a candidate is well on the way to joining the EU, the costs of losing ground or reversing course became prohibitive – for any government. At the same time, the fact that qualifying for EU membership is such a mammoth project of domestic politics compelled all mainstream political parties to reach a consensus about the underlying thrust of political and economic reform.[47] The

---

[44] Stephen Haggard and Steven B. Webb, "Introduction." In *Voting for Reform: Democracy, Political Liberalization, and Economic Adjustment*, pp. 1–36, 21 (New York: Oxford University Press, 1994).

[45] Peter A. Hall and Rosemary C. R. Taylor, "Political Science and the Three New Institutionalisms." *Political Studies*, 44 (1996). pp. 936–57, 955.

[46] Jon C. Pevehouse, "Democracy from the Outside-In? International Organizations and Democratization." *International Organization*, 56, No. 3 (2002), pp. 515–49.

[47] For the related argument that liberal democracies make more durable alliance commitments to one another, see Kurt Taylor Gaubatz, "Democratic States and Commitment in International Relations." *International Organization*, 50, No. 1 (1996), pp. 109–39.

EU's good opinion also became a direct factor in the decisions of foreign investors, whereas credit rating agencies such as Moody's and Standard and Poor adjusted credit ratings in reaction to EU assessments and to the release of the EU's Regular Reports.[48] The exigencies of the EU's preaccession process thus assured economic actors that the commitment to liberal economic reforms would be protected from two threats: from economic downturns and from government turnover. Continuing economic reform becomes clearly the most likely ongoing strategy for current and future governments.

The credibility of the commitment to ongoing economic reform in the context of the EU's preaccession process thus serves as a very important signal for domestic and international economic actors, promising them a stable business environment and access to the entire EU market.[49] Lisa Martin argues that the forms of international cooperation that offer states the highest benefits require them to make credible commitments to one another. She finds that for democracies the concerns of economic actors about the credibility of commitments are decreased by the participation of legislatures in international cooperation. In the case of EU candidates, progress in the preaccession process signals a seriousness of commitment not only to the EU itself as it weighs a candidate's suitability for membership, but also to a range of economic actors as they weigh a country's suitability for investment.[50] Progress in the preaccession process builds credibility in the eyes of economic actors using a similar mechanism as legislative participation; namely, it makes extrication from and violation of international agreements very difficult.

All together, the reforms of the economy that are implemented as part of the effort to qualify for EU membership, and the credible commitment to ongoing reform that comes from moving toward membership in the EU's preaccession process, bring significant economic benefits. These include a better business environment, higher regulatory quality,[51] higher levels of domestic and foreign investment, and greater opportunities for trade. They overlap, of course, with the economic benefits of being an EU member. But the two mechanisms I have emphasized here – conditionality and credible commitment – highlight the benefits of the process of joining the EU for candidates, as opposed to the benefits they get once they are in. And the drive to EU membership, by forcing economic restructuring, improves performance in the world economy over the long run. Most important, the mechanisms of conditionality and credible commitment help explain why, as discussed above, future governments in the

[48] Joly Dixon, European Commission, interview in Brussels, 1998.
[49] For the related argument that voters who are "winners" from the economic transition support EU membership as a guarantee that economic reforms will not be reversed, and therefore cast their vote for pro-EU parties, see Tucker, Pacek, and Berinsky, "Transitional Winners and Losers."
[50] Lisa Martin, *Democratic Commitments, Legislatures and International Cooperation* (Princeton, NJ: Princeton University Press, 2000).
[51] Walter Mattli and Thomas Plümper, "The Internal Value of External Options." *European Union Politics*, 5, No. 3 (2004), pp. 307–30.

candidate states, despite their very different political profiles, do not halt or reverse reform. Indeed, these mechanisms trigger another wave of *adapting* as formerly illiberal (or even authoritarian) political parties, such as the HDZ in Croatia, transform themselves and adopt positions that are consistent with Western liberal democracy and economic reform.

IS THE EUROPEAN UNION REALLY NEEDED?

My aim in this chapter is to identify the specific mechanisms that translate international influence into domestic political change, breaking the hold of illiberal rulers on power and sustaining democratic and economic reforms in the context of EU enlargement. The open question is whether the prospect of EU membership is a necessary condition for postcommunist states to transition toward liberal democracy and comprehensive economic reform. We can point to recent democratic breakthroughs in Ukraine and Georgia as cases where illiberal leaders have been unseated by civic democratic movements in countries that have no officially recognized prospect of becoming EU members.[52] What remains to be seen, however, is whether comprehensive reforms can be sustained without the discipline of the EU's preaccession process and the ultimate carrot of full membership.

Following on the Orange Revolution in the autumn of 2004, the government of Ukrainian president Viktor Yushchenko pledged comprehensive political and market-oriented reform and sought the prospect of EU membership as an anchor for Ukraine's democratic revolution.[53] The EU refused to recognize Ukraine as a prospective EU member, and explicitly stated that the Action Plan signed with Ukraine as part of the European Neighborhood Policy (ENP) is *not* a first step toward membership. At the close of 2004, Ukrainian leaders refused to sign a five-year ENP Action Plan that did not recognize Ukraine as a credible future candidate for EU membership; the time span of the Action Plan was consequently reduced to three years.[54] Given the economic costs alone for Ukraine of being excluded from the internal market, it is not surprising that Ukraine's new Western-oriented leaders would have such an intense preference for EU membership.

The ENP can be credited with providing an established framework that the European Commission could use to respond immediately to Ukraine's aspirations for closer relations after the October 2004 Orange Revolution. The ENP gave the EU a way to pledge political and economic support for Ukraine, without forcing the EU to respond with a yes or a no to Ukraine's membership bid at a time when EU governments were in no mood to take on a new candidate.

[52] Michael Mc Faul, "Transitions from Postcommunism." *Journal of Democracy*, 16, No. 3 (2005), pp. 5–19. See also Demeš and Forbrig,"Reclaiming Democracy."

[53] See Lucan Way, "Ukraine's Orange Revolution: Kuchma's Failed Authoritarianism." *Journal of Democracy*, 16, No. 2 (2005), pp. 131–45.

[54] Interview with official of the European Commission, Brussels, December 2004.

Indeed, with a little imagination, the ENP can be understood as a way for the Commission to help Ukraine begin the long and laborious preparations for EU membership on the gamble that once it is (more) fit to enter, EU leaders will find it impossible to reject it.

Three positive scenarios are possible for Ukraine as well as Moldova and perhaps Georgia. The first is that the ENP will only be a stopgap measure and the EU will recognize them as future candidates. The second is that the carrot of full participation in the internal market will become a credible reward for more limited compliance with EU rules, and that this will sustain at least some momentum in the reform process. The third is that reform will be maintained without any significant EU involvement, opening up a different trajectory of political change and opening up the possibility that the illiberal regimes in this study did not need EU leverage to maintain a new course.

The preliminary evidence from Ukraine, however, is not very promising: The Yushchenko government's plans for reform became bogged down in Ukraine's fractious parliament and its incompetent and corrupt public administration. Both the *conditionality* and the *credible commitment* mechanisms might have helped, though the time span has been too short to conclude that there is not durable forward momentum to reform without them (consider how slowly Serbia has made progress since 2000). In the parliamentary elections in March 2006, Yushchenko's party lost its majority in parliament. It remains to be seen whether all of the mainstream political parties in Ukraine will adapt to a Western agenda and successfully implement the reforms of the state and the economy that would have to precede any serious bid for Ukraine to become a candidate for EU membership.

CONCLUSION

I have made the case for the important independent effect of EU leverage on domestic political change in illiberal democracies under quite different domestic conditions. By no means does EU leverage erase or even diminish many domestic differences: but it does improve the quality of political competition, whereas it narrows the parameters of domestic policymaking as states comply with EU rules in order to qualify for membership. We see significant – though certainly far from complete – convergence among candidates as they get closer to qualifying for EU membership.[55] Under the right conditions, free and fair elections provide opposition parties and civic groups the opening they need to end illiberal rule. Working in synergy with such forces, the EU's leverage has had a hand, over time, in creating those conditions and making the political systems of the illiberal states more competitive. On many fronts, keeping ruling elites within the parameters set by the EU's preaccession process signifies an outstanding success: respect for basic democratic standards, more robust

---

[55] For a discussion of the high levels of dissatisfaction with democratic institutions in many postcommunist states, see Cameron, "The Quality of Democracy."

political competition, better protection of ethnic minority rights, ongoing reform of the economy, and, in some cases, cooperation with the ICTY.

All of this, however, does not by itself guarantee a high quality of democratic policymaking or governance. We certainly see a great deal of variation in political and economic performance once illiberal rulers are unseated. It is clear that the EU's leverage cannot work alone *but only in synergy with the efforts of domestic political elites and groups*. And despite the progress these states are all making toward a common goal, what stands out on final analysis is the diversity that stems from three main factors: (1) the nature and competence of domestic elites; (2) the effectiveness of civic groups that push for reform, accountability, and transparency; and (3) the domestic conditions that have to be addressed. There can be no comparison to the challenges faced by the ex-Yugoslav states that have to come to terms with the wars and overcome the ethnic divisions and the economic backwardness that they have caused. Because the problems are so diverse, this chapter has instead focused on the relative progress that each state has made since watershed elections took place. If ten years from now the EU has coaxed Serbia and even Bosnia–Herzegovina down the road to where Slovakia stands today, then there will be no doubt about the effectiveness of EU leverage in overcoming illiberal rule.

PART III

CHOOSING REGIME CHANGE: DEMOCRATIZING ELECTIONS

5

A Postcommunist Transition in Two Acts

The 1996–7 Antigovernment Struggle in Bulgaria
as a Bridge between the 1989–92 and 1996–2007
Democratization Waves in Eastern Europe

Tsveta Petrova
Cornell University

With the collapse of the Soviet Union, some of its former republics (Latvia, Lithuania, and Estonia) and some of the Central European satellites (the Czech Republic, Hungary, and Poland) quickly entered the ranks of capitalist democracies. The remaining majority of new post-Socialist states have carried on as hybrid regimes[1] or as autocracies with mixed marketization records.[2] Among them Bulgaria stood out with its unique coupling of a quick transition to parliamentary democracy and a lack of sustained commitment to economic reforms. Only at the beginning of 1997 did the country resolve the economic regime question by achieving a consensus on a larger "civilizational" choice to wholeheartedly seek admission to the European Union (EU) as a way to make the transition to a market economy irreversible in the immediate term and to acquire a new liberal democratic home in the international system in the long run.

What explains this critical juncture? How were the country's illiberal incumbents and their antireform agenda defeated? This chapter argues that by capitalizing on public discontent with and mass mobilization against the social consequences of the Left economic governance (the "Socialist third way"), the Right forged a consensus in favor of a prodemocratic, promarket, and pro-Western political agenda. This in effect ended the parity between the ex-Communists (the Left) and their former opposition (the Right) – a balance of

---

[1] On hybrid regimes, see T. Carothers, "The End of the Transition Paradigm." *Journal of Democracy*, 13, No. 1 (2002), pp. 5–21 and L. Diamond, "Thinking About Hybrid Regimes." *Journal of Democracy*, 13, No. 2 (2002), pp. 21–35.

[2] On the diversity of transitions away from postauthoritarianism in the region, see K. Dawisha and B. Parrott, eds., *The Consolidation of Democracy in East-Central Europe* (New York: Cambridge University Press, 1997) and C. Offe, *Varieties of Transition: The East European and East German Experience* (Cambridge, MA: MIT Press, 1997).

power that had frustrated the economic transition and the consolidation of democracy within the country.[3]

The severe economic crisis that took place in Bulgaria in 1996 compelled unions and other civic groups to mobilize thousands to protest, which served to undermine the legitimacy of Left governance while the opposition parties – with the help of transnational and international actors – articulated accession to the EU as a credible alternative to the Socialist third way. Inspired by popular mobilization in neighboring Serbia and reassured of the tacit moral and political support of the West for their cause, the Right party eventually assumed leadership of the protests. The protests of the now united civic and political opposition not only paralyzed the country but also threatened the Socialists' political future, forcing them to concede to preterm elections. However, the 1996–7 antigovernment struggle in Bulgaria was not limited to a regular turnover in power; it was rather a fundamental realignment in Bulgarian politics – a mandate for radical reforms and a triumph over the unreformed ex-Communists.

The Bulgarian case thus presents a bridge between the first and the second and third democratization waves in Eastern Europe. The opposition coalition used the 1996–7 campaign to conclusively resolve the economic regime question placed on the table with the fall of Communism in Bulgaria in 1989. Moreover, the campaign benefited from the demonstration and diffusion effects of the 1996 trial electoral revolution in neighboring Serbia. At the same time, the lessons of the defeat of the unreformed Bulgarian Left served to inspire opposition leaders in Slovakia in 1998 and in Serbia in 2000 to replace their illiberal incumbents with proreform and pro-Western elites. And the success of the Bulgarian struggle and its linkage to the successive successes in Slovakia and Serbia added to the clustering of events that influenced the future actions of illiberal leaders and their oppositions throughout the region.[4]

In addition to regional players, Western actors, too, played an important role in the process of economic regime change in Bulgaria. The Serbian opposition protests demonstrated to the Bulgarian Right that domestic mass mobilization had gathered enough momentum to create a mandate for radical change and offered a set of strategic and tactical innovations for the Bulgarian opposition coalition to carry their campaign to success. The West, on the other hand, had been granting assistance and legitimacy to aligned domestic actors, thus differentially empowering them. Critical of the Left's mid-1990s antireform rule, Western rhetoric and actions (exclusion from the first EU eastern enlargement and denial of International Monetary Fund bailout loans) helped to discredit the regime. At the same time, Western money, advice, and support to the Right

---

[3] M. McFaul, "The Fourth Wave of Democracy and Dictatorship: Noncooperative Transitions in the Postcommunist World." *World Politics*, 54, No. 2 (January 2002), pp. 212–44 and T. Frye, "The Perils of Polarization: Economic Performance in the Postcommunist World." *World Politics*, 54, No. 3 (April 2002), pp. 308–37.

[4] After M. Beissinger, *Nationalist Mobilization and the Collapse of the Soviet State* (New York: Cambridge University Press, 2002).

allowed it to develop organizationally as well as to position itself credibly in the pro-EU space by presenting EU membership[5] as an alternative to the Socialist third way. By reassuring the country of its belonging to Europe, the West further legitimized the opposition's reform agenda and claim to power. In the end, domestic consensus on EU membership and Bulgaria's dependence on the International Monetary Fund (IMF) magnified the impact of these organizations, whereas the weakness of the Left and the Right, as well as their parity, combined with their different ideological proximity to the West allowed external players some influence on the 1996–7 fundamental realignment in Bulgarian politics.

Finally, the Bulgarian case is also interesting because it exposes "the elite bias of the democratic transitions literature"[6] by highlighting the interaction of masses and elites in producing critical junctures[7] in politics. The role of popular mobilization in the process of transition to democracy remains the subject of some controversy. Still debated are the timing, content, and amount of mass mobilization that favor democratization.[8] Some scholars focusing on Latin America[9] warn that participation by the masses not only increases the costs of suppression but also may raise the cost of toleration of participation.[10] Demobilization, after the old order is weakened, is believed by these authors to allow parties to emerge as agents for moderation who would ensure that the transition ran its course.[11] In contrast, popular protest is argued to have been

---

[5] On the democratization effects of EU accession, see M. Vachudova, *Europe Undivided: Democracy, Leverage, and Integration after Communism* (New York: Oxford University Press, 2005); G. Pridham, "EU Enlargement and Consolidating Democracy in Post-Communist States – Formality and Reality." *Journal of Common Market Studies*, 40, No. 5 (2002), pp. 953–73; F. Schimmelfennig and U. Sedelmeier, "Governance by Conditionality: EU Rule Transfer to the Candidate Countries of Central and Eastern Europe." *Journal of European Public Policy*, 11, No. 4 (August 2004), pp. 661–79; and H. Grabbe, *Enlarging the EU Eastwards* (Herndon, VA: Pinter, 1998).

[6] For a critique of the elite bias of the democratic transitions literature, see G. Ekiert and J. Kubik, *Rebellious Civil Society: Popular Protest and Democratic Consolidation in Poland, 1989–1993* (Ann Arbor: University of Michigan Press, 1999) and M. Osa, "Contention and Democracy." *Communist and Post-communist Studies*, 31, No. 1 (1998), pp. 29–42.

[7] On the importance of elections as critical junctures for the emergent regime type in Eastern Europe, see S. Fish, "The Determinants of Economic Reform in the Postcommunist World." *East European Politics and Societies*, 12 (Winter 1998), pp. 31–78.

[8] N. Bermeo, "Myths of Moderation: Confrontation and Conflict during Democratic Transitions." *Comparative Politics*, 29, No. 3 (1997), pp. 305–22.

[9] G. O'Donnell and P. Schmitter, *Transitions from Authoritarian Rule: Tentative Conclusions about Uncertain Democracies* (Baltimore: Johns Hopkins University Press, 1986); T. Karl, "Dilemmas of Democratization in Latin America." *Comparative Politics*, 23 (October 1990), pp. 1–21; and A. Przeworski, *Democracy and the Market: Political and Economic Reforms in Eastern Europe and Latin America* (Cambridge: Cambridge University Press, 1991).

[10] On democratization as increasing the costs of suppression and decreasing the costs of toleration, see R. Dahl, *Polyarchy: Participation and Opposition* (New Haven, CT: Yale University Press, 1971).

[11] P. Oxhorn, "Where Did All the Protesters Go?: Popular Mobilization and the Transition to Democracy in Chile." *Latin American Perspectives*, 21, No. 3 (Summer, 1994), pp. 49–68. However, some Latin Americanists do recognize that popular protest may have pushed

crucial in convincing old-regime elites not only to begin regime negotiations but also to sustain reforms in a number of East European and African cases.[12] In the 1996–7 opposition campaign in Bulgaria, broad mass mobilization discredited the current regime[13] and created a sense that change was necessary and possible, as a result persuading the Right to assume leadership of the protests. Popular contention can thus alter elite expectations about the success of a potential struggle between incumbents and their political opposition. Just as important, it is not just domestic mass mobilization that invites the articulation and eventual institutionalization of an alternative regime. Where a minimal sense of shared identification between struggles is established[14] – directly and/or by brokers, such as the media – foreign contention, too, can alter expectations about the possibilities for the future actions of domestic incumbents and their oppositions alike. The Bulgarian case further points to the importance of a strong opposition, capable of articulating a compelling alternative and translating popular discontent into a mandate for radical change in the name of this alternative.[15] At this stage, mass mobilization demonstrates popular support for the opposition's alterative and thus legitimates it.[16]

This chapter begins by describing the collapse of Communism in Bulgaria and suggests that the balance of power between ex-Communists and former dissidents produced a consensus on democracy but not on economic reforms. Next, the chapter sketches the political and economic consequences of this parity – political instability and partial market reforms – as the context for Left economic governance in the mid-1990s. The economic crisis that ravaged the country as a result of the Left's antireform policies is also briefly presented. The next section of the chapter is devoted to the 1996–7 Left–Right struggle,

---

democratization farther and faster than regime elites initially intended. See, for example, B. Geddes, "What Do We Know about Democratization after Twenty Years?" *Annual Review of Political Science*, 2, No. 1 (1999), pp. 129–48; and D. Collier and J. Mahoney, "Adding Collective Actors to Collective Outcomes: Labor and Recent Democratization in South America and Southern Europe." *Comparative Politics*, 29 (1997), pp. 285–303.

[12] On Africa, see M. Bratton and N. van de Walle, *Democratic Experiments in Africa: Regime Transitions in Comparative Perspective*, pp. 198–200 (Cambridge: Cambridge University Press, 1997). On Eastern Europe, see V. Bunce, "Rethinking Recent Democratization." *World Politics*, 55 (January 2003), pp. 167–92.

[13] On the loss of legitimacy as a political opportunity for democratization, see A. Oberschall, "Opportunities and Framing in the Eastern European Revolts of 1989." In *Comparative Perspectives on Social Movements: Political Opportunities, Mobilizing Structures, and Cultural Framings*, D. McAdam, J. McCarthy, and M. Zald, eds., pp. 93–121 (Cambridge: Cambridge University Press, 1996).

[14] On "attribution of similarity" between transmitter and adopter as a precondition for diffusion, see D. McAdam and D. Rucht, "The Cross National Diffusion of Movement Ideas." *Annals of the American Academy of Political and Social Sciences*, 528 (1993), pp. 36–59.

[15] On the importance of regime alternatives in the process of democratization, see A. Przeworski, "Some Problems in the Study of the Transition to Democracy." In *Transition from Authoritarian Rule: Prospects for Democracy*, G. O'Donnell, P. Schmitter, and L. Whitehead, eds., pp. 47–63 (Baltimore: Johns Hopkins University Press, 1986).

[16] On the role of mass mobilization of reducing uncertainty during the transition, see V. Bunce, "Rethinking Recent Democratization."

which began as a protest against the social consequences of the economic crisis but evolved into a campaign that shifted the balance of power to the proreform and pro-Western agenda represented by the Right. In conclusion, the chapter reflects on domestic and international factors that contributed to the campaign's success.

THE COLLAPSE OF COMMUNISM IN BULGARIA: UNREFORMED COMMUNISTS AND WEAK OPPOSITION

Bulgaria was a latecomer to the 1989–92 wave of democratic revolutions. Although Bulgarians were dissatisfied with their current living standards, the country's Communist regime still retained some legitimacy, and opposition to it was very small, weak, disorganized, and fractionalized.[17] Even though some dissident organizations and the independent union CL Podkrepa were formed in 1989 and openly criticized the regime on a number of ecological, economic, and political issues, pressure from below was not the primary cause for the fall of Communism.[18]

The beginning of the Bulgarian transition resulted primarily from the political lessons learned by the Communist leadership, who witnessed the dramatic changes in the Soviet bloc and launched political and economic reforms in an attempt to maintain a central role in the postcommunist reality.[19] Compelled by a small majority within the Bulgarian Communist Party Politburo, the first party secretary, Todor Zhivkov, "retired" on November 10, 1989 (the day after the fall of the Berlin Wall). Zhivkov's successors – the coup's organizers – initially moved not to dismantle Communism but to "endow it with a human face." However, opposition groups, now federated in the Union of Democratic Forces (UDF), were calling for the introduction of a fully competitive democratic system. In support of its demands, on December 14, 1989, the UDF organized a thousands-strong demonstration. The Bulgarian Communists had been closely following developments in the other former Soviet satellites, so they feared a similar popular backlash against Communism in Bulgaria. But when the UDF proved capable of mobilizing popular discontent, the ruling circle saw democratization as imminent. To control the process, the Communists invited the still-weak UDF to roundtable negotiations in the first week of January 1990.

However, although popular mobilization against the Communist regime was sizable enough to force its leadership to concede to democratization, it was not large enough to marginalize the Communist Party's successor or to compel it to reform. The Communist Party was renamed the Bulgarian Socialist Party (BSP), and the reformist leaders were able to pass a party program that supported democratic capitalism. Still, these changes were pushed from the top

---

[17] V. Dimitrov, *Bulgaria: The Uneven Transition* (London: Routledge, 2001).

[18] E. Giatzidis, *An Introduction to Post-communist Bulgaria* (Manchester, UK: Manchester University Press, 2002).

[19] N. Vassilev, *Bitkata za Bulgaria* (Sofia: Lice, 2001).

in an almost autocratic fashion and were baffling to most party members.[20] Unlike their Hungarian or Polish colleagues, most BSP cadres had not been exposed to alternative ideas in the course of the 1980s, and only a small portion of the party's members sided with those who wanted to see the BSP become a "modern left (social-democratic) party."[21] The Communist Party underwent a superficial and purely tactical remodeling, which left it internally divided into a reformist and a conservative camp.

At the same time, the young and inexperienced UDF faced the challenge of transforming itself from a coalition of civic groups into an organized political force. After several waves of splits, the groups that remained in the UDF concentrated on establishing the coalition as the anti-Communist opposition by adopting an increasingly strident ideological tone[22] (rather than displaying competence and responsibility, as their Hungarian counterparts did[23]). The UDF leadership, however, was unable to create a unified and effective organizational structure; therefore, internal conflicts surfaced during elections and important policy debates.

The unreformed Communists and the weak opposition sought to legitimize themselves and to reshape the Bulgarian political landscape through constitution-making. Amid continuing public demonstrations, organized by the UDF to pressure the ex-Communists, the roundtable agreed on the basic rules of the new political order and scheduled multiparty elections for June 1990. The Communist Party immediately legalized private property, but the roundtable failed to address the urgent economic problems the country faced. Given the disagreements about the nature and pace of much-needed but painful economic reforms, neither party was willing to risk its popularity by associating itself with them.[24]

DEMOCRACY WITHOUT THE MARKET: THE MID-1990S ECONOMIC CRISIS

The collapse of Communism produced a balance of power between two internally divided camps – the unreformed Communists and the weak opposition. Both groups sought legitimacy by embracing democracy, but they could not agree on an economic agenda for the country. Because under Communism the political and the economic were linked, the result was political instability, executive deadlock, a stop-and-go market transition, and only partial economic reform. The country was wracked by political instability and labor unrest.

[20] N. Vassilev, *Bitkata za Bulgaria.*
[21] G. Pridham, "Patterns of Europeanization and Transnational Party Cooperation: Party Development in Central and Eastern Europe." Paper for Workshop on European Aspects of Post-Communist Party Development, ECPR Sessions, University of Mannheim, 26–31 March 1999.
[22] V. Dimitrov, *Bulgaria: The Uneven Transition.*
[23] A. Grzymala-Busse, *Redeeming the Communist Past: The Regeneration of Communist Parties in East Central Europe* (New York: Cambridge University Press, 2002).
[24] V. Dimitrov, *Bulgaria: The Uneven Transition.*

TABLE 5.1. *Acronyms*

BSP	Bulgarian Socialist Party
CITU	Confederation of Independent Trade Unions
(CL) Podkrepa	Confederation of Labor "Podkrepa"
EU	European Union
IMF	International Monetary Fund
IRI	International Republican Institute, USA
MRF	Movement for Rights and Freedoms
UDF	Union of Democratic Forces

At the first democratic elections in 1990, the Socialists received nearly 53 percent of the vote, whereas the UDF received only about a third; the remaining votes went to the Movement for Rights and Freedoms (MRF), which had emerged to represent the interests of the country's one million ethnic Turks. (See Table 5.1 for political acronyms.) The Socialist cabinet, led by Andrei Lukanov, passed sweeping legislation that created a liberalized legal framework for wages and prices, foreign exchange transactions, and a two-tier banking system, as well as national monetary and fiscal policies. However, the cabinet's Balcerowicz-style shock-therapy reform agenda failed to receive the support of conservatives in the party and the BSP's electorate.[25] Amid union-organized protests, the government collapsed only a few months after coming to power. In December 1990, the replacement government of Dimitar Popov, an unaffiliated technocrat, was appointed with an ambitious program of economic liberalization reforms, many of which it implemented. The National Assembly passed a new constitution in July 1991, and new parliamentary elections followed in October 1991. The next coalition government, of the UDF and the MRF under Filip Dimitrov, focused on ideological offensives against the BSP and the remnants of Communism.[26] With restitution under way but a botched land reform and slow progress on privatization, Bulgaria's economy continued to deteriorate, and unemployment continued to grow as uncompetitive industries failed.[27] In late 1992, the internally strained Right ruling coalition fell apart. The Dimitrov government was replaced by a minority coalition of the Socialists, the MRF, and some defecting UDF deputies – the caretaker cabinet

---

[25] USAID, *Bulgaria Assessment Report: Seventeen Years of Partnership in Transition: 1990–2007* (USAID, Bulgaria, July 2007).

[26] V. Dimitrov, *Bulgaria: The Uneven Transition*.

[27] To undermine the rural bases of socialist support, the government embarked on an effort to break up the collective farms and return the land to the original owners. However, the agricultural reform led to continual legal uncertainties and a dramatic drop in production. Moreover, the cabinet gave priority not to privatization but to returning assets seized by the Communists after WWII. The UDF also blocked ongoing privatization deals in an attempt to stop insiders from enriching themselves.

of Lyuben Berov, which survived for 15 months, and by which little was accomplished. The cabinet fell in May 1994 when faced with a general strike.[28] In the meantime, the BSP managed to achieve at least temporary consolidation when the newly elected party leader, Zhan Videnov, sought to present a dynamic and competent image to the electorate. Pledging to defend ordinary citizens against market excesses, the BSP and its two nominal coalition partners won an absolute majority in the 1994 elections.

Videnov rejected "capitalism," "the egoism of the market," and "the neocolonialism of international financial and political institutions."[29] He claimed to be promoting a "socially sensible left modernization," or a "Bulgarian third way," which was to be a middle ground between rapid marketization and recommunization. The list of controlled prices was dramatically expanded – by the end of 1996, approximately half of all consumer products were subject to some form of price control. Recollectivization of farming did nothing to reverse the decline of Bulgarian agriculture and only aggravated the administrative chaos that crippled the countryside. Instead of inviting foreign companies to address the dire investment needs of the Bulgarian economy, Videnov reversed the planned cash privatization because it "squandered national wealth" to the advantage of "foreign influences."[30] The cabinet's flagship policy of voucher/mass privatization, meant to advance long-delayed structural reforms and to promote social justice, was repeatedly delayed and was implemented only after most of the enterprises on offer were in desperate financial straits, thus generating escalating unemployment instead.[31] In addition, instead of asserting control over the state sector, the government itself was overrun by shadowy interests: spiraling corruption and crony capitalism reigned. Inefficient state enterprises were encouraged to work at full capacity, even though there were no markets for their goods; and all of their losses, which in 1995 amounted to 15 percent of GNP, were absorbed by the still largely state-owned banking sector.[32]

In early 1996 the economy began to unravel. The artificially supported exchange rate collapsed in March, which in turn fueled inflation. The inflationary spiral, however, was reinforced by the simultaneous crisis of the banking system, which led to the bankruptcy of one-third of all Bulgarian banks in May 1996. Furthermore, the government failed to generate enough resources to repay the country's foreign debt. The Bulgarian currency collapsed in November. By the end of 1996, inflation hit the 300 percent mark, and the GNP

---

[28] N. Daskalova and T. Mikhailova, "Industrial Disputes and Strikes in Bulgaria – Legislation and Trends." *South-East Europe Review*, 1 (2001), pp. 113–26.

[29] V. Ganev, "Bulgaria's Symphony of Hope." *Journal of Democracy*, 8, No. 4 (1997), pp. 125–39.

[30] N. Vassilev, *Bitkata za Bulgaria*.

[31] Trade union archives report that 70 percent of the firms to be privatized were bankrupt. CITU, *Hronologia: Subitia, Pozicii, Stanovishta, Dokumenti, 1990–2000* (CITU Archives: Sofia, 2000).

[32] N. Vassilev, *Bitkata za Bulgaria*.

shrank by a staggering 9 percent. Between January 1996 and January 1997, the average monthly salary had fallen almost tenfold, from $118 to $12.[33]

THE ANTIGOVERNMENT CAMPAIGN: FROM CRISIS TO CONSENSUS[34]

The Left–Right struggle progressed in four stages: (1) *A crisis of legitimacy*: the economic crisis fueled internal, civic, and parliamentary opposition to the government, but Videnov was able to buy time by reshuffling his cabinet because his opponents pursued different goals and preferred different tactics. (2) *An alternative to the Socialist third way*: the opposition parties united behind a charismatic presidential candidate who articulated an appealing message of proreform and pro-Western political change and whose victory served as a referendum on the Left's governance. (3) *A united opposition*: the cabinet collapsed when the Left fell into disarray and when the Right united and led the parliamentary and civic antigovernment forces to translate this popular mandate for change into a commitment to far-reaching (IMF- and EU-required) reforms. (4) *Institutionalization of the new consensus*: unable to contain the protests, the Left split and later agreed to preterm elections, thus effectively institutionalizing the shift in power toward the reform agenda represented by the Right.

Early Popular Mobilization: The Politicization of Economic Discontent

As economic problems began to have an effect in early 1996, the nation's unions began to criticize the government vocally and publicly for failing to keep its promises to defend the interests of workers and the socially weak.[35] By May, the unions were calling for the cabinet to resign: they organized the first mass workers' protest of the year under the slogan "We want jobs and life with dignity NOW!" and submitted a petition signed by 164,000 people to protest the inadequate governance of the economy.[36] The country's unions not only had established themselves as defenders of the working class but also were also structurally well positioned to organize the citizenry to demand price stability, better material compensation, and savings protection.[37] Although the

---

[33] V. Ganev, "Bulgaria's Symphony of Hope."

[34] The discussion of the antigovernment struggle is based on interviews with participants in the events studied, a review of the secondary literature on Bulgaria's political history, the private archives of the organizations from the anti-Left coalition, and, most importantly, newspaper accounts for the period analyzed. Because newspapers provide the most complete accounts of protests in 1996–7, data collection was based on two national prestige dailies with established reputations for being relatively neutral and politically unaffiliated – *24 Chasa* and *Trud*.

[35] CITU, *Hronologia*.

[36] *Trud*, 2 May, 1996, p. 3.

[37] The establishment of the anticommunist union Podkrepa in early 1989 was inspired by the history and accomplishments of the Polish Solidarity. Podkrepa grew rapidly in its first year because of its role as a charter member of the UDF – and therefore a participant in the roundtable – and as the organizer of numerous strikes and demonstrations at that time. In

unions managed to focus public attention on the deficits of the Socialist third way and thus expanded the political opportunities for opposition parties to act, the UDF was reluctant to join the unions' campaign. The party preferred to act through institutional channels and was preoccupied with trying to overcome its internal divisions in preparation for the upcoming presidential elections.[38] Moreover, reformers within the BSP were beginning to openly criticize the government, and the Right feared that a collapse of the Videnov government would strengthen the Left by resolving its internal crisis.[39] Thus the unions and the UDF continued to criticize the socially costly, antireform governance of the country separately.

After the collapse of the banking system in late May, the country's macroeconomic stability very much depended on the IMF loans being negotiated by the government. The IMF offered an assistance package that included suggestions for restructuring the economy and cabinet changes.[40] The reformers vying for control within the BSP saw the crisis as an opportunity to reform and redefine the Bulgarian Left as a modern social democratic party and as the only way to avoid the Left's complete marginalization.[41] They called for Videnov's resignation during a meeting of the party's high council and demanded leadership changes. Struggling to remain in power, the prime minister announced the government's intention to shut down several hundred factories and to free utilities' prices as part of the measures imposed by the IMF.

The trade unions, however, boycotted the process because the cabinet had no plans to address the raging price instability and unemployment (both of which, the unions argued, were a direct result of the government's inept restructuring efforts so far).[42] Podkrepa organized a series of protests throughout the country and sent an open letter to opposition MPs urging them to leave parliament and to demand early parliamentary elections. The MRF was ready to support the unions. The other trade union, the Confederation of Independent Trade Unions (CITU), decided to join CL Podkrepa in demanding that the government resign

---

1990 communist organizations were banned from the workplace and the trade union system, renamed the Confederation of Independent Trade Unions (CITU), was declared independent of the Communist Party. CITU, whose membership of 3 million dwarfed the 400,000 of Podkrepa, soon began mobilizing workers against government inactivity and even in the strikes initiated by Podkrepa. When external and internal criticism was raised of the political role of both labor organizations in 1990, Podkrepa emancipated itself from the UDF. However, CITU continued to receive criticism from the Right for its continued ties with the BSP and from the Left for its aggressive reformist stance. Still, both unions remained strong well into the mid-1990s, in part because slow economic reform had left their membership bases intact and in part because union activities had contributed to the collapse of every postcommunist cabinet to date. D. Jones, "The Transformation of Labor Unions in Eastern Europe: The Case of Bulgaria." *Industrial and Labor Relations Review*, 45, No. 3 (April 1992), pp. 452–70.

[38] Interview with CL Podkrepa President Konstantin Trenchev.
[39] *Trud*, 14 May, 1996, p. 4.
[40] *Trud*, 4 June, 1996, p. 3.
[41] *Trud*, 13 May, 1996, p. 1.
[42] *Trud*, 2 May, 1996, p. 3.

but was not willing to call for preterm elections. The UDF moved to keep the stakes high – not only to topple the Videnov cabinet but also to remove the BSP from power.[43]

On June 5, the opposition parties announced that they would submit in parliament a vote of no confidence in the government and asked for union and civil-society support for an effective national strike that could lead to "preterm elections in the fall and a change in the political and economic regime in the country."[44] The next day, the CITU, Podrepa, and the UDF organized a mass demonstration in the capital. On June 7, with support from the European Trade Union Confederation as well as 58 union organizations from 28 countries, the Bulgarian unions coordinated a national one-hour warning strike.[45] The opposition parties, too, asked their members and sympathizers to participate in the union protest. A total of 850,000 people were reported to have participated in the union strike that day.[46] On June 8, amid continuing protests, the High BSP Council decided to back Videnov but agreed to a few cabinet and some party-leadership changes. Somewhat pacified, and mostly fearing that a party split would mean the Left's demise, the reformers within the BSP supported the cabinet when on June 13 the opposition submitted the no-confidence vote in parliament. Many of the organized protests subsided; however, individuals and small groups of local citizens continued to protest throughout the summer against the high prices of basic goods, rising inflation, low wages and wage arrears, and factory closings.

Return to Institutional Politics: The Victory of the Right Alternative in the Presidential Elections

Because little changed when the new BSP government assumed power, a new cycle of the macroeconomic crisis began in July 1996. The government, however, managed to secure an agreement with the IMF. So, in a series of meetings with IMF representatives, the unions sought the Fund's help in compelling the cabinet to implement not only the much-needed structural reforms but also some measures to address their social costs. Recognizing the difficulty of mobilizing labor and the general population in the summer, CL Podkrepa and the MRF began negotiations for joint protests in the fall in an attempt to bring about preterm elections. Yet, once again, the CITU did not want to go so far as calling for a turnover in power. And once again, the UDF feared that further anticabinet protests would unite the Left and might hurt the presidential candidate of the Right. Even though teachers, health workers, college students, and miners struck to protest the poor financing of their sectors, the UDF managed

---

[43] *Trud*, 31 May, 1996, p. 2.
[44] *Trud*, 4 June, 1996, p. 2.
[45] *Trud*, 9 June, 1996, p. 3.
[46] CITU, *Hronologia*.

to convince the unions to withhold coordinated antigovernment actions until after the 1996 presidential elections.

After losing the parliamentary elections in December 1994, Filip Dimitrov had resigned as chairman of the UDF Party Council and, after a series of splits, was succeeded by Ivan Kostov, who set out to turn the coalition into a modern Christian Democratic party. To that end, the UDF received much foreign assistance (mainly from the United States and Germany).[47] Many Western capitals were concerned about the resurgence of the unreformed BSP and therefore invested substantial resources in propping up the UDF through election training as well as policy and organizational advice and, sometimes, financial support.[48] Indeed, instead of trying to unite the UDF's constituent parties and movements through ideological radicalism, Kostov sought to give the UDF factions stakes in working together, focused on building a party bureaucracy, and implemented a program of organizational reform. In addition, at the recommendation of the International Republican Institute (IRI), the party implemented primary elections as a way to unite the UDF behind a single presidential candidate.[49] Thousands participated in the UDF primaries and elected the little-known but charismatic lawyer Petar Stoyanov. He took an agrarian vice president, who was hoped to attract some of the BSP's disillusioned rural supporters.

The Right ran a fairly sophisticated (and innovative for the Bulgarian context) political campaign. With some U.S. help and funding, the UDF took advantage of preelection assessments and public opinion polling to improve its political appeal and to better target the electorate. At the recommendation of his Western advisers, and with their help, Stoyanov sought to project a pragmatic, proreform, pro-Western image.[50] Stoyanov continued to criticize the high social costs of the Socialist third way but also articulated accession to the EU as a credible alternative to the antireform rule of the former Communists. Such campaign promises were especially appealing to the Bulgarian electorate because the country had been left out of the first EU eastern enlargement and was in the midst of a raging economic crisis. The appeal and credibility of Stoyanov's candidacy were further strengthened by his warm reception in the West, where Videnov was no longer welcomed.[51] Because the UDF (and its international benefactors) had invested in the organizational development of the party, Stoyanov's campaign reached even the remotest corners of the country. The network of the UDF's local structures was harnessed in coordinated get-out-the-vote and election-monitoring efforts. Moreover, the party reached out to civic groups to involve them in the elections in order to educate the public and monitor the election. Unions and student groups also sponsored a few national

[47] A. Todorov, *The Role of Political Parties in Bulgaria's Accession to the EU* (Sofia: Center for the Study of Democracy, 1999).

[48] Interview with H.E. U.S. Ambassador to Bulgaria (1996–7) Avis Bohlen.

[49] USAID, *Bulgarian Assessment Report.*

[50] Stoyanov started his campaign with visits to Germany, the United States, and the United Kingdom. *Trud,* 22 November, 1996, p. 4.

[51] Interview with a student leader at the time, Dimitar Bechev.

and local protests under the slogan "We want a future for Bulgaria."[52] And special attention was paid to engaging young people, for whom concerts and happenings were organized.

The final boost for Stoyanov's campaign came in early September when the Board of Elections ruled the presidential candidacy of the popular Socialist Georgi Pirinski unconstitutional. The divided BSP struggled to find a replacement on such short notice and in the end fell back on Pirinski's little-known vice president, Ivan Marazov. He lost to Stoyanov in the second round, held on November 3, 1996. Even though in Bulgaria executive power rests with the prime minister and not the president, the UDF saw in Stoyanov's victory a growing popular consensus around the proreform and pro-Western agenda on which their candidate had campaigned. The UDF publicized Stoyanov's election as a "referendum" on the Socialists and their "third way."[53] Equally damaging to the Left's rule was that on November 5, the IMF declined the government's request for a much-needed loan and justified this decision by the cabinet's failure to enact structural reforms. Triumphant, the UDF proclaimed, "The IMF voted no confidence in the government!"[54]

Collapse of the Videnov Government: Civic and Parliamentary Oppositions Unite under UDF Leadership

After the presidential elections, the BSP fell into disarray, engrossed in internal struggles and unable to produce alternative policies. The reformers within the BSP demanded that a new cabinet be voted in to implement the necessary reforms, but a party plenum decided in an 87-to-59 vote to retain Videnov.[55] However, because about two-thirds of all municipal party conferences demanded that a new set of policies be implemented, a party congress was scheduled for late December.[56] In the meantime, the country faced another cycle of the macroeconomic crisis. To stabilize the country and save the cabinet, Videnov declared on November 14 that the government would begin negotiations with the IMF on accepting a currency board and invited the unions to participate. The latter, however, argued that Videnov lacked the necessary popular support and IMF trust to carry out the needed reforms.

Podkrepa was pushing the opposition to incite a parliamentary crisis, which would then be backed by street protests.[57] Even the CITU had come to accept preterm elections as the only solution to the country's economic crisis. On December 4, 953,000 Bulgarians from 3,242 union organizations and many local businesses participated in a 24-hour national strike called by the CITU.[58]

---

[52] *Trud*, 16 October, 1996, p. 4.
[53] *24 Chasa*, 3–6 November, 1996.
[54] *Democracya*, Newspaper 263, 1996.
[55] *24 Chasa*, 13 November, 1996.
[56] *24 Chasa*, 13 November, 1996.
[57] *Trud*, November 8 1996, p. 4.
[58] *Trud*, December 5 1996, p. 1.

Their demands included cabinet resignation, preterm elections, and humanitarian assistance to the thousands of Bulgarians who could no longer afford food or heat. The government responded with emergency transfers to cover some of the unpaid wages in the state sector. However, the opposition parties failed to back the protesters with any parliamentary action and even somewhat distanced themselves from the protest.[59] Having negotiated with current Left MPs a possible no-confidence vote against the government, the opposition leaders realized that, despite much internal opposition to Videnov and his policies, most of the BSP parliamentarians feared going against the party line and were instead awaiting the decisions of the December party congress.[60]

The economic crisis practically paralyzed the country, so students, doctors, and miners continued to strike with little centralized organization. Moreover, the currency collapse and the country's escalating unemployment rate prompted individuals and small groups throughout the country to engage in numerous spontaneous protests and symbolic displays of disapproval of the Left governance. A few examples should illustrate this point: laid-off miners from Balkanbas threatened to barricade the nearby highway because they had not received their severance pay; demanding that heat and running water be restored, 800 students and faculty occupied the philosophy department building at Sofia University; a retiree from Blagoevgrad called a popular local radio show to urge others to join her in front of the municipality to remind the political elite how difficult life had become by clanging empty pots and pans; and people waiting in line for bread in Pernik started a riot when they learned that the price of bread had nearly doubled overnight.

In addition to reacting to the Left's mismanagement of the Bulgarian economy, such protesters were also drawing strength and inspiration from a wave of dissent across the Balkans. Like their Bulgarian counterparts, the Romanian liberal opposition had united to replace their illiberal incumbent president and organized massive rallies in support of the proreform and pro-Western Romanian presidential candidate. On the day of his victory (November 17, 1996), there were local elections in Serbia, followed by massive protests against Slobodan Milošević's attempt to deny the opposition its significant victories. News reports about those three overlapping and interconnected struggles created the sense of a prodemocratic flow of events in the Balkans. The domestic Bulgarian media not only picked up the stories but, in editorials, also called on the opposition to learn from their counterparts in Serbia.[61] Unlike the Bulgarian Right, the Serbian opposition parties had not hesitated to use extrainstitutional

---

[59] *Trud*, 6 December, 1996, p. 10.
[60] *Trud*, 6 December, 1996, p. 1.
[61] M. Bakalova, "The Serbian 'Velvet Revolution' in the Mirror of Bulgarian Media." In *The Awakening: A Chronicle of the Bulgarian Civic Uprising of January–February 1997*, E. Dainov, ed., pp. 57–72 (Democracy Network Program: Centre for Social Practices, NBU, Sofia, 1998).

mobilization to challenge the authorities when the formal political institutions did not reflect the votes and preferences of citizens as they were intended to.

The Right undertook a series of consultations with foreign diplomats in the country, who advocated moderation and a peaceful resolution to the Bulgarian crisis but also reminded the opposition leaders that they had the moral support and political sympathies of the West.[62] After some hesitation, the UDF decided that the "people's revolt against their odious and unresponsive government"[63] had gathered enough momentum to overturn the Left. The Right sought to lead the civic and political antigovernment forces by systematically cooperating with the unions and later on with student groups in the streets and by translating this popular mandate for change into an institutionalized commitment to IMF-imposed reforms in the short term and EU-required ones in the long run.

In anticipation of the BSP party congress, the UDF declared on December 20 that the opposition parties would not support the implementation of a currency board until (1) a new government was elected, (2) a new executive council of the National Bank was appointed, and (3) a committee was elected by the National Assembly to negotiate with the IMF. The opposition also promised to compile these demands into a "Declaration for National Salvation" and to submit it to a parliamentary vote. Later that day, thousands of UDF and Promiana[64] (a UDF-sponsored union set up in the fall) members marched in the capital, asking the government to resign. Unable to unite the party around a plan to address the country's economic crisis and the rising political and social tensions, Videnov resigned. He had hoped to continue controlling the party from behind the scenes: in exchange for his resignation as a much-needed safety valve against mounting social pressure, he staffed the executive council with trusted and conservative Socialists.[65] Georgi Parvanov (rather than the more liberal Georgi Pirinksi) was to replace Videnov as a party leader, and Nikolai Dobrev was to lead the new BSP cabinet. On December 28, the Socialist majority in parliament accepted the cabinet's resignation but postponed the voting in of a new government in the hope that the social tensions and protests would subside.

[62] Interview with H.E. U.S. Ambassador to Bulgaria (1996–7) Avis Bohlen.

[63] I. Dimitrov, *Edin Dobre Kamufliran Durzhaven Prevrat*, pp. 9–11 (Sofia: Obrazovanie i Nauka, 1997).

[64] Having realized the mobilization capacity of unions and that the CITU and Podkrepa were too powerful to be easily manipulated, in the fall of 1996, the UDF sponsored the efforts of 23 unions and professional associations to establish a new trade union – Promiana. It never became a trade union in the classical sense because it remained the "union arm" of the UDF: its activity was mostly political and its membership small but radical. As a result the union withered away after the collapse of the Videnov government in February, especially because the majority of its leadership were given administrative positions under the UDF government. Indeed, the union was never recognized as a representative workers' organization. *Sega*, 103/04.05.1999, p. 3.

[65] N. Vassilev, *Bitkata za Bulgaria*.

Defeat of the Unreformed Socialists: A New Proreform and Pro-Western Consensus

Videnov's resignation allowed the now united political and civic opposition to consolidate in demanding preterm elections as a step toward "a change in the political and economic regime in the country."[66] The coalition hoped to institutionalize the growing popular reform consensus and to translate it into political consensus or to marginalize the Socialists as long as they remained unreformed. The UDF's tactical inspiration came from the strategy used by the Serbian opposition coalition. When the BSP majority refused to vote on the UDF's Declaration for National Salvation on January 3, the Right's leadership announced that the "solution of the crisis is not in parliament but in the streets."[67] "By Belgrade's example,"[68] the opposition parties threatened to protest every day until their conditions were accepted. That same day, members of the Right demonstrated in front of BSP headquarters. For the first time, demonstrators were carrying "UDF in power" signs in addition to the most widely seen so far "No to the economic crisis" signs. A few days later, Podkrepa, too, called on its members and sympathizers to participate in civil disobedience and protests against the BSP government. Inspired and shamed by the impressive participation of youth groups in the Serbian protests, Bulgarian student associations were also galvanized to mobilize as the third pillar of the opposition.[69]

On January 8, Dobrev accepted in parliament the BSP nomination to form the next Socialist government. While Dobrev was negotiating the cabinet's composition, protests organized by the opposition coalition intensified. They escalated on January 10, when the Declaration for National Salvation was to be voted on. The UDF, Promiana, and Podkrepa and the confederation of student associations organized a live chain around the National Assembly. The protesters announced that they would not allow the MPs to leave the building unless the UDF's demands were met. Because the BSP majority refused to accept the opposition's terms, the UDF and MRF declared that they were withdrawing from parliament and called for a national strike. In addition, the still-acting Right president Zhelyu Zhelev announced that he would not authorize the formation of another BSP government.

As Left MPs attempted to leave parliament, the demonstrators stormed the building. After the police had secured the MPs' way out of the Assembly and

---

[66] *Trud*, 20 December 1996, p. 2.

[67] *Trud*, 20 December 1996, p. 2.

[68] I. Dimitrov, *Edin Dobre Kamufliran Durzhaven Prevrat*, pp. 9–11. The movement in Bulgaria could and did identify itself with their Serbian counterparts because the Bulgarian opposition saw itself as fighting the last remnants of the old communist order in Bulgaria, as the Serbian opposition declared it was doing in their country. Therefore, the Serbian strategy and tactics seemed relevant and appropriate to the Bulgarian goals and borrowing them was borrowing legitimacy and a further validation of the Bulgarian movement.

[69] Interview with a student leader at the time, Dimitar Bechev.

the rally was over, the police brutally dispersed the few remaining demonstrators. Several MPs, dozens of demonstrators, and a few policemen were wounded. Even though Dobrev immediately publicized his written orders forbidding police brutality against demonstrators, the opposition declared the Bulgarian transition a bloody one.[70] Several times throughout 1996, union structures across the country had complained that the local authorities were trying to intimidate union members into not participating in industrial conflicts and civic protests,[71] but media coverage of the January 10 events lent reality to such complaints. Because the regional norm had been one of declining repression,[72] the opposition coalition felt that the Left had lost the moral battle, so its defeat was imminent.

Protests continued with elections as the most frequent demand. This call for preterm elections was not only a demand for turnover in power; it also symbolized the growing popular consensus on liberal reforms (including the IMF conditions) and a larger "civilizational" commitment to EU accession as the only future that would guarantee that such a crisis would not be repeated. After the UDF assumed leadership of the protests, the campaign strengthened; the opposition parties (UDF and MRF), the unions, and student groups were now working together in the streets and through established institutional channels.[73] However, this unity also transformed the struggle because it now transcended narrow partisan interests and pure economic concerns. The post–January 10 marches were no longer just a collection of hungry and angry people who felt robbed of their dignity by a government that had profited from their misery; these protests had also become a celebration of the new pro-Western and proreform direction in which the protesters urged their elites to take the country.[74]

---

[70] There were speculations in the Bulgarian media that the protesters had provoked the police into using force to discredit the Left for trying to quell peaceful protests. Yet there were also speculations that the police had intentionally allowed the demonstrators to attack parliament to discredit them for abandoning peaceful protest. In fact, on the very next day, foreign diplomats were invited to the National Assembly to personally witness the "barbarity of the protestors" (Interview with H.E. U.S. Ambassador to Bulgaria (1996–7) Avis Bohlen) but instead they "made it clear enough that they though of Bulgaria differently, badly" (N. Koichev, "Riot, Violence, Provocation and Disorder." in *The Awakening*, E. Dainov, ed., pp. 75–9 Centre for Social Practices, NBU, Sofia).

[71] CITU, *Hronologia*.

[72] V. Bunce and S. Wolchik, "Favorable Conditions and Electoral Revolutions." *Journal of Democracy*, 17, No. 4 (2006), pp. 5–18.

[73] It is noteworthy that although they coordinated their antigovernment actions and strove to create the perception of a united front, the members of the oppositional coalition often distrusted each other, sometimes acted somewhat independently, and made conscious efforts to resist being coopted and subordinated by the UDF. The opposition coalition also lacked a charismatic leader and even the UDF remained stretched between three different leaders – the party head, who was desperately trying to streamline the party; the right presidential candidate, who projected the image of an honest and incorruptible politician desired by the party; and the right mayor of Sofia, who was instrumental in giving the opposition coalition the right to protest in the most favorable locations.

[74] E. Dainov, ed., *The Awakening*: Centre for Social Practices, NBU, Sofia.

Even though the general population was at first afraid to participate in the daily rallies organized by the united opposition, after the storming of parliament much decentralized and spontaneous organizing by ordinary citizens and, especially, young people took place. Before January 10, most of the demonstrators were middle-aged union members and core sympathizers of the opposition parties.[75] After January 10, not only college students but also high school students constituted a critical mass in the daily rallies organized by the opposition. Media coverage of these peaceful and even festive crowds helped encourage others to participate, thus creating the conditions for a mobilization cascade. With their timely reaction and "new CNN-style of news delivery," the media facilitated protest organization. Moreover, just as the Bulgarian media had covered the events in Serbia as a battle between the government and its people, so Bulgarian journalists described their incumbents as a government that was not supported by "the people" and cast the protestors as "the conscience and the future of the nation."[76] Public acceptance of this interpretation of the events is obvious from opinion polls taken in January 1996 in which only 15 percent of the people assumed a negative stance regarding the events.[77]

On January 13, the IMF declared that it would not negotiate a new loan until a new, "stable" government was elected.[78] The UDF was also publicizing the political support the opposition had received from many Western embassies (U.S., German, French, Austrian, and Belgian, among others) for the call for preterm elections. "The world and Europe are with us!" the UDF declared.[79] On January 14, a national one-hour daily warning strike, organized by Podkrepa, Promiana, and the CITU and negotiated with the opposition parties, took off. Participants in the protest included transportation workers, schoolteachers, medics, national television and radio journalists, and employees of other major industries (mining, energy, oil, steel, engineering).[80] The unions received political support from the European Trade Union Confederation, the International Confederation of Free Trade Unions, the World Confederation of Labor, the Polish Solidarnosc, and the American Federation of Labor and Congress of Industrial Organizers.[81] The BSP announced that it would accept the protestors' demands for preterm elections on the condition that a new government – possibly a coalition one, led by Dobrev – prepare them. The UDF rejected the BSP's proposal. The BSP fell apart: ten parties, movements, and

---

[75] P. Bay, "The Young Did Not Follow the Leaders." In *The Awakening*: Centre for Social Practices, E. Dainov, ed., pp. 69–70 (NBU, Sofia, 1998).

[76] M. Bakalova, "The Serbian 'Velvet Revolution' in the Mirror of Bulgarian Media."

[77] M. Yanova and Z. Velcheva, "January 10th – One Year Later in the Public Opinion Polls." In *The Awakening*: Centre for Social Practices, E. Dainov, ed., pp. 45–50 (NBU, Sofia, 1998).

[78] *Trud*, 13 January, 1997, p. 1.

[79] *Trud*, 14 January, 1997, p. 2.

[80] It should be noted, however, that counterprotests in a dozen cities and towns were also organized.

[81] CITU, *Hronologia*.

factions within the BSP set up an executive committee to help create an alternative Left party – a social democratic "Euroleft."[82] With the resurgence of the conservatives after the December party congress and the escalating crisis, the reformers within the BSP saw the party's marginalization as imminent, so they finally moved to independently "restore socialism, its new value and new respect."[83]

With the inauguration of Stoyanov on January 19, all parties represented in parliament began joint consultations under the new president on the composition of the next government – caretaker or coalition. During the negotiation period, foreign diplomats urged a compromise and assured the country that it belonged in Europe. On January 28, the president had to invite Dobrev to form the next cabinet. All three unions declared a general national strike. The daily march rallies organized by the opposition parties, the student associations, and the unions continued. National airports and ports and many border checkpoints and major highways were closed off by protestors. In Sofia alone, 25 barricades were erected, and more than 300 barricades went up throughout Bulgaria.

Concerned with the escalation of the crisis, the IMF and the European Bank for Development and Reconstruction offered $500 million in aid if the warring parties would hammer out an agreement for preterm elections and a macrostabilization agreement with the IMF. Protests had brought the country to a near halt; yet the BSP still insisted on waiting them out. After desperately trying to coopt the strikers by promising a 100 percent increase in wages for all state employees and pensioners, and then trying to coerce them by threatening that strikers would be fired, the BSP gave up the right to form a cabinet. Even though a party plenum had decided on February 3 that Dobrev would form a new Left cabinet, during the February 4 meeting of the National Security Council under the president, Dobrev and Parvanov returned the mandate, hoping to save the unreformed and disunited party from being altogether marginalized. All parties signed a political agreement to form a caretaker government until elections could be held in mid-April. That same day, the unions called off the general strike, but some local protests continued until the demonstrators' demands (usually for higher wages) were met. On February 12, the National Assembly elected a caretaker government, headed by the UDF mayor of Sofia, Stefan Sofiansky, to negotiate with the IMF on adopting a currency board. The National Assembly was disbanded, and new elections were called for April 19.

---

[82] The new party stated its aspiration to legitimize itself as a Bulgarian social democracy of a European type and hoped to do so credibly because a majority of the BSP leaders who had up to then been involved in maintaining the Left's international contacts with the Socialist International and the Party of European Socialists (PES) left the BSP to set up the Euroleft.

[83] Pridham, "Patterns of Europeanization and Transnational Party Cooperation."

THE ROLE OF REGIONAL AND WESTERN ACTORS

Several external actors participated directly or indirectly in the 1996–7 events in Bulgaria: the EU and the IMF, the U.S. embassy and the agencies that granted USAID assistance to Bulgaria, the European (but especially German) party foundations, and the Serbian opposition. This chapter now turns to their contributions.

For Bulgarian society, EU accession was part of the country's political and economic transformation; the Union would guarantee Bulgaria's social, economic, and national security.[84] EU membership was one of the few issues on which the Bulgarian political parties agreed. However, the EU was far less eager to formalize its relationship with Bulgaria. Although the EU opened association negotiations with the Visegrád countries in December 1990, it was not until the August 1991 attempted coup in the Soviet Union that the EU declared its intentions to expand cooperation with Bulgaria (and Romania) in order to draw those countries closer to the West.[85] Following up on its promise, in 1993 the EU signed an Association Agreement with Bulgaria that was economic/trade-related in nature, although it contained some political elements such as pledged respect for democracy and human rights. Accordingly, most of the assistance the EU provided to Bulgaria before 1997 was aimed at helping the country meet the agreement's objectives.[86] Although the agreement helped set the tone for the liberalization the EU expected of Bulgaria, EU aid was a demand-driven portmanteau program, which gave the Bulgarian government leverage on how EU funds were spent, thus reducing their impact during periods of antireform cabinets. Moreover, democratization assistance was practically nonexistent.[87]

Thus, in the early transition years, exclusion from EU membership afforded the Union a much greater – if indirect – influence on the Bulgarian transition. Although the BSP cabinet submitted an application for Bulgarian membership in the EU, in less than a year after he came to power, Videnov had completely reversed the proreform and pro-Western policies of previous governments.[88] His rule alarmed the West and led to the country's exclusion from the first wave of EU applicants. With this, the EU signaled that only parties with certain agendas would be acceptable partners for Bulgaria's "return to Europe." Given the

---

[84] E. Giatzidis, "Bulgaria on the Road to European Union." *Southeast European and Black Sea Studies*, 4, No. 3 (September 2004), pp. 434–57.

[85] Giatzidis, "Bulgaria on the Road to European Union."

[86] P. Nikolova, "The Implementation of Phare, Ispa and Sapard in Bulgaria." Paper prepared for the Workshop "A Roadmap for the Western-Balkans: Using IPA and Other EU Funds to Accelerate Convergence and Integration," Brussels, 11 October 2007.

[87] By the end of 1996 Bulgaria had received €491 million in Phare grant aid; however, only €2.7 million of it went to civil-society and democratization projects. Such assistance was awarded only in 1994 (€1.2 million) and in 1996 (€1.5 million) and was mostly for the organizational development of civil-society groups. P. Nikolova, "The Implementation of Phare, Ispa and Sapard in Bulgaria."

[88] N. Vassilev, *Bitkata za Bulgaria.*

strong public support for EU membership, this served to delegitimize the Left. Moreover, ending this exclusion from Europe and securing EU membership as a way to complete the transition became the core of the opposition's claim to power as well as their reform agenda. At the same time, EU diplomats insisted on further reforms and reassured the country of its belonging to Europe, thus indirectly supporting the UDF's claims to power and strengthening the case against the Left.

Representatives of Western international institutions, governments, and nongovernmental organizations also helped opposition politicians credibly position themselves in the increasingly attractive pro-EU space. In fact, Western party foundations – mostly the German Konrad Adenauer Foundation but also the French Robert Shuman Foundation and the British Westminster Foundation – were instrumental in the UDF's evolution from a federation of parties and movements to a Christian Democratic party.[89] These European party foundations organized many seminars, conferences, and campaigns to assist the UDF in forming and educating a party activist core, in introducing "conservative" ideas to the party debate, in developing a Christian Democratic party profile, and in disseminating knowledge and skills among the party-nominated members of parliament. It should be noted, however, that similar assistance by Social Democratic party foundations, especially the German Friedrich Ebert Foundation, was available to the BSP as well. In fact, given the long tradition of borrowings from foreign political models, all major political parties in Bulgaria, including the BSP, have been strongly inclined to legitimize themselves through association with their Western counterparts.[90] BSP cooperation with the Socialist International and the Party of European Socialists intensified between 1992 and 1994, but relations were frozen soon thereafter as a result of the disappointment of international social democrats in the Videnov government's failure. And during the campaign for the 1996 presidential elections, the Socialist International sent an open letter of support to the UDF candidate.[91] Moreover, the UDF masterfully leveraged its Christian Democratic networks to gain access to and political support from Western elites. Some prominent politicians such as the Bundestag president at the time, Christian Democrat Rita Zusmut, were involved as advisers to Stoyanov's campaign. Others lobbied their governments to or themselves publicly did renounce the antireform governance of Videnov, while at the same time praising the UDF's ambitions to make Bulgaria part of the Western world, and later encouraged the BSP to give up its right to form a new cabinet.[92]

Even though successive Bulgarian governments focused their attention on developing good relations with Europe, the United States remained an important factor in Bulgarian foreign policy and the largest bilateral donor. A USAID

---

[89] A. Todorov, *The Role of Political Parties.*
[90] A. Todorov, *The Role of Political Parties.*
[91] *Trud*, 3 May, 1996, p. 2.
[92] *Trud*, 10 January, 1997, p. 1–2.

regional program for emergency aid and support for the transition process was set up in 1990. In addition to assistance for free markets and private enterprise, the United States invested in the development and strengthening of democratic institutions – public administration, parliament, local governments, independent media, civil society, and political parties. Several of those programs helped sustain democracy in the country and contributed indirectly to the 1996–7 proreform campaign: support for the UDF, assistance to the Federation of Independent Student Associations, election and civic education including that through Podkrepa and Bulgarian Association for Free Elections and Civil Rights, preelection assessments, and international election-observer missions. UDF leaders found most valuable the transition-process assessments and the IRI's help with the basics of party functioning, political campaigning, and electoral processes.[93] In addition to training the UDF and its local chapters in campaign tactics, constituency building, issue identification, candidate recruitment, organizational structure, and communication strategies, the IRI also worked with the UDF and the MRF to organize a primary in 1996 in order to help unite the democratic opposition behind a single presidential candidate. In addition to such assistance, U.S. diplomats provided moral support to the opposition and firmly opposed further IMF loans while Videnov was in power.

Despite Bulgaria's dependence on the IMF since 1991, when the Lukanov cabinet stopped servicing the country's foreign debt, very few IMF-sponsored policy proposals were implemented. Even in 1996, when the survival of the BSP possibly hinged on the next IMF loan, Videnov stubbornly continued to reject all IMF conditions, until the very moment of his resignation in December 1996. Yet the IMF's role in the events of 1996–7 was important in several ways. The organization's lending decisions were interpreted by the public and used by the opposition as a referendum on Videnov's policies, and the mere withholding of funds accelerated the country's economic crisis, thus facilitating the BSP's collapse. Moreover, much like EU accession, IMF negotiations with Bulgaria created for the opposition coalition a blueprint for short-term economic reforms as well as an opportunity to challenge the BSP on its ability to implement them. The IMF further aided (intentionally or not) the opposition's claim to power by suggesting cabinet changes in some of the loan proposals and by declaring in January 1997 that it would negotiate the currency board after the election of a new, "stable" government.

If the West helped delegitimize the Left third way and assisted the UDF in credibly positioning itself within the increasingly attractive proreform and pro-Western space, it was the demonstration effects of popular mobilization in neighboring Serbia that convinced the opposition coalition's political elites to assume opposition leadership against the Left. The UDF had contacts in

---

[93] On the first point former president Zhelyu Zhelev, and on the second former prime minister Filip Dimitrov, cited in USAID, "Bulgarian Assessment Report."

Belgrade and was following the unfolding of the Serbian struggle. The comparison of the Serbian and Bulgarian protests convinced the Right that mass mobilization in the country had gathered enough momentum to overturn the Left. The UDF no longer worried that it would be caught up in protests with dwindling support.[94] The inspiration was strategic as well as tactical. The UDF began cooperating with the MRF and the unions, which changed the nature and scope of the campaign. The united opposition also called on its supporters to come to the streets and to remain there until the BSP conceded to early elections.

Moreover, student associations, also inspired by their Serbian counterparts, emerged as a third pillar of the campaign to mobilize demonstrators. However, in addition to the demonstration effect, diffusion was also in play for the student groups. In mid-January, a small delegation of Bulgarian student organizers visited Belgrade. As a result, the Bulgarian students imported many theatrical protest tactics such as blowing whistles at police or lining up young women holding flowers at the frontline to keep the protests peaceful. They further improved on these tactics by playing music at police cordons and acting out events such as the death of Bulgaria or the prime minister having coffee with protesters. Student groups also abandoned occupations in favor of blockades and combined them with marches throughout the capital to create a demonstration cascade.[95]

In sum, critical to the Left's rule, Western rhetoric and actions helped to discredit the third way. At the same time, through (EU and U.S.) assistance for marketization and through (EU and IMF) agreements that included clauses on economic liberalization, the West signaled its support for economic reform and the actors who uphold it. Moreover, the political conditions attached to those agreements also contained blueprints for such reform, which helped set the policy agenda for the opposition parties eager to cooperate. In addition, whereas European politicians and nongovernmental officials helped shape the Christian Democratic profile of the UDF, the United States invested in improving the party's organizational capacity. Finally, the most geographically immediate contributions to the success of the opposition campaign were the demonstration and diffusion effects of the Serbian opposition: from inspiring the Right to lead the struggle to offering a set of strategic and tactical innovations for the opposition coalition to carry the campaign to success.

CONCLUSION: THE BULGARIAN 1996–7 STRUGGLE IN THE CONTEXT
OF THE 1996–2007 DEMOCRATIZATION WAVES IN EASTERN EUROPE

To briefly summarize the 1996–7 events in Bulgaria: the antigovernment campaign was set in motion in the spring of 1996 by the country's macroeconomic crisis, which brought into active contradiction Socialist promises for reforms

---

[94] Interview with H.E. U.S. Ambassador to Bulgaria (1996–7) Avis Bohlen.
[95] Interview with a student leader at the time, Dimitar Bechev.

with low social costs (the so-called Bulgarian third way) and the resultant acute pauperization of the majority of Bulgarians. The disgruntled population appropriated union structures at the local, regional, and national levels to express their dissatisfaction with the Left's governance. The protests were quickly politicized: by the summer the unions were calling for a new Socialist cabinet. The reformers in the BSP began arguing for a redefinition of Bulgarian Socialism and the Right stepped in to escalate the protests in the hopes of achieving a turnover in power.

Even though the reform demands of internal, parliamentary, and civic opposition to the Socialists were implicitly supported by the conditions that the IMF attached to the much-needed macrostabilization loans, conservatives agreed to a few cabinet and party leadership changes but remained in control of the Socialist party. At this stage of the struggle, the opposition to the government was divided by different campaign goals (party reform, cabinet change, preterm elections) and disagreements on tactics (institutional or extrainstitutional). As a result, the internal opposition to the Socialists and their parliamentary opponents could not bring themselves to work together, and the civic and parliamentary oppositions cooperated with each other only sporadically. Still, such early experiments served to undermine the legitimacy of the Socialist third way and were a valuable rehearsal for later campaign activities.

In the next stage of the struggle, coordinated union protests subsided and the opposition parties turned their attention to the upcoming presidential elections. The UDF focused on articulating a credible alternative to the Socialist third way through the proreform and pro-Western campaign of their presidential candidate. With the help of their Western allies, the Right ran a strong campaign, casting their victory as a referendum on the Left's governance and as a sign of a growing popular (but not yet elite) consensus on their political vision for the future of the country.

The victory of the Right's presidential candidate, the deepening of the economic crisis in the late fall, and the refusal of the IMF to bail out the cabinet threw the Left into disarray. The cabinet's unwillingness and inability to manage the crisis brought all unions together in demanding preterm elections as the only solution to the country's economic problems. In addition, spontaneous protests and symbolic displays by individuals and small groups, expressing disapproval of the Left's governance, erupted throughout the country. Reassured of the West's moral and political support and emboldened by popular mobilization in neighboring Serbia, the Right focused popular discontent into a struggle for early parliamentary elections. Under UDF leadership, the unions, student groups, and opposition parties finally began working together to commit the country to reforms. The coalition contested the BSP's capacity to implement the much-needed short-term reforms suggested by the IMF for the economic stabilization of the country. The UDF also argued for a more long-term commitment to EU accession, including all the reforms membership requires – a policy alternative whose appeal was successfully pretested during the presidential elections.

In a desperate attempt to regain control over the party from behind the scenes and to appease internal, parliamentary, and civic opposition to the Socialists, the prime minister resigned in late December. As they had done in the past, the Socialists were hoping to wait the protests out and then to vote another Socialist cabinet in. In a strategy borrowed from neighboring Serbia, the antigovernment coalition threatened to protest every day until preterm elections were negotiated. The Socialists gave up their right to form a second Left cabinet after a month of countrywide protests and a national strike had paralyzed the country. The upcoming elections were to institutionalize the ideological bankruptcy of the Socialist third way and thus to allow for democratic consolidation through economic reform and EU accession.

The success of the Bulgarian case highlights the importance of several factors that seem crucial in struggles against illiberal incumbents throughout the region. Most important was the *strong opposition coalition* of political parties and civic groups working together toward democratic consolidation (through economic reform and EU accession). Those efforts began as loosely coordinated activities of different actors in different sectors within *civil and political society* to create the perception of an *unpopular regime* by linking the economic crisis to the corrupt and incompetent antireform Left governance. But it was only after all groups united behind the *compelling alternative* for political change, (re-)presented by the Right, that this broad coalition could translate popular *discontent into a mandate* for radical change (rather than just another turnover in power). Achieving this new consensus, which in effect shifted the balance of power to the Right, was facilitated by a second factor – the *weakness of the incumbent party* itself – internally divided, isolated from society, and unable to produce alternative self-image and policies.

Finally, a supporting role was also played by the Bulgarian *media*, which *facilitated popular mobilization* as well as *brokering regional diffusion*. The portrayal of protesters was mostly positive. It weakened the popularity of incumbents and created mobilization momentum. Moreover, some journalists were actively drawing parallels between the Bulgarian and the Serbian struggles and calling on the Right leaders to assume leadership. That helped embolden the political opposition and unite it with its civic counterpart, which in turn created a strong coalition that transcended narrow partisan interests and isolated civic efforts and that was able to act in the streets as well as within the established democratic institutions.

The Bulgarian case, although temporally linked to the cycle of electoral revolutions in the region, differed from them in several ways. Bulgaria is the only case in which democratization accomplishments were very high even before the struggle. Moreover, public protests did not accompany but demanded the elections that marked a turning point in the country's democratization trajectory. Mobilization occurred not in support of democratization but rather in protest against the economic crisis brought about by the antireform governance of the Left. The subsequent involvement of the IMF in the 1996–7 struggle was unique among the other cases in the 1996–2007 democratization waves in

Eastern Europe. Also, even if it was internally divided, the UDF was a single party representing the Right political space in Bulgaria, whereas in a majority of the other cases the Right was inhabited by different parties with little or no history of cooperation in an opposition movement against the ex-Communists. And in no other context were labor unions as prominent as they were in Bulgaria. Not only were the unions key in supplying protestors for the Bulgarian antigovernment coalition, but also their impressive political activism preceded and was crucial in allowing the Right political elites, long reluctant to assume leadership of the protests, to eventually do so.

Finally, as in other struggles against illiberal incumbents throughout the region, international and regional actors provided critical moral, material, and technical support, which contributed to discrediting the Left and legitimizing the Right. Borrowing *legitimacy for their agenda and/or credentials* from the West, and especially the EU, was important given the exhaustion of the Left partial reform and the lack of other viable international (or regional) ideological alternatives. The political and economic norms institutionalized in the EU served as a credible alternative to the current regime in Bulgaria. They presented the UDF with the opportunity to challenge the status quo with reference to the reforms required for EU accession and thus channel popular discontent into a commitment to well-defined promarket and prodemocratic long-term change. In Bulgaria as in some of the other Central and South East European cases, *domestic consensus* on EU membership increased the appeal and therefore the leverage of the Union and the intergovernmental and transnational networks associated with it. *Bulgaria's dependence* on the IMF presented a similar opportunity, but its impact was rather short-term; it was overshadowed by the implications of membership in the more proximate and more influential EU, which offered much greater benefits for the social, economic, and political development of the country.

The *domestic weakness* of the Left (unreformed) and the Right (inexperienced) increased the importance of international legitimation for both parties. However, it was their *parity* combined with the *ideological distance* of the Left from and the ideological acceptability of the Right to the West that allowed it some influence in the 1996–7 fundamental realignment in Bulgarian politics. Western party foundations were divided on whether to engage the BSP, which was struggling between socialism and social democracy, and the Socialists themselves were unevenly receptive to international assistance. The conservatives within the BSP only seriously considered complying with transnational pressures when accession was tangible in the early 2000s. At the same time, Western work on strengthening the ideological profile and the organizational capacity of the UDF were formative for the Right. Such international cooperation was facilitated and intensified by the UDF challenges to the Videnov government but also contributed to *positioning the Right favorably* to shift the power scales. However, this international investment paid off poorly in the long run, as the UDF could not survive after its exit from power but split on pragmatic grounds of expediency. It should also be noted that in the critical events in 1996–7, moral support from the Right's Western allies was important in *emboldening the UDF* to assume leadership of the protests, but it was probably the example of the more proximate Serbian struggle that clearly demonstrated to the UDF the historical potential of mass mobilization in their own backward and legitimated the use of extrainstitutional *strategies* to achieve this potential.

6

Defining and Domesticating the Electoral Model

A Comparison of Slovakia and Serbia

Valerie Bunce
Cornell University

Sharon Wolchik
George Washington University

A key theme in this book is that the spread of democracy in postcommunist Europe and Eurasia over the past two decades has taken place through two successive waves of political change that, although differing from one another in certain respects, share nonetheless one overarching commonality: a convergence between international and domestic support for democratic development.[1] The initial wave of democratic change in this region took place as communism and communist states were unraveling from 1989 to 1992, and it rested on the deployment of several approaches to breaking with authoritarian rule and building democratic orders – in particular, large-scale protests against communism and in support of democracy and/or the formation of pacts between authoritarians and democrats in order to guide a transition to democratic politics. This initial round of democratic change, although far from fully regional in its reach, generated nonetheless fully democratic polities in seven of the twenty-seven countries that made up the region at the time: Poland, Hungary, the Czech Republic, Slovenia, and the Baltic states. What advantaged these countries in particular with respect to democratization was the distinctive character of their communist-era legacies, that is, the ability of citizens and oppositions in these contexts to capitalize on the development during communism of a strong liberal (and often nationalist) opposition and the formation of a popular consensus around three key issues: rejection of the communist model of politics and economics, substitution of liberal political and economic regimes for this model, and integration with Western economic, political, and security institutions.[2]

---

[1] Valerie Bunce, "Rethinking Recent Democratization: Lessons from the Postcommunist Experience." *World Politics*, 55 (January 2003), pp. 167–92.

[2] Valerie Bunce, "The Political Economy of Postsocialism." *Slavic Review*, 58 (Winter 1999), pp. 756–93; Valerie Bunce, *Subversive Institutions: The Design and the Destruction of Socialism and the State* (New York: Cambridge University Press, 1999).

The second wave, which ran from the mid-1990s to 2004, had two distinct dynamics. Thus, this wave saw not only the solidifying of these early successes and change in other regimes, such as Bulgaria and Romania, where the transition from communism had produced more mixed political results (see, especially, the chapters by Vachudova, Mungiu-Pippidi, and Petrova in this volume)[3] but also the use of elections to oust semi-authoritarian leaders in several countries in the region. Here, the key factors were the incentives for domestic change prompted by the prospect of membership in the European Union and NATO, and the considerable investments in the development of democracy and capitalism provided by these Western-based international institutions. Again, the number of democracies in the region increased, but many of the regimes in the postcommunist area were left on the political sidelines. Thus, we still find in this period a large number of regimes that featured either democratic decline or continuity in authoritarian politics or in regimes that mixed authoritarian and democratic elements. However, a number of such regimes experienced democratic openings during this period.

It is this aspect of the second wave that is of interest in this chapter. Here, the focus was on converting elections nto opportunities for democratic change through the defeat of authoritarian leaders and the empowerment of the democratic opposition. This wave of electoral change followed a classic pattern of diffusion, wherein a new model using an ensemble of creative and demanding electoral strategies was developed in Bulgaria, Romania, and Slovakia and then exported to Croatia, Serbia, Georgia, and Ukraine.[4] Once again, although this wave added to the number of democracies in the region, it fell far short of moving all the remaining authoritarian and competitive authoritarian regimes into the democratic camp – even when popular protests after stolen elections pressured regimes to admit defeat or hold new elections.[5] Indeed, as the chapters by Radnitz, Stoner-Weiss, Silitski, and Way remind us, this wave also had the effect of putting authoritarian leaders in the region on guard, even in countries, such as Kyrgyzstan, where a long-serving leader had left office following a parliamentary election and public protests.

---

[3] Also see Milada Vachudova, *Europe Undivided: Democracy, Leverage and Integration after Communism*, (Oxford: Oxford University Press, 2005).

[4] Valerie Bunce and Sharon Wolchik, *American Democracy Promotion and Electoral Change in Postcommunist Europe and Eurasia* (2008); Valerie Bunce and Sharon Wolchik, "Democratizing Elections in the Postcommunist World: Definitions, Dynamics and Diffusion." *St. Antony's International Review*, 2, No. 2 (February 2007), pp. 64–89; Valerie Bunce and Sharon Wolchik, "Favorable Conditions and Electoral Revolutions," *Journal of Democracy*, 17 (October 2006), pp. 7–18; Valerie Bunce and Sharon Wolchik, "International Diffusion and Postcommunist Electoral Revolutions." *Communist and Postcommunist Studies*, 39, No. 3 (September 2006), pp. 283–304.

[5] Valerie Bunce and Sharon Wolchik, "Opposition versus Dictators: Explaining Divergent Election Outcomes in Post-communist Europe and Eurasia," In *Democratization by Elections*, Staffan Lindberg, ed. (Johns Hopkins University Press, 2009).

The purpose of this chapter is to explore this wave of democratic change by comparing two key participants: Slovakia and Serbia.[6] These cases are of interest for two reasons. First, like most instructive comparisons, this one features a combination of similarities and differences. For example, although both of these countries shifted in a decidedly democratic direction in response to pivotal elections held in 1998 and 2000, respectively, the course of their transitions before these electoral breakthroughs was rather different. Although Slovakia featured more competitive politics and more turnover in the years before the 1998 election, it experienced a decline in the quality of democracy as a result of the politics and policies of Vladimír Mečiar. In contrast, Serbia was governed by the same individual from 1989 to 2000, and it featured a competitive authoritarian regime that had become even more authoritarian in the years preceding the 2000 election.

Second, this comparison is illuminating because it helps us understand not just how democratic change can take place through elections, but also the more general question of how democracy diffuses within regions.[7] Thus, Slovakia and Serbia are of interest because of their role in developing, amending, applying, and sharing a distinctive and highly successful model of defeating dictators, empowering democratic oppositions, and thereby laying some of the groundwork for democratic change. This model combined such actions as forging a more united liberal opposition, building ties between oppositions and civil society groups, conducting sophisticated campaigns, expanding voter registration and turnout, and placing pressures on regimes to improve the quality of elections through such innovations as exit polls, parallel vote tabulation, and external and internal vote monitoring.[8] Although these activities are commonplace in established democracies, they were in fact unprecedented in Slovakia and Serbia.

---

[6] Although the state has been variously called Yugoslavia, the former Yugoslavia, and Serbia and Montenegro, it is in fact developments within Serbia that are of interest in this study – though Milošević, it is important to note, moved from being President of Serbia to being President of Yugoslavia in 1997 and the election of interest in 2000 was in fact an election for the presidency of the state as a whole, not Serbia. However, we will nonetheless refer primarily to Serbia in the analysis that follows. First, the central political actor in the federation is Serbia, given that this is precisely where Milošević focused most of his career and power (since 1986, when he became head of the Serbian party) and because Serbia contains an overwhelming majority of the population of Serbia and Montenegro. Second, both the timing and the approach to democratization were different in Montenegro than in Serbia, with Montenegro best understood as a sideshow to Serbian developments – though a sideshow that is in the process of becoming a sovereign state, depending upon the outcome of the referendum in summer 2006. Finally, it is fair to argue that there could be in effect no democratization in Serbia and Montenegro until politics underwent a dramatic shift in Serbia.

[7] See Daniel Brinks and Michael Coppedge, "Diffusion Is No Illusion: Neighbor Emulation in the Third Wave of Democracy." *Comparative Political Studies*, 39, No. 7 (September 2006), pp. 1–23.

[8] For elaboration, see Valerie Bunce and Sharon Wolchik, *American Democracy Promotion*, Chap. 4; Valerie Bunce and Sharon Wolchik, "Democratizing Elections."

What made this model particularly important was not just its success in clearing away important obstacles to democratic development in these two countries, but also the fact that it was easily transferred to new sites, such as Croatia in 2000, Georgia in 2003, and Ukraine in 2004.[9] Moreover, this model has a long lineage, having been applied first in the Philippines and Chile in 1986 and 1998, respectively, and it has been successfully deployed since that time in other countries, such as Lebanon and Madagascar. The model, in short, lends itself to diffusion, and this linkage helps us understand not just the third set of democratic changes within the postcommunist region, but also the more global understanding of the third wave outlined by McFaul in chapter one of this volume. As a result, this comparative case study provides insights into two questions left dangling in studies of the diffusion of democracy, that is, the nature of the innovation itself that sponsored democratic change, and the processes involved in moving democratic change from one political setting to others.[10]

Our comparison proceeds in three stages. We begin our analysis by setting the regime context within which these electoral challenges took place in Slovakia and Serbia. This comparison focuses on two issues: the origins and structure of authoritarian rule in the Mečiar and Milošević regimes and the evolution of these two regimes over time. We then turn to the development and evolution of the electoral model in 1998 in Slovakia and 2000 in Serbia. We conclude by discussing why these efforts succeeded, at least in the minimal, but nonetheless critical sense of producing a transition from illiberal to liberal governance.

SLOVAKIA AND SERBIA UNDER MEČIAR AND MILOŠEVIĆ

In some ways, Slovak politics under Mečiar and Serbian politics under Milošević resembled each other. Both states came into being (though both, especially Serbia, had historical antecedents as states) as the result of a two-step process. One was the accumulating costs over time of ethnofederation under communism – for example, the tendency of this form of state to create in its constituent republics both nations and states in the making and to create a chain of dependencies, both economic and political, between each republic and the center, rather than among the republics. As a consequence, over time republics followed increasingly varied political and economic trajectories; competed with one another for the support or control of the central, federal government; and found it easy to develop resentments about their status within the ethnofederal state and the payoffs of state membership.[11] All of these effects were exaggerated by economic frustrations and the short-term opportunities for changes in regimes and state boundaries as a consequence of expanding

---

[9] Bunce and Wolchik, *American Democracy Promotion*; and see the chapters by Welt and McFaul.

[10] See Brinks and Coppedge, *Diffusion Is No Illusion*.

[11] Bunce, *Subversive Institutions*.

debates throughout the communist area in the second half of the 1980s about the future and form of political and economic liberalization. These debates, not surprisingly, played out differently in the constituent republics of Yugoslavia, while dividing and weakening the party and state apparatus at the center. In Czechoslovakia, where the political system remained far more repressive and rigid, it was only in the last two years of communist rule that experts and intellectuals could begin to discuss reform again. Although Czechoslovakia was ostensibly a federation, the center in fact held most of the power; Slovak dissatisfaction with the perceived neglect of Slovak interests was thus added to the general discontent with the communist system. As a consequence, the transition from communism in both Yugoslavia and Czechoslovakia created a combustible combination of political struggles within the republics over the nation, the state, and the regime, and the agenda of transition in both Serbia and Slovakia included not just the familiar choices between liberal and illiberal political and economic regimes and between rule by the communists and the opposition, but also between an expansive and a narrow definition of the nation and between existing state boundaries and republican sovereignty.[12]

The struggles over nation, state, and regime divided what had been in fact a relatively large liberal opposition in Serbia during the communist era and a much smaller group of liberal intellectuals and more traditional, nationalist, Catholic lay leaders in Slovakia. These issues created, as a result, an opportunity for enterprising communist politicians, whether at the top of the party or at lower levels, to seize upon nationalism as a way either to maintain power (in Serbia) or to gain power (in Slovakia) through nationalist and populist appeals and, perhaps more importantly, through the division, cooptation, and demobilization of both other communist elites and the liberal opposition.[13]

Thus, although in fact exceptional in the postcommunist region (in contrast to widespread assumptions), both Mečiar and Milošević became the prototype of the proverbial communists who became nationalists. They accumulated power and avoided liberal reforms (or, in Slovakia, amended those in place) by pursuing an agenda that played on the economic frustrations of the public and that, at the same time, played up threats to the nation, used minority populations as scapegoats, and created among many elites and publics a "bunker" mentality, given increasingly conflictual relations with their neighbors, minorities, and the West. In the Serbian case this conflict involved the aggressive use of military power and violence to challenge existing borders. The appeal to nationalism was more overt in Serbia than in Slovakia, where Mečiar, although posing as a champion of the neglected interests of Slovakia, was outflanked on the right by a small but very vocal extreme nationalist party, the Slovak National Party. Thus, although trumpeting the need to take

---

[12] And in the Serbian case, the boundaries of the new state.

[13] See especially Valere Philip Gordon. *The Myth of Ethnic War: Serbia and Croatia in the 1990s* (Ithaca: Cornell University Press, 2004).

Slovakia's particular history and needs into account in decision-making at the federal level, Mečiar did not call openly for the disintegration of the common state until he and Klaus negotiated its end after the June 1992 elections.[14]

However, the game Mečiar and Milošević pursued was even more complex.[15] They combined these appeals, attacks, and policies with a politics that, despite tolerating regular, competitive elections and some civil liberties (far more extensive in Slovakia), nonetheless took advantage of constitutional loopholes while increasing the political and economic dependency of parliament and thereby weakened its powers, centralized their own executive powers, and amended the constitution and laws in ways that divided and weakened those who would challenge them, from within or outside the official political arena.[16]

If these regimes had similar logics, however, they diverged from one another in two important respects. Czechoslovakia had an early and clear-cut break with the communist past as a result of the overwhelming victory of the Civic Forum and Public against Violence in the 1990 elections and the economic reforms that quickly followed. By contrast, the Serbian elections of 1990 provided no such break with the past – in terms of the specific parties or the individuals who emerged victorious or the economic agenda that followed. Moreover, whereas in the following years Slovakia had turnovers in government that led to several single terms for Mečiar and his ouster by parliament for a period in 1994, Serbia experienced remarkable governmental continuity. Milošević came to power in 1986 as head of the Serbian League of Communists and stayed in power under various guises for fourteen more years. During those years, he survived a remarkable number of threats, including no less than six national or federal elections from 1990 to 1998 (and a number of local elections); the violent dissolution of the Yugoslav state; protracted wars in Croatia and Bosnia–Herzegovina; the Dayton Peace Accords of 1995; Serbian attacks on Kosovo; NATO bombing in 1999; and the end of authoritarian politics in Croatia in early 2000. Moreover, under Milošević's direction, by

---

[14] See Martin Bútora and Zora Bútoro, "Slovakia after the Split." *Journal of Democracy*, 4, No. 2 (April 1993); Michael Kraus and Allison Stanger, *Irreconcilable Differences? Explaining Czechoslovakia's Dissolution*, (New York: Rowman & Littlefield, 2000); Sharon Wolchik, "The Politics of Ethnicity in Post-Communist Czechoslovakia." *East European Politics and Societies*, 8 (December 1993), 153–88.

[15] See for example Dusan Pavlovic, *Akteri I modeli: Ogledi o politici u Srbiji pod Milosevic* (Belgrade: B92, 2001); Dusan Pavlovic, "Serbia during and after Milosevic." Unpublished manuscript, September 27, 2004; Dusan Pavlovic, "Polaricacija stranackog system a nakon 2000 godine." In *Politicke stranke u Srbiji. Struktura I funkcionisanje*, Zoran Lutovac, ed. (Belgrade: Friedrich Ebert Stiftung/Institut drustvenih nauka, 2005); Damjan de Krnjevic-Miskovic, "Serbia's Prudent Revolution." *Journal of Democracy*, 12, No. 3 (July 2001), pp. 96–110; Sarah Birch, "The 2000 Elections in Yugoslavia: The 'Bulldozer' Revolution." *Electoral Studies*, 1 (2002), pp. 473–533.

[16] On the importance of strong legislatures for democratization, see M. Steven Fish, *Democracy Derailed in Russia. The Failure of Open Politics* (Cambridge: Cambridge University Press, 2005).

2000 the Serbian economy had shrunk to approximately forty percent of its size a decade earlier – a feat only equaled in the region by Georgia and Moldova.[17] By contrast, Slovak economic performance under Mečiar was, especially by the standards of the region, relatively robust. However, the dislocations produced by the shift to the market and the decline in production and incomes in the early postcommunist period were significantly greater in Slovakia than in the Czech lands. Unemployment rates in Slovakia were thus several times higher than those in the Czech lands in the early to mid 1990s. Foreign direct investment also lagged. As the 1998 election approached, it became clear that Slovakia was no longer on the fast track to EU membership and its anticipated benefits, largely due to the illiberal, antidemocratic actions of the Mečiar government.[18]

These differences in leadership tenure, regime continuity from communism to postcommunism, foreign policy, and domestic economic performance translated, not surprisingly, into differences in the nature of the Milošević and Mečiar regimes. Two distinctions are critical here. One is that the peaceful breakup of Czechoslovakia compared to the violent end of Yugoslavia (and the central role of the Serbian leadership in that process) meant that, whereas Slovakia never left Europe, Serbia did. Although former U.S. Secretary of State Madeline Albright once noted that Slovakia was in danger of becoming the black hole of Europe, the United States and Western Europe continued to be engaged with and active in Slovakia, particularly with the NGO community, but also with the government. Western leverage in Slovakia was thus far greater than it was in Serbia – a situation exaggerated by the incompetence of the West in dealing with the wars in Yugoslavia and the peculiar consequences of Dayton in both legitimating ethnic cleansing in Bosnia and raising the stature of Milošević.

Mečiar also had to operate within a far more liberalized and more institutionalized democratic environment than Milošević – though Milošević did adhere, where convenient, to the 1990 Serbian Constitution (which he had in effect written). In practice, this meant that, rather than just playing at the margins of the political rules, Milošević was more free to change them when he needed to do so. Milošević also went much further than Mečiar in combining the power generated by his formal roles as President of Serbia and then Yugoslavia, and his institutional ties, as a result, to the police, the security apparatus, the Socialist Party, and the military – with informal powers based upon chains of dependency that radiated out from him – including his family (his wife was in Parliament until 2003), the Serbian mafia, and the heads of banks and enterprises. Serbia was still a socialist economy, and the war plus

---

[17] Valerie Bunce and Sharon Wolchik, *American Democracy Promotion*, Chap. 6; Boris Begovic, *Post-Conflict Reconstruction of Serbia: A Political Economic View*, (Washington, DC: Center for International Political Economy, 2005); Birch, "The 2000 Elections in Yugoslavia."

[18] For an analysis of the impact of potential EU membership in Slovakia, see Milada Vachudova, *Europe Undivided: Democracy, Leverage and Integration after Communism*, (Oxford: Oxford University Press, 2005).

Western sanctions generated market dynamics that gave considerable power to those who could control and manipulate shortages, capitalize on weak state boundaries, and dominate illegal trade.[19] These dynamics, the sheer duration of Milošević's rule, and the impact of the wars and sanctions translated, not surprisingly, into an economic tailspin, hyperinflation, and extraordinarily high levels of corruption. Milošević was both the cause of these externalities and, ironically, their primary beneficiary.

In sum, on the eve of their ousters, the Milošević regime was more authoritarian, less constrained by other institutions, far more aggressive and isolated in external terms, and far more corrupt and violent than the Mečiar regime. However, there were nonetheless always pockets (hard-won and hard-maintained) of political autonomy in Serbia, including some independent media; an active, if beleaguered civil society; and elections that, surprisingly enough, remained competitive and became more competitive over time.[20] Perhaps most importantly, outbreaks of public protest were a consistent feature of the Milošević era – especially in Belgrade, where Milošević was consistently unpopular throughout his rule. Each round of protests left traces of popular resentments about his violations of accepted political norms (and these became more extreme over time); lessons for the opposition to apply in the future; and new recruits to the opposition (such as new generations of young people and people living in small and medium-sized towns).[21]

These costs became particularly pronounced when Milošević's regime became more hardline, beginning in 1997 and continuing throughout 2000 right up to the September election. Between May and August 2000, more than one thousand members of Otpor (Resistance), the Serbian youth movement, were arrested, including some as young as thirteen. These actions made Milošević appear toward the end of his rule to be a leader who was both desperate and despotic.

Milošević, like Mečiar, also began to face serious international constraints. The Open Society had played a critical role in Serbia since the early 1990s, but it did so largely alone until 1999 – when, for example, support by the National Endowment for Democracy jumped threefold, with an additional fifty percent increase the following year.[22] Finally, if the duration of Milošević's rule was helpful to the survival of his regime in some respects, it was harmful in others. It is a cliché that long-serving authoritarian regimes are undermined by

[19] See Peter Andreas, "Criminalizing Consequences of Sanctions: Embargo Busting and Its Legacy," *International Studies Quarterly*, 49, No. 2 (June 2005), pp. 335–60.

[20] See Vitali Silitski, "The Long Road from Tyranny: Post-communist Authoritarianism and Struggle for Democracy in Serbia and Belarus," Unpublished book manuscript, 2005; Bunce and Wolchik, *American Democracy Promotion*, Chap. 6.

[21] Also see Mladen Lazić and Liljana Nikolić, *Protest in Belgrade: Winter of Discontent* (Budapest: Central European University Press, 1999); Valere Philip Gordon, *The Myth of Ethnic War*.

[22] See especially Freedom House, *Freedom House Support to Free and Fair Elections in Serbia*, (Belgrade: Freedom House, 2005); and see Bunce and Wolchik, "International Diffusion and Postcommunist Electoral Revolutions."

growing corruption and isolation from critical feedback about their support and performance. However, this cliché applies to the last years of the Milošević regime.

Even toward the end of his rule, however, Milošević could still rely on some formidable assets. These included his ability to situate himself in the ideological middle (conveniently flanked by the extremist Seselj on the one hand, and on the other, by moderate nationalists, such as Vuk Drašković, and the liberal opposition, including a sizeable antiwar movement). This allowed him to sell himself as a compromise candidate who, nonetheless, was protecting the Serbian nation – a stance that was aided, for example, by the radicalization of politics in Kosovo, the seeming stability of the authoritarian regime in Croatia, and the actions of the West, including sanctions and the 1999 bombing, which led to a sizeable, although temporary increase in his popular support. He was also, almost to the end of his rule, exceedingly successful in preventing defections from the ruling circle and coopting, compromising, and dividing the opposition. The latter successes made it hard for voters to support the opposition – because so many members were compromised, so many protests had failed, and many citizens assumed that their votes could not lead to an actual change in government. Finally, Milošević was able to protect his power by practicing a relatively soft form of authoritarianism (though it became harder the last three years of his reign), while avoiding running for office (he only did so twice) and exploiting the difficulties of the European Union in particular in carrying out a consistent foreign policy that challenged his right and capacity to both rule and wage war.

Vladimír Mečiar's situation on the eve of the 1998 elections differed from that of Milošević in a number of ways. In contrast to Milošević, who achieved his position by manipulating the electoral process to mask his real source of power as head of the former communist party with the trappings of elected office, Mečiar emerged onto the national political scene in the context of the Velvet Revolution of 1989 when his later opponents in the liberal opposition put him forth as prime minister of the government that Public against Violence formed in 1990. He soon (in April 1991) quarreled with his former allies and founded his own movement, which twice (in June 1992 and September/October 1994) gained the most votes in free and fair elections. But, although Mečiar remained the dominant figure on the Slovak political scene for almost a decade, by the 1998 elections, he faced an opposition that had learned a lesson from its failure to unite for the elections in 1994 after forcing Mečiar to temporarily leave the position of prime minister and forming a broad coalition government that ruled for several months. In addition, Mečiar faced an NGO community that was unusually self-organized and cohesive. Due in part to Mečiar's dominance of the sphere of partisan politics and in part to the energy and organizational abilities of some of the third sector's dominant personalities, the NGO community attracted many of the most active and democratically oriented leaders in Slovakia. By the late 1990s, the community had a *Gremium*, or coordinating committee, that included representatives of all of the main sectors of NGO activity and an established tradition of yearly conferences. It also could rely on longstanding ties of friendship that, in some cases, stretched back to common participation in the para-opposition groups and activities of the communist period. Facing frequent verbal attacks by the government and hampered in its activities by laws designed to restrict its activities and influence, the third sector in Slovakia was well equipped to play a role in mobilizing opposition to Mečiar in 1998. Its leaders were also very well connected in the West and skilled in dealing with international donors and other supporters.

At the same time, however, Mečiar had a stable core of well-disciplined supporters who could be counted on to vote for him. Largely older, less educated, and rural, these voters could be expected to be resistant to calls for change, whether couched in terms of the need to restore democratic politics or the need to ensure Slovakia's integration into European and Euro-Atlantic institutions. Mečiar also had considerable influence in the police and security forces and controlled much of the media. Although his flagrant abuses of power were not as frequent or as costly as the genocide Milošević set in motion, Mečiar also engaged in his share of dirty tricks and antidemocratic behaviors, ranging from the kidnapping of then President Kováč's adult son and his transport across the border into Austria, where he was wanted for fraud, and the firebombing of the car of the main inspector investigating this incident, to sporadic harassment of political opponents. He also used his power in Parliament to attempt to manipulate the election by creating a single electoral district in Slovakia and increasing the percentage of the vote needed by coalitions to seat deputies in Parliament, among other actions.

By the late 1990s, these behaviors, as well as the manipulation of the privatization process to favor Mečiar's cronies and the restrictive policies his government adopted toward the sizeable Hungarian minority, resulted in increasingly clear signals from the West that Mečiar had become a liability to Slovakia. The demarches of the United States and other governments and assessments by EU and NATO officials made it obvious to the informed public that Mečiar's reelection would very likely result in Slovakia's exclusion from these organizations and isolation within Europe.

Thus, on the eve of the decision to hold parliamentary elections in Slovakia in 1998 and presidential and parliamentary elections in rump Yugoslavia in 2000, there were some good reasons to expect that, although vulnerable in certain respects, both the Mečiar and Milošević regimes would be able to withstand challenges to their power. Indeed, for Milošević, this was a rational assumption, given, for example, the brevity of opposition collaboration in 1996 to 1997. Thus, when Milošević engineered constitutional changes for the direct, rather than indirect election of the President of Yugoslavia (which he had become through parliamentary voting in 1997) in the summer of 2000 and then called for early presidential and parliamentary elections to take place in late September 2000, he was proceeding from the logical assumption that the opposition would have too little time to prepare for an election, and that he would benefit by holding elections before the winter came, with its promise of unusually severe heating shortages.[23] However, like Mečiar, Milošević miscalculated. To understand why, we turn to an analysis of the electoral model of regime change as it was developed and applied in the Slovak and the Serbian cases.

THE ELECTORAL MODEL

Several premises underlie the electoral model of regime change. One is that elections in authoritarian settings provide a contradiction between unaccountable power and power derived from public support.[24] Second, elections are a global norm, even more than other aspects of democracy. Citizens resent elections being stolen, especially when they are exposed to clear differences between the official tabulation and tabulations offered by other, more trusted groups. Although vote fraud can demobilize voters, it can also generate strong resentments when the alternative vote count comes before the official one, election commissions and courts issue ever-changing rulings (as they did in Serbia), and there is other evidence of fraud, such as knowledge of how others voted, extreme media attacks on the opposition during the campaign, and voter intimidation. Finally, elections are useful devices for producing regime change because they occur within a short span of time, ask little of citizens, encourage them to think about their future, and provide a moment when the reality of political rights and choices and the legitimacy of the regime are all put to a visible and quantifiable test.[25]

From the vantage point of American electoral politics, the electoral model of democratization seems largely a matter of "politics as usual." However, it was new to both of these countries, and it rested in practice on a number of key factors often in short supply, even in the United States: optimism, extraordinarily hard work, innovative ideas, and considerable planning and coordination. To understand how the electoral model played out, however, we need to focus, first, on developments that occurred prior to the campaign season. These include the long-term expansion of civil society, which was aided in part by the international community. As noted above, civil society was far more developed in Slovakia than in Serbia, in part because Slovakia was more

---

[23] On his addiction to elections, see especially Pavlovic, *Akteri I modeli*. Ellen Lust-Okar (2004a, 2004b) also argues, for a different part of the world, that authoritarian leaders use elections as a way of estimating the distribution of power among their allies and enemies, the utility of certain networks, and future payoffs.

[24] See Andreas Schedler, "The Nested Game of Democratization by Elections," *International Political Science Review*, 23 (2002), pp. 103–22; Andreas Schedler, ed., *Electoral Authoritarianism: The Dynamics of Unfree Competition*, (Boulder, CO: Lynne Rienner, 2006); Mark R. Thompson and Philipp Kuntz, "Stolen Elections: The Case of the Serbian October." *Journal of Democracy*, 15, No. 4 (2004), pp. 159–72.

[25] Also see Joshua Tucker, "Enough! Electoral Fraud, Collective Action Problems, and the Second Wave of Post-Communist Democratic Revolutions," *Perspectives on Politics* (September 2007), pp. 537–53; Mark Beissinger, "Structure and Example in Modular Political Phenomena: The Diffusion of Bulldozer, Rose, Orange and Tulip Revolutions," *Perspectives on Politics* (June 2007), pp. 259–76.

democratic than Serbia and participation in the work of civil society groups was thus less risky, in part because of the longer-term investment of the international community in Slovak democracy, and in part because of the constraints on such developments in Serbia, especially between 1997 and 2000.[26]

Previous rounds of elections, which gave the opposition electoral experience, confidence, and sometimes even office, were also important. Zoran Ðinđić, for example, was elected mayor of Belgrade – though he was deposed by Milošević and Drašković – and both Ðinđić and Koštunica served in the parliament from 1990 to 1997. The Slovak opposition succeeded in ousting Mečiar as prime minister and formed a broad coalition government for several months in 1994. Defeats in previous elections, as in Slovakia in the fall of 1994, also illustrated to the opposition the political costs of their lack of unity. Finally, earlier elections produced, especially in Serbia, previous rounds of political protest and growing knowledge about the falsification of election results and the methods used to carry out election fraud.

There are also some medium-term influences that foreshadow the application of the electoral model. These include exploitation of media openings, which was more difficult in Serbia, given the crackdown on some opposition papers and the radio station, B-92; building cooperative ties among a dispirited opposition divided along both personal and ideological lines and with an elite culture resistant to compromise for the sake of winning power; developing public opinion polling, which was relatively sophisticated in both Slovakia and Serbia and documented clearly that the regime was vulnerable; and expanding both the generational and the geographical reach of the opposition. Earlier elections produced, especially in Serbia, previous rounds of political protest and growing knowledge about the methods used to carry out election fraud. A strong performance in the local elections in 1996, the impact of three months of protests thereafter, and clear evidence of fraud in these elections and in two subsequent elections before 2000 helped bring the Serbian opposition together; gave them some practice in carrying out campaigns, voter registration, and electoral monitoring; and provided publics with a sense that the regime in fact might be vulnerable, that it was certainly corrupt, that votes mattered, and that the opposition, as a result, had the potential to win elections and perhaps even political power. In Slovakia, cooperation in several nationwide actions, including the failed referendum in 1997 on NATO membership, helped the NGO community coalesce.

The most distinctive example of these dynamics common to both Serbia and Slovakia was the rise of large numbers of young people committed to political change. Otpor in Serbia originated in 1998 when students organized in opposition to educational reforms that threatened to end the autonomy of Serbian universities. By 2000 Otpor had approximately 30,000 to 40,000

---

[26] See, for example, Robert Herman, "NGO Sustainability in a Time of Hope and Apprehension," in *The NGO Sustainability Index for Central and Eastern Europe and Eurasia*, USAID, ed. (Washington, DC: USAID, May 2005).

activists and approximately 120 branches throughout Serbia – despite a significant crackdown throughout 2000. Otpor played a pivotal role, not just
in exposing the weakness of the regime through street theater, concerts, rallies, and an unusually large-scale distribution of pamphlets, posters, and other
materials that mocked the regime and in reaching out to very young people
throughout the country, but also in pressing the opposition to work together
and to focus on a leader who could win. Otpor also brought in substantial
new supporters for the cause of ending the Milošević era, such as pensioners,
union members, and even portions of the military and the police, as well as
citizens from smaller towns. Otpor received the support of the Serbian Orthodox Church, which had been a clear supporter of the Milošević regime since
its beginning. In Slovakia, young people played a key role in the march across
Slovakia, which the opposition used to get their message to voters in light of
media manipulation by Mečiar. They also worked with the Rock the Vote campaign, which, together with other actions of OK98 (Citizens' Campaign 98),
resulted in an eighty percent turnout rate of first-time voters, a key element of
the opposition's victory.

This leads us to short-term dynamics: the electoral campaigns. Two developments here were crucial: the formation of a coalition of opposition parties and
massive get-out-the-vote campaigns carried out by NGOs.[27] In Serbia, no less
than eighteen parties in Serbia united (though five candidates did run for the
Presidency), and in Slovakia, seven "parties" (many of which were themselves
coalitions of parties). In Serbia, the remarkable decision by Zoran Đinđić to
drop out of the contest (despite heading the largest party within the coalition)
and support Koštunica, who public opinion pools showed was the more popular opposition candidate, was a critical step. In Slovakia, conflict over which
established party leader should lead the coalition was resolved through the
choice, which would prove to be inspired given his youth and charisma, of
Mikulas Dzurinda, a second-level official of one of the coalition's parties.

Once the opposition succeeded in coming together in both Slovakia and
Serbia, the electoral model went into full gear. Actions included significant voter
registration and mobilization drives, given considerable financial support by
Freedom House and others, to encourage first-time voters, who were known to
have anti-Mečiar attitudes, in Slovakia, and voters in areas outside of Belgrade
and members of women's groups, in Serbia. Pressure was also put on the
regimes to open up the media to the opposition (which meant in practice
relying primarily on the independent media in both Slovakia and Serbia and
on the "pamphlet and poster" mania that had served the Bulgarian opposition
so well in 1996–7) and to improve the quality of voter lists, and on central
election commissions to be more representative in their membership, tighten up
their procedures, and be more transparent. NGOs and the political opposition
also distributed campaign materials that advertised the costs of the incumbent

---

[27] See Valerie Bunce (with Sharon Wolchik), "Getting Real about Real Causes: A Reply to Lucan
Way." *Journal of Democracy*, No. 20, (2009).

regime and attempted to empower voters by assuring them that their ballots were critical.

Opposition leaders also engaged in campaigns that were far more ambitious than in the past or those of the incumbents. In Slovakia, the newly formed Slovak Democratic Coalition's leaders held hosts of face to face meetings with voters organized by NGOs; its leader and the future Prime Minister, Mikulas Dzurinda, also bicycled through Slovakia. And, in contrast to the situation in the 1994 elections, members of the coalition remained united throughout the campaign, despite their very real differences in policies in many areas. In Serbia there was a sharp contrast between the one-week campaign by Milošević in a few towns, coupled with a short-term priming of goods in the stores, and Koštunica's much longer campaign throughout Serbia – a style of politicking that was new to the behavior of both liberal and illiberal candidates in Serbian elections.

There were also very ambitious get-out-the-vote campaigns before and on election day – which led to record turnouts in both Slovakia (an increase from seventy-five percent in 1994 to eighty-four percent in 1998) and Serbia (from sixty-seven percent in the previous election to seventy-five percent). In Slovakia, these activities were carried out as part of a citizens' campaign, OK98, organized by leaders of the third sector. This campaign, which was conceptualized over the Christmas 1997 holiday and initiated in March 1998, coordinated and supported individual actions by a multitude of NGOs. Ranging from the hosting of citizens' meetings with candidates from a variety of political parties to the distribution of literature emphasizing the rights of citizens in a democracy to actions, including rock concerts in the squares of large cities and media campaigns to make voting "cool." Directed toward youth, these activities heightened the salience of the elections. Although the campaign's leaders and spokespersons scrupulously maintained that they were acting in a neutral, nonpartisan manner, there were close links between the leadership of the campaign and the opposition coalition, and it was clear that increased voter turnout would benefit the opposition, given the stability of Mečiar's voter base.

The activities of civil society groups were coupled in both countries with measures focused specifically on highlighting any irregularities in the vote. These included rapid tabulation of votes, often advertised repeatedly during election day through, for example, press conferences; election monitoring (only internal in Serbia and organized in sophisticated fashion by CeSID, the Center for Free Elections and Democracy); and extensive use of parallel vote tabulation, which provided a comparative standard against which "official" results could be contrasted.[28] In Serbia, polling stations had long been required by law to post the number of votes outside the station. CeSID then allocated workers

---

[28] See Larry Garber and Glenn Cowan, "The Virtues of Parallel Vote Tabulations," *Journal of Democracy*, 4 (April 1993), pp. 95–107; Zoran Lukic, Nebojsa Vasiljevic, and Dragisa Bjeloglav, *Iskustvo parallelnog prebrojavanja glasova* (Belgrade: CeSID, 2002).

to every constituency to phone in the numbers, thereby making it harder for vote fraud to occur through the last-minute generation of new ballots. CeSID activists, who were very worried about turnout by the late afternoon of voting day, were also able to send volunteers to targeted constituencies very quickly to get out the vote. This turned out to be critical, because the margin of victory for Koštunica was barely over fifty percent, and fifty percent plus one was required for election in this first round of a two-round system.

Finally, in Serbia in particular, the opposition prepared for public protests in the likely event that the regime lost, but refused to vacate office. This preparation built on popular mobilization and protest techniques used in the past and on training during the election period (albeit uneven) in techniques for nonviolent struggle.[29] Preparations for protest also capitalized on linkages already made outside the capital and large cities – through the campaign and through the work of civil society organizations.

Despite minor irregularities in certain localities, election monitors and international election monitoring groups judged the 1998 Slovak elections to be free and fair. Although Mečiar had tried to manipulate the results of the elections in numerous ways prior to the elections, including new legislation that hindered the opposition, passed one month before the elections, he did not resort to blatant fraud on election day. He also accepted the outcome of the elections once they were held. His concession speech, though delayed and very emotional, left no doubt that he would leave office peacefully once a new government was formed. There was thus no need for his opponents in Slovakia to take to the streets – except to celebrate. Mečiar's actions undoubtedly reflected the more constrained nature of public life in Slovakia than in Serbia under Milošević. They may have also reflected the fact that, although his government had engaged in actions that violated the spirit and at times the letter of Slovak law as well as democratic norms, Mečiar was not, as Milošević was, facing the threat of being indicted for war crimes and delivered to The Hague by his political successors.

In Serbia, the Milošević regime did not give up as easily. In the face of widespread election fraud and manipulation, the opposition turned to street protests. The success of such protests depended upon many of the factors we have discussed above, but also included the ease of moving from a celebration of victory into demonstrations demanding recognition of that victory. It also reflected another very important development: conversations during the campaign between opposition groupings and security forces (facilitated by well-established linkages between Otpor and members of the military and the security apparatus) that reminded the police and the military that they had also paid dearly for the actions of the regime. The security forces, even when pressed by the regime to act against protesters, backed off from repression at two key

---

[29] See Peter Ackerman and Jack Duvall, *A Force More Powerful: A Century of Nonviolent Conflict*, (New York: Palgrave, 2000); Thomas Carothers, *Critical Missions: Essays on Democracy Promotion*, (Washington, DC: Carnegie Endowment, 2004).

stages: when the miners in Kolabara went on strike (protected by the quick mobilization of citizens) in reaction to Milošević's declaration of victory, and a week and a half later, when hundreds of thousands of people from throughout Serbia converged on the Parliament in Belgrade to bring an end to the Milošević era.[30]

All of these developments – including the creation of a unified opposition, sophisticated campaigning, voter registration and voter turnout drives, and even preparations for political protest – were aided by the support of the United States, Canada, Japan, and several European countries. This occurred both through institutionalized channels, such as Freedom House, the National Endowment for Democracy, the Foundation for a Civil Society, the Open Society Fund, the National Democratic Institute, and the International Republican Institute, the Westminister Foundation for Democracy, the British Know How Fund, The Foundation for the Support of Civic Activities funded by the EU, the Canada Fund for Slovakia, the Sasakawa Peace Foundation, the Jan Hus Educational Foundation, and the Carpathian Foundation, and more informally – in particular, through the actions of the ambassadors to these countries.[31] Although such assistance is common to most of the successful uses of the electoral model in the postcommunist region, it is important to remember that both the United States and the Europeans (though the latter were less engaged) had become strongly committed by 1997 and 1999, respectively, to ending the Mečiar and Milošević regimes.

WHY DID THESE EFFORTS SUCCEED?

Why did these two applications of the electoral model of regime changes succeed – at least in the minimal sense of ending authoritarian rule and bringing liberal oppositions into power? A full answer to this question requires a systematic comparison between successful and nonsuccessful uses of the model. This is an issue we have addressed in other work.[32] However, we can nonetheless highlight some factors as critical to the democratic outcomes in Slovakia and Serbia.

One is the fact that both Serbia and Slovakia, despite the contrasts between Mečiar and Milošević, were the "right" types of regime for the electoral model to be applied successfully, that is, competitive authoritarian regimes.[33] Such regimes typically hold regular, though often not free and fair, elections in which the opposition, although disadvantaged, is able to participate. Such regimes are repressive enough to invite public resentment, but liberal enough to be open to the development of an opposition. The tensions inherent in such regimes also

---

[30] Milan Stoyan Protich, *Izneverena revolutiutsija: 5 Oktobar 2000*, (Belgrade: Chigoya, 2005).
[31] The U.S. embassy was closed in Serbia after the 1999 bombing, but the Canadian embassy functioned as a substitute.
[32] Bunce and Wolchik, *American Democracy Promotion*; "Opposition versus Dictators."
[33] See the chapter by Way in this volume.

make it far easier for incumbents to miscalculate; supporters to defect; and oppositions and citizens to transform symbolic exercises into competitive ones.

On a less theoretical level, the elections held in 1998 and 2000 occurred when the incumbents, although still resourceful, were nonetheless vulnerable. The costs of the Milošević and Mečiar regimes, although different in certain respects, were nonetheless increasing, and there was evidence that their ability to control their allies and political outcomes and to deliver results to important constituencies was declining. Indeed, it is striking how public opinion data for both countries on the eve of the pivotal elections suggested that the nationalist and populist games played by Mečiar and Milošević were resonating less and less with either their allies or the citizenry.

There are a number of factors beyond regime context, more short-term in nature and less common, that help opposition groups to carry out successful ousters of autocrats using the electoral model. One key consideration is the mounting cost of authoritarian rule and a pattern of increasing violation of social and political norms. Given secure jobs, privileged access to economic resources, and insulation from feedback (especially negative) about their performance, authoritarian leaders can become both corrupt and careless – which invites public resentment and defections from the ruling circle. In the Serbian case, for example, Milošević ignored trends in earlier elections with respect to his popularity and the commitment and capacity of the opposition to defeat him, and he underestimated the power of two NGOs in particular: Otpor and CeSID. In Slovakia, Mečiar was also vulnerable because U.S. and European leaders had made it clear that Slovakia would not be considered for NATO or EU membership so long as he was prime minister.

Vulnerable regimes can endure, however, if both civil society and the opposition are demobilized. Other factors that contributed to the successful use of the electoral model in these two cases include the gradual, but sustained growth in the size and diversity of civil society; the accumulation of experience, both negative and positive, by opposition groups through earlier rounds of mobilization, protest, and success in local elections; and cooperation among various elements of the opposition that lasted through the election period and allowed them to mount a serious campaign that convinced publics to participate and register their dissatisfaction with the regime, encourage institutional supporters of the regime either to maintain their distance or to defect, and prepare for protests should the incumbents or their designated successors try to steal the election.

Change in the behavior of the opposition as it moves from fragmentation to unity is obviously key here, but also the hardest piece to put into place.[34]

---

[34] See Marc Marje Howard and Philip G. Roessler, "Liberalizing Electoral Outcomes in Competitive Authoritarian Regimes." *American Journal of Political Science*, 50, No. 2 (2006); Nicolas Van de Walle, "Tipping Games: When Do Opposition Parties Coalesce?" In *Electoral Authoritarianism: The Dynamics of Unfree Competition* Andreas Schedler, ed., pp. 77–94 (Boulder, CO: Lynne Rienner, 2006).

Most oppositions, most of the time, in hybrid regimes proliferate, rather than concentrate, and they squabble with one another for reasons of personality and personal histories, competing networks, successful actions by the regime to divide and conquer, and less often, significant ideological disagreements. All of these constraints, it is important to remember, were evident in both Slovakia and Serbia prior to the 1998 and 2000 elections. Oppositions are often concentrated in the capital and care little about the provinces. They also find it all too easy to avoid the hard and often boring work of putting together successful campaigns for political office. Their inclination to tackle these tasks in fact was influenced in both Slovakia and Serbia by another factor that was critical to the success of the electoral model in these cases, which we will analyze next, the role of outside actors.

OUTSIDE ASSISTANCE

As we have argued, the United States's democracy assistance efforts have given preference to the postcommunist region.[35] U.S. funding for the development of civil society, citizen education, and the development of strong political parties began soon after the end of communism in Slovakia and continued, in somewhat modified form, through the ouster of Mečiar in 1998. The direct U.S. role in fostering the development of civil society and supporting the formation of a political opposition was more limited in Serbia, due to the nature of the Milošević regime and the sanctions against Serbia. However, by funding civil society activists from other parts of the region to work in Serbia and identifying Milošević as the key individual responsible for Serbia's status as an international pariah, the United States played an important if indirect role in bolstering the opposition.

European governments and foundations also were involved in supporting civil society and working with political parties in both cases, with the German party foundations, for example, providing assistance. As Vachudova's chapter in this volume illustrates, the possibility of EU membership also contributed indirectly to the victory of the opposition, particularly in Slovakia, as citizens became aware of the impediments Mečiar and the policies of his government posed to Slovakia's eventual integration into European as well as Transatlantic organizations.

If the United States and other outside actors played an important role in both the Serbian and the Slovak electoral revolution, does that mean that they engineered the downfall of both Mečiar and Milošević? Because the United States was more active than the Europeans in both of these cases, and because it is the United States that is most often accused of having dictated these developments, we will focus on the U.S. role in our discussion.

[35] Bunce and Wolchik, "International Diffusion and Postcommunist Electoral Revolutions."

On the one hand, it is true that especially since the end of the Cold War the United States has been in the business of promoting democracy abroad (especially when it converges with security interests); that it has been in this game longer and has devoted more resources to this goal than other countries, private foundations, or international organizations; and that American democracy promotion efforts are in both per capita and per state terms particularly concentrated on the postcommunist region, with respect to both programs such as the development of civil society, free and fair elections, and rule of law and policies such as signaling considerable dissatisfaction with the quality of purportedly democratic elections and promises of support for more liberal governments, should they come to power.[36] It is also true that of all USAID outlays, electoral assistance stands out as the one most strongly associated with improved democratic performance.[37] Finally, there is in fact a correlation between American commitment to regime change and the success of electoral revolutions in the postcommunist world. The contrast between American reactions to the elections in Azerbaijan in 2005 and Ukraine in 2004 and the different outcomes of the two elections are a case in point, as is the contrast between the outcomes of the 1996 elections in Serbia (where the United States was not involved) and the 2000 elections (where the defeat of Milošević was a clear priority).[38] It is clear that the United States was also strongly committed to the electoral defeat of Mečiar.

However, the key factors in the successful ouster of Mečiar and Milošević were domestic, as outlined earlier. First, as we argued above, local groups did the hard, tedious, and often dangerous work of implementing the model. Second, as a number of studies have documented and as our research supports, international democracy promotion – whether by the United States, the European Union, the German foundations, or the Organization of American States – cannot work in the absence of domestic democracy promotion.[39] The United States, in short, cannot substitute for a lack of domestic will and capacity.

Third, the most important international actors in these events were not necessarily democracy promoters from the United States. Rather, they were the graduates of successful uses of the electoral model or elements of it who shared

---

[36] Bunce and Wolchik, "International Diffusion and Postcommunist Electoral Revolutions."

[37] Steven F. Finkel, Anibal Perez-Linan, Mitchell A. Seligson, and Dinorah Azpuru, *Effects of US Foreign Assistance on Democracy Building: Results of a Cross-National Quantitative Study*, Final report, Version 22 (USAID, September 2005).

[38] See Bunce and Wolchik, "Opposition versus Dictators."

[39] Carothers, *Critical Missions*; Thomas Carothers, *Assessing Democracy Assistance: The Case of Romania*, (Washington, DC: Carnegie Endowment for International Peace, 1996); Jaba Devdariani, "Building democracy in Georgia: 'The Impact of International Assistance.'" IDEA Web site and conference, May 2003; and Sarah E. Mendelson, "The Seven Ingredients: When Democracy Promotion Works," *Harvard International Review* 26, No. 2 (Summer, 2004), p. 88.

their ideas and strategies with oppositions and NGO activists in neighboring countries who were committed to using elections to oust nondemocratic rulers in their own countries. Thus, Bulgarians and Romanians were critical to the ideas behind and the success of the OK98 campaign in Slovakia, and Slovaks played a key role in the campaign against Milošević as well as in the victory of the Croatian opposition in 2000. Indeed, the importance of these "rooted cosmopolitans," as Sidney Tarrow has termed them, has also been recognized by authoritarian leaders.[40] Just as Kuchma blocked visits by Georgians and Serbs to Ukraine, so Lukashenka did the same in Belarus, and then jailed the few who managed to get to Minsk. One of the most important roles the United States and other European actors played, in fact, was to support contact between the graduates and activists in other countries seeking to emulate their success. Outside actors, then, were important in so far as they facilitated the development of and acted as part of transnational networks that supported democratization that included domestic opposition leaders and NGO activists.

Finally, there is a certain logic to American democracy promotion that returns us to the importance of domestic factors. American democracy promotion efforts tend to specialize in places where there are favorable conditions for democratic change. Favorable conditions, in short, lead to playing favorites. Thus, what may seem to be a powerful role for the United States in the success of the electoral model, in Slovakia and Serbia, is in reality a decision based on collaborative opportunities that nudges along already promising situations.

CONCLUSIONS

The purpose of this chapter has been to compare the use of elections to oust autocratic leaders and promote democratization in Slovakia in 1998 and in Serbia in 2000. Rather than repeating our arguments, let us conclude with one key point. It is easy with hindsight to assume that both regimes were quite vulnerable, and that this vulnerability was the key to their downfall. As we argued in this chapter, this interpretation is wrong.[41] Both regimes had considerable assets, and their defeat spoke to the remarkable properties of the electoral model as an agent of democratic change; the painstaking work of the political oppositions and NGO activists in Slovakia and Serbia, their planning, and the risks they were willing to take; and the surprising willingness of jaded voters, new and old, to participate in large numbers in choosing a new government. In this sense, the electoral model can be seen as a mechanism of transition that surmounts a number of obstacles posed by hybrid authoritarian

---

[40] Sidney Tarrow, *The New Transnational Activism*, (Cambridge: Cambridge University Press, 2005).

[41] Compare Lucan Way, "The Real Causes of the Color Revolutions." *Journal of Democracy*, 19, No. 3 (2008), with Valerie Bunce, "Getting Real about Real Causes: A Reply to Lucan Way" (with Sharon Wolchik).

regimes – in particular, the tendency of such regimes to be effective at dividing the liberal opposition and demobilizing voters. The value of the model in achieving these results clearly is one of the reasons, in addition to the diffusion process, that the model has been used by opponents of authoritarian leaders in other hybrid regimes, including those in which conditions have been less favorable.

7

Georgia's Rose Revolution

From Regime Weakness to Regime Collapse

Cory Welt
Georgetown University

INTRODUCTION

Georgia's August 2008 war with Russia put an end to a string of spectacularly unexpected successes for Georgian President Mikheil Saakashvili. It might have been unrealistic for Saakashvili to think that Georgia could defend itself in South Ossetia against the might of the Russian armed forces. Yet Saakashvili had already surmounted a number of challenges previously thought to be insurmountable. In the fall of 2007, it was unrealistic for Saakashvili to think that he could efficiently extricate himself from a political crisis that arose after his forcibly dispersing antigovernment protesters; in 2004 and 2006, that he would be able to establish an armed Georgian presence in the disputed regions of South Ossetia and Abkhazia; and in 2004, that he could force without bloodshed the retirement of regional despot Aslan Abashidze.

Indeed, despite the considerable vulnerabilities of Georgia's *ancien régime*, even the Rose Revolution that catapulted Saakashvili to power in November 2003 was unexpected. The opposition to Georgian President Eduard Shevardnadze entered the 2003 parliamentary election disunited, promising the regime an opportunity to play parties off each other and prevent them from forming an effective resistance movement. The nature of the electoral contest – an election to parliament in a presidential system – also did not offer much hope for radical change. The election was mainly about defining the process and actors for the 2005 presidential election, a race in which Shevardnadze was constitutionally barred from taking part. Most observers assumed that opposition parties would enjoy a respectable showing, even given fraud, and that they would accept their seats in a flawed but improved electoral process.

To explain the Rose Revolution, therefore, requires that not only the regime's vulnerability prior to the elections be addressed but also the dynamics of the postelectoral process itself, when the interaction between Saakashvili and other nonstate actors committed to exposing and protesting fraud and a weak state scrambling to maintain order dramatically magnified the latter's vulnerability, ultimately providing an opening for regime change. Often neglected is the fact that protests during the Rose Revolution were generally not that large – 5,000 demonstrators or less and only on two occasions substantially greater. As this slow-moving mobilization suggests, it is a mistake to assume that regime weakness alone engenders successful electoral breakthroughs.

In this context, two external forces are said to have contributed to Georgia's electoral breakthrough: the diffusion effect of copycat mobilization, and U.S. assistance and diplomacy. On the first, there is no doubt that the student movement Kmara and associated NGOs, as well as some political leaders – Saakashvili in particular – sought to emulate the success of electoral breakthroughs elsewhere, especially the popular mobilization in Serbia against President Slobodan Milošević. Adhering to an electoral model that proved successful in Serbia and elsewhere in Eastern Europe, these NGOs and political figures helped expose the regime's vulnerability before and after the election.

These efforts, however, operated only in conjunction with other factors that cannot be ascribed to diffusion. The most important of these was Mikheil Saakashvili himself. Saakashvili's decision to have his followers peacefully storm the parliamentary building to prevent the new parliament from convening was a decisively "counterdiffusion" effect that was necessary to force the government to admit defeat and allow Saakashvili's own rapid ascendancy to the presidency.

The role of U.S. assistance and diplomacy was also mixed. On the one hand, declining U.S. support for the Georgian government heightened perceptions of regime vulnerability before the election and, most importantly, afterward. On the other hand, U.S. efforts were geared not toward the resignation of President Shevardnadze but toward the less objectionable goals of strengthening Georgia's democratic process through technical assistance for elections and support for political party and civil society development. With regard to its goals of promoting a democratic election and, failing this, a postelectoral compromise, the United States did not succeed.

This chapter first briefly discusses indicators of regime vulnerability before Georgia's parliamentary election. These included a severely fragmented political elite and the rump ruling party's inclination to ally with marginal political forces; prior defeat in local elections and opinion polls; relatively free broadcast media with the capacity and interest to cover dissent; and a lack of state will to engage in repression against citizens seeking to exercise democratic rights. This vacuum of state vulnerability set the context for Georgia's electoral breakthrough.

The chapter then analyzes in greater detail the set of interactions between nonstate actors and the state that magnified these indicators of regime vulnerability after election day. First, NGOs and media produced postelectoral vote counts that asserted the regime's defeat. Second, Shevardnadze joined forces with a widely reviled regionally based despot, dramatically demonstrating the hollowness of authority at the center. Third, the postelectoral protests shifted beyond the bounds of political partisanship, as two opposition parties united in protest and were joined not only by NGOs but also by a broad spectrum of Georgia's professional and cultural elite, as well as a number of regime elites. Fourth, after election day the broadcast media continued to have the capacity and interest to cover protest and regime defections. Finally, political elites and state security organs proved their lack of resolve to use force against peaceful protesters. Together, these factors turned a weak regime into a collapsing one.

The chapter then assesses the impact on the Rose Revolution of diffusion and U.S. assistance and diplomacy. Key actors in the Rose Revolution, Saakashvili included, received training and consciously sought to replicate electoral break-throughs elsewhere. U.S. assistance and diplomacy actively sought to bring about a democratic parliamentary election in Georgia. However, the *success* of the Rose Revolution and its particular outcome did not depend on these external factors; the outcome, in fact, was contrary to U.S. government intentions. Ultimately, it was Saakashvili's determination *not* to rely on external influences that brought about the Rose Revolution.

THE VULNERABILITY OF THE REGIME

Even if the Rose Revolution was unexpected, by November 2003 the Georgian government was at least highly vulnerable. Years earlier, the population had already become disenchanted with Eduard Shevardnadze, the former Soviet foreign minister (1985–90) and first secretary of the local Communist Party (1972–85), who came to power in independent Georgia in 1992. Popular discontent was directed at increasing criminalization within the regime, massive corruption, and an inability to deliver to the population basic social services, including gas and electricity.

Still, a combination of public apathy, fear of upheaval, and Shevardnadze's own nimble political deal making contributed to the regime's survival. By 2003, however, these factors no longer counted for much. Political elite fissures before the election were palpable, with the regime forced to rely on a hodgepodge of marginal political figures to shore up its power base. As well, the ruling party surrendered electoral superiority in local elections a year before parliamentary elections and, on the eve of the election, could not (or did not care to) prevent the publication of opinion polls that suggested that this outcome could be repeated. Next, an independent and popular television station emerged victorious from a battle with the government two years before the election and continued to criticize the regime up until election day. Finally, the government openly lacked the resolve to use force against peaceful protesters.

Grasping at Straws: Divided Elites and Replacement Alliances

The regime's most visible sign of vulnerability was the implosion of the ruling party, the Citizens' Union of Georgia (CUG), in the three years before parliamentary elections. In 2000, a group of parliamentary deputies representing the business community were the first to defect from a government that had already begun to be viewed as impotent and captured by a handful of corrupt and criminal officials.[1] Shevardnadze himself resigned from his position as chairman of the CUG in September 2001. Days later, Mikheil Saakashvili, who had served as Georgia's minister of justice for a year, resigned, complaining of an inability to make a dent in Georgia's political culture of corruption.[2] Zurab Zhvania, the chair of the Georgian parliament since 1995, departed from the government in November, after a student-led demonstration of several thousand demanded the government's resignation in the wake of a scandalous operation against the independent television channel Rustavi-2 (see below).[3] Nino Burjanadze, Zhvania's successor as parliamentary chair, made her final break from the regime in 2003. With each defection, the ruling party retreated further into its shell. By the 2003 election, the CUG had become a camp of senior apparatchiks, joined by a handful of younger powerbrokers, mainly based in the regions, accumulating illegal wealth through their government positions.

To make up for the vulnerability that resulted from these defections, the government tried to rebuild a power base to contest parliamentary elections by allying with a number of former opposition parties and figures whose popularity had long peaked and whose decision to join with the ruling party was widely met with derision. These included the previously staunch oppositionist Irina Sarishvili-Chanturia and her National Democratic Party; businessman Vakhtang Rcheulishvili's Socialist Party; and the extreme religio-nationalist Guram Sharadze. Although CUG leaders may have calculated that such diverse alliances would enable it to pick up additional votes among these factions' core supporters, this was at the expense of increasing the perception that the CUG was unable to stand on its own.[4]

[1] The author thanks interns Miranda Der Ohanian, Erica Lally, and David Riddy at the Center for Strategic and International Studies for their research assistance. For an account of the NRP's defection, see Irakly Areshidze, *Democracy and Autocracy in Eurasia: Georgia in Transition*, pp. 53–5 (East Lansing: Michigan State University Press, 2007).

[2] "Saakashvili Dissociates From Shevardnadze's Corrupted Government." *Civil.Ge United Nations Association of Georgia Magazine* (Tbilisi), September 20, 2001, available at http://www.civil.ge/eng/article.php?id=225&search=; accessed December 28, 2006.

[3] Though Zhvania was not implicated in the operation, he agreed to leave office as a result of a deal in which the ministers of security and internal affairs, the key offenders, also resigned. Although Zhvania fought with supporters of Shevardnadze to retain legal title to the CUG, the courts eventually ruled in the latter's favor. See "Government Was Forced to Leave." *Civil.Ge*, November 1, 2001, available at http://www.civil.ge/eng/article.php?id=562&search=; Jaba Devdariani, "Reformists Vie To Establish Power Base in Georgian Local Elections." *Eurasia Insight*, May 29, 2002, available at http://www.eurasianet.org/departments/insight/articles/eavo52902a.shtml; Mikhail Vignansky, "Georgian Reformer Faces Political Oblivion," Caucasus Reporting Service No. 129, Institute for War and Peace Reporting (IWPR), May 17, 2002, available at http://www.iwpr.net/index.php?apc_state=hen&s=o&o=p=crs&l=EN&s=f&o=160866; all accessed December 28, 2006.

[4] In referring to the CUG's coalition partners, Nino Burjanadze recounts how she told Shevardnadze he was "doing a really strange thing . . . going against everything [he had] done" when he "gathered around him people who were corrupt, people who had no authority among Georgians, people who were hated by Georgians. It was really unbelievable how President Shevardnadze

Precedents of Defeat: Local Elections and Opinion Polls

By the time of the parliamentary elections, the ruling party's vulnerability at the polls had also been demonstrated – through both past local elections and preelection opinion polls. Thrown into disarray by its initial series of defections, the CUG lacked the wherewithal or ability to engineer a convincing show of strength in 2002 local elections. Despite substantial disorganization and voting improprieties, the ruling party's incapacity to mobilize supporters or to engineer decisive electoral fraud was exposed in these elections. Out of a total of approximately 4,850 seats, candidates formally affiliated with the CUG won just 70 seats, barely one percent of total mandates.[5] Coupled with the estimated 600 party supporters who ran as independents, the CUG total came to approximately fourteen percent of total seats.[6] In the city council of Tbilisi, Georgia's capital and home to more than one-third of the country's population, the CUG did not obtain a single seat.[7]

- Independent candidates – 2,754 seats, 56.80 percent;
- New Rights Party – 558 seats, 11.51;
- Industry Will Save Georgia – 485 seats, 10.00;
- Revival Party – 201 seats, 4.15;
- Socialist Party – 189 seats, 3.90;
- Labor Party – 167 seats, 3.44;
- National Democratic Party – 86 seats, 1.77;
- Citizens' Union of Georgia – 70 seats, 1.44
- National Movement – 29 seats, .60;
- Christian Conservative Party – 4 seats, 0.08;
- Other parties – 306 seats, 6.31.

could surround himself with such people, but it was his choice. I absolutely can't explain it." Similarly, in the words of parliamentary deputy and NGO representative Ivliane Khaindrava, the progovernment bloc "looked like a ghastly mutant even in the Georgian reality. The cocktail of failures, bankrupt politicians and dubious individuals who had nothing to do with politics was too much for the people to stomach." Zurab Karumidze and James V. Wertsch, *"Enough!":The Rose Revolution in The Republic of Georgia, 2003,* p. 45 (New York: Nova Science, 2005); and Ivlian Haindrava, "Georgia: Through Elections to the 'Rose Revolution.'" In *Election Assessment in the South Caucasus (2003–2004),* p. 107 (Stockholm: International IDEA, 2004), available at http://www.idea.int/publications/ea_caucasus/upload/BookEng.pdf; accessed December 28, 2006.

[5] Central Election Commission of Georgia, "Percentage Allotment of Sakrebulo Members Elected among Election Subjects throughout Georgia (Results by June 24, 2002)." Central Election Commission of Georgia, available at http://www.archive.cec.gov.ge/Cfdocs/sablooshedegebi/gasulebiENG.cfm?contact=0; accessed December 28, 2006.

[6] Areshidze, *Democracy and Autocracy in Eurasia,* p. 71.

[7] For more on the local elections, see Irakly Areshidze, "Early Review of Georgia's Local Elections," *Eurasia Insight,* June 6, 2002, available at http://www.eurasianet.org/departments/insight/articles/eav060602.shtml; and IFES, "Technical Assessment of Election Day Administration 2002 Local Government Elections of Georgia," July 2002, available at www.ifes.ge/files/assasments/techn_ass_eng.pdf; both accessed December 28, 2006.

With a full fifty-seven percent of the seats (2,754) filled by "independent" candidates, the chief significance of the results was that the ruling party was vulnerable, not that an obvious competitor was rising to take its place. The party that received the most votes on the basis of party affiliation was the opposition New Rights Party (NRP), formed on the basis of the initial pro-business CUG defectors, which received approximately twelve percent of total seats (eighteen percent if informally affiliated independent candidates are included). Four parties that served formally or informally as CUG allies in the 2003 parliamentary elections – Industry Will Save Georgia (ISG), the Socialist Party, the National Democratic Party, and Revival, the party of Aslan Abashidze, head of the autonomous republic of Adjara – received twenty percent of the seats.[8] The opposition Labor Party, led by Shalva Natelashvili, received only three percent, and Mikheil Saakashvili's National Movement, formed with several of his supporters in November 2002 and which campaigned almost exclusively in Tbilisi, received less than one percent.[9] In the Tbilisi city council, however, the Labor Party and the National Movement each won approximately twenty-five percent of the vote, finishing in first and second place, respectively.[10] Zhvania and his parliamentary allies ran on the platform of the little-known Christian Conservative Party, which received seven percent of the vote in the Tbilisi City Council.

Public opinion polls in the last two months of the election campaign also demonstrated the government's vulnerability. Polling, commissioned by Rustavi-2 and, for one final poll, by the George Soros–funded Open Society Georgia Foundation, was carried out regularly and the results were publicized weekly on at least Rustavi-2. According to these polls, the progovernment bloc For A New Georgia (FNG) had the support of just six to nine percent of the population; on questions of trust, government leaders also ranked at the bottom.[11]

---

[8] ISG received 485 party-affiliated seats (ten percent), whereas the other three parties cumulatively received an additional 476 party-affiliated seats (another ten percent).

[9] The remaining six percent of seats were filled by seven other parties, three of which received more party-affiliated seats than either the CUG or the National Movement. A complete analysis of the approximately 1,845 independent seats that were not affiliated with the CUG or NRP is needed to determine relative party strength more precisely. See Central Election Commission of Georgia, "Percentage Allotment of Sakrebulo Members."

[10] When Saakashvili demanded a recount that ultimately did not change these results, the Labor Party agreed to support his bid to become head of the city council. According to Natelashvili, the Labor Party supported Saakashvili's candidacy to prove to the population that he lacked governing ability and also "so [that] afterward people won't say that Saakashvili could have saved Tbilisi and Georgia and we did not give him a chance." See "Georgian Labour Party brands its ally in Tbilisi city council 'bogus opposition.'" Prime News Agency (Tbilisi), June 25, 2002, trans. in *BBC Worldwide Monitoring*; and Java Devdariani, "Opposition Leader Poised to Become Tbilisi Council Chairman." *Eurasia Insight*, June 19, 2002, available at http://www.eurasianet.org/departments/insight/articles/eavo61902.shtml; accessed December 28, 2006. Also see Areshidze, *Democracy and Autocracy in Eurasia*, p. 79.

[11] "Georgian Parliament Speaker's Election Bloc Leads Opinion Polls." Rustavi-2 TV (Tbilisi), September 17, 2003; "Georgian Opposition Parties Leading Opinion Polls." Rustavi-2 TV, October 4, 2003, "Georgian Opposition Parties Maintain Steady Lead in Opinion Polls."

Nearly all opposition parties ranked higher than the FNG. A new alliance of Burjanadze and Zhvania, the "Burjanadze-Democrats," led the polls for most of this time with gradually rising support of sixteen to twenty percent, almost exclusively linked to Burjanadze's relatively high popularity (Zhvania ranked barely above government leaders on lists of trusted politicians). The National Movement rocketed from eight to twenty-three percent over the eight-week period. Polls showed the Labor Party at fourteen to eighteen percent, and the New Rights at five to ten percent. They also showed the level of support for Revival gradually declining over this period from thirteen to eight percent.

The Victory of the Media

Prior to the elections, the opposition had a key media ally in the independent television channel Rustavi 2. In an overall climate of relative media freedom, the channel had been recognized as the most professional in Georgia and had gained widespread popularity "as a result of several years of open and fearless criticism of the Shevardnadze regime."[12] Rustavi-2 became associated most visibly with antigovernment sentiment in July 2001, when a popular 25-year-old television news anchor, Giorgi Sanaia, was shot to death in his apartment. A former interior ministry official was found guilty of his murder. The prosecution's belabored justification of the crime on personal grounds was believed by many to mask a directive to eliminate Sanaia in response to Rustavi-2's reporting on corruption. Sanaia's death caused an uproar and brought thousands onto the streets for his funeral.[13] Three months later, tax

Rustavi-2 TV, October 10, 2003; "Opposition Parties Lead Opinion Polls in Georgia." *Caucasus Press* (Tbilisi), October 27, 2003, trans. in *BBC Worldwide Monitoring*.

[12] David Usupashvili, "An Analysis of the Presidential and Parliamentary Elections in Georgia: A Case Study, November 2003–March 2004." In *Election Assessment in the South Caucasus*, 94. The rise of Rustavi-2 need not be interpreted solely as a case of a plucky independent medium defending the principle of free speech and public criticism. The station was developed not as an opposition channel, but with Shevardnadze's full support and the active assistance of Zhvania in the mid-1990s as a platform for reform and an example of Georgian democracy. Although it did benefit from startup grants from the Eurasia and Soros Foundations, as well as assistance and training from the U.S. government-funded NGO Internews, it was also a business venture that procured financial support from a variety of private domestic sources. See Areshidze, *Democracy and Autocracy in Eurasia*, pp. 42–3, 105–7. In a prepublication version of his article on the Rose Revolution (see note 19), Kandelaki discusses the development of Rustavi-2 in similar terms. Giorgi Kandelaki, "Rose Revolution: A Participant's Story." Unpublished manuscript, United States Institute of Peace, July 2005, 16–17; also David Anable, *Role of Georgia's Media – and Western Aid – in the Rose Revolution*. Joan Shorenstein Center on the Press, Politics and Public Policy, Harvard University, 2005, 8, available at http://www.hks.harvard.edu/presspol/publications/papers/working_papers/2006_03_anable. pdf; accessed December 28, 2006.

[13] See "Giorgi Sanaia, A Famous Georgian Journalist, Was Found Murdered in His Own Flat." *Civil.Ge*, July 27, 2001, available at http://www.civil.ge/eng/article.php?id=94&search=; "Murder of Giorgi Sanaia – What Was the Reason and What Will Happen Next." *Civil.Ge*, July 28, 2001, available at http://www.civil.ge/eng/article.php?id=98&search=; "Georgia Mourns

police raided Rustavi-2's offices, whether as an attempt to shut the station down, buy it out, or deter it from airing reports on corruption.[14] The operation failed spectacularly, however, leading instead to the government's resignation. The operation also did not rein in Rustavi-2. Prior to parliamentary elections, Rustavi-2 openly sided with the opposition, actively encouraged the public to participate, and cosponsored preelection opinion polls. In 2003, Rustavi-2 was joined by two more independently financed stations: Imedi, owned by oligarch Badri Patarkatsishvili, and Mze, owned by Vano Chkhartishvili, a leading banker and former minister of economy, industry, and trade. Whereas Imedi remained largely apolitical in the run-up to the election, Mze was willing to broadcast criticism of the regime, if to a lesser extent than Rustavi-2.[15]

The Absence of Fear

Whatever its faults, the Georgian government was strongly conditioned against using force to prevent or disperse legitimate protests prior to election day. Police brutality, official complicity in kidnapping crimes, and the unresolved murder of Sanaia in 2001 pointed to the regime's ability to engage or tolerate isolated instances of violence. As well, in the two years before parliamentary elections, the government had made some effort to pressure critics – lawsuits against the media, the tax raid against Rustavi-2, a hardening of the libel law, and proposed reviews of foreign-sponsored organizations.[16] Overall, however, the Georgian political scene was not characterized by repression – criticism freely emanated from a number of sources, including political parties across the spectrum, NGOs such as the Georgian Young Lawyers' Association and the Liberty Institute, and print and broadcast media. Antigovernment demonstrations had never been dispersed, and no leading opposition figure had ever been arrested or seriously harassed. In addition, many Georgians took for granted that the memory of April 9, 1989, when Soviet troops forcibly dispersed pro-independence demonstrators on Tbilisi's central Rustaveli Avenue, was a powerful restraint against government officials and members of the security forces participating in

---

Murdered Journalist," Caucasus Reporting Service No. 92, IWPR, July 31, 2001, available at http://www.iwpr.net/?p=crs&s=f&o=160363&apc_state=henicrs2001; and "Georgia: Sanaia Murder Inquiry Slated," Caucasus Reporting Service No. 110, IWPR, December 18, 2001, available at http://www.iwpr.net/?p=crs&s=f&o=158809&apc_state=henicrs2001; all accessed December 28, 2006.

[14] "Ministry of State Security Enters Rustavi-2." *Civil.Ge*, October 30, 2001, available at http://www.civil.ge/eng/article.php?id=531&search=; "Free Speech, Democracy Is Being Ignored." *Civil.Ge*, October 31, 2001, available at http://www.civil.ge/eng/article.php?id=540&search=; "Protests Widen as More Students Hit the Streets." *Civil.Ge*, October 31, 2001, available at http://www.civil.ge/eng/article.php?id=543&search=; all accessed December 28, 2006.

[15] Areshidze, *Democracy and Autocracy in Eurasia*, pp. 105–6, 111, 124, 133.

[16] See Laurence Broers, "After the 'Revolution': Civil Society and the Challenges of Consolidating Democracy in Georgia." *Central Asian Survey* 24, No. 3 (September 2005), pp. 333–50, at p. 339.

efforts to prevent or suppress legitimate protest. Indeed, Shevardnadze himself encouraged Georgians to participate in the election without fear. In a message broadcast on state television four days earlier, the president insisted that "every person has a free choice" and should "vote as their conscience dictates."[17]

In sum, prior to Georgia's 2003 parliamentary elections, several indicators pointed to the vulnerability of the regime. The regime was fragmented and dependent on discredited allies; it had lost local elections and ranked low on opinion polls; it had lost a showdown with independent media that were beginning to expand; and it was unwilling to threaten or use force to discourage the population from exercising its democratic rights. Under such conditions, the political arena was wide open to competition and protest.

FROM VULNERABILITY TO COLLAPSE

No Rose Revolution: A Plausible Outcome

Even given the regime's vulnerability, an electoral breakthrough, especially one predicated on successful mass mobilization, was not a foregone conclusion. Georgians have a history of popular mobilization, having protested against separatist movements and for independence in the last years of the Soviet Union and, immediately after, for and against the first Georgian president, Zviad Gamsakhurdia. A decade later, however, Georgians appeared to have developed an antagonism toward popular mobilization, whether because the benefits of past mobilization proved so uncertain (including ethnic and civil war and the corruption and lethargic development of the Shevardnadze years) or because the stability they had managed to achieve through past mobilization appeared so fragile. Perpetual power shortages finally led to mild street protests in 2000, and the tax raid against Rustavi-2 in the fall of 2001 prompted a significant demonstration of several thousand. In June 2003, another demonstration was mounted against government resistance to election commission reform.[18] Although these demonstrations signaled a renaissance of popular mobilization in Georgia, their limited size (probably no more than 5,000 at their height) and duration also suggested that the appeal of popular mobilization had limits.

In the lead-up to parliamentary elections, then, it was a real question whether a sufficient number of Georgians would come out to the streets in the event of electoral fraud. According to Giorgi Kandelaki, a leading member of the youth organization Kmara, "breaking through the...political apathy" of a public that tended to believe that all elections were unfair was Kmara's central

---

[17] "Georgian President Interviewed on Forthcoming Parliamentary Elections." Georgian State Television Channel 1 (Tbilisi), October 29, 2003, trans. in *BBC Worldwide Monitoring.*

[18] On the June 2003 demonstration, see Irakly Areshidze, "Opposition Organizes Political Protests across Georgia." *Eurasia Insight,* June 3, 2003, available at http://www.eurasianet.org/departments/insight/articles/eavo60303.shtml; accessed December 28, 2006; and Areshidze, *Democracy and Autocracy in Eurasia,* pp. 111–12.

function. According to Kandelaki, Georgians' attitude toward both the political process and political parties was "nihilistic and distrustful."[19] This meant that no matter how vulnerable the government was, and how obvious the fraud to secure victory, the people could not be relied upon to defend their vote. Mikheil Saakashvili himself later estimated that up to ninety percent of the population would have said before the 2003 elections that they would not come out to the streets in the event of electoral fraud.[20]

Indeed, mostly forgotten after the Rose Revolution is the fact that street demonstrations were not that large or sustained. On ten of the twenty-one days between the election and Shevardnadze's resignation (November 3, 6, 7, and 15–21), there were no demonstrations to speak of. On eight days, November 4 and 5 and November 8–13, the number of demonstrators probably did not exceed 5,000.[21] The first of three days of major demonstrations was November 14, when at least 20,000 demonstrators went to the streets. After this, street protest subsided for several days, although a civil disobedience campaign began throughout the country. A single, massive demonstration was convened on November 22 prior to the peaceful rushing of parliament by opposition supporters, which interrupted the new parliament's opening session and sent Shevardnadze into retreat. This demonstration extended into the next day. Once Shevardnadze resigned, it transformed into an enormous street celebration, the image of which, after the parliamentary storming, is most symbolic of the Rose Revolution – after it had already happened. Estimates for the size of the precelebration component of this demonstration vary wildly – between 20,000 and 100,000 people.[22]

To explain Georgia's electoral breakthrough, therefore, we must be careful not to link preelectoral indicators of regime vulnerability directly to a successful electoral breakthrough. Instead, we need to explain how the interaction between nonstate actors and the state magnified the regime's vulnerability in the days after the election, ultimately paving the way for regime change. In Georgia, this occurred in several steps. First, NGOs and media quickly produced tabulations of the vote, which suggested that the government had lost the election. Second, the regime chose to rely on regional despot Aslan Abashidze to stay in power, revealing its desperate position and provoking a strong counter-reaction in the Tbilisi population. Third, two political parties were joined

---

[19] Giorgi Kandelaki, *Georgia's Rose Revolution: A Participant's Perspective*. Special Report 167, United States Institute of Peace, July 2006, pp. 5, 8, available at http://www.usip.org/files/resources/sr167.pdf; accessed December 28, 2006.

[20] Karumidze and Wertsch, *"Enough!"* p. 23.

[21] Lincoln Mitchell, director of the National Democratic Institute office in Tbilisi from 2002 to 2004, says that for most of that time, there were far fewer. Lincoln Mitchell, "Georgia's Rose Revolution." *Current History* 103 (October 2004), pp. 342–8, at p. 345.

[22] One source that consistently overestimated the sizes of earlier protests reported that day a figure of 60,000. "Saakashvili Meets Shevardnadze, Saakashvili Says Shevardnadze Prepares for Resignation." *Civil.Ge*, November 23, 2003, available at http://www.civil.ge/eng/article.php?id=5620&search=; accessed December 28, 2006.

in postelectoral protest not only by NGOs but also by a broad spectrum of Georgia's professional and cultural elite and even a number of regime elites. Fourth, Rustavi-2 and, eventually, other broadcast media communicated and legitimized protest to as broad an audience as possible. Finally, the government demonstrated its lack of resolve to use force against peaceful protesters, neither issuing credible threats of force to deter protesters nor contemplating seriously the use of force to limit or disperse protests. Through these interactions, the regime shifted from being vulnerable to being on the brink of collapse.

Evidence of Defeat: Exit Polls, the Parallel Vote Tabulation, and Official Results

The vulnerability revealed by local elections and opinion polls was confirmed immediately after the parliamentary election by exit polls and an NGO-organized parallel vote tabulation (PVT), a statistically significant parallel vote count at the precinct level.[23] The results of two exit polls, both of which established a victory for opposition parties, were released on election night. The first results to reach the airwaves were from a poll jointly funded by the Open Society Georgia Foundation, the USAID-supported Eurasia Foundation, the British Council, and Rustavi-2 and organized by a U.S. company in collaboration with Georgian pollsters. Preliminary results of this poll placed the National Movement on top with twenty-one percent of the vote, making it the leading party to fill the 150 (out of 235) parliamentary seats reserved for party lists, followed by the FNG at thirteen percent (later amended to fifteen percent).[24] According to the poll, the Democrats came in a disappointing fourth with eight percent, behind the Labor Party's thirteen to fourteen percent.[25] (See Table 7.1).

---

[23] Together with the exit polls, which help to counter election day fraud in its earliest stages (e.g., ballot box stuffing), a properly administrated PVT increases the certainty that late-stage fraud (i.e., manipulation of the vote count above the precinct level) will be detected. For more on parallel vote tabulations, see Larry Garber and Glenn Cowan, "The Virtues of Parallel Vote Tabulations." *Journal of Democracy* 4, No. 2 (April 1993), pp. 95–107.

[24] Eighty-five seats were assigned to the winners of single-mandate districts, though in place of the eight allotted to districts in breakaway Abkhazia were ten that were filled by formerly elected Georgian representatives from Abkhazia, now internally displaced.

[25] Interestingly, even the state television held an exit poll that confirmed the overall strength of the opposition. Although the poll predictably identified FNG as the leading electoral bloc with twenty-two percent of the vote, it gave the Democrats a second-place finish with sixteen percent and put the National Movement in fourth with thirteen percent (and also suggested that the Adjara-based Revival Party would not receive enough votes to even make it into parliament). The poll thus acknowledged that, combined, the soon-to-be leaders of the protest movement had been victorious. "Georgian Opposition Bloc Wins Most Votes in Parliamentary Election – Exit Poll." Rustavi-2 TV, November 2, 2003; "'Updated' Exit Poll Results Released in Georgia." Rustavi-2 TV, November 2, 2003; "Official Georgian Election Results at Odds with Parallel Vote Count Figures." Rustavi-2 TV, November 3, 2003; "Progovernment Bloc Wins Parliamentary Election in Georgia – State TV," Georgian State Television Channel 1, November 2, 2003, trans. in *BBC Worldwide Monitoring*.

TABLE 7.1. *Independent and Official Exit Polls*

Rustavi-2 Exit Poll	Channel One (State TV) Exit Poll
National Movement – 20.8 percent	FNG – 22.1 percent
FNG – 15.0	Democrats – 16.4
Labor Party – 13.8	Labor Party – 13.5
Democrats – 8.2	National Movement – 13.2
Revival Party – 7.1	NRP – 558 seats, 11.3
——— (threshold)	——— (threshold)
NRP – 5.6	Revival Party – 4.2
ISG – <3	ISG – 4.2

The results of the PVT, run by the U.S.-funded NGO International Society for Fair Elections and Democracy (ISFED) in collaboration with the National Democratic Institute, were released the next day and reinforced the findings of the exit polls.[26] According to the PVT, the National Movement received twenty-seven percent of the vote, whereas the FNG came in second place with nineteen percent. The Democrats came in fourth place with ten percent; two other opposition parties, Labor and the NRP, received twenty-five percent total, coming in third and sixth place respectively. Revival received eight percent, in fifth place, whereas ISG received five percent, not enough to enter parliament. In short, the regime and its de facto allies received thirty-two percent of the PVT count, whereas opposition parties won sixty-two percent. Such data again established the government's defeat.

Even final election results, announced eighteen days after the election, conceded the pro-government bloc's poor performance at the polls. The Central Election Commission (CEC) gave the FNG just twenty-one percent of the vote (a total statistically in agreement with the PVT results); Revival was granted the second-place slot, with an exaggerated nineteen percent of the vote. At the same time, the four leading opposition parties received forty-seven percent of the vote, including twenty-eight percent for the future ruling bloc of the National Movement and Democrats – a combined total more than that for the FNG itself. For supporters and detractors of the opposition alike, the outcome of the election was clear – the government had lost the vote.[27] (See Table 7.2).

---

[26] "Official Georgian Election Results at Odds with Parallel Vote Count Figures," Rustavi-2 TV, November 3, 2003, trans. in *BBC Worldwide Monitoring*.

[27] The discrepancy between the official results and the PVT translated into a difference of twenty-five seats in favor of FNG and Revival. By the official results, FNG and Revival combined would have seventy-one party-list plus twenty-five majoritarian seats, or ninety-six seats in all (forty-one percent), whereas the National Movement and Democrats would have forty-seven party-list seats, plus seventeen majoritarian seats (twenty-seven percent). The ten Abkhazian IDP seats would also go toward the ruling coalition, as would most if not all of twenty unaffiliated majoritarian seats and perhaps ISG's four majoritarian seats, granting progovernment forces a slim parliamentary majority. By the PVT, by comparison, FNG and Revival would only have had seventy-one seats in all (thirty percent), whereas the National Movement and the Democrats

TABLE 7.2. *Parallel Vote Tabulation vs. Official Results*

Parallel Vote Tabulation	Official Results
National Movement – 26.60 percent	FNG – 21.32 percent
FNG – 18.92	Revival – 18.84
Labor Party – 17.36	National Movement – 18.08
Democrats – 10.15	Labor Party – 12.04
Revival – 8.13	Democrats – 8.79
NRP – 7.99	NRP – 7.35
——————————— (threshold)	——————————— (threshold)
ISG – 5.20	ISG – 6.17

Adjara: The Ultimate Replacement Alliance

Aware of this fact, Shevardnadze relied on the blatantly falsified vote count in Adjara, an autonomous republic on Georgia's Black Sea coast, to maintain victory. Run Soviet style by its leader, Aslan Abashidze, Adjara was by far the most authoritarian region of Georgia, returning turnouts and tallies of over ninety percent for Abashidze's party, Revival, in every election. In 1999 parliamentary elections, Revival, in alliance with other parties including the Socialists, was virtually the only "opposition" bloc voted into parliament – and proceeded for four years to raise hardly a peep against the government. This arrangement reflected an informal agreement to support CUG governance at the center in exchange for Tbilisi's tolerance of Abashidze's rule in Adjara.

As became clear during the election, one reason for this alliance was Shevardnadze's fear of state collapse. Thanks to Russia's military presence in Adjara and other indicators of Russian backing for his state-within-a-state, Georgia's past secessionist losses in South Ossetia and Abkhazia, and Shevardnadze's own aversion to risk, Abashidze held sway over Shevardnadze as much as he did over Adjara. Shevardnadze was exceedingly wary of doing anything that could prompt Abashidze to try to move Adjara any further out of the central government's orbit (even though there were few signs of separatist sentiment among Adjara's bireligious Georgian population).

When the tally from Adjara was reported four days after the election, Revival's total share of the vote rocketed from the less than seven percent it had received until then to an absurdly high twenty-one percent of the vote count, temporarily entering first place nationwide. In addition to receiving an unrealistic ninety-five percent of the vote in Adjara, Revival benefited from inflation in the regional voter rolls, a twenty-two percent increase from the already inflated voter rolls of the 1999 parliamentary elections.[28]

would have had seventy-nine seats (thirty-four percent). To make up a majority in parliament, these parties would still have had to secure a coalition with the NRP and unaffiliated deputies.

[28] See the OSCE/ODIHR Election Observation Mission, "Post-Election Interim Report, 2–25 November 2003," p. 5, available at www1.osce.org/documents/odihr/2003/11/1593_en.pdf;

Whatever Shevardnadze believed about the need for caution in Adjara, most of Georgia's politically active population (mainly concentrated in Tbilisi) reviled the pro-Russian Abashidze and his Soviet-style regional dictatorship, anomalous even for less-than-democratic Georgia and associated with a return to Russian domination. Many observers note the outrage that developed among Tbilisi residents, once they realized that the government was going to depend on Abashidze for protection.[29] Protests began in force on November 8, two days after Adjara's official count was announced and a day after Revival's Tbilisi-based leadership organized its own demonstration in Tbilisi. These protests continued over the following days, as Shevardnadze traveled to Batumi, standing with Abashidze in front of a manufactured crowd to declare that "nothing will separate us, we will stand together."[30] After the large protest of November 14 subsided, protesters were given a new jolt by the appearance of Adjarans bussed into Tbilisi to demonstrate in support of the government.[31] Rather than confront the counterprotesters directly, opposition leaders announced a nationwide civil disobedience campaign.

In addition to serving as a catalyst for popular mobilization, Shevardnadze's alliance with Adjara helped bring about the Rose Revolution in two other ways: by interfering beforehand with reforms that could have produced a democratic election and by restricting the government's ability to annul fraudulent results afterward. Before the election, Abashidze was already a key spoiler of election commission reform. The reform, debated during the summer before the election, would have granted enough seats to opposition parties to shape commissions' preelectoral preparations and to block certification of fraudulent results.[32] Although Shevardnadze publicly expressed support for the reform,

---

accessed December 28, 2006. Areshidze estimates that the 284,000 votes allegedly cast in Adjara constitute "at least a third more" than the region's entire population. Areshidze, *Democracy and Autocracy in Eurasia*, p. 157.

[29] Karumidze and Wertsch, *"Enough!"* pp. 48, 63–4; Haindrava, "Through Elections to the 'Rose Revolution,'" p. 109; Areshidze, *Democracy and Autocracy in Eurasia*, pp. 158, 167.

[30] "Shevardnadze, Abashidze Pledge Cooperation." *Civil.Ge*, November 10, 2003, available at http://www.civil.ge/eng/article.php?id=5467&search=; accessed December 28, 2006. Also see Karumidze and Wertsch, *"Enough!"* p. 10. For an analysis of Shevardnadze's possible motivations in going to Adjara after election day, see Areshidze, *Democracy and Autocracy in Eurasia*, pp. 160–61.

[31] Before this happened, Revival's parliamentary leader, Jemal Gogitidze, announced that "Revival [would] go to Tbilisi to help" the president withstand the demands of the protesters. Areshidze, *Democracy and Autocracy in Eurasia*, p. 161; also see Karumidze and Wertsch, *"Enough!"* p. 10.

[32] The reform was going to give the progovernment bloc just five seats in all election commissions, whereas nine opposition parties would receive one seat each. This reform was opposed by Revival and one other party, the ISG, who claimed that as the only two parties to have surpassed the seven percent threshold to enter parliament in the 1999 elections, they should receive more seats than other opposition parties, which either did not surpass the barrier in 1999 or, as was the case for the NRP, the National Movement, and the Democrats, did not yet exist. "Parties Fail To Agree, Baker Plan Endangered." *Civil.ge*, July 23, 2003, available at http://www.civil.ge/eng/article.php?id=4626&search=; accessed December 28, 2006.

and the proposal passed a first reading in parliament, it was shot down in its second required reading, thanks to the influence of government officials who persuaded Shevardnadze to retreat.[33] The main trump card of the reform's opponents was Abashidze, who threatened to boycott the election if the proposal passed and implied to a Rustavi-2 interviewer that the authorities, which were responsible for losing two Georgian territories already, were taking the country down the road to further fragmentation.[34] After the reform was shot down, Shevardnadze explained that though the decision might leave some political players unsatisfied, this was not as bad an outcome "as leaving a whole region outside the election process and virtually beyond the country's jurisdiction."[35] If Shevardnadze had been willing to stand up to Abashidze, Georgia's electoral breakthrough may have ended up resembling the smoother transitions of power that occurred in countries such as Slovakia, Croatia, Romania, and Bulgaria.

After the election, Adjara again became the key sticking point preventing Shevardnadze from pushing for a recognition of democratic results, via a combination of recounts and revotes in districts that had suffered from egregious fraud. Soon after the election, political parties, together with the election-monitoring NGO ISFED and the Georgian Young Lawyers' Association, filed legal complaints in over 150 precincts and also lodged official protests against district commissions.[36] The courts even ruled for a recount in one of the most contested districts, as well as of absentee ballots, setting a potential precedent. Conducting recounts and revotes was an option that would have received the acceptance of some government officials and the approval of, most importantly among opposition parties, Saakashvili's National Movement.

Even if the opposition were able to overcome resistance at the center, however, the problem of Adjara still loomed. Although the vote for the FNG and other parties may have been sufficiently corrected to better resemble the PVT results, the government could not easily order a democratic revote in Adjara. Shevardnadze had no guarantee that Abashidze would play by the rules, and the FNG would have ended up in a leading alliance with Revival by default. If the government were to annul the results of the election in Adjara, on the other hand, Shevardnadze risked the prospect of Abashidze refusing to recognize the parliament's legitimacy, again raising the specter of Adjaran secession.

---

[33] The reform passed, but in a modified form that prevented opposition representatives from blocking fraud-related decisions. Three seats were awarded to Revival, two to ISG, and the remaining four to opposition parties. "Parliament Adopts Rule on CEC Composition, Contradicting Baker's Plan." *Civil.ge*, August 5, 2003, available at http://www.civil.ge/eng/article.php?id=4711&search=; accessed December 28, 2006.

[34] "Ajarian Leader's Party Threatens to Boycott Georgian Elections." Prime News Agency, July 24, 2003; "Leader of Ajaria Challenges Georgia's Central Government," Rustavi-2 TV, July 25, 2003, trans. in *BBC Worldwide Monitoring*.

[35] "Georgian President Reaffirms Loyalty to Pro-Western Course," Georgian Radio, August 11, 2003, trans. in *BBC Worldwide Monitoring*.

[36] Broers, "After the 'Revolution,'" p. 5.

Because Shevardnadze was not willing to challenge Abashidze to step in line, the postelectoral situation shifted further from the possibility of a negotiated outcome and closer toward the events that actually composed the Rose Revolution – the rushing of parliament and Shevardnadze's resignation.

A Winning Coalition: Unity and Division among the Elite

Additional mobilizing power came from the coalition-building of two opposition parties, together with Georgia's nonpolitical elite. This coalition-building transformed protest from a vehicle for narrow political aims into a defense of the national interest, successfully attracting a cross spectrum of the population rather than just partisan supporters. This, in turn, enabled protests to attract ever greater numbers of participants. Critically, it also demonstrated the fragility of the hardliners' position in a divided ruling elite.

The most obvious coalition building involved the street coalition of the National Movement and the Democrats. The two parties had made efforts to unite as a single electoral bloc before the elections but ultimately failed.[37] When street protests began after election day, the National Movement and Democrats held almost comically separate demonstrations at different ends of Tbilisi's main Rustaveli Prospect. For several days, their demands were distinct, with the National Movement calling for revised results that would validate their first-place finish and the Democrats, disappointed in their fourth-place finish, calling for new elections entirely. The two parties eventually agreed to support unified street protests, however.

At the same time, the protests found broad support among social leaders outside the political parties. Georgia's intellectual and artistic elite, traditionally well regarded by the Georgian public, were highly visible in the protests. Usupashvili argues that "the most popular writers, poets, singers, actors, sportsmen, lawyers, journalists, scientists, and others" were heavily critical of the government in television and news media before election day. He notes that this group encouraged "the leaders of the political opposition . . . to make braver and bolder moves against Shevardnadze's regime" and that they "played a crucial role in bringing people out on demonstrations." At an initial rally inside the Tbilisi Philharmonic Hall called by the Democrats, the audience was relatively small, only several thousand, but they arrived within two hours of being called and included, according to Zhvania, "the most famous intellectuals and scientists." Davit Zurabishvili, then head of the opposition NGO Liberty Institute, adds that the creation of postelection university disobedience committees

---

[37] In the final weeks of the election, Saakashvili launched attacks against the Democrats, accusing members of corruption and Zhvania and Burjanadze, in particular, of "Shevardnadze-like tactics." Areshidze says that these attacks were more successful than realized at the time, which, if true, helps explain the contrast between the Democrats' standing in the opinion polls and in the later Rustavi-2 exit poll and the PVT. Areshidze, *Democracy and Autocracy in Eurasia*, p. 129.

was spurred on not by Kmara or the Liberty Institute, but by a disobedience committee that came to be known as the Artcom (art committee), "comprised mostly of artists, movie directors, and writers."[38]

This kind of coalition-building was critical for the success of protest. Opposition political parties, acting separately and without broader social support, were not likely to succeed in bringing many people to the streets. Leading opposition parties as a whole were not even committed to mobilization. Two opposition parties representing by the PVT one-fourth of total votes and a full forty percent of the opposition vote – the Labor Party and the NRP – opted out of street protest altogether. The Labor Party set itself apart from the other opposition parties at the start of October, when it accused Rustavi-2 of carrying out a "dirty campaign" against it and of openly supporting the Democrats.[39] Subsequently, party leader Natelashvili denounced street protests as a destructive struggle for power. He even joined Revival and ISG in a boycott of Rustavi-2 and called on Shevardnadze, Burjanadze, Zhvania, and Saakashvili all to resign from politics.[40]

The NRP, although more staid, also rejected street protests, setting for itself the narrow aim of "protecting the votes that [the party] had received."[41] The NRP pushed for a compromise to hold new elections within six to nine months, although it supported first convening the new parliament (which was at least more representative than the old parliament and the first to which the NRP had been elected).[42] Ultimately, however, the NRP went further than Labor in acting against the protest movement, agreeing to allow its CEC representative to certify official election results.[43] Although the NRP was reluctant to join the

---

[38] Kandelaki also comments that "groups of well-known . . . artists, poets, and musicians started campaigning throughout the country, mainly in different universities, calling on students to join the protest." Usupashvili, "An Analysis of the Presidential and Parliamentary Elections in Georgia," p. 93; Karumidze and Wertsch, *"Enough!"* pp. 36, 66; Kandelaki, "A Participant's Perspective," p. å8.

[39] "Georgian Labour Party Accuses Independent TV Station of 'Dirty Campaigning,'" *Caucasus Press*, October 2, 2003, trans. in *BBC Worldwide Monitoring*.

[40] "Georgia: Opposition Leader Accuses President of Masterminding Protests," *Caucasus Press*, November 8, 2003; "Three Parties Decide to 'Boycott' Independent Georgian TV Station." *Caucasus Press*, November 10, 2003; "Georgian Labour Party Urges both Government and Opposition Leaders to Resign," Imedi TV (Tbilisi), November 12 2003, trans. in *BBC Worldwide Monitoring*.

[41] Areshidze, *Democracy and Autocracy in Eurasia*, pp. 154–5, 329 (n. 30).

[42] The NRP reportedly shared the idea with Saakashvili on November 17 and with visiting U.S. diplomat Lynn Pascoe and National Security Council official Matthew Bryza by e-mail two days later. Ibid., pp. 168, 171.

[43] Ironically, then, even in the absence of the original CEC reform, the changes that had been made to the CEC's composition almost produced the reform's intended effect. The two representatives of ISG, whose progovernment vote had been taken for granted, ultimately refused to certify the election results, presumably in protest at failing to surpass the election threshold, together with the single representatives of the National Movement, the Democrats, and the Labor Party. It was the NRP that went along with the five presidential representatives, the three Revival representatives, and the CEC chairwoman to certify the results. If the NRP had refused to

opening session of parliament, they agreed to do so at the last minute, allowing the new parliament to legitimately convene.[44]

Left to lead mobilization were the National Movement and the Democrats, representing (by the PVT) thirty-seven percent of votes and sixty percent of the opposition vote. Even these parties, however, could not be relied upon to mount a successful protest movement. The National Movement was not extraordinarily popular; its top percentage on any measure (the PVT) was twenty-seven percent. Alone, Saakashvili might not have been able to mobilize enough supporters, lacking not only numbers but also the more important quality of being able to compellingly represent a popular rather than partisan movement. As for the Democrats, they and their followers could have been expected to simply accept defeat, with the Rustavi-2 exit poll and the PVT handing them half the vote public opinion polls suggested they would receive.[45] Their decision to join with the National Movement to lead protests helped put the already wobbly regime on the defensive.

Within the halls of power, rather than closing ranks and insisting on victory, members of the government and the FNG were themselves divided regarding how to deal with protests. Although many politicians and officials insisted on pursuing a fraudulent victory, some were consistently in favor of promoting a clean election, whereas others expressed willingness after the election to negotiate an alternative vote tabulation or a new election. Government officials even took the unusual step of calling in the head of the local NGO that had conducted the parallel vote tabulation (PVT) to discuss the mechanics of it with them.[46]

---

certify, as was expected, the CEC would not have had the necessary two-thirds majority to certify the results.

[44] If the NRP had not joined the opening session, the government, which together with Revival had fewer than 100 deputies, might not have been able to muster the 118 deputies needed to make a quorum. Areshidze, *Democracy and Autocracy in Eurasia*, p. 176.

[45] When Burjanadze consulted with some party members regarding possible courses of action, she paraphrases the responses of some as "[y]ou know, we should just try to exceed the seven percent barrier and be in parliament." At the same time, though some Democrats had little desire to take their seats in a parliament where they would be in an insignificant minority position, they also had no incentive to push for a revised vote tally that would still relegate them to at best fourth place. Burjanadze herself explains that the Democrats "decided not to participate in parliament because I knew quite well that it was not possible to do anything if you had only fifteen members there. It would mean that the president had given you the chance to be in parliament and you should be grateful to him for this, but I really didn't want to do that." See Karumidze and Wertsch, *"Enough!"* pp. 45–6.

[46] On November 6, three members of the FNG bloc (including Sarishvili-Chanturia and Rcheulishvili) accused authorities of "immorally" negotiating a manipulation of the vote count to satisfy the opposition. Six days later, even Rcheulishvili admitted that acknowledging the National Movement's victory was the only way out of the current political crisis. "Georgian Pro-government Bloc Leaders Warn against Deal with Opposition." Georgian State Television Channel 1, November 6, 2003; "Georgia: Pro-government Official Ready to 'Cede First Place' to Opposition Bloc," Imedi TV, November 12, 2003; "Georgian Authorities 'Take Interest' in Parallel Vote Count," Rustavi-2 TV, November 12, 2003, trans. in *BBC Worldwide Monitoring*.

In the end, the government publicly lost numerous supporters from within its ranks. These included the chair of the state broadcasting company, Zaza Shengelia, presidential legal advisor Levan Aleksidze, and, most importantly, National Security Council head and former ambassador to the United States Tedo Japaridze. On November 20, before the CEC released its results, Japaridze says he already favored the holding of new elections. He drafted a speech for Shevardnadze to announce this decision, but the president refused to take it. Rebuffed, Japaridze read a revised statement on television the next day, acknowledging election fraud and the damage it had done to Georgia's reputation.[47] He warned authorities against using force and expressed support for a form of the NRP's compromise solution, in which the new parliament would temporarily convene and announce the holding of new elections. He was the last official Shevardnadze ever fired.

Broadcasting Vulnerability: The Television Media

Almost unanimously, Georgian observers emphasize the role of the broadcast media in mobilizing protest. Usupashvili characterizes Rustavi-2 as "the most active part of the opposition political coalition" and goes so far as to say that the channel "frequently determined the most important decisions of the political leaders." Two other observers, Ivliane Khaindrava and Ghia Nodia, contend that the Rose Revolution could not have happened without the media's participation.[48]

Rustavi-2 openly sided with the opposition after election day and actively encouraged public involvement in protests. As Lincoln Mitchell, director of the National Democratic Institute's Georgia office during the Rose Revolution, puts it, "Rustavi 2's coverage of the protests was almost nonstop, except to provide periodic interviews and roundtables with opposition leaders – who often used the opportunities to inform Georgians about upcoming demonstrations and actions."[49] Rustavi-2's director-general, Erosi Kitsmarishvili, later admitted that "[w]e gave a one-sided coverage of the events in Tbilisi."[50]

---

[47] See Karumidze and Wertsch, *"Enough!"* pp. 55–8; and "Georgian Security Chief Warns of Bloodshed, Distances Himself From Elections," Imedi TV, November 21, 2003, trans. in *BBC Worldwide Monitoring*.

[48] Others have also noted the importance of the media in comparison to NGOs. Then head of the opposition NGO Liberty Institute Davit Zurabishvili notes that media played a larger role than NGOs. Saakashvili concurs, calling Rustavi-2 in particular "extremely important," an opinion Burjanadze has echoed. U.S. Ambassador Richard Miles also remarked that Rustavi-2 was "in a little different category" than NGOs, the role of which he believed was exaggerated, because "many people in Georgia pay attention to Rustavi-2, and it did play what can almost be called an inflammatory role." Usupashvili, "Presidential and Parliamentary Elections in Georgia," p. 95; Haindrava, "Through Elections to the 'Rose Revolution,'" p. 108; Ghia Nodia, "The Parliamentary and Presidential Elections in Georgia, 2003–2004," in *Election Assessment in the South Caucasus (2003–2004)*, p. 120; Karumidze and Wertsch, *"Enough!,"* pp. 25, 51, 65, 78.

[49] Mitchell, "Georgia's Rose Revolution," p. 345.

[50] "Rustavi-2 Admits Losing Viewers' Confidence," ITAR-TASS News Agency, December 2, 2003, trans. in *BBC Worldwide Monitoring*.

Rustavi-2 also cosponsored preelection opinion polls and an exit poll, releasing preliminary results as soon as possible. It also provided rapid exposure of the PVT results.

In addition to Rustavi-2, other television channels, including, surprisingly, state television, were also important. Imedi and Mze, which had not sided with the National Movement and the Democrats, eventually came to provide regular coverage of the demonstrations and publicized the exit polls and PVT results. Most importantly, even state-controlled Channel One provided access to "anti-Shevardnadze political forces, NGOs and independent experts" and provided footage of the demonstrations.[51] Strikingly, and rarely discussed, the staff of Channel One revolted on November 19, a day before official election results were issued, when Shevardnadze criticized the channel for "[assuming] a neutral and not pro-government position in this difficult political situation."[52] The head of the state broadcasting corporation resigned in protest, criticizing Shevardnadze for operating in a "vacuum." Channel reporters followed his lead, openly criticizing the government on television and cutting the day's news broadcast short. Popular television host Koka Qandiashvili addressed Shevardnadze directly on live television, accusing him of making a difficult situation "even more difficult today."[53] This kind of coverage dramatically confirmed the vulnerability of the regime, and ensured that dissent was transmitted to as wide and politically diverse an audience as possible.[54]

In addition to taking sides and communicating to the population at large what was happening, media coverage also served tactical functions, whether in collaboration with or used instrumentally by NGO activists and opposition parties. Usupashvili observes that the opposition "had much more sophisticated and innovative methods of using the media than the government."[55] Laurence Broers elaborates that media and activists employed a variety of techniques designed to make people believe protests were larger, more representative, and more successful at breaking down the regime than they were, and thereby

---

[51] Usupashvili, "Presidential and Parliamentary Elections in Georgia," p. 95.

[52] "Georgia: President Appoints New Chairman of State TV," Interfax, November 20, 2003, trans. in *BBC Worldwide Monitoring*.

[53] In a move that heralded a decisive shift in the balance of power away from the government, Qandiashvili announced that Shevardnadze was calling into the show while it was being broadcast, but that he would only take his call once he went off the air. "Georgian State TV News Staff Go on Strike," Georgian State Television Channel One, November 19, 2003, trans. in *BBC Worldwide Monitoring*.

[54] Usupashvili also notes that "[w]ith seven television stations covering election-related political events daily, this election was the most exhaustively covered election in Georgian history. This coverage eventually supported the mobilization of the citizens and focused their attention on political events." Usupashvili, "Presidential and Parliamentary Elections in Georgia," p. 95. At the same time, given the power shortages that plagued all of Georgia and, in particular, areas outside Tbilisi, the mechanisms of television media influence – its live broadcasts may not have even been viewed by all demonstrators – need to be further investigated.

[55] Ibid., p. 94.

get people out on the streets who would otherwise have been hesitant. Such techniques included, according to Broers,

judicious use of camera angles, the shifting of the same crowds around different locations, the attaching of other parties' insignia to National Movement buses to give the impression of a wider support base, and the encouraging by protesters of security forces to remove their helmets, thereby giving the impression in television coverage of the "breaking" of the police line and the implication that the police had "turned."[56]

Most dramatically, on the night of November 21, before the large demonstration and the rushing of parliament the next day, Rustavi-2 (and probably other channels) displayed the most dramatic display of resistance so far, a nighttime convoy of cars and buses descending on Tbilisi from the countryside and led by Saakashvili, who had traveled to the western Georgian region of Mingrelia to mobilize supporters. It was, in Burjanadze's words, "famous footage [that] was so exciting... you can't watch it without feeling emotion." Saakashvili himself downplayed the importance of the convoy, claiming that it was "more a symbolic thing" that "brought in something like 5,000 people to Tbilisi, not more."[57] His admission that the event was more symbolic than substantive speaks profoundly to the importance of the media as a spur for mobilization.

The Absence of Force

Most importantly, Georgia's security forces never cracked down on protesters. The government did not seek to deter protesters credibly with the threat of force, limit or crack down on early protests, or use force to restore order during or after the rushing of parliament on November 22.

At the first sign of street protest, there were a few indications that the government might consider brandishing force. In anticipation of the first significant rally on November 8, the government deployed hundreds of police and interior forces to block roads into Tbilisi and to line Rustaveli Avenue. A spokesperson for the Ministry of Internal Affairs warned that the police were

[56] Mitchell elaborates on Rustavi-2's use of camera angles: "[T]he station always showed images of demonstrators tightly packed together, shying away from aerial shots that might have shown that the protestors were crowded in a relatively small space. Rustavi 2's image of the vigil differed just enough from reality to give viewers the impression that there really was a mass movement actively supporting Saakashvili and the opposition." Broers, "After the 'Revolution,'" p. 342; Mitchell, "Georgia's Rose Revolution," p. 345.

[57] As other observers have put it, "[t]he television images were stunning: with headlights on, the cars moved like a huge blazing river." Having watched these images, I can attest to their impact at the time; they heralded the end of the regime. Zurabishvili says that "[t]he idea for the now famous mass arrival of people from the provinces and rural regions of Georgia in Tbilisi belongs to Levan Ramishvili, one of the founders of the Liberty Institute. It was his idea to imitate the actions taken by the opposition in Yugoslavia. After hearing this suggestion, Saakashvili went to the regions and started to summon people to come to Tbilisi." Karumidze and Wertsch, *"Enough!"* pp. 5, 13, 25, 30.

prepared to use force "if the situation gets out of control."[58] During the next significant demonstration of November 14, when protesters neared the heavily guarded state chancellery building where Shevardnadze's offices were located, Minister of Internal Affairs Koba Narchemashvili warned that in the event "armed opposition members" appeared in front of the building, the police would be compelled to respond and that this would "end very badly for the opposition."[59]

At the same time, the official armed presence and warnings of force were diluted by other signals. The smaller demonstrations that continued around the clock between November 8 and 14 encountered no opposition from security forces, and Narchemashvili specified at least twice that peaceful demonstrations would not be dispersed, a sentiment echoed by Shevardnadze and Georgia's prosecutor-general.[60] During the November 14 demonstration, the interior minister again announced that force would not be used. That day, security forces were even less visible than during the last major rally, and they concentrated their efforts on protecting government buildings and deploying on the outskirts of Tbilisi. Ultimately, any threat of force during the November 14 demonstration was grossly undermined the day before when on state-run Channel One deputy national security council chairwoman Rusudan Beridze specified that force would never be used against peaceful protesters:

The use of violence by the government . . . was always considered absolutely unacceptable at any stage of the process, unless there were instances of overt violence, such as the use of arms. Then, perhaps, the government would have had to resort to such steps. However, even then such steps would have been regarded as a last resort. . . . Narchemashvili's statement that, if needed, force would be used, was just talk, since this possibility – that is the use of violence – was completely ruled out behind the scenes.[61]

Finally, security forces failed to use force to restore order when it would have been the most justified, during and after the November 22 rushing of parliament. Shevardnadze ordered the government to enact a state of emergency at this time. His order, however, was never implemented, and he retreated the following day. The most obvious explanation for this retreat is that Shevardnadze was unable to rely on his security organs to implement the decree.

[58] "Georgian Interior Ministry: Police May Be Forced to Fire at Protesters." *Caucasus Press*, November 8, 2003, trans. in *BBC Worldwide Monitoring*.

[59] "Georgian Opposition Leader Urges Crowd to March on President's Office," *Agence France Presse*, November 14, 2003. Also see "Political Confrontation in Georgia Can Break Out into Civil War"; "Georgian Authorities to Use Force if State Office Is Stormed," *ITAR-TASS*, November 14, 2003; and "Georgian Interior Minister Expects 'Act of Provocation' Near President's Office." *Caucasus Press*, November 14, 2003, trans. in *BBC Worldwide Monitoring*.

[60] "Georgian Interior Minister Says Situation under Control." *Caucasus Press*, November 9, 2003; "Georgia: Internal Troops Deployed in Tbilisi," *Prime News Agency*, November 10, 2003, trans. in *BBC Worldwide Monitoring*.

[61] "Georgian Official Rules Out Violent End to Street Protests," Georgian State Television Channel One, November 13, 2003, trans. in *BBC Worldwide Monitoring*.

Japaridze reports that his initial reaction to the state of emergency was that it was "not only morally unacceptable" to implement but "physically impossible." Police forces were, by then, "neutral" and "different units in [the] army were staying out of the whole process from [the start.]" According to Kandelaki, by that day the opposition already "knew that some security units would not intervene."[62] Japaridze also says that at a meeting with Shevardnadze that included the defense, security, and interior ministers, in response to the urgings of some to impose a state of emergency, the chief of presidential security, Sulkhan Papashvili, started "almost shouting": "Why are you lying to the president? Tell him that it's impossible!" Given such responses, Japaridze said, who exactly "was supposed to implement this decree of a state of emergency?" Petre Mamradze, Shevardnadze's chief of staff, phoned the president in front of Japaridze and told him "there is no way to implement this state of emergency decree."[63]

There is some speculation that Shevardnadze still commanded enough security forces to have been able to engage in a crackdown if he so wished. On November 22, Narchemashvili said that "the internal troops and police were ready to act on the president's orders and would undertake all necessary measures envisaged by [a] state of emergency."[64] Kandelaki also notes that "the risk of violence was still great with no word from a number of special forces units loyal to the president."[65] Shevardnadze himself insisted that although the opposition claimed "they were the ones who actually controlled the military and special police forces," even if this were true it did "not mean that they were in control of one hundred percent of them. Enough troops would still remain to implement the emergency decree."[66]

So why then did Shevardnadze retreat? He insists he changed his mind after his wife and son urged him to reconsider, given that there would probably be casualties. Committed to avoiding bloodshed, Shevardnadze says he made up his mind to resign. In addition, Shevardnadze probably realized that given the relatively small base of loyalists among his security forces, there was a high

---

[62] Burjanadze also noted that the opposition had "supporters...active inside the army and police." Saakashvili adds that after Burjanadze declared herself interim president, she called the heads of army regiments, who did not openly acknowledge her authority but hinted at their neutrality: "Don't worry. We are not going to take any radical steps. We will look into it." Kandelaki, "A Participant's Perspective," p. 11; Karumidze and Wertsch, *"Enough!"* pp. 27, 47, 54.

[63] Karumidze and Wertsch, *"Enough!"* p. 55. Mitchell similarly argues that "Shevardnadze resigned because, finally realizing his own weakness, he became aware that he no longer controlled the military and security forces. Bloodshed was avoided largely because the president was too politically weak to command it." Mitchell, "Georgia's Rose Revolution," p. 348.

[64] "Georgian Interior Minister 'Ready to Act' on President Shevardnadze's Orders." *Caucasus Press*, November 22, 2003, trans. in *BBC Worldwide Monitoring*.

[65] Burjanadze adds that she thought Shevardnadze would "never give an order to use violence" but that she "was not sure about those surrounding him." Kandelaki, "A Participant's Perspective," p. 11; Karumidze and Wertsch, *"Enough!"* p. 48.

[66] Karumidze and Wertsch, *"Enough!"* p. 30.

possibility that a special-forces crackdown would be of limited effectiveness, ultimately risking failure and leaving Shevardnadze's reputation in tatters and his family vulnerable to retribution. Whatever the reason, Shevardnadze let his decree on the state of emergency lapse. The day before, he hastily denied to Mamradze that he had even ordered it, fearing (correctly) that Mamradze and Japaridze were already in discussions with opposition representatives. The next morning, Japaridze paints a picture of a frightened and desperate Shevardnadze, scolding one of his inner circle: "What was this talk about plans for a decree of a state of emergency? There was no reason for us to implement this."[67]

With this final absence of an order to suppress the demonstrations, the security organs at last defected en masse to the opposition. Zhvania explains that while "a couple [of] army units had started to join [the opposition] on the 22nd" (i.e., before Shevardnadze ordered the decree to impose a state of emergency), "the situation was very uncertain. There were no guarantees."[68] By the early afternoon of November 23, a cascade of army units declared loyalty to Burjanadze as interim president. They were followed by police units and, at last, the Tbilisi chief of police. The opposition had won. Shevardnadze resigned that night.

THE ROLE OF EXTERNAL FACTORS

Assuming the significance of the above factors – alternative vote counts, the government's dependence on the local despot Abashidze, the broad social coalition spearheading protests, the engagement of broadcast media, and the government's reluctance to use force – what role may be ascribed to external factors? Two, in particular, are often cited as critical to the unfolding of the Rose Revolution: the diffusion effect of democratic resistance models elsewhere, in particular in Serbia, and U.S. government assistance and diplomacy.

Diffusion: Assessing the "Serbia" Factor

A diffusion effect on the Rose Revolution was certainly in evidence. A handful of prominent Western-funded nongovernmental organizations (the Liberty Institute, Kmara, ISFED and the Fair Elections Foundation, and the Georgian Young Lawyers' Association) received support and training from prodemocracy NGOs in the United States and Europe and were active at all levels – promoting democratic institutions and participation and the message of regime vulnerability; pressing for legal redress; and encouraging people to come to the streets. To the extent that open and frequent criticism of the regime, exit polls and the PVT, and NGO tactics and organization led to a public perception of

---

[67] Shevardnadze says that the next morning he "even avoided meeting some of my colleagues who were very bellicose and demanded the use of force." Karumidze and Wertsch, *"Enough!"* p. 30, 55.

[68] Ibid., p. 39.

government vulnerability, the organizations involved were instrumental in this success.[69]

The argument for a specifically Serbian diffusion effect stems from the fact that activists and, among politicians, Saakashvili in particular directly sought to reproduce the Serbian popular movement in Georgia. According to Kandelaki, the Serbian youth group Otpor "served as [an] inspiration and model for Kmara," a Georgian student organization formed in the spring of 2003 to promote democratic elections. In the fall of 2002, Otpor activists, as well as some from civic movements in Slovakia, visited Tbilisi for consultation with and training of local NGOs. Representatives from the Liberty Institute and other NGOs went to Belgrade (as well as Bratislava) on an Open Society Foundation–funded study tour at the start of 2003.[70] Inspired by these exchanges, NGO leaders helped stimulate the creation of Kmara on the basis of two preexisting student groups, an elected student body organization that fought corruption in Tbilisi State University beginning in 2000, with the assistance of the National Democratic Institute, and the Student Movement for Georgia, formed from students who participated in the 2001 protests to defend Rustavi-2.[71] Kmara's role in the Rose Revolution sparked considerable interest after observers became aware of the role of the Open Society Foundation in facilitating the Otpor visit to Tbilisi and the NGO trip to Belgrade.[72]

Kandelaki has argued that Kmara was one of three actors that "played a crucial role in making the Rose Revolution possible" (the other two being the National Movement and Rustavi-2) and that it "succeeded in breaking through the public's political apathy."[73] Its methods included "non-violence, discipline, coordination, promoting its brand [as well as the myth of a powerful organization], and making skillful use of humor." Its activities included marches, antigovernment theatrical or humorous displays, graffiti campaigns, rock concerts, and social services (including book donation campaigns and trash collections) before the election; leaflet distributions and television commercials before and after election day; and involvement in university disobedience committees (representing the universities, not Kmara) during postelectoral protests.[74]

---

[69] Kandelaki makes the useful point that the quality of election monitoring allowed Kmara and other opposition groups "to concentrate all their resources in promoting political participation." Kandelaki, "A Participant's Perspective," 10.

[70] Kandelaki, unpublished, pp. 9–10.

[71] Kandelaki, "A Participant's Perspective," p. 6.

[72] See Hugh Pope, "Pro-West Leaders in Georgia Push Shevardnadze Out." *Wall Street Journal*, November 24, 2003; Peter Baker, "Tbilisi's 'Revolution of Roses' Mentored by Serbian Activists," *Washington Post*, November 25, 2003; Mark MacKinnon, "Georgia Revolt Carried Mark of Soros." *Globe and Mail* (Toronto), November 26, 2003; and Natalia Antelava, "How to Stage a Revolution." *BBC News*, December 4, 2003, available at http://news.bbc.co.uk/2/hi/europe/3288547.stm; accessed December 28, 2006.

[73] Kandelaki, "A Participant's Perspective," p. 5.

[74] Ibid., pp. 5, 6–8.

That Kmara actively pressed for democratization, resistance to fraud, and eventually revolution is not in dispute. Initially, the 3,000-strong Kmara organization, together with other opposition groups, hoped only to achieve enough success to influence the later 2005 presidential elections. Although Kandelaki does not emphasize it, Kmara, again together with other opposition groups, planned to try to mobilize sufficient support after election day to pressure the government into conceding defeat or at least nullifying fraudulent results.[75] According to Kandelaki, once it became clear the government was determined to validate the fraudulent elections, the opposition "radicalized their demands and began to use the word *revolution*."[76]

How much did Kmara's efforts contribute to Georgia's electoral breakthrough? Kandelaki asserts that its success was chiefly in mobilizing Georgian youth. He estimates that they managed to mobilize more than 10,000 "previously inactive university students" through their work in the disobedience committees. Even so, how significant the activity of 10,000 students was in overthrowing the regime must be considered. With regard to promoting broader public mobilization, Kandelaki says that Kmara "sought to fight political apathy among all Georgian voters" and that its members proved "capable of carrying their pleas for more political involvement to all parts of Georgian society."[77] He stops short, however, of insisting that Kmara was critical to mobilizing protesters more broadly. There is good reason for this modesty. A survey taken among Tbilisi residents immediately after the Rose Revolution polled attitudes toward Kmara specifically. In this poll, where exuberance appears to have led to self-reporting extremes on many questions, just twenty-six percent of those polled expressed approval for Kmara's goals and methods. Another thirty-three percent of respondents voiced approval for Kmara's goals *but not their methods*, whereas fifteen percent expressed "a negative attitude" toward the youth organization.[78]

[75] David Zurabashvili, former head of the Liberty Institute, notes that the "second point" Kmara made in its preelectoral activities was that in case "elections were rigged people should speak up, and we [the Liberty Institute] carried out a lot of activities in this regard, both in the capital and in the provinces." Ibid., p. 5; Karumidze and Wertsch, *"Enough!"* p. 65.

[76] Zurabashvili elaborates that "revolution" at that point meant regime change; after it became clear that the government "was not going to give up" (i.e., intended to validate the fraudulent results), "we had no other option. Either we would move ahead and make them resign and make Shevardnadze step down, or the nucleus of Shevardnadze's bloc . . . would grab all power, and democracy would be finished completely." Even then, however, opposition groups, including Kmara, recognized that government concessions, even in the form of nullifying only the results where fraud was "absolutely obvious," would have limited their capacity to effect a revolution (and, for most, would still have been an acceptable outcome). Zurabishvili admits that some of the opposition were "worried about what would happen if Shevardnadze [conceded since they] really wanted to go the way of the revolution." Kandelaki, "A Participant's Perspective," p. 4; Karumidze and Wertsch, *"Enough!"* p. 62.

[77] Kandelaki, "A Participant's Perspective," p. 8.

[78] Twelve percent claimed neutrality, and fourteen percent did not answer the question. Nana Sumbadze and George Tarkhan-Mouravi, "Public Opinion in Tbilisi: In the Aftermath of the

Georgian political actors deliver mixed verdicts about the impact of Kmara and associated NGOs. Saakashvili said that Kmara and other NGOs were "not that important," especially compared to the role of the media, in bringing most students out to the streets. Others, however, are more willing to emphasize Kmara's achievements. Khaindrava highlights the ambiguity of Kmara's role:

Noisy and annoying, [Kmara's] activists sometimes irritated the ordinary citizen, but they managed to build up their campaign. When during the post-election protests the activism of the general public subsided temporarily, Kmara revived popular enthusiasm for its un-self-seeking activity.[79]

Similarly, when speaking of Kmara's role, Burjanadze reveals that she "didn't always support them," and that their "reactions and...methods were not acceptable" to her. At the same time, she argues that "what they did, their activities and emotional feelings and emotional preaching...they did a lot with the people and somehow to mobilize the people. I think it would be unfair not to speak about their very important role."[80] Kandelaki himself emphasizes that it was not through their extraordinary capacities that NGOs helped to reveal government vulnerability but precisely because of their limitations: though the NGO community was "weak and fragmented," the government demonstrated its incompetence on a wider scale because it could not manage to respond to its accusations in a persuasive and authoritative manner.[81]

Whatever the impact of diffusion via Kmara and associated NGOs, however, they were not the only ones seeking to emulate the Serbian model. As it happens, OSI also sent Saakashvili, together with Zhvania and Gamkrelidze, to Belgrade at the start of 2003 on a "study trip" to learn more about the movement that toppled Milošević. Although the Serbian mobilization model had little appeal to Gamkrelidze, and only limited and belated attraction to Zhvania, Saakashvili embraced it. In January, Saakashvili told a television interviewer that the opposition should unite to achieve victory in the upcoming parliamentary elections, "[j]ust as it happened in Yugoslavia where they first defeated Milosevic." At a public meeting in Washington, DC in April, Saakashvili referred "several times" to the Serbian comparison and called himself a "successful version of [assassinated Serbian Prime Minister and former

Parliamentary Elections of November 2, 2003," In *NISPAcee News* (Bratislava), 11, No. 1 (Winter 2004), pp. 1–14, at p. 7, available at http://unpan1.un.org/intradoc/groups/public/documents/NISPAcee/UNPAN014817.pdf; accessed December 28, 2006.

[79] Zurabishvili and Nodia also contend that NGOs were important but do not privilege them as they do the media. Haindrava, "Through Elections to the 'Rose Revolution,'" p. 109; Karumidze and Wertsch, *"Enough!"* p. 65; Nodia, "The Parliamentary and Presidential Elections in Georgia, 2003–2004," p. 120.

[80] Karumidze and Wertsch, *"Enough!"* p. 51.

[81] In general, he notes that the role of NGOs in the Rose Revolution was overestimated. He says that Georgian NGOs were "constrained by elitism" and their foreign funding sources, keeping both their agenda foreign and preventing them from achieving "the local legitimacy necessary to gain public support." Kandelaki, "A Participant's Perspective," p. 10.

Belgrade mayor Zoran] Djindjic." The next month, he warned Shevardnadze against trying to play the ethnic card in Georgia, noting that this had already "been tried by Milosevic" and warning that the latter had been defeated by Otpor.[82]

Rustavi-2 was also inspired by the Serbian example, twice during the election crisis airing a documentary on the fall of Milošević. Later, National Movement member (and eventually interior minister) Ivane Merabishvili asserted that "[a]ll the demonstrators knew the tactics of the revolution in Belgrade by heart because they showed . . . the film on their revolution. Everyone knew what to do. This was a copy of that revolution, only louder."[83]

To answer the question of diffusion effects on popular protest, then, not only should Kmara and associated NGOs be considered a conveyor of the "Serbian" model but also Saakashvili's National Movement and, ultimately, Rustavi-2 should be so considered. Whether the twenty-six percent of survey respondents that backed Kmara overlapped entirely or only partially onto the support base for the National Movement – and whether in aggregate they formed the bulk of street protesters – is difficult to tell. So, too, is it difficult to know how many demonstrators saw or were informed of the documentary broadcast on Rustavi-2. Still, the diversity of elements inspired by Milošević's downfall and their role in spearheading the protests indicate that popular mobilization, if not its success, stemmed at least in part from a diffusion effect.

Ironically, in the end a diffusion effect appears to have played its greatest role in bringing about the Rose Revolution through actors' awareness of the *differences* between Georgia and sites of previous electoral breakthroughs. Saakashvili's decision to rush parliament, the proximate cause of the Rose Revolution, lay decidedly outside a "copycat" framework of popular street mobilization. Although Saakashvili drew inspiration from the overthrow of Milošević in Serbia, he also realized that Shevardnadze's convening of parliament risked shifting the balance of power back toward authorities and reducing the momentum of the protest movement. Rather than allow the resistance – and the emulation of Serbia – to fail, Saakashvili made the unexpected and unwritten move to rush parliament, radically exposing the government's vulnerability and forcing Shevardnadze to concede defeat. Thus, by the "counterdiffusion" act of rushing parliament, Saakashvili made the Rose Revolution occur and established it as something decidedly different from the electoral breakthroughs that had come before.

---

[82] "Georgia's Two Leading Opposition Parties Call for Broad Antigovernment Alliance." Rustavi-2 TV, January 22, 2003, trans. in *BBC Worldwide Monitoring*; "Stability in Georgia: After the War in Iraq, Prior to Elections," The Nixon Center, Washington, DC, April 14, 2003, available at www.nixoncenter.org/publications/Program percent 20Briefs/PBrief percent 202003/041403saakashvili.htm; accessed December 28, 2006. "Opposition Accuses Georgian Authorities of Fanning Ethnic Strife." Rustavi-2 TV, May 4, 2003, trans. in *BBC Worldwide Monitoring*. Also see Areshidze, *Democracy and Autocracy in Eurasia*, pp. 100–101.

[83] Baker, "Tbilisi's 'Revolution of Roses' Mentored by Serbian Activists."

Foreign Intervention: Assessing U.S. Influence

The role of the United States in bringing about the Rose Revolution is similarly nuanced. Certainly, U.S. democracy promoters pursued a number of policies aimed at improving the chances that a democratic election would occur in Georgia. The U.S. Agency for International Development budgeted more democracy-related assistance to Georgia in 2002 and 2003 than to any post-Soviet state except the considerably larger Russia and Ukraine. This assistance included funding for voter list reform, PVT training and implementation, the cultivation of local election-monitoring NGOs, and civil society advocacy training. Together with the Soros-funded Open Society Foundation funding for NGOs, study trips, and training, U.S. aid is commonly cited as a factor that increased pressure on the government to hold a democratic election, and increased the likelihood of voter participation and postelectoral detection of fraud.

In addition to assistance, the level of U.S. diplomacy in support of democratic elections was striking. It included a number of letters from President George W. Bush to Shevardnadze encouraging clean elections; a June 2003 visit of former Secretary of State James Baker, serving as a special presidential envoy, who urged the regime to adopt a ten-point plan for elections, including the main task of reforming election commissions as well as allowing a PVT; and delegations to Georgia a month before the election led by Senator John McCain and, via the National Democratic Institute, former deputy secretary of state Strobe Talbott and former chairman of the Joint Chiefs of Staff John Shalikashvili.

In addition to these efforts at persuasion, U.S. officials also used diplomatic pressure. In mid-August, U.S. Ambassador Richard Miles told a Rustavi-2 interviewer that if parliamentary elections were "not conducted in an open and honest and transparent manner," this would not only "be very bad for Georgia," it would "also be bad for the American–Georgian relationship."[84] In late September, Thomas Adams, then deputy coordinator of U.S. assistance to Europe and Eurasia, announced from Tbilisi that the United States would be scaling down its foreign aid to Georgia, citing dissatisfaction with corruption and abuse of power. Several days later, Ambassador Miles told a Georgian television interviewer that the United States would "probably further reduce the assistance" to Georgia in the next six months "if progress is not achieved" in areas the United States was helping finance.[85]

---

[84] "US Ambassador to Georgia Hails Ties, Urges Fair Elections," Rustavi-2 TV, August 15, 2003, trans. in *BBC Worldwide Monitoring*.

[85] Prior to Adam's announcement, the International Monetary Fund (IMF) declared that it was also suspending assistance to Georgia. "USA Set to Cut Aid to Georgia," Rustavi-2 TV, September 24, 2003, trans. in *BBC Worldwide Monitoring*; Natalia Antelava, "United States Cuts Development Aid to Georgia," *Eurasia Insight*, September 29, 2003, available at http://www.eurasianet.org/departments/insight/articles/eav092903.shtml; accessed December 28, 2006; "Georgian Election to Determine 'Quality of Relations' with USA." Rustavi-2 TV, October 5, 2003, trans. in *BBC Worldwide Monitoring*.

U.S. assistance and diplomacy promoted at least *more* democratic Georgian elections than there would have been if these efforts had been absent. U.S. intervention, through funding and diplomacy, might have been critical, for instance, in implementing vote-monitoring mechanisms such as the exit polls and PVT. To be certain, we would have to determine whether civil society groups could have found domestic sponsors and trainers and whether the Georgian government would have agreed to these mechanisms in the absence of external pressure. For the PVT, at least, U.S. intervention was probably decisive, as other possible sponsors and trainers were not immediately apparent. The independent exit poll, on the other hand, had more diverse sources of funding, including funding from domestic sources (Rustavi-2), and the government might very well have permitted it to be conducted in the absence of U.S. support.

At the same time, U.S. efforts did not achieve their main objective: a free and fair election. In one of the two biggest controversies prior to the elections, the Georgian government backtracked on its agreement with Baker to provide a blocking minority of seats to opposition parties on the election commissions. In addition, despite the tremendous organizational effort on the part of the USAID contractor International Foundation for Electoral Systems (IFES), the process of revising, updating, and computerizing voter lists was riddled with difficulties, including repeated delays by the Ministry of Internal Affairs in providing necessary data.[86] Despite all U.S. urging, the Georgian government ultimately carried out, and validated, a fraudulent election.

In determining the U.S. impact, however, we should consider whether the American aims in Georgia were even more ambitious than the pursuit of high-level democracy promotion prior to election day. Did the U.S. government plan to respond to electoral fraud with conventional criticism and a downgraded relationship with Georgia, or did it actually hope to help bring about a resistance movement that would compel the Georgian government to submit to the people's will? Certainly, U.S. diplomacy was geared toward producing a compromise resolution to the crisis – which, in this context, likely meant getting the Georgian government to concede its loss. In addition to a stream of critical remarks in the State Department's daily press briefing, U.S. officials were in regular communication with both government and opposition representatives in the days before official results were announced. U.S. Ambassador Richard Miles characterized his role less as one of direct mediation, than of encouraging communication between the two sides in the hopes that they would work

---

[86] In the final days before the election, when it became apparent that the computerized lists still contained obvious inaccuracies, the CEC ruled to use original handwritten lists and to amend them as necessary on election day. This last condition – allowing individuals to vote even if they were not on the registered lists – accommodated voters who had been disenfranchised by the confusion, but it also opened the door to election day fraud. For a discussion of the voter lists, see Usupashvili, "Presidential and Parliamentary Elections in Georgia," pp. 82–4. Also see Areshidze, *Democracy and Autocracy in Eurasia*, pp. 126–9.

out a compromise solution.[87] Government officials in Washington, DC were also following events closely, with at least one in regular contact with both reform-minded government representatives and the opposition, Saakashvili in particular.[88]

Although these efforts were unsuccessful, U.S. diplomacy could conceivably have been successful in weakening the government's resolve to use force against protesters, thereby (intentionally or not) creating the opening for a peaceful change of power. More than on his role as facilitator, Miles placed value on his role as restrainer – urging the government (and opposition representatives) to resolve the crisis peacefully. Miles says he spoke with authorities at length about "the need to avoid the use of force and in particular the use of lethal force." He also specifies that he spent "[h]ours in repeated conversations with the power ministers [i.e., security, internal affairs, and defense], as did other people in the embassy who had working relationships with the people in those ministries."[89] In addition, Pentagon officials, who had been working in close collaboration with the Georgian defense ministry since 2002 with the initiation of the Georgian Train-and-Equip Program, are said to have appealed to defense officials to keep the army neutral.[90]

Did U.S. urgings restrain government officials, particularly those in the security organs, from using force?[91] Miles said that he "would like to hope that [his involvement] helped keep the whole exercise nonviolent."[92] At the same time, the Georgian government and security forces were already disinclined to use force against protesters. Still, the references of some Georgian participants to army units that could be counted on not to get involved were likely in reference to forces undergoing U.S. training at the time. Thus, even if diplomacy was not the critical factor, security linkages to the United States may still have been relevant to the government's inclination to pursue restraint.

Declining U.S. support for Georgia's government also likely reinforced regime vulnerability more generally, by increasing the confidence of opposition supporters that mobilization would succeed and the incentive of government officials receptive to political change to defect. For months, the specter of losing U.S. support was evident, including most prominently the announcement of a reduction in foreign aid. The most powerful effect, however, was at the very

[87] Karumidze and Wertsch, *"Enough!"* p. 72.

[88] Personal communication, February 13, 2004.

[89] Karumidze and Wertsch, *"Enough!"* p. 72.

[90] See Charles H. Fairbanks, Jr., "Georgia's Rose Revolution." *Journal of Democracy*, 15, No. 2 (2004), pp. 100–24, at pp. 117 and 123. The United States was also closely engaged with the Georgian Ministry of Security, though I have no information regarding the nature of communication to the ministry during this period.

[91] A second question is whether those urgings had the strategic intent of shifting the balance of power in favor of the opposition, precisely in order to achieve an electoral breakthrough (even if U.S. officials were hoping for a breakthrough of a more moderate sort), or were motivated by the straightforward belief that the important thing was that the security organs stay out of the conflict, regardless of its outcome.

[92] Karumidze and Wertsch, *"Enough!"* p. 72.

end of the crisis. On November 20, after official election results were issued, State Department deputy spokesman Adam Ereli informed journalists that "we have seen the results released today.... [and] are deeply disappointed in these results, and in Georgia's leadership. The results... reflect massive vote fraud in Ajara and other Georgian regions." He noted that the results "revealed an effort by the Central Election Commission and the Georgian government to ignore the will of the people."[93] This was, one analyst asserted, the "first time ever that the U.S. has openly accused the leadership of a former Soviet republic of rigging an election."[94]

The State Department statement was circulated throughout Georgia, repeated by newscasters on several television news channels and printed in full on the screen. The following day, the implication of this message was clear: the United States, which Georgia looked to as a patron, did not, and would not, support the regime.

What would have happened if the United States had backed the Georgian government? What if officials had quickly congratulated the ruling party, while issuing only mild condemnation of fraud; had not openly persuaded the government to negotiate; and did not have the kinds of linkages that made it plausible for them to urge security organs to refrain from the use of force? Would the government have felt itself stronger, the opposition weaker? Would officials who were on the fence have been encouraged to stick with the government and not, as it actually happened, jump off the evidently sinking ship? It is at this level that one should determine whether the role of U.S. diplomacy was decisive – whether, given definitive U.S. support for the government, the Rose Revolution would have failed.

At the same time, there is no evidence to suggest that the U.S. government sought or expected specifically *regime* change (as opposed to fair elections) in Georgia in November 2003. Shevardnadze's resignation and the ascent of Mikheil Saakashvili to the presidency were not part of the game plan. U.S. assistance and diplomacy sought to promote free and fair elections in Georgia and, at most, weaken the Georgian government's will and/or ability to uphold fraudulent results that would maintain its dominance in parliament. In these aims, it did not succeed.

In the end, to reiterate, it was Saakashvili's own determination to go outside the script and peacefully storm parliament that spectacularly boosted the popular movement's chance of success. Without this denouement, a failed but externally supported popular movement might still have led a weakened

---

93 Daily Press Briefing, U.S. Department of State, November 20, 2003, available at www. state.gov/r/pa/prs/dpb/2003/26502.htm; accessed December 28, 2006. For the formal White House reaction to the election, see "Presidential Election in Georgia," Press Statement, U.S. Department of State, November 21, 2003, available at www.state.gov/r/pa/prs/ps/2003/ 26539.htm; accessed December 28, 2006.

94 Liz Fuller, "Shevardnadze's Resignation Resolves Constitutional Deadlock," RFE/RL Caucasus Report, November 24, 2003, available at www.rferl.org/reports/caucasus-report/2003/11/41–241103.asp; accessed December 28, 2006.

government to make concessions toward the opposition, and perhaps even facilitated a democratic presidential election scheduled for 2005.[95] However, the Rose Revolution – and Mikheil Saakashvili's rapid ascent to power – would not have occurred.

CONCLUSION

Georgia's Rose Revolution stemmed from Georgians' discontent with an ineffective, criminalized, and corrupt ruling regime. Georgia's ruling party was not only unpopular before the 2003 election, but also weak. The ruling party had fragmented and was forced to rely on marginal and discredited political forces; it had performed poorly in past local elections and opinion polls; it faced criticism from popular broadcast media; and it lacked the will to use force against protesters and political opponents.

That said, before election day it was clear that the government was vulnerable, not that it could be defeated. The Rose Revolution was the product of a set of interactions between social and political forces and the state that magnified the government's vulnerability after election day and ultimately led it to the brink of collapse. The conjunction of exit polls and a parallel vote tabulation weakened the ruling regime's ability to insist on its outright success; the government depended on a flagrantly fraudulent vote count in one region, provoking widespread indignation among the Tbilisi population; two political parties joined with civil society activists and Georgia's intellectual and cultural elite to set a nonpartisan tone for protest; the broadcast media broadly covered the protests, with the most popular station publicly backing the opposition; and political elites refused to support the use of force to restore order. Together these developments created the context for opposition leader Saakashvili and his supporters to successfully rush Georgia's parliamentary building and break up the new parliament's opening session, forcing Shevardnadze to concede defeat.

---

[95] Leading opposition figures all agree that if Shevardnadze had agreed to rerun the election, he would never have had to resign. The only realistic possibility to this effect appears to be that proposed by the NRP and backed by Japaridze – to convene the new parliament but schedule an early election for the coming months. Even the head of the FNG, Vazha Lortkipanidze, went on record in support of the New Rights proposal. Areshidze says that Shevardnadze initially refused to consider this option but, desperate for a quorum at the parliament's first session, at the last minute agreed to back a proposal to hold new elections, after which the newly elected NEP deputies agreed to join the parliamentary session. Saakashvili and his followers rushed into the parliament building, however, before anyone had a chance to discuss the issue. It is impossible to know whether Shevardnadze was going to go ahead with the alleged agreement and announce new elections, and if so whether new elections would have been more democratic. On the opportunity for Shevardnadze to stay in power, see Karumidze and Wertsch, *"Enough!"* pp. 35, 44, 59, 62. The NRP's perspective is in Areshidze, *Democracy and Autocracy in Eurasia*, pp. 176–80. On Lortkipanidze, see "Georgian Pro-government Bloc Leader Supports Early Parliamentary Elections," *Caucasus Press*, November 21, 2003, trans. in *BBC Worldwide Monitoring*.

External influences promoted this outcome, even if they were not decisive. Saakashvili and a number of civil society activists sought to replicate past electoral breakthroughs in eastern Europe and planned to use popular mobilization to pressure the government to accept defeat if it refused to acknowledge its loss. This diffusion effect operated in conjunction with factors that were not exported across borders to help produce the Rose Revolution, the most important of which was Saakashvili's own determination to go outside the script. At the same time, the most obvious effect of U.S. assistance and diplomacy was not in promoting a democratic outcome – in this, the United States did not succeed – but in heightening perceptions of government vulnerability.

Georgia's Rose Revolution highlights a central paradox of electoral breakthroughs. They happen in countries that have moved further down a democratic pathway than those that have not. In neighboring Armenia and Azerbaijan, for example, opposition forces sought to resist fraud in various electoral races in 2003, 2005, and 2008 and were even able to mount substantial protests. In all these cases, however, they were defeated by strong regimes. In Armenia and Azerbaijan, ruling regimes went into elections neither fragmented nor reliant on discredited political forces; they had not previously lost local elections or (with one Armenian exception) received poor ratings in publicized opinion polls; they did not allow free broadcast media; and they maintained a credible threat of force. Unsurprisingly, after election day, the interaction between social actors and the state in Armenia and Azerbaijan reinforced regime strength rather than magnify their vulnerabilities, with the state, in particular, able and willing to use force to deter and break up protests. The lesson for electoral breakthroughs is thus two-sided – as in other revolutions, electoral revolutions require the emergence of proper conditions within the state as much as they require dedicated revolutionaries.

8

Importing Revolution

Internal and External Factors in Ukraine's 2004 Democratic Breakthrough

Michael McFaul
Stanford University

The fall 2004 Ukrainian presidential election led to one of the seminal moments in that country's history. Initially, the campaign and election results resembled other tainted and fraudulent votes in semiauthoritarian regimes around the world. The incumbent president, Leonid Kuchma, and his chosen successor, Prime Minister Victor Yanukovych, deployed all available state resources, national media, and private funding from both Ukrainians and Russians to defeat the opposition candidate, Victor Yushchenko.

When this effort to win the vote failed, Kuchma's government tried to steal the election, allegedly adding more than 1 million extra votes to Yanukovych's tally in the second round of voting held on November 21, 2004. In response to this perceived fraud, Yushchenko called upon his supporters to come to the Maidan, the Independence Square in Kyiv, and protest the stolen election. First thousands, then tens of thousands, then hundreds of thousands answered his call. They remained on the square, with some living in a tent city on Khreshchatyk, Kyiv's main thoroughfare, until the Supreme Court annulled the official results of the second round on December 3, 2004 and set a date for the rerunning of the second round for December 26, 2004. In this vote, Yushchenko won fifty-two percent of the vote, compared to forty-four percent for Yanukovych. Although most domestic and international observers declared this third round of voting to be freer and fairer than the fist two, Yanukovych nonetheless contested the results in the courts, but with no success. On January 23, 2005, the Supreme Court affirmed the validity of the December 26 vote, and Yushchenko took the presidential oath of office. The victors in this dramatic struggle commemorated this set of events by calling it the Orange Revolution.

These events in Ukraine inspired most people living in the free world. Ukrainian citizens stood together in the freezing cold to demand from their government what citizens in consolidated democracies take for granted: the right to elect their leaders in free and fair elections. But not all observers of Ukraine's Orange Revolution were so elated. Instead of democracy's advance, some saw a U.S.-funded, White House-orchestrated conspiracy aimed at undermining Ukrainian sovereignty, weakening Russia's sphere of influence, and expanding Washington's imperial reach.[1] In reaction to the Orange Revolution, autocratic regimes in Belarus, China, Ethiopia, Kazakhstan, Russia, Uzbekistan, and Zimbabwe initiated crackdowns on civil society organizations and further constrained the freedom to maneuver for independent political actors more generally.

What role did external actors, and the United States in particular, play in fostering the Orange Revolution? An answer to this question is not only important as a factual response to the critics of the Orange Revolution. The case is also an important one to be studied by those interested in understanding how external actors can influence democratization. Tracing the causal impact of democracy assistance programs on the consolidation of liberal democracy is very difficult, because the process of liberal democratic consolidation is incremental, complex, and long-term. The Orange Revolution, however, was a defined, concrete outcome, which therefore can be more easily explained. This essay attempts to offer such an explanation, with special attention devoted to isolating the distinctive contributions to the Orange Revolution of programs funded by the U.S. Agency of International Development.[2]

To structure the analysis, this chapter is organized as follows. Section I begins by characterizing the nature of the regime in Ukraine on the eve of the 2004 presidential elections. The argument in this section is that Ukraine's semiautocratic regime created the conditions permitting the Orange Revolution to occur.

Section II then catalogs the proximate causes of the Orange Revolution: an unpopular incumbent, a successful opposition campaign, the ability to create the perception of a falsified vote, the means to communicate information about the falsified vote, the ability to mobilize masses to protest the fraudulent election, and sufficient divisions among the "guys with guns" to cast doubt on the success of repression. To this list of necessary conditions for success are then added three facilitating conditions: an independent parliament, a relatively independent Supreme Court, and a roundtable negotiating effort that included Yushchenko, Yanukovych, and Kuchma. After the importance of each of these proximate causes is identified, the role of external actors and the United States in particular in facilitating the development of these factors is discussed.[3]

Section III pushes the story back one step further in the causal chain and analyzes the deeper structural features that may have produced the proximate causes outlined in Section II. Here the analysis focuses on broader, variables

---

[1] See, for example, Jonathan Steele, "Ukraine's Post-Modern Coup D'Etat" *The Guardian*, Nov. 26, 2004.

[2] In focusing on the causes of the Orange Revolution, this essay does not assume that the struggle to consolidate liberal democracy in Ukraine is over. Such a claim would be absurd. Rather, the focus here is only on explaining this one outcome, motivated by the more modest claim that the Orange Revolution or "democratic breakthrough" in Ukraine will have a positive impact on democratic development in Ukraine more generally.

[3] To date, the inordinate focus on the American role is only a function of research completed. Further work requires a more full accounting of all external actors.

such as economic growth, the rise of the middle class, the development of civil society more generally, an educated and informed electorate, and the role of ideas and culture. This section then also attempts to map the potential international contributions to the structural factors outlined. As this analysis is far removed from the actual events of the Orange Revolution, the conclusions are more suggestive of future research than definitive in making causal claims.

Section IV concludes.

I. SEMIAUTHORITARIANISM AS A CONDITION PERMITTING DEMOCRATIC BREAKTHROUGH

The literature on democratization contains several different arguments about the relationship between the kinds of autocracy, on the one hand, and the probability of successful democratic regime change, on the other.[4] Of course, all autocratic regimes are vulnerable to collapse at some point, but which kinds of autocracies are more vulnerable than others? To date, the debate has not been resolved. Some posit that semiautocratic or competitive authoritarian regimes better facilitate democratization than full-blown dictatorships.[5] Others argue that semiautocracies or partial democracies actually impede genuine democratization to a far greater degree than more rigid autocracies because liberalized autocracies can partially diffuse societal pressures for change and thereby avoid regime collapse more effectively than more rigid dictatorships.[6] Scholars also disagree about which autocratic institutional arrangement is most conducive to political liberalization.

To this debate, Ukraine offers confirming evidence that semiautocracy, competitive autocracy, or partial democracy can be conducive to democratic breakthrough. These are regimes in which the formal rules of democracy and especially elections were never suspended and competition, to some degree, still mattered.[7] They are also regimes in which some political institutions and organizations had some autonomy from the autocratic ruler. This particular regime type allowed pockets of pluralism and opposition within the state, which proved critical to democratic breakthrough.

In Ukraine, President Leonid Kuchma constructed a semiautocratic or semidemocratic regime, which was neither a full-blown dictatorship nor a

---

[4] Juan Linz and Alfred Stepan, *Problems of Democratic Transition and Consolidation*, (Baltimore: Johns Hopkins University Press, 1996); Jeane Kirkpatrick, *Dictatorship and Double Standards: Rationalism and Reason in Politics*, (New York: Simon and Schuster, 1982).

[5] Michael McFaul, "Transitions from Postcommunism." *Journal of Democracy*, 16, No. 3 (2005), pp. 5–19.

[6] Daniel Brumberg, "Liberalization versus Democracy," In *Uncharted Journey: Promoting Democracy in the Middle East*, Thomas Carothers and Marina Ottoway, eds., (Washington: Carnegie Endowment for International Peace, 2005), pp. 15–36.

[7] On this regime type, see Larry Diamond, "Thinking about Hybrid Regimes." *Journal of Democracy*, 13, No. 2 (2002), pp. 21–35; Steven Levitsky and Lucan Way, "The Rise of Competitive Authoritarianism." *Journal of Democracy*, 13, No. 2 (2002), pp. 51–65.

consolidated democracy. Kuchma aspired to construct a system of "managed democracy" – formal democratic practices, but informal control of all political institutions – similar to Putin's in Russia. But the Ukrainian president never achieved as much success as his Russian counterpart.[8] Because Kuchma in his second term never enjoyed the overwhelming public support that Putin garnered in the first years of his rule in Russia, the Ukrainian president was more constrained when trying to limit political autonomy and opposition. In addition, Kuchma's inept and blunt attempts to squelch opposition voices – his alleged collusion in ordering the murder of journalist Giorgy Gongadze, his jailing of former energy minister Yulia Tymoshenko, and his dismissal of the successful and popular prime minister Viktor Yushchenko – served to mobilize even greater opposition. This societal response to bad and autocratic government is what most distinguishes Ukraine from its neighbors. The "Ukraine without Kuchma" campaign from December 2000 to March 2001 and the results of the March 2002 parliamentary elections demonstrated that Ukrainian society was active and politically sophisticated. Especially after the electoral success of Our Ukraine in the 2002 parliamentary vote, Ukraine's opposition also had a foothold in an important institution of state power. As discussed below, a Rada speaker not totally loyal to the president, and opposition representation within the Rada, proved to be critical factors in defusing the political stalemate during the Orange Revolution. Finally, Ukraine's business tycoons or oligarchs were not completely united by the *ancien régime*.[9] Ukraine's three largest oligarchic groups did back Kuchma and wielded their media and financial resources on behalf of Kuchma's candidate in the 2004 presidential election, but significant if lesser oligarchs did decide to back Yushchenko, as did tens of thousands of smaller business people, meaning that Ukraine's economic elites were divided, not united, in the fall of 2004. The regime, in other words, had elements of competition and pluralism, which created the space for the mobilization of an effective democratic opposition.

II. THE PROXIMATE CAUSES OF THE ORANGE REVOLUTION AND EXTERNAL FACILITATORS OF THESE CAUSES

In this case of democratic breakthrough, several factors are *necessary* for success. None were external actors. Ukrainians made the Orange Revolution. This obvious observation cannot be stressed enough. Equally important, for almost all external actors involved in Ukraine, there was not an explicit goal of fostering "revolution." Rather, the focus for most Western organizations was to

---

[8] Michael McFaul, Nikolai Petrov, and Andrei Ryabov, *Between Dictatorship and Democracy: Russian Post-Communist Political Reform*, (Washington, DC: Carnegie Endowment for International Peace, 2004).

[9] Anders Åslund, "The Ancien Régime: Kuchma and the Oligarchs," In *Revolution in Orange: The Origins of Ukraine's Democratic Breakthrough*, Anders Åslund and Michael McFaul, (Washington, DC: Carnegie Endowment for International Peace, 2006), pp. 9–28.

make the 2004 presidential election as democratic as possible and/or to promote democratic development more generally. It is difficult to assign credit (or guilt, depending on one's perspective) to an actor for an outcome if that actor was not seeking to achieve that outcome. At the same time, external factors did influence – both positively and negatively – the ability of Ukrainians to make the Orange Revolution successful.[10]

1. Unpopular Leader and Unpopular Regime

An unpopular regime was a necessary condition for democratic breakthrough in Ukraine in the fall of 2004. This factor may seem obvious, but it also a feature that distinguishes this case from countries such as Russia, where former President Putin was still popular, or countries such Mexico during the heyday of semiauthoritarian rule when the Institutional Revolutionary Party (PRI) could manufacture electoral victories without major voter fraud.

Leonid Kuchma won presidential elections in 1994 and 1999, which were judged to be relatively free and fair by the standards of the region. Moreover, during Kuchma's second term in office, Ukraine witnessed record economic growth, reaching a twelve percent increase in GDP between 2003 and 2004. However, high levels of corruption in Ukraine denied Kuchma the popular support that twelve percent growth should have generated for him. When asked on the eve of the 2004 presidential vote, only 8.4 percent of Ukrainian voters assessed Kuchma's tenure in a positive manner, whereas 62.2 percent gave him a negative assessment.[11] Kuchma's unwillingness to fight corruption was a central factor driving his unpopularity, but another important factor in his low public approval ratings had to do with the murder of journalist Giorgy Gongadze, the founder of the Internet publication *Ukrainskaya Pravda*. Tapes of conversations between Kuchma and subordinates leaked to the press strongly suggested that the Ukrainian president played a role in ordering Gongadze's execution. More than any other single event, Gongadze's murder exposed the illegitimacy of Kuchma and his allies.

Kuchma's failures as a president could only adversely affect the popularity and legitimacy of his regime if his actions were communicated in some way

---

[10] The Kremlin coordinated and sponsored various activities aimed at helping Yanukovych win the election and creating the impression that he won the election. At the urging of the Kremlin, Russian businesspeople contributed to Yanukovych's campaign, Russian PR consultants worked for several factions within the Yanukovych campaign, and Putin personally traveled twice to Ukraine in the fall of 2004 to help Yanukovych. The Ukrainian prime minister and his financial backers also hired American law firms and public relations specialists to help with the campaign, including Barbour, Rogers, and Griffith and DBC Public Relations Experts. A Russian-sponsored election-monitoring group also observed the Ukrainian vote and declared the first and second round free and fair. Due to space constraints, however, antidemocratic external actors are not fully examined here. See Petrov and Ryabov, "Russia's Role in the Orange Revolution," in Åslund and McFaul, eds., *Revolution in Orange*, pp. 145–64.

[11] Razumkov Centre Sociological Survey, as reported in "2004 Presidential Elections: How Ukrainians Saw Them," *National Security and Defence*, No. 10 (2004), p. 19.

to the voters. Any media reporting, think tank publication, Our Ukraine press release, or parliamentary hearing that provided an objective analysis of the Gongadze affair or corruption played some role in decreasing popular support for the Kuchma regime. During the campaign period itself, several civic groups took direct aim at Kuchma in their GOTV publications and activities. Black Pora organized the most famous of these anti-Kuchma campaigns, called "Kuchmizm"; Yellow Pora pushed the slogan "Time to understand – they lie."

Kuchma was not running for office in 2004, but his handpicked presidential candidate, Prime Minister Yanukovych, did little to inspire hope for a break with past corrupt practices. Yanukovych was a convicted criminal, who still maintained ties with criminal circles in his hometown region of Donetsk. Had Yanukovych become president, it is not at all certain that he would have maintained the delicate equilibrium between Kuchma's presidential office, the parliament, and the oligarchs. Yet, among voters, he was perceived as the candidate who would preserve the status quo, not change it.

In the rerun of the second round of the presidential election held on December 26, 2004, Yanukovych captured more than forty-four percent of the popular vote. This significant level of support reflects both the success and the limits of Yanukovych's campaign strategy. The prime minister and his campaign consultants deliberately tried to accentuate ethnic and regional divisions within Ukraine, mobilizing the Russian-speaking voters in the East against the Ukrainian-speaking supporters of Yushchenko in the West.[12] In large measure, although aided of course by fraud, the campaign strategy worked. For instance, in the eastern regions, Yanukovych won smashing victories in the December round of voting in a few eastern regions, winning 93.5 percent of the vote in Donetsk, 91.2 percent in Luhansk, and 81.3 percent in the Crimea. Conversely, in the Western regions of Ternopil, Ivan-Frankivsk, Lviv, and Volyn, Yanukovych failed to break into double digits. However, this strategy of fostering regional polarization did not help Yanukovych win votes in the center of Ukraine, including Kyiv, which swung decidedly toward the challenger, Yushchenko. In the capital, for instance, Yushchenko won 71.1 percent of the vote, compared to 17 percent for Yanukovych. Given the economic boom underway throughout Ukraine in 2004, but especially in Kyiv, this strong popular support for change suggests a deep, genuine rejection of the regime constructed by Kuchma in the 1990s.

External Facilitators of an Unpopular Ancien Regime. Kuchma's own actions and independent media monitoring and reporting on these actions contributed most directly to the decline in popularity of his government. Indirectly, though difficult to document, Western reactions to Kuchma's behavior did contribute to his image as an illegitimate and criminal leader. Most importantly, Bush administration officials strongly denounced the manner in which Kuchma

---

[12] Author's interview with Mikhail Pogrebinsky, Director of the Kiev Center for Political Studies and Conflictology, November 2005.

handled the investigation into Gongadze's murder. When Oleksandr Moroz released tapes implicating Kuchma in Gongadze's murder, the U.S. government granted the producer of these tapes, Yuri Melnichenko, asylum. Miroslava Gongadze, Gongadze's widow, as well as his two children, also received asylum. After the murder, the Bush administration never invited Kuchma to the United States and tried hard to avoid and marginalize Kuchma at international gatherings. For instance, at a NATO meeting to which Ukraine was invited, U.S. government officials deliberately requested that the French spelling of countries be used so that Bush would not have to sit next to Kuchma. The Bush administration further downgraded contacts with the Kuchma regime after it become known that the Ukrainian government had tried to sell its Kolchuga air defense radar system to Iraq.[13] Kuchma did receive some praise from the White House for his decision to send Ukrainian troops to Iraq. However, the general message coming out of Washington and the American embassy in Kyiv was that Kuchma and his regime were not held in high regard.

As already stressed above, media reporting, think tank publications, Our Ukraine press releases, and parliamentary hearings that provided an objective analysis of the Gongadze affair or corruption, played some role in decreasing popular support for the Kuchma regime. This list of critical sources of reporting on the Kuchma regime included several organizations that received Western technical assistance or financial support, including *Ukrainskaya Pravda*, the Razumkov Center, and the Rada.[14] Freedom House provided direct assistance to Znayu and indirect assistance to Yellow Pora and the Freedom of Choice coalition by sponsoring and helping to organize a summer camp for Yellow Pora activists (as well as for activists from other organizations). Another USAID grantee, the U.S.–Ukraine Foundation, funded and organized the major portion of the Znayu campaign. Indirectly, all of these efforts contributed to more critical coverage of the Kuchma regime and a lowering of his government's popularity.

In addition, independent analysis and reporting from these sources helped to inform U.S. government officials and analysts, who in turn influenced the way that their own government perceived Kuchma. For instance, an article about corruption would be published in *Ukrainskaya Pravda*, which would be read by an analyst at the Carnegie Endowment for International Peace in Washington, who in turn might speak out on television, in the op-ed pages, or in briefings to government officials about corruption in Ukraine, and thereby influence the way that the Bush administration or the U.S. Congress thought and acted on Ukraine. Such information flows also influenced Ukraine's Freedom House scores, which in turn helped to shape Western assessments of the Kuchma

---

[13] Michael Wines, "Report of Arms Sale by Ukraine to Iraq Causes Consternation," *New York Times* (November 7, 2002).

[14] The Indiana University Parliamentary Development Project facilitated the development of professional hearings within the Rada, which in turn helped to generate information about corruption within the Kuchma government.

regime. This pattern in the trajectory of media influence is regularly observed during the last years of the Kuchma administration. Ukrainian publications, which had the resources to translate a portion of the work into English, including *Zerkalo Nedelya*, *Ukrainskaya Pravda*, and Razumkov's journal, *National Security and Defence*, were especially effective in reinforcing U.S. campaigns to expose Kuchma's illegitimacy.

During the final weeks of the campaign and then during the Orange Revolution, e-mails sent and Websites operated by the CVU, Pora, Our Ukraine, Internews-Ukraine, and several others also helped to inform the outside world about the machinations of Kuchma and Yanukovych.

2. Organized Opposition

A strong and well-organized opposition – or the perception of a united front – was a second precipitating factor crucial for democratic breakthrough in Ukraine in the fall of 2004. In the previous decade, Ukraine's democratic forces had struggled with division and disorganization. Opposition unity was complicated by the presence of a strong and legitimate Socialist Party, which made cooperation with Ukrainian liberals difficult. For many years, there also was not a single, charismatic leader of the opposition who stood out as an obvious first among equals with the sufficient wherewithal and political cachet to unite the opposition and rally public support. Ironically, Kuchma helped to create such a leader when he dismissed Viktor Yushchenko as his prime minister in 2001. At the time, Yushchenko's image was that of a technocratic economist, not a stump politician. Those who knew him best did not believe that he had the drive or temperament to become a national political leader. But he was a popular prime minister with a record of achievement while in office and an image of not being corrupt, making him a dangerous opponent to the party in power.

The first critical step for forging a united front was the 2002 parliamentary election, which in effect acted as a primary for aspiring presidential candidates. To participate in these elections, Yushchenko succeeded in creating a new electoral bloc, Our Ukraine, which captured one-fourth of the popular vote in the 2002 parliamentary elections. Our Ukraine's success in 2002 made Yushchenko the focal point of a united front for the presidential election in 2004. Most importantly, Yulia Tymoshenko – an opposition leader with more charisma than Yushchenko but also more baggage – agreed not to run independently for president, but instead backed Yushchenko.[15] Socialist Party leader Alexander Moroz did decide to participate in the presidential vote, but won only 5.8 percent in the first round, after which he quickly endorsed Yushchenko for the second round.

Unity behind a single candidate, especially after the first round, was an essential ingredient for electoral success in 2004 for Ukraine's opposition. Without

[15] Interview with Timoshenko, February 2006.

electoral victory in the second round of the presidential election, there would have been no Orange Revolution. Beyond acknowledging the importance of unity behind a common candidate, however, assessing the relative salience of other ingredients for Yushchenko's successful electoral campaign is more difficult. The second round of the vote essentially became a polarized referendum on the *ancien régime*.[16] Compared to parliamentary votes, presidential elections with runoffs are structurally polarizing in that they force voters to make a choice between two candidates. But this election was especially polarized, as it was not so much a contest between opposing campaign promises about the future as a referendum on the past performance of Kuchma and his regime.[17] As already mentioned, the vote was polarized first and foremost along geographic lines. The most robust predictor of voting behavior in the second (and third) round of voting was not age, education, wealth, or the rural–urban divide, but geographic location: the farther west one lived, the more likely one was to support Yushchenko, whereas the farther east one lived, the more likely one was to support Yanukovych.[18]

Therefore, although always difficult to trace in normal elections, the causal impact of campaign messages and techniques in this election is particularly difficult to measure. In *normal* elections, the success of a campaign is measured by assessing the deployment of campaign assets such as effective party organization, the personal appeal of the candidate, targeted messages, and the financial resources to pay for national television airtime, campaign staff, leaflets, and get-out-the-vote activities.[19] Without question, Yushchenko and his campaign staff deployed these kinds of resources in a manner sufficient to win in 2004.

By 2004, Our Ukraine had developed into a national organization, with party representatives throughout the country, even if its local party organizations were much weaker in the east than the west. The organizational reach of Our Ukraine was deeper than any other proreform political organization in Ukraine since independence.

Yushchenko was not a fiery campaigner. But in electoral terms, he had a very appealing biography, including his birthplace and work experience, an impeccable reputation for not being corrupt (despite having worked for Kuchma for many years), and a handsome appearance. His enemies ruined his physical appearance when they poisoned him in September 2004; but this event,

---

[16] Compared to parliamentary votes, presidential elections with runoffs are structurally polarizing in that they force voters to make a choice between two candidates.

[17] Morris Fiorina, "Economic Retrospective Voting in American National Elections: A Micro-Analysis." *American Journal of Political Science*, 22 (1978), pp. 426–43.

[18] Razumkov Centre Sociological Survey, as reported in "2004 Presidential Elections," p. 9. See also Taras Kuzio, "Everyday Ukranians and the Orange Revolution," in Åslund and McFaul, *Revolution in Orange*, pp. 45–68.

[19] For an attempt to measure these variables in a Russian electoral cycle, see Timothy Colton and Michael McFaul, *Popular Choice and Managed Democracy: The Russian Elections of 1999 and 2000*, (Washington, DC: Brookings Institution Press, 2003).

however painful and tragic for Yushchenko personally, did help to bolster his appeal as a tough and embattled candidate.

After the Orange Revolution, it seems as if no other leader could have united the opposition and toppled the regime. But this "fact" only seems obvious after success. The pivotal role of Yushchenko as an individual is not easy to discern.[20] Only months before victory, several leaders within the Ukrainian democratic movement questioned whether Yushchenko had the political and campaign skills to win.[21]

Regarding messages, Yushchenko on the campaign trail did not push a comprehensive agenda of policy changes.[22] Rather, his campaign messages attempted to cast the vote as a choice between two different systems of government, one that was corrupt, authoritarian, and criminal, and his regime, which would be "for the truth," "for freedom," and "for our rights." Printed and broadcast campaign messages explicitly stated that he and his team were "against the bandits in power," yet Yushchenko personally tried to keep his own speeches positive. The word Tak! (Yes!) and the color orange were positive symbolic images. Detailed statements about policy changes were not used. To the extent that a negative message developed, it was to say *enough* of the current regime.

Geographically, the Yushchenko campaign concentrated on the center of the country. In contrast to both the far east and far west, campaign officials believed that these regions, including Kiev, were home to Ukraine's swing voters, that is, voters who may have voted for Kuchma in the past but could be persuaded to vote against his candidate and his regime after a decade in power.

Voter mobilization was also a factor in Yushchenko's success. In the second round of the presidential elections, voter turnout reached an amazing 80.4 percent; in the rerun of the second round (the third time Ukrainians were asked to go to the polls that fall), turnout was still very high, 77.2 percent. The Yanukovych and Yushchenko campaigns both devoted serious resources to get-out-the-vote activities. In addition, several nongovernmental organizations made voter participation a central focus of their fall 2004 activities. NGO leaders and party activists interviewed by the author singled out the Znayu campaign (supported by the U.S.–Ukraine Foundation and Freedom House) in particular as the most extensive nonpartisan effort to get out the vote.[23] Black Pora, Yellow Pora and its closely affiliated Freedom of Choice Coalition,

[20] On the misplaced emphasis on leaders more generally in such situations, see Kurt Schock, "Nonviolent Actions and Its Misconceptions: Insights for Social Scientists," *PS: Political Science and Politics*, 36, No. 4 (October 2003), pp. 705–12.

[21] Author's interviews with Our Ukraine campaign officials, November 2005.

[22] Of course, he did have a program, including a list of presidential decrees that he promised to enact should he be elected. These actions of the future, however, were not emphasized. For instance, after the election, two-thirds of the electorate reported that they had never heard about these decrees. See Razumkov Centre Sociological Survey, as reported in "2004 Presidential Elections," p. 10.

[23] This essay is informed by over 100 interviews done mostly in Ukraine in March 2005, November 2005, and February 2006, listed in the Appendix at the end of this chapter.

and the Committee of Ukrainian Voters (CVU) also organized extensive get-out-the-vote campaigns, and groups such as Internews-Ukraine, the Center for Ukrainian Reform Education, Freedom House, and ABA/CEELI (American Bar Association/Central European and Eurasian Law Initiative) placed public service announcements on television educating Ukrainian voters about their electoral rights, which indirectly was also a method for increasing voter turnout.

It is often asserted that those more democratically inclined are more likely to vote. However, the role that democratic ideas played in mobilizing voters (for either candidate) is not easy to determine. In several interviews conducted by the author, many Yushchenko supporters claimed that his electorate were more enthusiastic supporters of democratic ideas than Yanukovych supporters. The hypothesis seems plausible, but difficult to prove.

Assessing the role of external actors in the formation of an effective opposition in Ukraine is a most difficult task, in part because of the nature of the work and in part because of the sensitivity of the work. The nature of the work is difficult to evaluate because the process of making an impact occurs over extended periods of time, indirectly, and in parallel with many local inputs. The transfer that takes place between groups such as the International Republican Institute (IRI) and the National Democratic Institute (NDI) on the one hand and Our Ukraine on the other is essentially one of ideas and know-how, the most difficult variables to trace systematically. Assessing this work is sensitive, because Ukrainian actors do not want to taint their reputations or legitimacy by reporting that Western actors contributed to their domestic success, whereas Western actors want to protect their partners and also maintain a claim of acting as nonpartisans. With these huge constraints recognized, several observations about the role of external actors in the development of Ukraine's opposition coalition can still be made.

First, there is no evidence that NDI, IRI, or any other American NGO supported by USAID contributed financial resources directly to the campaign of Viktor Yushchenko and Our Ukraine.[24] Claims to the contrary are based on false information or political motivations. Our Ukraine did receive financial contributions from citizens living in the United States and Canada, though the greatest source of foreign funding for the Yushchenko campaign came from Russia. (Yanukovych also received financial support from abroad, including Russia first and foremost.) The Yushchenko campaign hired American and Russian campaign consultants; Yanukovych also hired Russian *and* American consultants. No U.S. government group paid for the professional public relations specialists hired by Yushchenko.[25]

---

[24] Authors' interviews with IRI and NDI officials and Our Ukraine campaign organizers.

[25] Aristotle International did some work for the Yushchenko campaign. The head of the NDI's office in Kyiv, David Dettman, used to work for Aristotle International. In the 2006 parliamentary election, however, this company worked for Kuchma's former chief of staff, Viktor Medvedchuk. Likewise, Yanukovich and his Party of Regions dumped the Russian consultants for the 2006 contest and hired one of Washington's most prominent Republican firms, Davis

As discussed above, the Our Ukraine campaign had greater organizational reach than any other party in Ukraine. Our Ukraine leaders accomplished this feat primarily on their own through years of hard work. At the same time, Our Ukraine political leaders reported that the development of their organizational capacity benefited from years of close relationships with the NDI and the IRI.[26] Well before the formation of the Our Ukraine Yushchenko bloc in 2002, the IRI and NDI also worked closely with many of the individuals who later assumed senior positions in the Our Ukraine organization and campaign. After the creation of the party, the NDI and IRI provided additional party training assistance, though using different strategies. IRI conducted multiparty training programs focused almost exclusively on regional party leaders outside of Kyiv. NDI provided trainers to programs organized by Our Ukraine, a service they provided to other parties as well. In contrast to IRI, NDI staff also focused more of their efforts at working with Our Ukraine's senior leadership in Kyiv. The close ties between NDI staff and senior Our Ukraine leaders were apparent during interviews conducted with Our Ukraine officials. Measuring the results of these interactions, be it NDI's engagement with senior party officials or IRI regional training efforts, was simply beyond the scope of this study.

In other countries, NDI and IRI have helped their counterparts develop campaign techniques, providing technical assistance with everything from how to conduct a focus group to how to make television ads. IRI and NDI most certainly did provide these kinds of technologies to party organizers in Ukraine at some stage in Ukraine's transition from communism. By the time of the 2004 presidential campaign, however, Our Ukraine leaders had constructed an experienced and professional team of campaign experts. In the expert community, no one interviewed for this project was particularly impressed with the components of Our Ukraine's campaign, but as discussed above, clever slogans, well targeted messages, and slick television ads were less important in the campaign than in normal elections because this vote was more a referendum about regime types than a contest of ideas, platforms, or even personalities. Nonetheless, no one believes that Our Ukraine ran a truly bad campaign and some innovations, such as the color orange, were striking. (By contrast, no one could explain the importance of the horseshoe as a symbol, though it was pervasive in all Our Ukraine materials.)

Indirectly, both NDI and IRI also helped to increase the respectability of Yushchenko in Washington. IRI organized a trip to Washington for Yushchenko and his senior staff in February 2003, at which time the Ukrainian presidential candidate met with key Bush administration officials and members of Congress, including Senator Lugar, who would eventually play a key role in helping to undermine U.S. endorsement of the second-round result of the 2004 vote. Former Secretary of State Madeleine Albright, chair of NDI's board,

Manafort, which had previously worked for Ronald Reagan and George W. Bush. See Jeremy Page, "Revolution Is Reversed with a Little Spin from the West," *The Times*, March 28, 2006.

[26] Interviews with Stetskiv and Katarynchuk.

traveled to Ukraine in February 2004 to meet with Yushchenko and other Our Ukraine officials. Upon her return to Washington, she also spoke favorably about Yushchenko as a candidate. These kinds of contacts helped to assure the Bush administration that the Ukrainian opposition was viable and worth supporting – a reputation that other opposition movements have failed to nurture in similar pivotal elections (e.g., in Azerbaijan in the fall of 2005).

Forging the Our Ukraine coalition was a difficult feat that did not survive the Orange Revolution. NDI staff seemed particularly involved in helping to maintain the coalition during the 2004 campaign (as NDI had been involved in a similar effort in Serbia in 1999). Measuring the impact of such efforts, however, is nearly impossible and to date beyond the analytical skills of this author.

Turnout in regions supportive of Yushchenko was much higher in this election than in previous elections. Several American organizations, including IRI, NDI, Freedom House, Internews, and the Eurasia Foundation, contributed directly and indirectly to get-out-the-vote projects organized by their Ukrainian partners.

3. Creating the Perception of a Falsified Vote

A third condition critical to success of the Orange Revolution was the ability of NGOs to provide an accurate and independent account of the actual vote quickly after polls had closed. Although several organizations, including international groups, monitored the vote count, the Committee of Ukrainian Voters (CVU) played the central role in monitoring all rounds of the 2004 presidential vote. The CVU also conducted a parallel vote tabulation (PVT) during all three rounds. Yushchenko's party, Our Ukraine, also tried to organize a parallel vote tabulation. In addition, the Ukrainian NGO Democratic Initiatives coordinated the National Exit Poll (NEP), conducted by four polling firms: the Kyiv International Institute of Sociology (KMIS), the SOCIS Center, the Social Monitoring Center, and the sociological service of the Razumkov Center.[27]

These Ukrainian organizations had years of experience; the CVU had ten years of experience, whereas the Democratic Initiatives Foundation orchestrated the first exit polls in Ukraine in the 1998 parliamentary elections.[28] At the same time, compared to earlier elections, these groups also faced a much more sophisticated vote manipulator in 2004. Kuchma and his allies successfully executed two novel methods for obscuring the actual tally, which

---

[27] The Ukrainian Institute of Social Research, a government-sponsored organization, and the Russian firm Foundation for Social Opinion (FOM) also conducted exit polls. FOM discontinued its exit poll in the first round because more than forty percent of all voters asked were refusing to reveal how they voted. See Tetiana Sylina, "Exit Poll: A Long Ordeal," *National Security and Defence*, No. 10 (2004), pp. 24–8.

[28] Available at http://www.dif.org.ua.

frustrated attempts by independent actors to expose fraud. First, Kuchma's regime falsified the vote at the level of precincts, and not between the precinct level and higher levels of counting, where fraud traditionally occurs.[29] A PVT attempts to expose fraud by sampling the actual vote count at the precinct level. But if the precinct numbers are already fraudulent, then a PVT will also reflect the result of the falsified vote, an outcome that the Committee of Ukrainian Voters had to face. Because the CVU figures from their PVT did not expose significant fraud, they did not release their second-round results.

Second, the legitimacy of the NEP came into question when two firms in the consortium decided to use a tallying method different from that used by the other two. As a response to the intense polarized atmosphere of the 2004 presidential vote, preelection opinion polls recorded very high no-response rates, exceeding seventy percent in some regions and over fifty percent nationwide. As a corrective to this unacceptable no-response, two consortium partners, KMIS and the Razumkov Center, agreed to switch from the face-to-face method of asking exiting voters how they voted and adopt the more anonymous method of collecting exit poll data using, in essence, a second ballot box placed outside the polling station, into which voters could report on how they voted without the interviewer seeing how they voted. However, the SOCIS Center and the Social Monitoring Center refused to adopt this new method. Not surprisingly, the two methods produced different results: using the more anonymous method, KMIS and the Razumkov Center reported higher levels of support for Yushchenko than SOCIS and the Social Monitoring Center using results collected by the open method. The consortium dissolved for the second round of the vote. In this second round, results released by KMIS and Razumkov showed that Yushchenko received 52 percent of the vote, compared to 44.2 percent for Yanukovych, whereas the official CEC results released claimed that Yushchenko won only 46.6 percent of the vote, and Yanukovych won 49.5 percent of the vote. This discrepancy played a key role in mobilizing citizens to come to Maidan to protect their votes.

When these quantitative or macro methods for exposing fraud yielded ambiguous results, qualitative micro methods came to the rescue. Individual election monitors, fielded by Our Ukraine, CVU, and other NGOs, reported hundreds of instances of irregular procedures. So too did international monitors (discussed in detail below). Their efforts to gather evidence of falsification were facilitated by the multiparty composition of the local election commissions. This method of forming election commissions put Our Ukraine members and supporters in the room in most election districts (but not all) in the country when counts were taking place. In addition, turnout levels in some regions in the east were so outrageously high that election analysts knew they could not be true.

---

[29] Author's interviews with Igor Popov, chairman of the Committee of Ukrainian Voters, Kyiv, Ukraine, March 10, 2005, and Yevgen Poberezhny, Deputy Chairman of the Board, Committee of Voters of Ukraine, November 15, 2005.

This combination gave a few members of the Central Election Commission the courage not to certify the final count, sending the issue to the parliament. The parliament did not ratify the official results, but instead sent the issue to the Supreme Court.[30] The Court then used evidence of fraud collected by the CVU and other NGOs to overturn the official results on December 3, 2004 and call for a replay of the second round of the presidential election late that month.

It is unlikely that either the defecting members of the CEC or the majority of the Supreme Court would have acted the way they did if hundreds of thousands of protestors were not in the streets by the time of their deliberations.[31] In a different political context with no major societal mobilization, the Supreme Court might easily have responded very differently to the handful of cases regarding fraud brought before them.

Many of the Ukrainian activities that contributed to the exposure of fraud had significant assistance from external actors. In fact, the West's central contribution to the Orange Revolution was to this critical factor. This took the form of long-term support and cultivation of voters' rights groups, think tanks, youth groups and other civil activist organizations, and media organizations that would be instrumental in monitoring, polling, PVT, and disseminating information about voters' rights and violations of those rights, especially during the second round of voting.

Even with the mixed results of the parallel vote tabulation, CVU still played a leading role in exposing fraud (and creating the perception of electoral fraud) during the second round of the presidential vote, first through its network of 10,000 monitors (this is the number cited in CVU press releases), second through the legal actions that CVU lawyers initiated that helped to challenge the legitimacy of the official results, and third through the evidence of falsification gathered by CVU officials and used then by the Our Ukraine legal team before the Supreme Court. Based on its experiences first in the Philippines and later in other countries in postcommunist Europe, NDI provided the original idea for a Ukrainian election-monitoring organization and then provided substantial technical and financial assistance to the CVU throughout its development, including support for the 2004 election.[32] In 2004, other Western donors, including most importantly the International Renaissance Foundation, also contributed major financial resources to the CVU.

The CVU was the largest and most visible NGO effort supported by Western funds dedicated to exposing fraud, but not the only effort. At the end of its voter education and voter mobilization campaigns, the Znayu campaign (supported by the U.S.–Ukraine Foundation and Freedom House) also turned to exposing fraud, including one leafleting campaign that warned/threatened CEC

---

[30] Author's interview with CEC member Roman Knyazevich, Kyiv, Ukraine, March 12, 2005.
[31] Ibid.
[32] On the evolution of this technology, see Eric Bjornlund, *Beyond Free and Fair: Monitoring Elections and Building Democracy*, (Baltimore: Johns Hopkins University Press, 2004).

officials about the legal consequences of committing electoral fraud. Yellow Pora, Black Pora, Chysta Ukraina, and hundreds of smaller NGOs also used various tactics to expose fraud. Through its small grants program, Freedom House funded many of the NGO activities at the regional level through its Citizen Participation in Elections in Ukraine program. A key effort was an emergency round of grants made before the third round of elections to prevent fraud by ensuring that the public was educated about changes in the election laws that had been made after the second round.

Our Ukraine also worked hard to expose fraud, first by training its party representatives serving on CEC commissions on the rules for vote counting and mechanisms for recording irregularities in the process, and second by organizing a parallel network of election monitors. The NDI played a major role in the training of Our Ukraine monitors.

Democratic Initiative's exit poll, which also played a critical role in undermining the legitimacy of the official results in the second round, was funded almost entirely by a consortium of Western donors, including the Eurasia Foundation, Counterpart, and the Europe XXI Foundation.

In addition to Ukrainian poll watchers, the IRI, the NDI, and the U.S.–Ukrainian Foundation deployed international election monitoring teams to observe the Ukrainian election. The United States government also funded American participants in the 600-person observer mission fielded by the OSCE. And most innovatively, the NDI and Freedom House cooperated to bring to Ukraine the European Network of Election Monitoring Organizations (ENEMO), which was composed of 17 electoral monitoring organizations from countries in the former communist world. After reviewing initial international observational plans, the U.S. ambassador, John Herbst, called upon USAID and its grantees to generate an additional 1,000 international volunteers. ENEMO was the creative and efficient response – creative because it brought to Ukraine trained electoral monitors experienced in exposing postcommunist vote rigging (and many of these foreign observers also spoke Russian) and efficient because 1,000 volunteers from neighboring countries could be brought to Ukraine at a fraction of the cost that it would have taken to bring Americans in. All of these international teams released critical reports about the election process, which in turn played an instrumental role in generating a unified condemnation of the voting procedures from Europe and the United States.

Another successful innovation in the Ukrainian observation efforts was the presence of a special envoy representing President Bush personally, Senator Richard Lugar. A moderate Republican, an experienced foreign affairs specialist, and the chair of the Senate Foreign Relations Committee, Lugar had the international authority to make his judgments meaningful in Washington and European capitals. USAID did not support his trip directly but USAID grantees, especially the IRI, informed his assessments. His press statement on the vote was scathing, which in turn bolstered the negative evaluation and tone of Secretary of State Colin Powell's first remarks on the vote. Powell was unequivocal in declaring the official results illegitimate. In interviews, Our Ukraine leaders and NGO activists reported that Powell's statement provided a major boost of inspiration for the Maidan demonstrators. The statement also raised doubt within the president's entourage about their ability to make the official results stick.

4. A Modicum of Independent Media

As discussed in greater detail below, the creation of a foothold for independent media was another important ingredient in creating momentum for the Orange Revolution years before the 2004 presidential vote. Independent media played a facilitating role, preparing the public for the development of many of the Orange Revolution precipitants, including weakening the popularity of incumbents and strengthening the support for the opposition.

During the 2004 campaign, Kuchma's regime controlled or enjoyed the loyalty of most national media outlets. By 2004, Ukraine boasted several independent television networks, but all the major channels were owned or controlled by oligarchs loyal to Kuchma and Yanukovych. The Russian television stations ORT, RTR, and NTV, which enjoyed considerable audiences in Ukraine, also gave favorable coverage to Yanukovych. In 2003, a wealthy Yushchenko ally, Petro Poroshenko, acquired the rights to a small television station and then transformed it into Channel 5. Unlike all other networks, Channel 5 did provide positive (or, they would say, "objective") coverage of the Yushchenko campaign, but Channel 5's audience was much smaller than those for the major channels, roughly 8 million viewers, and its signal reached only approximately 30 percent of the country.[33] Regarding radio, Radio Era did provide news that was not shaped by the government. External stations such as Radio Liberty, the BBC, and the Voice of America were also important channels of independent news for those with the ability to receive short wave broadcasts – a small fraction of the Ukrainian population.[34] Some important print newspapers such as *Zerkalo nedeli, Ukrayna moloda, Vecherny visty,* and *Silsky visty* (controlled by the Socialist Party), as well as Internet news outlets such as *Ukrainska pravda* (the independent online publication founded by Gongadze) and Telekritika – a Web-based forum for discussing television coverage of the campaign – also provided sources of news about the election campaign not controlled by the state or oligarchs closely tied to the state. But all had limited circulations. It should be noted that Internet access is still too expensive for the average media consumer in Ukraine, and much of that audience – just

---

[33] Adrian Karatnycky, "Ukraine's Orange Revolution," *Foreign Affairs*, 84, No. 2 (March/April 2005), pp. 35–52.

[34] Some FM stations, such as Radio Continent, Radio NART, and Radio Takt in Vinnytsia did rebroadcast Radio Liberty. Radio Liberty officials claimed that eight percent of the Ukrainian population were listening to their broadcasts, a very large number. See Olena Prytula, "The Ukrainian Media Rebellion," In Åslund and McFaul, eds., *Revolution in Orange*, pp. 113–15.

over fifty-five percent – is in Kiev.[35] Every region also had at least one opposition newspaper, including such famous regional papers as *Kafa*, *Hrviyna*, and *Vechirney Cherkassy*. The media playing field for the 2004 was skewed in favor of Yanukovych, but independent and pro-Yushchenko outlets did exist.

If the impact of independent media outlets on the campaign results are difficult to measure, their role in facilitating popular mobilization after the vote was much more obvious. Independent media played a positive and critical role in communicating news about the falsified vote and helping in turn to mobilize popular opposition to the regime after the vote. Channel 5 played the central role, first in communicating the results of the exit polls and in reporting on the hundreds of cases of electoral fraud. Channel 5 then served the especially vital function of providing live, 24-hour coverage of the events on Maidan, broadcasts that helped to encourage others to join the protests, especially when viewers saw the peaceful, festive nature of the crowds.[36] By the end of the demonstration, Channel 5 catapulted from thirteenth to third in the national ratings. Channel 5 coverage also put pressure on the other channels to stop spewing their propaganda. By the fourth day of protests, the staffs at most other stations had joined forces with the street demonstrators. Radio Era, Radio Kyiv, and Radio Gala also provided around-the-clock reporting from Maidan.

Compared to the previous electoral breakthrough in Georgia in 2003, Ukraine's opposition had one major advantage – the Internet. In fact, the Orange Revolution may have been the first in world history organized in large measure on the Web. During the critical hours and days after the second-round vote, *Ukrainskaya Pravda* displayed the results of the exit poll most sympathetic to Yushchenko, as well as detailed news about other allegations of fraud. The website also provided all sorts of practical information to protestors. During the second round of voting, *Ukrainskaya Pravda* readership grew to 350,000 readers and one million hits a day.[37] Other portals also provided critical information that helped to create the Orange Revolution. The Maidan site was a clearinghouse of information and coordination for protestors. The student group Pora and Our Ukraine also had important Web sites and Web masters that blasted out informational and motivational e-mails to supporters and observers all over the country and all over the world (including to this author) during the critical moments right after the vote. Telekritika was also a popular site for independent journalists during the campaign, which played an instrumental role in pressuring journalists working at Kuchma-friendly outlets to withdraw their support once tens of thousands had mobilized on the streets. As a technology of mobilization and coordination, text messaging was

35 IREX, *Media Sustainability Index 2004*, pp. 208–9, 211 (Washington, DC: IREX); available at http://www.irex.org/msi/2004/MSI-2004-Ukraine.pdf.

36 One poll showed that ten percent of the people in Maidan Square had no political motives whatsoever but came instead just to enjoy the party.

37 Prytula, "The Ukrainian Media Rebellion," p. 110.

an essential device for those on Maidan and in the tent city where people did not have access to e-mail.

The development of a cadre of independent-minded professional journalists in Ukraine contributed over time to the exposure of corruption and crimes committed by the Kuchma regime, which in turn made it possible for Yushchenko to win the 2004 presidential vote. Training programs conducted by Internews-Ukraine, in partnership with IREX (U-Media Program), the Ukrainian Newspaper Publishers Association, and Telekritika, nurtured the emergence of this professional class over years of work. Internews also helped to organize the Independent Association of Broadcasters (IAB), which has played an instrumental role in defending professional journalists against state attacks since its formation. USAID implementers also helped the development of the Ukrainian Association of Press Publishers (UAPP) and a network of twenty-four regional press clubs, run by the Center for Ukrainian Reform Education, both which have also helped to develop and defend independent media. In this long period of nurturing independent journalism, Internews and its partners, such as IAD, UAPP, the IREX/Legal Defense Education Program, and the Media Law Institute, also helped to provide the legal framework for defending independent media outlets against state attacks (such as revoking licenses) and bringing Ukrainian media practices into line with international standards.

During the campaign, Internews subsidized and supported a whole series of activities, including the production of public service announcements, television talk shows, press conferences around the country, and funds to support local coverage of the national campaign and voters' rights in the print media. It must be stressed, however, that these activities only occurred in the margins of the national campaign, because pro-Kuchma forces still dominated the national electronic media.

During the Orange Revolution, several journalists, including Andrei Shevchenko and Roman Skrypin at Channel 5 and Natalia Dmytruk, the famed official sign-language interpreter for state-run television, assumed heroic roles in their coverage of the campaign and the civic resistance triggered by the fraudulent voter.[38] At various stages in their careers, many of these people had contact with USAID-funded media projects. As already discussed, *Ukrainskaya Pravda* played a central role in the Orange Revolution, and this Internet publication received major support from the National Endowment for Democracy (not USAID). Telekritika, an Internet publication sponsored by Internews, was also cited by many as a useful source of information and debate during the 2004 campaign and its immediate aftermath. Discussions on Telekritika were especially instrumental in spurring the "journalists' rebellion" on October 28, 2004, when forty journalists from five different television stations declared that

---

[38] When translating the spoken broadcast into sign language, Dmytruk told her viewers through her hands that the announcer was not telling the truth. Her deviance was a pivotal moment in spurring other journalists to defy dictates from the state.

they would no longer obey the secret instructions (*temniki*) that the Kuchma administration provided them.

5. Popular Mobilization to "Protect the Vote"

Months in advance of the presidential election, Our Ukraine campaign leaders made plans to organize street demonstrations in the likely (in their view) event that the election results would be falsified.[39] At the last minute, the location of their protest changed. And some planned tactics of mobilization, such as a planned parallel vote count to be conducted in the tents on Maidan Square, did not succeed. However, the central idea of calling on Yushchenko supporters to come to the streets and then remain there until the fraudulent vote was overturned did succeed. Several components produced success.

First, after initially considering the streets outside of the Central Election Commission as ground zero of the protest, Our Ukraine leaders decided instead to make their stand on Maidan Square, because policemen occupied the space surrounding the CEC. Early in the morning that day after the second round of voting, Our Ukraine MPs were swinging hammers to build a stage on Maidan. Amazingly, no one tried to stop them (though MPs were assigned this task specifically because they have immunity). Truckloads of tents, mats, and food supplies soon appeared as well, clearly demonstrating the opposition's preplanning.

Second, Our Ukraine leaders coordinated with Yellow Pora activists to set up a tent city downtown. This act created a quasi-permanent presence in downtown Kyiv immediately. The tent city and Maidan became as much major symbols of the revolution as the color orange.

Third, Yushchenko appeared on television to denounce the results of the second-round election and call upon his supporters to come to Kyiv and occupy the square. Strangely, Yushchenko's first postelection speech was covered on all major Ukrainian television stations. Later in the process of mobilization, as already discussed, independent media outlets helped to encourage demonstrators to come to Kyiv and also helped to coordinate the massive logistics required to keep a million people fed and warm.

Fourth, NGOs that focused on get-out-the-vote activities during the campaign also played an important role in urging voters to "protect their vote" after election day. The Znayu information campaign devoted particular attention to educating voters about their responsibility to ensure that their votes were accurately counted. This kind of message was widely distributed. Other NGOs developed and distributed similar messages during the campaign, helping indirectly to mobilize civic resistance to fraud after the official results of the second round were announced.

Fifth, regarding the logistics of Maidan, Yushchenko and his team benefited tremendously from the support of the Kyiv city government and the city's mayor, Oleksandr Omelchenko. Had political leaders loyal to the *ancien régime*

---

[39] Interviews with Stetskiv, others.

been in charge of the capital, the capacity to sustain the Orange Revolution would have been severely constrained.

Sixth, civil society and the middle class more broadly speaking helped to swell the numbers on Maidan from the several thousand who planned to show up to the million or so who spontaneously joined the protest. Our Ukraine and its partners made preparations for tens of thousands to protest a rigged election. They did not anticipate that their act of civil disobedience would swell to hundreds of thousands and eventually over a million people. To provide for such large numbers required volunteer work and donated supplies from thousands of individuals, who had no direct relationship with Our Ukraine previously.

Finally, a central feature of the mobilization's success was a commitment to nonviolence and a negotiated solution to the crisis. Our Ukraine organizers and Pora activists did not take any measures to prepare for an armed conflict. There were no guns in Our Ukraine headquarters and no pro-Yushchenko militias waiting in the wings in the event of violence. On the street, where protestors and soldiers stood eye to eye for days, Pora demonstrators used humor to defuse tension. Young women with flowers were deliberately asked to stand on the frontlines opposite the police as a method of making violence less likely.

At several moments during the seventeen-day standoff, some political leaders, including allegedly Yulia Tymosehnko and Yellow Pora leaders, wanted to end the crisis by storming the president's office.[40] They calculated, not without reason, that the government's armed forces would not stop them, Kuchma and his team would flee, and they could therefore seize power with a minimum amount of violence as the Serbian and Georgian oppositions had done in 2000 and 2003 respectively. Yushchenko, however, categorically rejected these tactics, and no one was prepared to act against the wishes of their leader.

Our Ukraine planned the first actions of civic resistance immediately after the second round of voting. There is no evidence that they received any Western assistance in making these preparations. Nor did U.S. government sources support their tremendous two-week operation on the Maidan. The assertion that demonstrators were paid a daily wage for their efforts is a complete myth. There is no evidence whatsoever to support this claim.

As discussed above, NDI and IRI did contribute, however difficult the contribution is to measure, to the expanded organizational capacity of Our Ukraine. Indirectly, therefore, one might argue that these Western organizations played some role in helping to make the Our Ukraine portion of the protest successful.

Yellow Pora worked closely with Our Ukraine in coordinating their efforts on the Maidan, and Yellow Pora did have significant contacts with civic resistance activists from Slovakia, Serbia, and Georgia, through the facilitating efforts of Freedom House and the German Marshall Fund. In their training programs, Znayu also used trainers from Serbia and Georgia. Exactly what knowledge about nonviolent resistance was transferred in these interactions is difficult to trace. That Ukrainian activists received inspiration from successful

---

[40] Interview with Kaskiv.

civic organizers from other countries is without question, and was reported frequently in interviews with participants in these training programs.[41] Moreover, nearly all of these training programs concerning civic mobilization received at least partial funding from Western sources, including the International Renaissance Foundation, Freedom House, the U.S.–Ukrainian Foundation, the German Marshall Fund, the NDI, the Westminster Foundation, SIDA, and grants from Western embassies in Kyiv.

6. Divisions among the "Guys with Guns"

In Ukraine, communication between opposition leaders and intelligence officials helped to remove violent suppression as an option for the Kuchma regime.[42] The defection of several Ukrainian police and intelligence units made clear that the guys with the guns – that is, the military and special forces with the intelligence services and police – could not be trusted to carry out a repressive order.[43] A week into the Maidan protest, special troops from the Ministry of the Interior did arm and mobilize, with the intention of clearing the square. But Orange Revolution sympathizers from within the intelligence services warned the Maidan organizers of the impeding attack, and then commanders within the regular army pledged to protect the unarmed citizens if these special forces tried to march into the center of town. These splits helped to convince Kuchma to call off the planned police activity, even though Yanukovych and his associates were urging the Ukrainian president to take action.

Divided loyalties within the security forces were closely intertwined with mass mobilization. Had there only been a few thousand demonstrators on the streets, Kuchma might have been less reluctant to use force. Major mobilization also meant that police and soldiers were more likely to have relatives on the square.

Identifying a direct Western impact on division within the security forces is difficult. Some have claimed that those soldiers who participated in NATO's Partnership for Peace programs were more likely to support the demonstrators than those who did not.[44] To date, however, the evidence marshaled to support this claim is far from convincing.

Western actors did contribute indirectly to keeping the peace during the standoff between armed forces and the Orange demonstrators. Well before the

---

[41] Interviews with Potekhin, Kosuchev, Kaskiv, Zolotarev.

[42] C. J. Chivers, "How Top Spies in Ukraine Changed the Nation's Path," *New York Times*, January 17, 2005.

[43] The causes of these divisions were many and predated the Orange Revolution. See Julie Anderson and Joseph Albini, "Ukraine's SBU and the New Oligarchy," *International Journal of Intelligence and Counterintelligence*, 12, No. 3 (July 1, 1999), pp. 282–324.

[44] See, for instance, comments of Major General Nicholas Krawciw, U.S. Army, ret., made at the American Enterprise Institute event "Ukraine's Choice: Europe or Russia?" (Washington, DC: December 10, 2004) during a panel discussion entitled "Ukraine's Armed Forces: On the Way to Join NATO?"

election, U.S. diplomats explicitly warned officials in Kuchma's government of the pariah status they would earn should the vote turn out to be unfree and unfair. Ambassador Herbst called upon visiting American dignitaries, such as Madeleine Albright, Henry Kissinger, Zbigniew Brzezinski, Tom Pickering, and Richard Holbrooke, to communicate threatening messages about the negative consequences of bad behavior should the election process become tainted.[45] As a signal of seriousness, the U.S. government denied a visa to Ukrainian oligarch Hryhoriy Surkis to warn Kuchma and his family (including, most importantly, his son-in-law, television media mogul and billionaire Viktor Pinchuk) that they too could face a similar fate of *persona non grata* status in the West. In the end, these threats did not prevent Kuchma and his team from trying to steal the vote. Yet the threats and warnings against using violence against the peaceful demonstrators did continue throughout the standoff, including a late night phone call from Colin Powell to Kuchma (which Kuchma refused to take) on the night when security forces were getting ready to try to clear the square. The U.S. embassy learned of these troop movements from an anti-Kuchma source within the SBU (Ukrainian security forces).[46] Throughout the crisis, Pinchuk was a consistent and accessible channel of communication for U.S. government officials wanting to get a message to Kuchma. Again, measuring the impact of these efforts is difficult. Even if it is impossible to measure how helpful, several participants in the standoff did report that the American interventions were helpful. Nevertheless, the number of protesters on the streets was the decisive deterrent to violence, not a phone call from Washington.

USAID and its grantees played very little role in these elite interactions. Individual Americans (some of whom were working on USAID grants) took advantage of their close ties with senior leaders in Our Ukraine to urge them to keep their demonstration nonviolent. In times of crisis, these personal relationships between internal opposition leaders and their external supporters can be morale boosters for those in the middle of a revolutionary situation. On the other side of the barricade, it does not appear that any foreign individuals were urging Ukrainian police, soldiers, or their bosses to show restraint.

7. Institutions and Mediation Efforts that Provided a Process for Peaceful Resolution of the Standoff

A final factor in the success of the Orange Revolution was the combination of a set of institutionalized procedures for finding a peaceful solution to the standoff and a process for mediating the crisis.[47] On November 23, Viktor Yushchenko stood in the Rada and took the presidential oath of office. At

---

[45] Interview with Herbst, November 2005.
[46] Interview with Herbst, November 2005.
[47] Whether this set of facilitating factors was necessary for breakthrough is disputable. For instance, in an interview with the author (February 2006), Timoshenko argued that the Western-anchored mediation efforts were not central to the outcome and actually tied the opposition's hands after breakthrough.

that moment, Ukraine had the essential ingredient of a revolutionary situation: two sets of political forces each claiming sovereign authority over the same territory.[48] In response to Yushchenko's actions and the demonstrators on the streets of Kyiv, several regional leaders in eastern Ukraine threatened to declare their independence from Ukraine and establish their own country. A few Russian leaders, including Moscow mayor Yuri Luzhkov, endorsed the idea and pledged to help the effort. Historically, these kinds of revolutionary situations are resolved when one side reasserts its authority over the other, often through the use of violence.

Ukraine avoided violence and civil war, however, in part because of a set of laws and institutions that helped to defuse the crisis and provide a mechanism for resolution. First, in contrast with leaders of full-blown autocracies, President Kuchma did not control the parliament (the Rada), or its speaker, Volodymyr Lytvyn. This institution, therefore, had the independence and authority to vote to reject the official CEC results of the second round of the presidential vote. The electoral law in place also gave the Rada the legal authority to rule on the CEC election results, another critical element in a positive outcome based on procedure and not simply political will. As elected officials, members of parliament were also particularly influenced by the crowds on the streets of Kyiv when making their decisions about the official vote tally.

Second, President Kuchma also did not have the Supreme Court fully under his thumb. Although many Yushchenko backers feared that these Court officials would be bribed and pressured into serving the will of the president, a majority of Court members voted on December 3 to annul the results of the second round of voting and called for a rerun of this election. This decision was absolutely critical in defusing the standoff, because this solution did not come from the Yushchenko or Yanukovych camp, but from a third party, and was therefore acceptable to both sides. Of course, Yanukovych and his allies wanted a different decision from the Court, but they were more willing to acquiesce to a process for ending the crisis coming from a third party than they would have been had the proposal come from the Yushchenko camp.

Explaining why the judges voted the way they did is an important and complex question beyond the scope of this study. Most certainly, some judges were more democratically inclined and prepared to do the right thing. In interviews with the author, participants in the Court's procedures also speculated that the size of the crowds and the tense situation on the streets of Kyiv played a role in influencing their deliberations. Without question, however, we do know that a necessary condition for the Court's decision was hard evidence that the results had been falsified. The results of PVTs or exit polls could not be used. This evidence came from Our Ukraine election monitors and commission members, CVU monitors, and several other NGOs. The effort to first document and

48 Charles Tilly, *From Mobilization to Revolution*, Chap. 9. (Reading, MA: Addison–Wesley, 1978).

record violations and then take legal action to prosecute offenders was much greater in this vote than in previous Ukrainian elections. This legal preparation to protect the rights of Ukrainian voters proved critical to the case presented by Our Ukraine lawyers before the Supreme Court.

In parallel to the law-based procedures followed by the Rada and the Supreme Court, a negotiation between Yanukovych, Yushchenko, and Kuchma also helped to end the standoff. With the assistance of international mediators (discussed in detail below), Ukraine's leaders eventually did agree to negotiate, a pact by which Kuchma and his side allowed the second round of the presidential election to be rerun and in return Yushchenko and his side agreed to changes in the constitution that would give the parliament and prime minister more powers and the president fewer. At the time of these roundtable talks, some leaders of Ukraine's opposition wanted to end discussions, follow the example of the Rose Revolution, and simply seize power. Less radically, others called on Yushchenko to simply stop participating in these talks, because Kuchma and Yanukovych had no legitimacy in changing the constitution. Yushchenko, however, rejected these calls for storming government buildings or boycotting the roundtable talks and insisted instead on the negotiated path. It is hard to know if Yanukovych and Kuchma would have agreed to a rerun of the second round of elections if this constitutional compromise had not been reached beforehand.

The first state institution that had the potential to play a heroic role was the CEC. As an institution, it did not. Instead, dozens if not hundreds of CEC officials, including a majority of the commissioners who ratified the official results, played a direct role in falsifying the vote. Assessing the positive contribution of the CEC's Western partners, therefore, is nearly impossible.[49] When push came to shove, many CEC officials did break the law and falsify the electoral results and no Western training program could stop this behavior. International actors can do little to help the cause of reform inside another country if they do not have willing domestic partners committed to reform. A critical mass of committed democrats (with a small d) within the CEC seemed to be missing in 2004.

---

[49] This observation is not a criticism of the goals or strategies pursued by Development Associates and its Strengthening Electoral Administration in Ukraine Project (SEAUP), the USAID implementing partner that worked most closely with the CEC officials. On the contrary, data collected by the author in interviews with DA employees and others familiar with their work, as well as DA documents and publications, suggested that the attempt at working with the CEC to make the 2004 election freer and fairer was a serious one, especially the work on cleaning up election registrars. DA/SEAUP's efforts were industrial in scale, including the training of 5,000 territorial election commissioners and 100,000 precinct-level commissioners, and the publication of 450,000 copies of training and instructional materials. Moreover, DA employees (to the best of this reviewer's knowledge) did not attempt to whitewash the work of their Ukrainian government partners after the official results were released, a phenomenon observed in other countries and other projects. What is also true is that a majority of CEC local commissions probably did report the vote accurately. It is also true, as discussed above, that a few CEC federal commission members refused to endorse the official results.

As discussed above, according to Ukraine's electoral law, the CEC's vote count had to be approved by the Rada. But as the number of demonstrators on the streets of Kyiv began hovering near 1,000,000, a majority of MPs in support of the CEC's official tally could not be constructed. Indirectly, a number of American activities contributed in the margins to the independence of the Rada. For many years, the Indiana University Parliamentary Development Project has contributed to the professionalism of the Rada and its staff. Tracing a direct link between this project's activities and the decision of the Rada not to ratify the CEC official results is impossible. Western organizations that worked to strengthen the organizational capacities of Our Ukraine, the Yulia Tymoshenko Bloc, and the Socialist Party also contributed indirectly to the Rada's ability to make an independent judgment about the vote, because it was these parties that voted not to approve the CEC's official results.

The U.S. embassy also sponsored a visit to Washington for Rada speaker Lytvyn, right before the election. The message hammered home to Lytvyn during his visit was to "do the right thing" if the Rada had a role to play in ensuring the freeness and fairness of elections.

The third institution to contribute to the process of annulling the official results of the second election was the Supreme Court. Again, it is simply not possible to trace a direct causal link between a U.S.-sponsored program and the Supreme Court's historic decision on December 3 to annul the second-round results and call for a rerun of the second round. Several Court members had long, positive, and developed relationships with ABA-CEELI, for instance, but it is not possible (at least with the data collected by this researcher) to trace a direct causal role between these Western training programs and the CEC decisions.

In parallel to these activities was a mediation effort between Kuchma, Yanukovych, and Yushchenko that was facilitated immensely by Presidents Aleksander Kwasnewski of Poland, Valdas Adamkus of Lithuania, and Javiar Solana of the European Union. Kwasnewski was especially influential in pressing for a negotiated but "right" solution to the crisis; Solana followed his lead. The Bush administration deliberately did not seek a public role in the negotiations, but stayed closely involved behind the scenes through contacts with Kwasnewski as well as Solana and Adamkus.

III. LONG-TERM SOURCES AND THE EXTERNAL FACILITATORS OF THE ORANGE REVOLUTION

1. Sources of Semiauthoritarianism

The U.S. government and USAID grantees played an indirect role in sustaining competitive authoritarianism and preventing a full-scale dictatorship from consolidating in Ukraine. Kuchma was a ruthless leader who established a corrupt and criminal regime, but he refrained from attempting to construct a truly repressive tyranny because he wanted a cooperative relationship with

Washington. Assistance and moral support provided by USAID grantees helped to sustain pockets of pluralism within the regime and independent, opposition actors outside of the state. Russian leaders and organizations, to varying extents, played the exact opposite role and encouraged autocratic methods as an effective strategy for holding on to power. Programs and activities that helped to sustain both the idea of checks and balances and the actual institutions that checked executive power were especially important in maintaining semiauthoritarianism and preventing full-blown autocracy.

Within the state, the independence of the Rada was an especially critical component for checking executive power. Technical assistance provided by the Indiana University Parliamentary Development Project helped to make this institution more effective. Party development efforts by the IRI and NDI were also critical in helping to ensure that Kuchma's party did not win an overwhelming majority of seats in the parliament as occurred in the Russian Duma during the Putin era. The NDI and IRI worked with *several* parties, which won representation in the Rada, and in turn helped to maintain this institution's independence from the presidential administration. But neither the IRI nor the NDI worked with *all* parties, official claims of nonpartisanship notwithstanding. Given the asymmetries of resources between those tied to the Kuchma regime and those not, as well as the extreme variation in commitment to democracy between those tied to Kuchma and those not, the decisions about selective engagement made by the IRI and NDI seem entirely justified if the central objective of their work is to promote democracy (and not just simply party development).

Beyond strengthening the capacity and independence of the Rada, the effectiveness of other efforts by external actors to promote democracy through working with state institutions is difficult to measure.[50] Over the years, USAID has sponsored several projects designed to strengthen the capacity and independence of the courts, yet the role of this third branch of government in checking the rise of authoritarian power is hard to document. The same must be said about technical assistance programs that engaged the various institutions and bureaucracies of the executive branch. Therefore, the decision by USAID to offer up for bid two RFPs (requests for proposals) – one for activities dealing with the state and another for working with society – was not only appropriate but necessary for working in Ukraine in the run up to the 2004 presidential vote.

2. Stimulating the Emergence and Persistence of Civil Society

The factors described above, which precipitated the Orange Revolution, did not appear overnight. Rather, they crystallized after years and years of nurturing. Even new groups such as Black Pora, Yellow Pora, and Znayu benefited from

---

[50] Regional legislative governments provided another soft check on executive power, but a serious analysis of their work (and the work of democracy assistance programs working with them) was beyond the scope of this study.

the efforts of civic organizations that had formed several years earlier. Some of the leaders of these Orange Revolution groups got their initial start in civic organizing in other NGOs, which may have played only an indirect role in the events in 2004. At a most general level, then, the emergence and development of civil society during the 1990s provided an enabling environment for the construction of organizations that led the Orange Revolution in 2004.

Indirectly, then, all Western-sponsored programs that promoted the development of civil society contributed in some way to the Orange Revolution. However, without using survey instruments, explaining how is nearly impossible. Nonetheless, in interviews conducted by the author with civil society leaders, a few general themes did emerge concerning the donor community's role in nurturing civil society. First, because Ukraine had developed a rather mature civil society over the fifteen years since independence, direct financial assistance in the forms of small grants was the most effective mechanism for sustaining and nurturing civil society; technical assistance mattered less. Second, external actors played a vital role in networking Ukrainian NGOs with each other and with other actors and institutions committed to deepening democracy. For instance, Internews played a direct and critical role in helping to form the IAB and the UAPP. Grant money given to Znayu organizers, the CVU, and Democratic Initiatives in turn gave these organizations leverage to induce others to cooperate with them. This is a crucial function that Ukrainian actors either were unwilling to initiate or lacked the contacts and resources to initiate effectively. Third, programs focused on promoting advocacy, concrete outcomes, and partnership with constituencies stimulated a particular kind of vibrant civil society in Ukraine.

At the same time, only a small portion of the NGOs supported by Western aid played any role – direct or indirect – in the Orange Revolution. These were the organizations described above in the discussion about precipitants. The vast majority remained focused on their individual projects and local concerns, and did not aspire or attempt to play a role in the events surrounding the Orange Revolution. General support for civil society development did not produce electoral breakthrough in Ukraine and is unlikely to do so in other countries. Rather, electoral breakthrough requires support for very specific kinds of activities, described above.

On an anecdotal level, there does appear to be some correlation between Ukrainians who studied in the West and those who became NGO leaders. Dozens of people working in the third sector interviewed by the author had spent some time studying in the United States and Canada or had participated in some sort of exchange program.

3. Economic Reform, Economic Growth, and the Rise of the Middle Class

In commentary and analysis, the rise of the middle class is frequently cited as a factor contributing to the Orange Revolution. The hypotheses about the role of the middle class in undermining the Kuchma regime are many. The middle class contributed in greater amounts to the Yushchenko campaign; the middle class voted in greater numbers for Yushchenko; the middle class participated in greater numbers on Maidan; and the middle class contributed directly to the financial and material support of the demonstrators on Maidan. A final hypothesis about Western aid therefore follows: if Western programs helped to nurture the rise of the middle class in Ukraine, then these programs also played a role in the Orange Revolution.

The first set of hypotheses about the causal relationship between the rise of the middle class and the Orange Revolution could be tested empirically using survey data. Regrettably, such survey data do not exist. This said, there is most certainly anecdotal evidence that the middle class, buoyed by several years of economic growth, did contribute to the Our Ukraine campaign. The evidence of in-kind and financial contributions to the Maidan demonstrations is even clearer. The effort was simply too massive and too decentralized to be funded by billionaires or coordinated by a single authority. Evidence about middle class voting behavior is thinner. On average, voters in the industrial East are richer than voters in the more rural West, yet Yanukovych captured the majority of votes in the East, and Yushchenko captured the majority of votes in the West. The pivotal regions were in the center of the country, where growth was also highest in recent years. But Kuchma and Prime Minister Yanokovych presided over the recent period of economic growth. If voters were simply casting their ballots based on pocketbook assessments, then those in the richer central regions should have voted in greater proportion for Yanukovych. Obviously, factors others than economic prosperity or even class consciousness played a role in determining voter preferences.

Even if a causal link could be identified between the rise of the middle class and the success of the Orange Revolution, tracing the role of Western assistance programs in the rise of this middle class is fraught with complexity. In interviews with organizations involved in economic reform issues such as Padco, the Center for Social Welfare "Dobrochin" (Chernigiv), the Local Economic Development project (administered by Chemonics), the Centre for Ukrainian Reform Education, and the Ukraine Land Titling Initiative in Chernigiv, none of the project managers interviewed claimed that their work contributed directly to the Orange Revolution. When pressed by the author to speculate about indirect contributions (such as the creation of farmers owning land, who in turn might have voted differently, or the stimulation of economic growth, which in turn might have influenced the behavior of citizens during the fall of 2004), no one dared. Untangling the complex relationship between economic transformation on the one hand and the political outcomes related to the Orange Revolution on the other hand is an important research question that would require the collection of data, survey data in particular, which is (so far) beyond the scope of this study.

Generally, in the literature on democratization, there is disagreement about this relationship. One school of thought contends that economic growth facilitates democratization, whereas another school argues that economic crises spark democratic change.[51] In the postcommunist world, there is no single pattern. Economic crisis helped to undermine Milošević in Serbia in 2000 and Shevardnadze in Georgia in 2003, but the absence of economic crisis in Ukraine in 2004 did not prevent the fall of the Kuchma regime. Kyrgyzstan also was experiencing economic growth when Akaev was ousted in the spring of 2005.

4. Demonstration Effects

In interviews, actors in the Orange Revolution reported favorably on the demonstration effects that Serbia 2000 and Georgia 2003 had on their own mobilization efforts. Contacts with youth activists from Serbia, Slovakia, and Georgia provided inspiration to their counterparts in Ukraine, even if the transfer of technical knowledge about civic resistance is more difficult to measure. Elite contacts between Ukrainian opposition leaders and their counterparts in Georgia, Poland, and the United States had a similar inspirational effect. Groups that facilitated such contacts, such as Freedom House, the German Marshall Fund, the NDI, and the IRI, therefore contributed in another way to the Orange Revolution.

5. The Pull of Western Institutions and Western Norms

Among those who supported Yushchenko in the election and then demonstrated in support of their votes for him after the second round, there is clear evidence that they supported the idea of Ukraine joining Europe. Among elites involved in the organizing the Orange Revolution interviewed by the author, this desire to make Ukraine look more European (and less like the autocracies in Central Asia and Russia) was a sentiment frequently expressed. Western aid programs that helped to advance this idea of Ukraine as a country in Europe therefore contributed indirectly to the Orange Revolution.

IV. CONCLUSION: THE LIMITS OF EXTERNAL ACTORS

In seeking to learn lessons from the Ukrainian democratic breakthrough, it is important to realize that the list of necessary conditions specified above is long. The presence of only a few of these factors is unlikely to generate the same outcome. A more popular or more ruthless autocrat might have been able to outmaneuver the democratic opposition. A less organized electoral monitoring effort might not have been able to convince people to take to the streets.

[51] Seymour M. Lipset, for example versus Stephan Haggard and Robert Kaufman in various writings.

Thousands on the streets, instead of tens or hundreds of thousands, might have produced a very different outcome. The stars must really be aligned to produce such dramatic events as the Orange Revolution.

Of this long list of factors, external actors can only play a positive role in influencing a few of them. The Ukrainian experience suggests that it is hard for outsiders to foster splits within an *ancien régime* and difficult for them to influence the popularity of the regime directly. Influencing the effectiveness of opposition candidates is also difficult, though not impossible. At the margins, external actors can encourage unity among the democratic opposition, but the real drivers of unity or disunity will always be local actors, not their foreign partners.

The greatest space for meaningful activity was regarding electoral observation, creating the perception of a falsified vote, and the development of societal organizations that then played a critical role in protecting the vote after election day. The Ukrainian experience underscored the importance of having a multipronged strategy, that is, supporting exit polls, a parallel vote tabulation, domestic monitors, and international monitors. Reliance on just one of these mechanisms would have been insufficient. The novel idea of bringing international monitors from the region (rather than from the United States), who are more familiar with the problems of elections in semiautocratic regimes, was a brilliant one. Developing the ENEMO should be a top priority for USAID and other democracy assistance organizations. In addition to expanding its work in the postcommunist region, ENEMO could help develop new electoral monitoring organizations in the greater Middle East.

External actors also played a significant role in underwriting the activities of civic organizations that helped to get out the vote and then protect it. In reference to the big debate over whether to support state institutions or civil society, the Orange Revolution is a clear example of the payoffs from maintaining sustained support for civil society.

External actors also contributed to the development of independent media in Ukraine. One of the most effective media outlets, *Ukrainskaya Pravda*, relied almost exclusively on external financial support. The Ukrainian experience affirms the wisdom of a strategy focused primarily on supporting societal actors, rather than state institutions, in a country ruled by a semiauthoritarian regime. Democratic change did not occur as a result of incremental changes within the old regime, but due to societal mobilization against the old regime. To be sure, the Orange Revolution did not eliminate all antidemocratic elements of the Ukrainian regime. But the rupture in the fall of 2004 has helped to accelerate the deepening of democracy.

The Ukrainian experience suggests that programs designed to foster the development of professional media, civil society, and political parties must be funded for long periods of time, as it is difficult to predict when the payoffs for democratization will come.

APPENDIX: INTERVIEWS

David A. Atwood
Director, Office of Democracy,
Governance and Social Transition
Bureau for Europe and Eurasia

Yarema Bachynsky
Chief of Party
Strengthening Electoral Administration
in Ukraine Project
Development Associates, Inc.

Oleksandr Barabash
Expert
Strengthening Electoral Administration
in Ukraine Project
Development Associates, Inc.

Roman Mikhailovich Barabash
Center Coordinator, Attorney
Ukraine Land Titling Initiative
Project
Chernigiv Center for Legal Aid to New
Land Owners

Iryna Bekeshina
Research Director
Democratic Initiatives Foundation

Markian Bilynskyj
Vice President
US-Ukraine Foundation

David Black
Office of Democracy and Governance
USAID

Tetyana Boiko
Member of Governing Board
Pora! (United)

Jeanne M. Bourgault
COO and Vice President for Programs
Internews Network

Eric David Boyle
Regional Director, Kiev Regional Office
The Eurasia Foundation

Aleksandra E. Braginski
Team Leader, Ukraine/Moldova/Belarus
Team
USAID

Svitlana Buko
IREX/Media Administrative Manager
IREX Kiev

Yevhen Bystrytsky, Ph.D.
Executive Director
International Renaissance Foundation

Irina Cherenko
Board Member
"Orange" Center for Progressive
Youth

Jeff Clark
Executive Associate
Development Associates, Inc.

Lorne Craner
President
International Republican Institute

David Dettman
Resident Director (Kyiv, Ukraine)
National Democratic Institute

Nadia Diuk
National Endowment for Democracy

Natalia Drozd
Director, NGO "Dobrochyn" (Good
Deed) Center for Social Welfare
(Chernihiv, Ukraine)

Serhiy Dyoma
Grants Manager, Open Media Fund
International Renaissance Foundation

Alisa Farah
Ukrainian Association of Publishers

Barbara Felitti
Country Director
Ukraine Citizen Action Network
Project

Volodymyr Fesenko, Ph.D.
Chairman of the Board
Center for Political Studies "Penta"

Susan W. Folger
Chief of Party
Internews Network

Svitlana Franchuk
Deputy Chief of Party
Civic Oversight of Election Program
Freedom House

Vadim Galaychuk
General Director, Moor &
Krosondovich
Coordinator for Our Ukraine Election
Monitoring Program

David Goldberg
Special Advisor, Democracy Programs
Office of the Coordinator for U.S.
Assistance to Europe and Eurasia
U.S. Department of State

Juhani Grossman
Senior Program Officer
Civic Participation in Elections in
Ukraine
Freedom House

Ihor Gryniv
Former Director
National Institute for Strategic Studies
Our Ukraine MP
(key campaign advisor to Yushchenko)

Kostyantyn Gryshchenko
Vice-Chairman of the Party, Republican
Party of Ukraine
Minister for Foreign Affairs of Ukraine
(2003–2005)

Sheila Gwaltney
Deputy Chief of Mission, Ukraine
Embassy of the United States of America

John Herbst
American Ambassador to Ukraine
Embassy of the United States of
America

Karen R. Hilliard
Deputy Director
USAID Mission for Ukraine, Belarus,
and Moldova
U.S. Embassy

Chris Holzen
Resident Program Director, Ukraine
International Republican Institute

Andrij Ihnatov
Board Member
Maidan Inform

Oleh Ilkiv
Head of the Board
"Your Right"

Assia Ivantcheva
Deputy Director
Office of Democracy and
Governance
USAID Ukraine

Sarah Jedrzejczak
Senior Program Manager
Freedom House

Laura Jewitt
Deputy Director of FSU Programs
National Democratic Institute

Serhii Kalchenko
Activity Manager
Strengthening Electoral Administration
in Ukraine Project
Development Associates, Inc.

Andrij Kartashov
Head of Parliamentary Center
Nash Dim

Vladislav Kaskiv
Yellow Pora/Freedom of Choice
Coalition

Mikhola Katarynchuk
Chairman of Our Ukraine

Daria Khabarova
PR Specialist, Translator
BBC World Service

Tanya Khmyz
Senior Project Officer
Civic Participation in Elections in
Ukraine
Freedom House

Yuri Kliuchkovsky
Deputy Head of the Committee
Committee on State Development &
Local Self-Government
Parliament of Ukraine

Roman Knyazevich
Member
Central Election Commission

Andriy Kohut
Member of Board
Pora! (Black)

Sergey Kokizyuk
Center for Ukrainian Reform
Education

Marta Kolomayets
Project Director
Community Partnerships Project
US-Ukraine Foundation

Petro Koshukov
LED Advisor, ERUM Project
(Chemonics)
(former co-director of Znayu
project)

Sergiy Kostiuk
Reporter
Ukrainskaya Pravda

Dr. Volodymyr Kovtunets
Deputy Chief of Party
Strengthening Electoral Administration
in Ukraine Project
Development Associates, Inc.

John M. Kubiniec
Regional Director (Poland)
Freedom House

Ilko Kucheriv
Director
Democratic Initiatives Fund

Sally Kux
Director of Democracy Programs
Office of the Coordinator for U.S.
Assistance to Europe and Eurasia
U.S. Department of State

Taras Kuzio
Visiting Professor
George Washington University

Konstyantyn Kvurt
Executive Director
Internews Ukraine

Iryna Kyselova
Monitoring and Evaluation Manager
USAID Implementing partner (ERUM
Project)

Tetyana Lebedeva
Head of the Board
Independent Association of
Broadcasters

Ambassador Nelson Ledsky
Director of FSU
National Democratic Institute

Oleh Levchenko
Member of the Board
Black Pora!

Natalya Ligachova,
Project Director and Chairman of the
Board
Telekritika

Yurii Lutsenko
Minister of Interior
Ukraine
(former MP from Socialist Party and one
of key organizers of Maidan events)

Iryna Manokha
Center for Political Education
(Znayu organizer)

Sergei Markov
Russian advisor to Yanukovich
campaign

Oksana Maydan
Grant Manager
Center for Ukrainian Reform Education

Leslie McCuaig
Vice President for Program Development
Institute for Sustainable Communities

H. Brian Mefford
Resident Program Officer, Ukraine
International Republican Institute

Vitaly Moroz
Program Officer
Civic Participation in Elections in
Ukraine
Freedom House

Kateryna Myasnykova
Executive Director
Independent Association of
Broadcasters

Mary Mycio
Media Law Adviser
U-Media Legal Defense and Education
Program
IREX

Hryhoriy Nemyria
Director
Center for European and International
Studies
(advisor to Yulia Tymoshenko)

Steve Nix
Director of FSU Programs
International Republican
Institute

Valeriy Oliynyk
Grant Programs Director
Urkaine Citizen Action Network Project
(UCAN)

Dr. Irina Paliashvili
President
Russian-Ukrainian Legal Group, P.A.

Yurii Papernyi
Political Observer

Volodymyr Parkhomenko
LED Advisor
USAID Implementing partner (ERUM
Project)

Dr. Roman A. Petrov
Board Member, Ukrainian Bar
Association
Associate Dean for International
Programs, Economics and Law Faculty
Donetsk National University

Inna Pidluska
President
Europa XXI Foundation

Yevgen Poberezhny
Deputy Chairman of the Board
Committee of Voters of Ukraine

Alexandr Podgorniy
Chairman of the Board
Center for Social Welfare "Dobrochin"
(Chernihiv)

Mikhailo Borisovich Pogrebinskiy
Director, Kiev Center for Political
Studies and Conflictology
(campaign advisor for Yanukovych)

Konstantyn Polsky
Center for Political
Education

Ihor Popov
President
Committee of Voters of Ukraine (CVU)

Dmytro Potekhin
Co-director Znayu campaign
U.S.-Ukraine Foundation

Antonina Prudko
Clinical Legal Education Program
Coordinator
ABA/CEELI

Olena Prytula
Editor
Ukrainskaya Pravda

Anatoliy V. Rachok
Director General
Ukrainian Center for Economic &
Political Studies Named After Razumkov

Edward Rakhimkulov
Associate Field Director
Indiana University Parliamentary
Development Project
USAID Democratic Parliamentary
Strengthening Program

Olga Romanyuk
Project Coordinator
PADCO

Kateryna Ryabiko
Program Management Specialist
Office of Democracy and Governance
U.S. Embassy to Ukraine/USAID
Mission for Ukraine, Belarus and
Moldova

Aly Farkhatovich Safarov
Attorney, Expert on Media Rights

Lyudmyla Safarova
Grant Manager
Freedom House – Ukraine

Bill Schlansker
Municipal Development Advisor, Office
of Economic Growth
U.S. Embassy to Ukraine
USAID Mission for Ukraine, Belarus,
and Moldova

Paula Schriefer
Director of Programs
Freedom House

James Schumaker
Ambassador/Project Coordinator in
Ukraine
OSCE

Valeriy Semenets
Chief Director
Ukrainian Social-Democratic Youth

Natalia Semiryazhko
Director
Center of the Women's Initiative "Belie
Zolnt"

Illia Shevliak
First Deputy Minster
Ministry of Ukraine for Family, Youth
& Sports
(former senior advisor to the OSCE)

Yuriy Stepanets
"Nash Podilya"

Nick Stevens
Director
Ukraine Citizen Action Network Project
(UCAN)

Tetiana Soboleva
Political Party Program Officer (Kyiv,
Ukraine)
National Democratic Institute

Alexander Sokolowski, Ph.D.
Senior Political Process Advisor
USAID

Anatoly Solovyov
LED Advisor
ERUM Project (Chemonics)

Oleksandr Sputay
NGO Program Coordinator
International Republican Institute

Taras Stepanovich Stetskiv
Member of Parliament, Ukraine
(One of key organizers of Maidan
events)

Kathryn Stevens
Director, Office of Democracy &
Governance
USAID Ukraine

Nick Stevens
Program Director
Ukraine Citizen Action Network Project

Volodimir Cheslavovich Sventitsky
Director
Public Education and Legal Assistance

Sergiy Taran
Ph.D. Candidate, Department of
Political Science
Duke University
Yellow Pora leader

Viatcheslav Tcherniavski
Financial Manager
Center for Social Innovations

Yulia Timoshenko
Former prime minister

Michael Uyehara
First Secretary
Embassy of the United States of America
(Ukraine)

Judy Van Rest
Executive Vice President
International Republican Institute

Olena Vasilchenko, Ph.D.
Project Director, Senior Legal Advisor
Planning and Development
Collaborative International
USAID Ukraine Pension Reform
Implementation Program

Oleksandr Vorobyov
Activity Manager
Strengthening Electoral Administration
in Ukraine Project
Development Associates, Inc.

Gavin Weise
ABA/CEELI

Charles R. Wise
Director
Parliamentary Development Project
USAID

Andriy Yaramenko
Board Member
City Charitable Organization "All
Together"

Yarna Yasynevych
Member of the Board
Pora! (Black)

Yevgen Zolotarov
Yellow Pora leader

PART IV

RESISTING REFORM: BACKSLIDING DEMOCRACIES AND ENDURING AUTOCRACIES

9

Resistance to Contagion

Sources of Authoritarian Stability in the Former Soviet Union

Lucan Way

University of Toronto

Why did the "third wave" of postcommunist transitions sweep away some autocrats but leave others untouched? A partial explanation is that hybrid or competitive authoritarian regimes (such as Ukraine or Georgia) were more vulnerable than fully closed regimes (such as Uzbekistan or Turkmenistan) to opposition challenges. As Steven Levitsky, Harvard University, and I have argued, the "coexistence of democratic rules and autocratic methods aimed at keeping incumbents in power creates an inherent source of instability."[1] Indeed, each of the color revolutions occurred in nondemocratic but relatively competitive political systems.[2] Yet, even among post-Soviet competitive authoritarian regimes, only some autocrats succumbed to opposition challenges.

This chapter examines the sources of authoritarian vulnerability through a comparison of the fate of autocrats in the seven post-Soviet countries that emerged as hybrid in the 1990s.[3] Why did some (Armenia, Belarus, Moldova, and Russia) survive the third wave in the early and mid-2000s whereas others (Georgia, Kyrgyzstan, and Ukraine) fell to opposition forces? A comparison of these cases suggests that incumbent state and ruling party capacity are key

---

[1] Valerie Bunce evocatively describes hybrid regimes as "unusually 'restless.'" Competitive authoritarianism is defined by the combination of authoritarian practices and meaningful democratic institutions. See Steven Levitsky and Lucan Way. "The Rise of Competitive Authoritarianism." *Journal of Democracy*, 13 (April 2002), pp. 51–65, esp. p. 59.

[2] Michael McFaul, "Transitions from Postcommunism." *Journal of Democracy* 16, No. 3 (2005), pp. 5–19.

[3] In the 1990s, Armenia, Belarus, Georgia, Moldova, Russia, and Ukraine were all competitive authoritarian in that executive-level elections, while highly unfair, offered the possibility of opposition victory. Kyrgyzstan at the time was arguably more authoritarian. Although, media and the legislature were notably more independent than in other Central Asian countries, elections to the executive were less clearly competitive. Belarus had ceased to be competitive authoritarian by the late 1990s. See Steven Levitsky and Lucan Way, "Competitive Authoritarianism: International Linkage, Organizational Power and the Fate of Hybrid Rule," Manuscript, Harvard University and the University of Toronto, 2009.

sources of authoritarian stability.[4] Autocrats have been more likely to hang on when they possessed at least *one* of the following pillars of incumbent strength: (1) a single highly institutionalized ruling party backed by a nonmaterial source of cohesion such as a revolutionary tradition or highly salient ideology; (2) an extensive, well-funded, and cohesive coercive apparatus; or (3) state discretionary control over the economy, generated either by the failure to privatize or by reliance on easily captured energy revenues. As we see below, each of these dimensions of incumbent strength can be measured ex ante and not just *after* incumbents have either succumbed to or survived opposition challenges.

State and party strength has shaped the balance of power between incumbent and opposition in two key ways. First, such capacity has affected the ability of incumbents to face down opposition challenges. Thus, leaders in powerful states such as Armenia have withstood even highly mobilized opposition challenges, whereas incumbents backed by weaker coercive apparatuses have faltered even in the face of modest opposition mobilization. Second, incumbent state and party capacity has often indirectly affected opposition strength. Thus, oppositions in Georgia, Kyrgyzstan, and Ukraine were powerfully bolstered by the weakness of ruling coalitions and weak state control over the economy, whereas oppositions in Russia and Belarus in the 2000s were severely undermined by state economic control. Certainly, incumbent weakness does not provide a complete explanation for authoritarian collapse. Yet, such weakness does make regimes vulnerable to a variety of more contingent factors – including diffusion, examined extensively by Valerie Bunce and others in this volume.

THREE PILLARS OF STABLE AUTHORITARIANISM

This chapter explores three sources of authoritarian organizational capacity that have affected the ability of leaders to preserve the loyalty of allies and to defuse, coopt, or crush protest. In the post-Soviet context, institutionalized ruling party structures, coercive capacity, and state economic control provided partially interchangeable sources of autocratic resistance to the postcommunist third wave.

Ruling Party Strength

Ruling party strength has been one key source of authoritarian durability. Until recently, most studies of postcommunist parties emphasized the ways in which they strengthened democratic consolidation by facilitating democratic

---

[4] This work draws heavily on my own work and work with Steven Levitsky. See Lucan Way, "Authoritarian State Building and the Sources of Regime Competitiveness in the Fourth Wave." *World Politics*, 57, No. 2 (January 2005), pp. 231–61. Lucan Way, "Failed Authoritarianism and the Sources of Political Competition in the Former Soviet Union," Unpublished manuscript, University of Toronto, 2009; Levitsky and Way, "Competitive Authoritarianism."

accountability and structuring political competition.[5] Yet students of authoritarianism have long noted that strong ruling parties are also key to authoritarian durability.[6] Indeed, Vladimir Putin in the early 2000s sought to strengthen party rule not to promote democracy but to increase vertical control over both the Duma and regional governments.[7] Strong ruling parties bolster authoritarian rule in several ways. First, as Barbara Geddes, Jason Brownlee, and Beatriz Magaloni emphasize, parties discourage elite defection. Parties structure and institutionalize the distribution of patronage, thereby making it more likely that elites will remain loyal even when they lose short-term battles over resources. In contrast, loosely organized and highly atomized nonparty ruling coalitions give executives a high degree of flexibility to dump allies; but they also make it less costly for allies to defect – often with their own organizational resources intact. This is particularly evident within the legislature, where patronage alone has been insufficient to maintain executive dominance. For example, Yeltsin's refusal to rely on any institutionalized party structure contributed to the rapid rise of a powerful parliamentary opposition in 1992–3 despite the President's overwhelming access to key administrative and patronage resources. By contrast, as Kathryn Stoner-Weiss notes in Chap. 10, Putin's United Russia has facilitated much more stable Kremlin control over the Duma. Similarly, Radnitz argues in Chap. 12 that President Kurmanbek Bakiev's creation of the ruling Ak Jol party in Kyrgyzstan has strengthened his control over the legislature.

Ruling parties also facilitate incumbent control by helping progovernment deputies to ride the coattails of popular incumbents and gin support in legislative elections. As Stoner-Weiss notes in her chapter, Putin's decision to openly back United Russia helped the party enormously in elections. On the other hand, the absence of such parties may undermine the election efforts of progovernment deputies. Thus, Yeltsin's failure to back the "Russia's Choice" cost the party an estimated ten to fifteen percent of the vote in 1993.[8]

---

[5] Cf. Herbertt Kitschelt and Regina A. Smyth, "Programmatic Party Cohesion in Emerging Postcommunist Democracies in Comparative Context." *Comparative Political Studies.* 35, No. 10 (2002), pp. 1228–56; M. Steven Fish, "Stronger Legislatures, Stronger Democracies." *Journal of Democracy*, 17, No. 1 (2006), pp. 5–20, esp. p. 16; Henry Hale, *Why Not Parties in Russia? Democracy, Federalism, and the State*, p. 20 (New York: Cambridge University Press, 2006). For a recent exception, see Ora John Reuter, and Thomas F. Remington. "Dominant Party Regimes and the Commitment Problem: The Case of United Russia." *Comparative Political Studies*, 42, No. 4 (2009), pp. 501–526.

[6] Cf. Barbara Geddes, "What Do We Know about Democratization after Twenty Years?" *Annual Review of Political Science*, 2 (1999); Jason Brownlee, *Durable Authoritarianism in an Age of Democratization* (New York: Cambridge University Press, 2007). Beatriz Magaloni, "Credible Power Sharing and the Longevity of Authoritarian Rule." *Comparative Political Studies*, 41, Nos. 4–5 (2008), pp. 715–41.

[7] V. Gelman, "Vozvrashchenie Leviafona? Politika Retsentralizatsii v sovremennoi Rossii," Unpublished manuscript, 2006; Vitalii Ivanov, *Partiia Putina: Istoriia 'Edinoi Rossii'*, (Moscow: Olma Press, 2008).

[8] Leon Aron, *Yeltsin: A Revolutionary Life* (New York: St. Martin's Press, 2000), p. 561.

We can classify party strength ex ante in the following way. First, a *weak* ruling party exists either when incumbents lack any ruling party, as in Ukraine under Kravchuk, or when executives are linked to multiple and competing ruling parties, as in Russia under Yeltsin or Ukraine under Kuchma. By contrast, a party with *medium strength* exists when leaders have access to a single dominant ruling party with an institutionalized system of patronage. Examples include United Russia, and Ak Jol in Kyrgyzstan. Finally, high party strength is defined by the existence of a single institutionalized ruling party that is bolstered by other, non-material sources of cohesion less vulnerable to economic crisis or swings in the ruling party's perceived strength. The strongest source of cohesion is elite solidarity forged during periods of violent revolutionary or liberation struggle that have allowed parties such as ZANU-PF in Zimbabwe and the Communist Party of Cuba to survive severe economic crises and powerful opposition challenges.[9] No party in the former Soviet Union approximates such high cohesion. Nonetheless, some parties such as the Party of Communists of the Republic of Moldova (PCRM) have been distinguished from pure patronage parties by the fact that they draw on an established ideological tradition. Such ideology provides a stable support base and motivates a strong core of activists that is likely to bolster regime stability.

State Coercive Capacity

A second source of autocratic stability is the autocrat's command over an extensive, cohesive, well funded, and experienced coercive apparatus that can reliably harass regime opposition and put down protest. Coercive state power affects the ability of incumbents to preempt opposition challenges and/or contain large-scale protest once it emerges. Coercive capacity has a critical impact on the strength of opposition required to topple autocratic incumbents. Where the state is weak, police are more likely to resist taking action against regime opponents and may simply dissolve in the face of even modest protest. Thus, in Kyrgyzstan, underpaid police simply stood by as a few hundred protestors stormed regional centers in the south – leading to the downfall of Akaev in 2005. By contrast, a more powerful coercive apparatus can confront even well mobilized opposition. Thus, in Armenia, war-hardened security forces put down protests ranging from 25,000 to 200,000 in 1996, 2003, 2004, and 2008 – shutting down opposition headquarters, sealing off the capital, and arresting hundreds of opposition leaders and activists.

The Soviet collapse left post-Soviet autocrats in the early 1990s with mixed levels of coercive strength. On the one hand, leaders benefited from extremely extensive and well-developed security services and organizational networks

---

[9] For an in-depth discussion of other sources of cohesion, see Levitsky and Way, "Competitive Authoritarianism."

that in most cases survived into the 1990s.[10] At the same time, though, leaders faced greater difficulty in controlling security and other coercive structures. Economic crisis and the absence of clear lines of authority in the wake of the Soviet dissolution contributed to significant insubordination in the early 1990s.[11] Such weakness directly undermined authoritarian consolidation. Thus in Ukraine, President Leonid Kravchuk backed away from efforts to shut down parliament in early 1994 after the heads of police and security services resisted. Similarly in Russia, Yeltsin was barely able to gain the cooperation of the military in his assault on the legislature in late 1993.[12]

By the late 1990s, post-Soviet states had emerged with varying levels of coercive strength. The first were *weak states* characterized by significant under-funding and/or large wage arrears. Other indicators of weakness included loss in war and evidence of open rebellion – expressed in the form of coup attempts or exceptionally weak central control. Thus in Kyrgyzstan in the early 2000s, police were severely underpaid and often not provided with basic equipment.[13] In Georgia in the early 2000s, the central state was unable to control significant portions of the country and could not pay its police for months on end.[14] In such cases, we expect that leaders will face greater difficulty in putting down even weakly mobilized protest.

At the other end of the spectrum, success in large-scale violent conflict combined with significant financing generated a *high state strength*. Success in war (or revolution) arguably produces a powerful coercive apparatus with the experience, cohesion, self-confidence, and "stomach" to use force and face down significant challenges.[15] In the former Soviet Union, the clearest example of a strong coercive state is Armenia, which possessed an extremely well-funded military and in 1994 successfully captured twenty percent of neighboring Azerbaijan in a war over the Nagorno-Karabakh region.[16]

Finally, other post-Soviet states emerged in the late 1990s with *medium coercive strength* characterized by extensive, well-paid, and well-equipped security services that lacked experience in a national-level victorious war or

[10] Amy Knight, *Spies without Cloaks: The KGB's Successors* (Princeton, NJ: Princeton University Press, 1997).

[11] Cf. Kathryn Stoner-Weiss, *Resisting the State: Reform and Retrenchment in Post-Soviet Russia* (New York: Cambridge University Press, 2006); Kahn, Jeffrey, *Federalism, Democratization, and the Rule of Law in Russia* (New York: Cambridge University Press, 2002).

[12] See Way, "Authoritarian State Building."

[13] Scott Radnitz, personal communication.

[14] Cory Welt, "A Return to Eurasia." *Transitions Online.* 11 January 2000.

[15] Along these lines, Mark Thompson has argued that Chinese leaders' experience in revolutionary struggle gave them the self-confidence and cohesion to put down protests in 1989 that Soviet leaders lacked at the time – resulting in regime survival in China and collapse in the Soviet Union. Mark R. Thompson, "To Shoot or Not to Shoot: Posttotalitarianism in China and Eastern Europe." *Comparative Politics* 34, No. 1 (2001), pp. 63–83.

[16] Thomas de Waal, *Black Garden: Armenia and Azerbaijan through Peace and War* (New York: NYU Press, 2003).

violent revolutionary struggle. In contrast to weak states, police and security services were likely to remain cohesive in the face of modest protest but
more likely to lack the cohesion, skills, and stomach to cope with sustained
and large-scale mobilization. Examples include Russia under Putin, Ukraine
under Kuchma, and Belarus under Lukashenka – where coercive forces were
well-financed in the early 2000s but lacked experience in recent national level
military conflict.

State Control over Wealth

Finally, authoritarian stability has been shaped by the extent to which leaders
have discretionary control over wealth in society – whether through formal
state control over the economy or through reliance on energy revenues that
are relatively easy for even weak autocrats to capture. Discretionary economic
control first gives leaders access to enormous resources to buy off opposition
and keep supporters in line. Thus, even in the context of economic decline,
leaders of centrally planned economies may tap into vast resources that they can
direct to allies.[17] Similarly, leaders in oil-based economies with weak market
institutions often have access to "budgets that are exceptionally large and
unconstrained."[18]

Even more critically, state economic control and/or mineral wealth gives
autocrats power over an overriding share of a society's wealth that they may
use to monopolize resource distribution. In this context, opposition parties may
be unable to gain sufficient monies to mount national campaigns or even survive as viable organizations. In extreme cases, the monopolization of resources
by the state creates significant barriers to activism at the individual level.
"[K]eeping one's job and even sheer economic survival require political circum-
spection and conformity."[19] Thus, both oil-rich states and centrally planned
economies are often able to prevent the formation of independent social
groups.[20]

Cases are considered to have *high state economic control* if states have either
retained dominant formal control over the economy or rely on mineral wealth

---

[17] M. Steven Fish, *Democracy Derailed in Russia: The Failure of Open Politics*, (New York:
Cambridge University Press, 2005).

[18] Michael Ross, "Does Oil Hinder Democracy?" *World Politics*, 53, No. 3 (April 2001),
pp. 325–61, esp. 333; Eva Bellin, "The Robustness of Authoritarianism in the Middle East:
Exceptionalism in Comparative Perspective," *Comparative Politics* 36 (January 2004); Nathan
Jensen and Leonard Wantchekon. "Resource Wealth and Political Regimes in Africa." *Comparative Political Studies*, 37, No. 7 (September 2004), pp. 816–41, esp. 819, 821.

[19] Jagdish Bagwati, 1992. "Democracy and Development," *Journal of Democracy*, 3, No. 3
(1992), pp. 37–44, p. 40; see also Robert Dahl, *Polyarchy: Participation and Opposition*
(New Haven, CT: Yale University Press, 1971); Kenneth Greene. *Why Dominant Parties Lose:
Mexico's Democratization in Comparative Perspective*, (New York: Cambridge University
Press, 2007).

[20] Ross, "Does Oil Hinder Democracy?" p. 333; Dahl, *Polyarchy*; Greene, "Defeating Dominance."

for more than fifty percent of their exports. Examples include Azerbaijan, Belarus, Russia, and Uzbekistan in the 2000s. Cases are considered to have weak state economic control if they lack access to significant mineral resources and have experienced extensive privatization. Examples include Armenia, Georgia, Kyrgyzstan, and Ukraine.

Organizational Power and Opposition Mobilization

State and party capacity has strongly influenced the balance of power between incumbents and opposition. First, as noted above, state coercive capacity affects the scale of opposition mobilization necessary to topple autocratic governments. Autocrats backed by powerful state and/or party organizations are able to face down even well mobilized and popular opponents, whereas weaker incumbents may fall to even weak opposition forces.

Second, organizational capacity has directly influenced the strength of opposition mobilization. As the literature on social mobilization makes clear, the scale of mobilization hinges to an important extent on incumbent strength.[21] On one hand, state economic control and extensive and well-funded security services in Belarus and Russia have arguably kept protest to a minimum. Here, states have been able to starve opposition and create overwhelming barriers to participation in protest. On the other hand, defections by regime elites and/or weak state repressive capacity have provided key political opportunities for protest. Ruling party weakness has directly facilitated mobilization. In Georgia and Ukraine, party weakness encouraged the defection of politicians who in turn led opposition protests in 2003 and 2004. In Ukraine, former proregime oligarchs promoted protest against election fraud in 2004 by funding activists' travel to the capital and providing food and lodging once they were there.[22]

ORGANIZATIONAL POWER AND THE COLOR REVOLUTIONS

Autocrats in the former Soviet Union witnessed very different fates in the early 2000s during the postcommunist "third wave" (see Table 9.1). One frequently cited explanation for variations in authoritarian survival is economic performance.[23] Indeed, successful autocrats among our cases benefited

---

[21] Sidney Tarrow writes that "[r]ational people do not often attack well fortified opponents when opportunities are closed." Sidney Tarrow, *Power in Movement: Social Movements and Contentious Politics*, 2nd ed., (New York: Cambridge University Press, 1997), p. 77; Doug McAdam, "Political Opportunities: Conceptual Origins, Current Problems, Future Directions," in *Comparative Perspectives on Social Movements*, Doug McAdam, John D. McCarthy, and Mayer N. Zald, eds., pp. 26–8 (New York: Cambridge University Press, 1996).

[22] Lucan Way, "Kuchma's Failed Authoritarianism." *Journal of Democracy.* 16, No. 2 (2005), pp. 131–45.

[23] Adam Przeworski and Fernando Limongi, "Modernization: Theories and Facts." *World Politics*, 49, No. 2 (1997), pp. 155–83.

TABLE 9.1. *Organizational Power in 1999–2001 and Incumbent Survival through the mid 2000s*

	Ruling Party Strength	State Coercive Strength	State Discretionary Economic Control	Incumbent Survival 2000–2008
Armenia	Low	High	Low	Yes
Belarus	Low	Medium	High	Yes
Georgia	Medium	Low	Low	No
Kyrgyzstan	Low	Low	Low	No
Moldova (under Lucinschi)	Low	Low	Low	No
Moldova (under PCRM)	Med-High	Low	Low	Yes[24]
Russia	Medium	Medium	High	Yes
Ukraine	Low	Medium	Low	No

from slightly higher average growth (+7.2 percent) than did autocrats who fell (+6.7 percent).[25] But overall growth levels were extremely high in the early 2000s – which would lead us to expect generalized stability. Every country but Kyrgyzstan had consistently positive growth that averaged at least 6 percent in the early 2000s. Ukraine, a case of instability, had the highest growth average among our cases.[26] Thus, to understand autocratic failure or success, we clearly need to look beyond economic performance.

The strength of autocratic state and party power is key. Table 9.1 shows that by 1999–2001, Armenia, Belarus, Kyrgyzstan, Moldova, Russia, and Ukraine had widely divergent patterns of organizational power. One set of cases – Armenia, Belarus, Moldova (under the PCRM), and Russia – possessed relatively high organizational power in at least one dimension discussed here. In contrast, the remaining cases – Georgia, Kyrgyzstan, Moldova (under President Petru Lucinschi), and Ukraine – lacked high strength in *any* area.

Autocratic survival was powerfully shaped by leaders' access to at least one of three key pillars of autocratic strength. First, a comparison of Ukraine and Moldova demonstrates the importance of party strength. The absence of strong ruling parties in Ukraine under Kuchma (1994–2004) and Moldova under Petru Lucinschi (1996–2000) contributed to large-scale defection of allies and autocratic failure in 2004 and 1999–2000. In contrast, the tightly organized

[24] At time of printing in the summer of 2009, the Communists appeared to be under serious threat of losing power.

[25] Averages calculated over previous executive term at election time in the early/mid 2000s: Armenia (2003): 8.6 percent; Belarus (2001): 4.1 percent; Belarus (2006): 9 percent; Moldova (2005): 8.5 percent; Russia (2004): 6 percent; Georgia (2003): 7 percent; Kyrgyzstan (2005): 3.8 percent; Ukraine (2004): 9.2 percent. In cases where elections were held in the last quarter of the year, I gave the executive credit/blame for growth in that year. Data from World Bank "World Development Indicators" (www.worldbank.org/data). Accessed January 2009.

[26] In addition, variation in outcome does not seem to be explained by levels of corruption, because all of these cases demonstrated exceptionally high levels of corruption in the 2000s. According to Freedom House Nations In Transit, all of the cases received corruption scores of 5.25 or higher in the 2000s (highest score = 7).

Communist Party (2001–) in Moldova was less prone to elite defection and successfully thwarted opposition challenges through the mid-2000s. Next, a comparison of Armenia, Georgia, and Kyrgyzstan suggests the critical importance of state power. Weak and severely underfunded states were unable to cope with relatively modest protests in Georgia in 2003 and Kyrgyzstan in 2005, whereas a strong coercive state in Armenia was able to put down powerful protests in Armenia in 1993, 1995, 1996, 2003, 2004, and 2008. Finally, a comparison of Belarus and Russia suggests the importance of state coercion and economic control. In both cases, incumbents had been able to starve the opposition and prevent large-scale mobilization by the late 2000s. While certainly not the only factor shaping autocratic success or failure, organizational power critically affected regime susceptibility to threats from within and abroad.

RULING PARTY STRENGTH AND AUTHORITARIAN STABILITY: UKRAINE AND MOLDOVA

Ukraine and Moldova illustrate the importance of an institutionalized party structure to authoritarian survival. First, Kuchma's Ukraine was characterized by medium coercive strength, relatively dispersed control over economic wealth, and a weakly organized ruling party. By the early 2000s, Kuchma had developed an extensive and well-funded security apparatus but lacked other sources of cohesion.[27] At the same time, like Yeltsin in Russia and Lucinschi in Moldova, Kuchma supported privatization and relied on a relatively diverse group of economic actors outside the state. By the early 2000s, major parts of the economy were controlled by quasi-autonomous business-politicians or "oligarchs" who had gained wealth through access to cheap privatization, state monopolies, and/or budgetary resources.[28]

This economic strategy was augmented by a decision to rely on support from a loose coalition of competing progovernmental parties rather than a single ruling party. Like Yeltsin, Kuchma refused to tie himself closely to any single group. In early 2000, support for Kuchma in parliament was divided among numerous mostly regionally based oligarchic parties, including Viktor Medvedchuk's Social-Democratic Party of Ukraine based in Kyiv and Zakarpatiya, Yulia Tymoshenko's Fatherland Party, and the Party of Regions created by the head of the tax administration, Mykola Azarov, and later taken over by Viktor Yanukovych. By distributing political and economic resources to multiple and competing groups, Kuchma hoped to prevent any single group from

---

[27] Taras Kuzio, "Non-military Security Forces in Ukraine," *Journal of Slavic Military Studies*, 13, No. 4 (2000), pp. 29–56.

[28] By 2002, an estimated sixty-five percent of the economy was controlled by the private sector (EBRD). Oligarchs are defined here as businesspeople who hold direct political power and use that power overwhelmingly to promote their own private business interests. In 2000, the head of the state tax authority estimated that 386 of 450 deputies in parliament were founders of 3,954 businesses – controlling twenty-five percent of Ukraine's imports and ten percent of its exports. Mykola Melnychenko, *Kto est Kto na divane Prezidenta* Kuchmy, (Kyiv: publisher not indicated, 2002).

becoming too strong and posing a challenge to his rule. By keeping his allies mutually antagonistic and competitive, the President sought to remain "the uniting, cementing force that keeps all of his allies together."[29]

Yet, in a context of weakened state economic control, this strategy under-mined Kuchma by generating a series of relatively autonomous parties backed by powerful economic actors only weakly controlled by the President. As a result, Kuchma often faced significant difficulties garnering the support of his own allies. For example in 2000, he was unable to gain parliamentary ratifica-tion of a law that strengthened executive power, despite the dominance of pro-governmental factions in the legislature, strong popular support for Kuchma, and a rapidly growing economy.[30] More critically, the proliferation of rela-tively autonomous progovernmental groups with their own economic bases of support gave politicians the potential resources to pose serious opposition challenges. In 2001, following the release of highly embarrassing tapes that implicated the President in corruption and abuse of power, Yulia Tymoshenko easily transformed her Fatherland Party from a progovernmental force into a major opposition party. In turn, Kuchma's dispersion of political and eco-nomic resources made it harder for him to isolate Viktor Yushchenko, the highly popular former Prime Minister fired in 2001. Thus Yushchenko was able to attract major pro-Kuchma financial figures such as Petro Poroshenko to support Yushchenko's "Our Ukraine" party, which handily beat pro-Kuchma forces in the 2002 parliamentary elections.

Going into the 2004 presidential election, Yushchenko benefited from signif-icant financial and organizational muscle that had essentially been seized from the Kuchma regime. Indeed, virtually the entire leadership of the "orange coali-tion" that defeated Kuchma's chosen successor in 2004 had been close allies of Kuchma just 2–3 years previously.[31] Former pro-regime oligarchs helped to finance a nation-wide election campaign and provided resources to facil-itate massive popular mobilization in the wake of the November fraudulent elections.[32] Subsequently, Kuchma's loosely organized ruling coalition disinte-grated. Five days after the protests began, parliamentary speaker Volodymyr Lytvyn, who had earlier commanded the pro-Presidential faction in parliament, declared the November election results invalid. By mid December, elite-level support for the regime softened considerably and repeat elections were held on December 26 – leading to Yushchenko's victory.

Next, Moldova illustrates the impact of both party weakness under Lucin-schi (1996–2000) and party strength under the Communists (2001–). Moldova

[29] Iulia Mostovaia "'Brestkii mir' Leonida Kuchmy," *Zerkalo nedeli* 23–9 March 2002.
[30] Serhyi Kudelia, "Intangible Asset: Society, Elites and the Politics of Constitutional Reform in Ukraine," Ph.D. Dissertation, SAIS, 2008.
[31] At least two-thirds of the Committee of National Salvation that was created to respond to the fraudulent elections in 2004 were former Kuchma allies – including almost all of the most prominent leaders of this group.
[32] Way "Kuchma's Failed Authoritarianism." Events surrounding the Orange Revolution are discussed in detail in Chap. 8 by McFaul.

has had a weak coercive state[33] and weak control over the economy.[34] At the same time, party strength differed significantly under Lucinschi and under the Communists. First, Lucinschi, who was elected President in 1996, tried to prevent the institutionalization of any single progovernmental political faction in the hopes of dividing potential opposition and preserving full leadership autonomy. He dispersed support across a range of political organizations while preventing the concentration of power in any single group.[35] For example, although the "Bloc for Democratic and Prosperous Moldova" had been created as a pro-Presidential party, Lucinschi openly promoted a number of competing groupings (the "Furnica" electoral bloc and the social democratic bloc "Speranta") and independent deputies in the 1998 parliamentary elections.[36] In the words of one former ally, "Lucinschi liked to break up any group – whether it backed the President or not – that was becoming too powerful."[37]

Yet, this strategy was self defeating and ended up alienating key allies – including Dumutri Diacov, a close supporter, who became head of parliament in 1998. Disenchanted with Lucinschi for dividing up support,[38] Diacov spear-headed efforts to undermine Lucinschi in mid-2000 by eliminating the popularly elected Presidency. Passed with ninety percent support of parliament, the new law dictated that the President would be chosen by parliament and Lucinschi was forced to leave power. Thus, as in Ukraine, the President's efforts to disperse resources among competing groups generated unreliable allies who directly and successfully challenged executive power.

Subsequently, splits in the majority ruling coalition undermined efforts to elect a president, and new elections were called that led to the overwhelming victory of the Communist Party (PCRM) in 2001. The PCRM, drawing on a Leninist organizational structure emphasizing party discipline,[39] was far better organized than any party that had existed in Moldova since independence.[40] It also drew on a well-established ideological tradition that motivated key

---

[33] In 1990–92, the Moldovan police and military forces – consisting of a rag-tag collection of policemen and nationalist activists, some armed with farm implements – lost control of the eastern Transnistrian region to Russian-backed forces. (Lucan Way, "Weak States and Pluralism: The Case of Moldova." East European Politics and Societies 17, No. 3 (2003), pp. 454–482.) Police forces have remained underfunded throughout most of the post cold war period (cf. *Basapress*, 26 April 2000).

[34] According to EBRD estimates, the private sector as a share of GDP increased from twenty percent in 1994 to sixty-five percent by 2006.

[35] Interview with Anatol Golea, journalist, Chisinau, 1 February 2002; interview with Dumutri Diacov, head of parliament 1998–2000, Chisinau, 1 February 2002.

[36] Interview with Dumutri Diacov, head of parliament 1998–2000, Chisinau, 1 February 2002.

[37] Interview with Alexandru Muravschi, Chisinau, 31 January 2002.

[38] Interview with Dumutri Diacov, head of parliament 1998–2000, Chisinau, 1 February 2002.

[39] Luke March and Graeme P. Herd. "Moldova between Europe and Russia: Inoculating against the Colored Contagion?" *Post-Soviet Affairs* 22, 4 (2006), pp. 349–79 esp. p. 358.

[40] In 2001, the PCRM had 10,362 reported members (taken from pcrm.md, accessed April 28, 2001) and had representatives in 1000 of Moldova's 1004 villages. Luke March, "The Moldovan Communists: From Leninism to Democracy?" *Journal of Foreign Policy of Moldova.* 9 (2005), pp. 1–25 esp. p. 13.

groups of supporters. As a result, the PCRM was "widely seen as the most disciplined party" in the country.[41]

The emergence of a well-institutionalized and cohesive ruling party eliminated key sources of contestation and contributed to much greater stability than had existed earlier. In the absence of the rampant elite defection that had characterized the 1990s,[42] "Moldova's national governance [was] marked by tight presidential control over the legislature, executive, and judiciary."[43] By the mid-2000s, the party had "become omnipresent in all public institutions, which makes it difficult to speak about effective checks and balances on the power of the ruling party."[44] For example, Moldovan media became increasingly subject to government censorship and by 2004 was rated by Freedom House as "not free."[45]

The party's organization and monopolization of state institutions were arguably critical to the PCRM's electoral success in 2005. Thus, the media were notably more biased than in previous elections,[46] whereas the party's extensive local presence and control over local governments helped mobilize voter support.[47] Partly as a result, the Communists became the first Moldovan political force to win reelection in the post-Cold War era.[48]

COERCIVE STATE POWER AND AUTHORITARIAN STABILITY: ARMENIA, GEORGIA, AND KYRGYZSTAN

State power has also been key to authoritarian persistence. Thus, a demonstrably powerful coercive apparatus in Armenia was able to face down large-scale antiregime protests following fraudulent elections in 1996, 2003, and 2008, whereas measurably weaker states in Georgia and Kyrgyzstan fell at the hands of more modest opposition challenges.

---

[41] Radio Free Europe/Radio Liberty, 2 July, 2009; March "The Moldovan Communists." pp. 2–3.

[42] Way, "Weak States and Pluralism."

[43] George Dura, *Nations In Transit: Moldova*, (New York: Freedom House, 2008).

[44] George Dura, *Nations In Transit: Moldova*, (New York: Freedom House, 2007).

[45] See Freedom House, "Freedom of the Press 2008: Moldova," In 2007, the government shut down the independent radio station Antena C.

[46] ODIHR, Moldova: *PARLIAMENTARY ELECTIONS Election Observation Mission Report*, pp. 12–13 (Warsaw: OSCE, 2005).

[47] William Crowther, "Moldova, Transnistria, and the PCRM's Turn to the West," *East European Quarterly*, 41, No. 3 (2007), pp. 273–304, esp. 290.

[48] At the same time, Communist hegemony looked to be under severe threat at the time of publication in mid 2009. While the PCRM had gained a substantial 60 of 101 seats in the April 2009 legislative elections; the party was unable to garner the *single* extra vote in parliament required to elect a President. This led to new elections in late July that – in part because of continued economic crisis and the defection of a major PCRM leader, Marian Lupu – resulted in a substantial loss of support with the Communists winning 12 fewer seats than in April. While confirming the critical role played by party cohesion in regime outcomes, these events – particularly Lupu's defection – suggest that party discipline was not as strong within the PCRM as many had thought.

First, in Armenia, the regime was characterized by a weak ruling party and weak economic control but a strong coercive state. President Kocharian (1998–2008) governed without a single ruling party – basing his support on three separate and often competing parties – the Prosperous Armenia Party and the Dashniaks, which supported Kocharian and the Republican Party, which had closer ties to Prime Minister Serzh Sarkisian.[49] As in Moldova and Ukraine, state control over the economy had been weakened by privatization in the 1990s and early 2000s.[50]

At the same time, nationalism and success in war helped to create a powerful coercive apparatus in Armenia. In the wake of conflict between Armenia and neighboring Azerbaijan in the late 1980s, Armenia's first president, Levon Ter-Petrosian (1991–8), successfully consolidated central state control and was able to build a powerful coercive apparatus that won control over Karabakh from Azerbaijan.[51] The government instituted a successful draft[52] and provided extensive financing to the military.[53] The Armenian central state also maintained firm control over regional governments and built an extensive coercive apparatus that penetrates the country.[54] In turn, military success in Karabakh generated a set of cadres highly skilled in violence and coercion that became an important bulwark for authoritarian stability.[55]

Regime developments have reflected conflicting dynamics caused by weakly organized ruling parties and elite divisions, on the one hand, and a strong coercive apparatus that efficiently put down mass protest, on the other. Thus, while the regime suffered major defections at key points throughout the post-Cold War era,[56] it was consistently able to block outside threats. Indeed, the

---

[49] Earlier, President Levon Ter-Petrosian (1991–1998) ruled via a relatively under-institutionalized Armenian National Movement (ANM) that combined a diverse collection of former dissidents, ex-communist nomenklatura, and younger activists. Mark Sarafyan, "Armenia." In *B. Szajkowski, ed. Political Parties Of Eastern Europe, Russia, and The Successor States.* pp. 29–36 (Stockton: Essex, 1994). Although the ANM had a salient ideology, it is scored as medium strength given its recent formation. See Levitsky and Way "Competitive Authoritarianism."

[50] The EBRD estimated that by 2004 the private sector as a share of GDP reached seventy-five percent.

[51] Suzanne Goldenberg, *Pride of Small Nations: The Caucasus and Post-Soviet Disorder*, p. 144 (London: Zed Books. 1994). Jonathan Aves, "National Security and Military Issues in the Transcaucasus." In *State Building and Military Power in Russia and the New States of Eurasia*, V. Parrott, ed., pp. 209–33 (Armonk, NY: M. E. Sharpe, 1995); de Waal, *Black Garden*, p. 111.

[52] Aves, "National Security," p. 223.

[53] De Waal, *Black Garden*, p. 127, 257. In the early 2000s, Armenia had the highest level of military expenditure (7.7 percent of GDP) in Europe. See *Military Balance*, pp. 398–9 (London: International Institute for Strategic Studies, 2006).

[54] Christoph H.Stefes *Understanding Post-Soviet Transitions. Corruption, Collusion and Clientelism*, pp. 114–16 (New York: Palgrave Macmillan, 2006).

[55] See Liz Fuller, "Armenia: Political Power Grows out of the Barrel of a Gun." *RFE/RL Caucasus Report.* 12 May Vol. 1, No. 11.

[56] For example, President Ter-Petrosian was challenged by former Prime Minister and Defense Minister Vazgen Manukian in Presidential elections in 1996. In 1998, Ter-Petrosian was forced to resign under pressure from Prime Minister Kocharian, who was elected President that year.

Armenian government was repeatedly challenged throughout the 1990s and 2000s by demonstrations on a scale unseen in other parts of the former Soviet Union – including protests of 100,000 in February 1993, 50,000 in July 1994,[57] 150–200,000 in 1996[58]; 25–100,000 in 2003,[59] and about 25,000 in March 2008.

The regime faced its most serious challenge in 1996, when Ter-Petrosian was forced to rely on fraud to secure a first round victory against former Prime Minister Vazgen Manukian.[60] In response, the opposition led a demonstration of 120–200,000 in front of the Central Election Committee and stormed parliament.[61] Yet the military – backed by a heavy contingent of Karabagh war veterans[62] – quickly defused the opposition by rapidly closing down opposition party offices and jailing as many as 250 antigovernment leaders.[63] In stark contrast to its counterparts in Ukraine in 2004 or Georgia in 2003, the Armenian state successfully sealed off the capital, thereby preventing an escalation of the protests.

The military and police were similarly effective at beating back protests of 25–100,000 following the first round of presidential elections in 2003 that eventually saw the reelection of Kocharian[64] and demonstrations of 10–25,000 in early 2004 inspired by events in Georgia.[65] Finally in March 2008, security forces were able to suppress protests led by Ter-Petrosian – now in opposition – against fraud in presidential elections that saw the victory of Serzh Sarkisian as Kocharian's successor. Kocharian declared a state of emergency in the capital

In 1999, Kocharian faced strong competition from his own Prime Minister, Vazgen Sarkisian. In 2008, key regime elites defected from the government following controversial presidential elections. See Marianna Grigoryan and Gayane Abrahamyan. "Deputy Parliamentary Speaker Resigns, Defections to Ter-Petrosian." *Eurasianet* (22 February 2008); Levitsky and Way, "Competitive Authoritarianism."

57 V. G. Mitiaev, "Vnutripoliticheskie protsessy v nezavisimoi Armenii." In *Armeniia: Problemy Nezavisimogo Razvitiia*, E. M. Kozhokina, ed., pp. 73–138, esp. 86, 91, 101 (Moscow: RISI, 1998).

58 Mikael Danielian, "Elections in Armenia: A Funeral for Democracy," *Uncaptive Minds*, 9, Nos. 1–2 (1996–7), pp. 125–31, esp. 128.

59 Susanna Petrosian, "Armenian Election Clash Looms: Government and Opposition Are Set on a Collision Course Following the Disputed First Round of Armenia's Presidential Election," *Caucasus Reporting Service* (online), No. 168 (27 February 2003).

60 See Emil Danielyan, "Ter-Petrossian Rigged 1996 Election, Fell Into 'Depression,' Says Top Ally," *RFE/RL Armenia Report* (30 December 1998).

61 Danielian, "Elections in Armenia" *RFERL Newsline* 25–26 September 1996. On a per capita basis, Armenia's largest opposition demonstration in 1996 was roughly twice as large as that in Ukraine in 2004.

62 Liana Minasian, "The Role of the Army in Armenia's Politics," *Caucasus Reporting Service* (online), No. 5 (4 November 1999).

63 Ian Bremmer and Cory Welt, "Armenia's New Autocrats," *Journal of Democracy*, 8, No. 3 (1997), pp. 77–91.

64 Susanna Petrosian, "Armenian Election Clash Looms: Government and Opposition Are Set on a Collision Course Following the Disputed First Round of Armenia's Presidential Election," *Caucasus Reporting Service* (online), No. 168 (27 February 2003).

65 Anna Hakobyan "Armenia: Authorities Hit Back as Opposition Campaign Mounts," Transitions Online (April 13 2004).

and arrested more than a hundred opposition supporters.[66] During each of these crises in 1996, 2003, 2004, and 2008, the security forces effectively closed off the capital and arrested key members of the opposition – thus preventing the opposition from growing strong enough to topple the regime.

Both Georgia and Kyrgyzstan, in contrast, combined weak ruling parties with weak coercive states that were often unable to suppress even modest protest. In Georgia, the Rose Revolution was to an important extent the outgrowth of moderate party strength and weak coercive capacity. President Shevardnadze (1992–2003) relied on a single ruling party – the Citizens' Union of Georgia (CUG) – a relatively loose coalition of Shevardnadze supporters without any clear ideology.[67] Simultaneously, Georgia experienced weakened state control over the economy[68] and, in stark contrast to Armenia, had a very weak coercive apparatus – suffering the loss of Abkhazia and Ossetia in 1990–92 and continued problems of underfunding and weak central control over much of the country through the early 2000s.[69]

Cory Welt, in this volume, cogently analyzes the full range of factors that caused the Rose Revolution and the fall of Shevardnadze in late 2003 – including the impact of Western assistance and the influence of previous electoral revolutions. Here, I want to highlight the critical role of two factors – Shevardnadze's reliance on a pure patronage party that was vulnerable to elite divisions and his access to a weak and underfunded coercive apparatus that was ill equipped to cope with even modest antiregime protest.

First, in 2001, in the absence of any serious economic or other crisis, the CUG disintegrated when Shevardnadze's popularity began to wane. Major regime officials – Justice Minister Mikheil Saakashvili, and Parliamentary Speakers Zurab Zhvania, and Nino Burdjanadze – broke with Shevardnadze and just 41 of an original 109 deputies remained in the ruling CUG by the end of the year.[70] The major opposition parties – referred to by some as the "new CUG" – were led by "Shevardnadze's top protégés."[71]

The opposition seriously challenged Shevardnadze in the 2003 parliamentary elections. According to official results, Shevardnadze's party won a plurality of the vote. However, a parallel vote count suggested that Saakashvili's National Movement had won the most votes. Saakashvili mobilized protestors

---

[66] Ten died in clashes on March 1–2, ODIHR *Final Report on the 19 February 2008 Presidential Election in Armenia*, pp. 27–8 (Warsaw: OSCE 2008).

[67] Jonathan Wheatley *Georgia from National Awakening to Rose Revolution: Delayed Transition in the Former Soviet Union*, Chap. 5 (Aldershot: Ashgate Publishing, 2005).

[68] Private sector control over the economy had reached sixty-five percent by 2002, according to EBRD figures.

[69] Stephen F. Jones, "Adventurers or Commanders? Civil Military Relations in Georgia Since Independence." In *Civil–Military Relations in the Soviet and Yugoslav Successor States*, C. Danopolous and D. Zirker, eds., pp. 35–52 (Boulder, CO: Westview, 1996); Cory Welt, "A Return to Eurasia." *Transitions Online* (January 11, 2000).

[70] Wheatley *Georgia*, p. 128.

[71] Lincoln Mitchell *Uncertain Democracy: U.S. Foreign Policy and Georgia's Rose Revolution*, pp. 48, 38 (Philadelphia: University of Pennsylvania Press, 2008).

in Tbilisi and stormed parliament on November 22, forcing Shevardnadze's resignation.

Mobilization was remarkably successful but also quite modest in size. Most observers estimate that the largest demonstrations reached 20–30,000 – about half as many per capita (and far less sustained and widespread) than in Ukraine.[72] As Welt notes, protests "were not that large or sustained."[73] The celebration on the streets *after* Shevardnadze's resignation was appreciably larger than the demonstrations that led to his downfall.[74]

In fact, the opposition's stunningly rapid defeat of Shevardnadze was rooted less in the scale of mobilization than in the fact that the police and security forces basically dissolved on November 22–3. When Saakashvili stormed parliament, police, who had not been paid in months, simply stepped aside – leaving the government defenseless.[75] Shevardnadze attempted to call martial law, but when security forces refused to comply, the President was forced to resign. Indeed, Shevardnadze "no longer controlled the military and security forces. Bloodshed was avoided largely because the president was too politically weak to command it."[76]

Finally, Kyrgyzstan also demonstrates the impact of state weakness on regime collapse. Askar Akaev's Kyrgyzstan was characterized by a weak party, weak state economic control, and a weak coercive apparatus. First, Akaev, like Kuchma and Lucinschi, was not represented in the legislature by a single progovernment party. Instead, the government was supported by a series of independent candidates and competing progovernmental parties – including the Adilet Party, the Democratic Party of Women and Youth, and Alga Kyrgyzstan! (Forward Kyrgyzstan), an amalgam of four small progovernmental groups formed in 2003. Next, as in Ukraine, Moldova, Armenia, and Georgia, the government had privatized much of the economy by 2004.[77] Finally, Kyrgyzstan possessed weak coercive capacity. Kyrgyz police were significantly underpaid and often had to buy their own fuel and uniforms.[78]

Weak state economic control, a weakly organized ruling party, and a weak coercive apparatus all contributed to the rapid collapse of the regime of Askar Akaev in March 2005. First, Radnitz notes in this volume that privatization and economic reform led to the growth of a large number of powerful actors "autonomous from the state and residing in diverse regions of the country.

---

[72] See, for example, *RFE/RL Caucasus Report*, (November 24, 2003), "up to 30,000"; *Independent on Sunday* (London) (November 23, 2003), "25,000." See also Thomas de Waal, "Caucasus after the Fall, Georgia after Shevardnadze," *The Financial Times* (July 9, 2004). Welt notes that one news-source that that had consistently overestimated the size of earlier protests reported 60,000.

[73] See Welt's chapter in this volume; also Lincoln Mitchell, "Georgia's Rose Revolution." *Current History* 103, No. 675 (2004), pp. 342–53, esp. p. 345.

[74] Welt's chapter in this volume.

[75] Zurab Karumidze and James V. Wertsch, eds., *Enough! The Rose Revolution in the Republic of Georgia 2003*, pp. 29, 15 (New York: Nova Science Publishers, 2005).

[76] Mitchell, "Georgia's Rose Revolution," p. 348.

[77] According to EBRD, the private sector accounted for 75 percent by 2004.

[78] Radnitz, personal communication.

Many new businessmen parlayed their wealth into political influence by running for parliament." These actors were in turn able to work together in forming tactical alliances that blocked Akaev initiatives and became critical in organizing against the government following parliamentary elections in February–March 2005.

Simultaneously, Akaev lacked any type of cohesive party organization that might have held the regime together in the midst of crisis. In the absence of partisan ties to the President, leading politicians readily abandoned the regime when Akaev seemed vulnerable. Thus, although Radnitz is certainly correct when he writes in this volume that the fragmentation of the Kyrgyz political system made it "easy for Akaev to keep the opposition divided and weak," this disorganization *also* left Akaev completely isolated when confronted with any kind of serious opposition.

Most critically, Akaev fell because the Kyrgyz state simply disintegrated under him. Kyrgyzstan's weak coercive apparatus made it possible for a fragmented opposition backed by relatively few protestors to capture key state institutions and overthrow the regime. Thus on March 18, 2005, a few hundred protestors were able to seize the regional government in Jalal-Abad in southern Kyrgyzstan. According to Radnitz,[79] the underfunded police had agreed with the protestors to stand aside as the protestors more or less spontaneously took control over the regional government. Within a week, protestors had seized control of about half the country. Finally, on March 24, about ten thousand (fewer than any other color revolution) rallied in the capital and stormed the government headquarters – forcing Akaev to flee the country and eventually resign.[80]

COERCIVE STRENGTH, STATE ECONOMIC CONTROL, AND AUTOCRATIC STABILITY IN BELARUS AND RUSSIA

Lukashenka in Belarus and Putin in Russia not only survived the postcommunist third wave but confronted almost no serious opposition challenges. In both cases, an extensive coercive apparatus combined with high de facto state control over the economy allowed incumbents to deprive regime opponents of virtually any life blood. Differences in de facto state economic control help explain why opposition was successfully marginalized in Belarus and Russia but not in Georgia, Kyrgyzstan, or Ukraine.

First, Putin's Russia was characterized by medium coercive capacity, high state economic control, and medium ruling party strength. Coercive state capacity increased markedly from the Yeltsin years. Amid economic crisis in the early 1990s, the state had been plagued by widespread wage arrears, open rebellion by regional leaders,[81] and rampant insubordination within the armed

---

[79] Personal communication.

[80] Erica Marat, 2006. *The Tulip Revolution: Kyrgyzstan One Year After*, pp. 5–7 (Washington, DC: The Jamestown Foundation, 2006).

[81] Stoner-Weiss, *Resisting the State*.

services.[82] Under Putin, however, improved fiscal health facilitated greater bureaucratic discipline and a "precipitous" decline in sub-national rebellions.[83] Putin successfully abolished a series of ad hoc agreements made with separate regions and reduced local control over key agencies, including tax and police.[84] At the same time, in contrast to Armenia, Russia lacked experience with national level military conflict that has generated a high degree of cohesion in other cases.[85]

Next, Putin sought to reestablish greater state control over the economy – the energy sector in particular. In 2000–2001, Putin reasserted Kremlin direct authority over Gazprom by ousting Yeltsin-era officials. In 2003, he arrested Mikhail Khodorkovsky and seized Yukos oil as well as other energy assets.[86] Between 2000 and 2007, the share of oil production under state control increased from sixteen percent to about fifty percent.[87] Over the course of the 2000s, high-level government officials were placed in key leadership positions in major enterprises in energy, the military, transportation, and communication – giving the government direct control over key sectors of the economy.[88] At the same time, as prices of oil increased, energy exports became increasingly important and accounted for over fifty percent of merchandise exports by 2000.[89]

Finally, Putin, in stark contrast to Yeltsin, invested significant resources in building a single progovernment party, United Russia, founded in 1999–2001.[90] Although the party was relatively absent at the highest reaches of power in the 2000s,[91] it incorporated an increasing share of the Russian mid-level political elite between 2000 and 2008.[92] At the same time, by the metric used in this chapter, United Russia is a classic medium-strength party – with a

---

[82] John P. Moran, "Praetorians or Professionals? Democratization and Military Intervention in Communist and Post-Communist Russia." *Journal of Communist Studies and Transition Politics*, 15, No. 2 (June 1999), pp. 41–68.

[83] Stoner-Weiss, *Resisting the State*, p. 62.

[84] Nikolai Petrov and Darrell Slider, "Putin and the Regions," In *Putin's Russia: Past Imperfect, Future Uncertain*, D. Herspring, ed., pp. 237–58 (Boulder, CO: Rowman and Littlefield, 2005); Gelman, "Vozvrashchenie Leviafona?"

[85] The war in Chechnya was costly in terms of lives lost but remained mostly localized.

[86] Marshall Goldman, *Petrostate: Putin, Power, and the New Russia*, pp. 104–23 (New York: Oxford University Press, 2008).

[87] Goldman, *Petrostate*, p. 99.

[88] Goldman, *Petrostate*, p. 133; Kryshtanovskaya, "Советизация России в 2000–2008 гг," p. 22.

[89] See World Bank, *World Development Indicators*, (www.worldbank.org/data) Accessed June 2009.

[90] Putin initially gave backing in 1999 to a party Unity, which combined with the Fatherland-All Russia Block to become "United Russia" in 2001. See Henry Hale, "The Origins of United Russia and the Putin Presidency: The Role of Contingency in Party-System Development," *Demokratizatsiya: The Journal of Post-Soviet Democratization* 12, No. 2 (2004), pp. 169–94.

[91] Thus in early 2008, just six of eighty-six ministers and one of thirty-nine Kremlin officials was a member of the party (Kryshtanovskaya, "Советизация России в 2000–2008 гг," p. 7).

[92] By 2008, the party had gained 315 of 450 seats in the Duma, had a majority in at least 72 of 86 regional legislatures, and encompassed 75 regional governors and 51.6 percent of district, city, and village heads. Over the course of the 2000s, official party membership rose enormously –

well-established patronage system but very little identifiable ideology. Thus, the party incorporated officials with "the most varied political views" and mostly resisted taking explicit positions on issues in order to give Putin maximum room for maneuver.[93]

Putin in the 2000s succeeded in virtually eliminating any kind of serious opposition in Russia. Putin won in the first-round Presidential elections in 2000 and 2004 against a highly fragmented opposition. By 2003, the government gained effective control of two-thirds of the legislature, and in 2007 United Russia captured sixty-four percent, whereas liberal parties – Yabloko, Union of Right Forces – were shut out. Today, the highly marginalized Communist Party is the only real opposition in the legislature. Protest mobilization has also been low. The most serious protests in early 2005 against the monetization of communal service benefits were never able to bring together more than 5–10,000 in any one place and never represented a serious threat to Putin's power.[94] Thus, by the mid 2000s, Russia had witnessed the "destruction without exception of all opposition parties" and the elimination of "meaningful alternatives to incumbent power."[95]

The successful consolidation of authoritarian rule in Russia was overdetermined. As a major regional power possessing key energy resources, Russia faced far less external democratizing pressure than did any other post-Soviet country.[96] Simultaneously, rising energy prices contributed to robust annual economic growth in the early 2000s of about six percent. Yet the absence of external pressure does not explain the striking dearth of mobilized domestic opposition. Further, Putin does not seem to have benefited any more from economic growth than did Shevardnadze or Kuchma. Kuchma in particular was awash in cash in the early 2000s before he was forced from power.[97] Thus, the key issue is not simply the availability of patronage resources in Russia, but Putin's ability to limit elite defection and concentrate control over these resources.

Putin's success in concentrating power is partly explained by the appearance of a relatively well-institutionalized ruling party and increasing state

from a reported 220,000 in 2000 to over 1.7 million at the end of 2007. Vitalii Ivanov, *Partiia Putina*, pp. 331–2, 66, 331.

[93] Vitalii Ivanov, *Partiia Putina*, pp. 194, 195.

[94] See RFE/RL newsline reports, 11 January–16 February 2005.

[95] Vladimir Gelman "Politicheskaia oppozitsiia v Rossii: vymiraiushchi vid?" in V. Gelman, ed., *Tretii elektoral'nyi tsikl v Rossii, 2003–2004 gody*. pp. 35–79, esp. p. 79 (St. Petersburg: European University in St. Petersburg Press, 2007).

[96] As one EU official put it, "You know what happens when [EU leaders] get in the same room with Vladimir Putin?.... [they] say 'I love you, Vladimir" (quoted in Thomas Friedman, "The Really Cold War," *New York Times*, 25 October 2006). See Levitsky and Way, "Competitive Authoritarianism."

[97] Economic growth was thirteen percent the year Kuchma's regime fell. Massive resources were distributed to encourage vote fraud. Thus, polling stations were given as much as US$5000 each election round. (There were about 33,0000 polling stations in Ukraine.) See Way "Kuchma's Failed Authoritarianism," p. 136.

control over the economy. First, the emergence of a relatively cohesive United Russia party both facilitated Putin's efforts to centralize power in the mid-2000s and eliminated the Duma as a staging ground for opposition challenges. In the 2000s, the party functioned as a "highly disciplined and centralized organization"[98] and "rivaled the Communists" in voting discipline.[99] The party's cohesion allowed Putin to centralize control with ease – eliminating elections for regional governors and imposing restrictions on civil society and political parties.[100] Dominated by a well-organized party under strict Kremlin control, the Duma no longer presented any serious challenge to Presidential control.[101]

Simultaneously, the concentration of resources in the energy sector[102] helped Putin to starve opposition and monopolize control. The fact that enormous resources were concentrated in a few large energy corporations – such as Gazprom – arguably made it easier for Russian leaders to dominate key centers of power. For example, NTV's dependence on Gazprom financing greatly facilitated Kremlin efforts to take over the station that had opposed Putin in 1999. Thus, Vladimir Gusinsky and NTV owed Gazprom US\$473 million – US\$262 million of which was coming due in July 2001.[103] The Kremlin was able to use NTV's vulnerable financial position to seize the station, thereby eliminating a major thorn in the President's side early in his first term.[104] In turn, increased state control over the economy in the early 2000s greatly hampered opposition development. In contrast to his counterparts in Georgia and Ukraine, Putin was able to significantly reduce business contributions to opposition forces and thus starve them of resources.[105] Parties such as Yabloko, for example, which had depended heavily on Khodorkovsky, lost critical support.

Belarus also illustrates the role of state economic control in sidelining opposition challenges. Under Lukashenka, Belarus was characterized by a weak ruling party, medium state strength, and high state economic control. First, Lukashenka did not create any ruling party.[106] Instead, the President relied

[98] Vladimir Gelman, "Party Politics in Russia: From Competition to Hierarchy." *Europe–Asia Studies*, 60: 6 (2008), pp. 913–30, esp. p. 921.

[99] Thomas Remington, "Majorities without Mandates: The Russian Federation Council since 2000." *Europe–Asia Studies*, 55, No. 5 (2003), pp. 667–91.

[100] Thomas Remington, "Patronage and the Party of Power: President–Parliament Relations under Vladimir Putin." *Europe–Asia Studies*, 60, No. 6 (August 2008), pp. 959–87, esp. 974–5.

[101] Ol'ga Kryshtanovskaia, *Anatomiia rossiiskoi elity*, p. 253 (Moscow: Zakharov, 2005).

[102] World Bank, *Russian Federation – From Transition to Development: A Country Economic Memorandum for the Russian Federation*. World Bank Report 32308 (Washington, DC: World Bank, 2003).

[103] David E. Hoffman, *The Oligarchs: Wealth and Power in the New Russia*, p. 482 (New York: Public Affairs, 2003).

[104] Masha Lipman, and Michael McFaul. "'Managed Democracy' in Russia: Putin and the Press." *The Harvard International Journal of Press/Politics* 6, No. 3 (2001), pp. 116–27.

[105] Michael McFaul and Nikolai Petrov, "What the Elections Tell Us." *Journal of Democracy*, 15, No. 3 (July 2004), pp. 20–31, esp. pp. 24, 27.

[106] Initially, after gaining power, Lukashenka sought to build his own political party – Civic Consensus (*Grazhdanskoe Soglasie*). However, the party quickly disappeared; see Stanislav

on an extensive security apparatus and state economic control to maintain power. As in Russia and Ukraine, Belarus never seriously scaled back the security services. Following the collapse of the Soviet Union, the security services remained virtually intact and established an extensive presence throughout the country.[107] In contrast to Georgia, Kyrgyzstan, or Moldova, the security services were relatively well financed, and state workers as a whole suffered far fewer wage arrears than their counterparts in neighboring countries in the late 1990s.[108] At the same time, in contrast to Armenia, Belarus had not recently won a national-level military victory.

Simultaneously, in contrast to Kuchma in Ukraine, Lucinschi in Moldova, or Shevardnadze in Georgia, Lukashenka did not privatize in the 1990s. Lukashenka essentially conceived of the Belarusian economy as a single enterprise – explaining to one of his advisors that "Belarus is a small country and should be managed from a single center like a good production collective."[109] Thus, almost two decades after the collapse of Communism, the private sector in Belarus still accounted for just about thirty percent of GDP in 2008.[110]

Like Putin, Lukashenka successfully sidelined the opposition in the 2000s. In 2001, official results gave Lukashenka a reelection victory of 75 percent to 15 percent over his nearest rival, Uladimir Hancharyk. In the runup to the 2006 presidential elections, the opposition united behind Alyaksandr Milinkevich and mounted larger than expected protests of up to 10–15,000 following the fraudulent vote. Nevertheless, as Silitski notes in this volume the opposition "could not count on sustained public support" and Milinkevich never presented a serious challenge to Lukashenka's rule.

The severity of authoritarian controls in the early 2000s makes Belarus less comparable to the other cases in this chapter. Thus, massive voter fraud,[111]

Sushkevich, *Neo kommunizm, v belorussii*, p. 94 (Smolensk: "skif," 2002). In the government-dominated House of Representatives in 2004–8, just 12 of 109 deputies represented political parties.

[107] Interview with Vladimir Alekseevich Reznikov, KGB official, Minsk, 13 July 2004. Ethan S. Burger, and Viktar Minchuk. "Alyaksandr Lukashenka's Consolidation of Power." In Joerg Forbrig, David R. Maples, and Pavol Demes, eds. *Prospects for Democracy in Belarus*, (Washington, DC. German Marshall Fund of the United States, 2006).

[108] Anastasia Nesvetailova, "A Friend in Need, Or a Friend in Need? Russia and the Belarusian Economy," in *The EU and Belarus: Between Moscow and Brussels*, A. Lewis, ed., pp. 215–27, esp. 222 (London: Federal Trust, 2002).

[109] Quoted in Feduta, *Lukashenko*, p. 202.

[110] EBRD estimates. The most recent available EBRD estimate from 1999 suggested that under twenty percent of the population weres employed in the private sector.

[111] In 2001, observers estimated that 20–25 percent of votes were stolen in the Presidential election. Exit polls suggested that Lukashenka failed to win in the first round. ODIHR *Final report on the presidential election in Belarus, 9 September 2001*, p. 24 (Warsaw: OSCE). As Alyaksandr Milinkevich, presidential candidate in 2006, put it, elections "are useless... merely another informational campaign, a mobilizational campaign. But they are in no way a means of acquiring power" (RFE/RL, "Milinkevich Discusses 'Schism' within Belarusian Opposition," June 6, 2007). In 2004 and 2008, opposition failed to gain a single seat in the legislature.

near-total media censorship,[112] and severe repression of opposition[113] virtually eliminated any serious political competition in the 2000s.[114]

Nevertheless, Belarus under Lukashenka provides a useful illustration of the ways in which state control over the economy may weaken opposition challenges. Although the virtual absence of any kind of party uniting Lukashenka's supporters has arguably made defection more likely, Lukashenka's control over the economy has given him highly effective tools to buy support and starve opposition. An important center of economic control was the Presidential Business Administration (*Upravleniia delami prezidenta*), which was reportedly the largest commercial structure in the country, controlling about one billion dollars.[115] The Presidential Business Administration benefited from monopoly import and export of a wide range of consumer products.[116] Simultaneously, the President accumulated significant resources in a special Presidential Fund. The Fund reportedly received profits from a range of arms sales carried out by the administration that did not show up in the official state budget[117] and was used as the source of a wide range of commercial investments. According to a Lukashenka official, this income was a key source of cohesion within the state – supplying local officials with bribes and foreign cars and providing benefits to certain "loyal" social groups.[118]

State economic control has simultaneously helped starve the opposition of resources and activists. Thus, Belarus never witnessed the emergence of a quasi-autonomous economic elite,[119] which was so critical in financing opposition in Ukraine in the 2000s as well as in Russia under Yeltsin. According to one former Lukashenka associate cited by Silitski, the President sought "to destroy every private company capable of independently financing the opposition presidential campaign."[120] Thus, opposition forces have found it almost impossible to find

---

[112] Broadcast media was completely monopolized by pro government fores while authorities "arrested and harassed independent journalists, confiscated equipment, and blocked distribution of independent newspapers." Committee to Protect Journalists "Attacks on the Press in 2008: Belarus," accessed at cpj.org in June 2009. During the 2008 parliamentary election, broadcast media presented the opposition "with no opportunity to present their own views." ODIHR *Final report on the 28 September 2008 parliamentary elections in Belarus.* p. 18 (Warsaw: OSCE, 2008).

[113] In 1999, four opposition figures disappeared, apparently at the hands of the government. See Silitski's chapter in this volume; Aleksandr Feduta, *Lukashenko: Politicheskaia biografiia* (Moscow: "Referendum," 2005).

[114] In addition, more than the other cases in this chapter, Belarus has benefited from extensive Russian energy subsidies. See Feduta, *Lukashenko.*

[115] *Belarusskaia delovaia gazeta* (Belarusian Business Newspaper), 16 June 2004.

[116] Feduta, *Lukashenko,* pp. 401–2.

[117] Kaare Dahl Martinsen, "The Russian Takeover of Belarus." *Comparative Strategy,* 21 (2002), pp. 401–16; Feduta, *Lukashenko,* pp. 403–14.

[118] Feduta, *Lukashenko,* pp. 414–15, 418–19.

[119] Alexander Lukashuk, 1998. "Yesterday as Tomorrow: Why It Works in Belarus," *East European Constitutional Review,* 7, No. 3 (1998).

[120] Vitali Silitski, *Post-Communist Authoritarianism in Eastern Europe: Serbia and Belarus Compared.* Manuscript 2004, p. 72. According to one Belarusian human rights organization, twenty percent of prison inmates in Belarus are former heads of state and private enterprises. See

domestic sources of financing. Simultaneously, state economic control allowed Lukashenka to greatly increase the costs of opposition mobilization. As Silitski notes in his chapter, a large section of the labor force works on fixed-term contracts for state firms. This allowed the government to threaten the livelihood of anyone who supported opposition initiatives.[121] As a result, activists often suffered enormous material costs.[122]

CONCLUSION

This chapter has highlighted a key set of factors that made some autocrats far more vulnerable than others to the third wave of postcommunist transitions examined in this volume. Those that survived did so in part because of their ability to rely on at least one of three pillars of autocratic strength – strong ruling party, strong coercive apparatus, and/or state economic control. The four cases of authoritarian stability in the early and mid 2000s – Armenia, Belarus, Moldova, and Russia – each relied on a somewhat different set of institutions to suppress opposition challenges. Thus, the Moldovan Communists were able to maintain tight discipline through the mid 2000s via a well-institutionalized and relatively ideological party despite access to a weak coercive apparatus and relatively weak state economic control. (Although events in mid 2009 suggest that party discipline was not as strong as many had thought.) In contrast, Lukashenka had no party, but was able to preempt and starve opposition challenges through dominant state control over economic resources, as well as an extensive coercive apparatus. In Armenia, weak economic control and a weak ruling party have facilitated elite fragmentation. Yet a strong coercive state created out of war with Azerbaijan in the early 1990s allowed the regime to beat back serious opposition challenges throughout the post–Cold War era. Authoritarian stability in Putin's Russia benefited from high state economic control, a relatively strong coercive apparatus, and a medium strength ruling party. Resting on these three pillars, Putin's regime may be the strongest of those examined.

In contrast, Kuchma in Ukraine, Shevardnadze in Georgia, and Akaev in Kyrgyzstan lacked critical tools to prevent collapse – a fact that made them more vulnerable to a variety of contingent forces, including external diffusion. In Ukraine, a weak ruling party combined with weak state economic control

---

"Samyi bol'shoi strakh belorusov – tiur'ma," available at www.charter97.org/rus/news/ 2006/10/24/turma. Accessed June 2008.

[121] Silitski *Post-Communist Authoritarianism*, pp. 73–4.

[122] Thus, the vast majority of lower-level opposition activists whom I interviewed in the March 2006 Presidential elections were either unemployed or employed in small trade. As one activist noted, "economics dictates politics." *Way*, interview with Natasha Poliakova, opposition activist, Mogilev, Belarus, 17 March 2006. In the words of one commentator, "This state controlled corporation, Belarus Inc., is a multiline conglomerate with revenues of about US$25 billion . . . It employs over 4 million workers and controls the services, health-care and education sectors" (Siarhej Karol, "The Belarusian Economic Model: A 21st Century Socialism?" *RFE/RL Reports* (13 March 2006)).

made it easier for powerful opposition challenges to emerge from within the regime. Finally, the bases of authoritarian stability were weakest in Georgia and Kyrgyzstan. The combination of a relatively weak ruling party, a weak coercive apparatus, and weak state economic control made both Shevardnadze and Akaev vulnerable to even modest opposition challenges.

At the same time, this analysis also points to potential future sources of regime vulnerability in each of our cases. As we see in Table 9.1, none of the countries had high capacity in all areas. Thus, the absence of any ruling party in Lukashenka's Belarus heightens the dangers of elite defection in the event of an economic or other crisis.[123] Similarly, party weakness in Armenia would seem to make the regime vulnerable to a serious challenge from within. On the other hand, state weakness in Moldova may make the regime especially susceptible to even modest popular mobilization. Finally, Putin in Russia possesses the most robust authoritarian regime discussed in this chapter. Nonetheless, the government's nearly exclusive reliance on patronage and the dearth of non-material sources of cohesion meant that United Russia will have a harder time surviving any kind of serious economic downturn or large-scale popular mobilization.[124]

In sum, this analysis suggests that while contingency will always play a role in regime development, we can still identify ex ante which authoritarian regimes are more vulnerable to collapse. This approach does a poor job of predicting the exact timing of regime collapse. Yet this theory may allow us to determine which regimes are more likely to collapse in the face of a variety of contingent shocks – ranging from successful opposition challenges in neighboring countries to economic crisis.

---

[123] Lukashenka's dependence on Russian economic assistance combined with recent increases in the price paid for Russian gas also make Lukashenka especially vulnerable. See Vitali Silitski, "Welcome to Post-populism?" *BISS Blitz*. 11 January 2009. Available at belinstitute.eu accessed January 2009.

[124] For example, in 2004–2005, the party witnessed "unusually widespread defection" in the Duma after housing sector reform stimulated small-scale demonstrations across country. See Remington "Patronage and the Party of Power," p. 976.

10

Comparing Oranges and Apples

The Internal and External Dimensions of Russia's Turn away from Democracy

Kathryn Stoner-Weiss
Stanford University

What we thought would be easy, turned out to be very difficult.
– Boris Yeltsin, December 31, 1999 upon resigning as President of Russia

When Vladimir Putin was elected president of Russia in March 2000, the country bequeathed to him by his predecessor, Boris Yeltsin, was an unconsolidated, often disorderly and raucous electoral democracy. Gradually, the Russian political system under Putin came to be described first as "managed democracy," then as "illiberal democracy" or "delegated democracy," and finally, by 2008, and the ascendancy of a new hand-picked Russian president, Dmitri Medvedev, as not really a democracy at all. What happened? Why did the fourth wave miss Russian shores? Is Russia immune to the diffusion effect of democratization that swept the East in the late 1980s and that again moved eastward from Serbia, Ukraine, and Georgia? What prospects are there for external factors to play a role in bringing about a rejuvenation of democracy in Russia?

I examine these questions in the three main sections of this chapter. Section I examines the internal political, social, and economic factors that have contributed to the growing momentum of the reverse wave in Russia. This section notes that most of the crucial factors that brought about the color revolutions elsewhere were for the most part absent within the Russian domestic political, social, and economic context. Section II then looks at the role of external factors and the international environment in promoting democracy versus an authoritarian reversal in the past and present. Finally, Section III examines regime vulnerabilities and the variables that would determine whether the tide will turn toward democracy again in Russia.

I. INTERNAL FACTORS EXPLAINING THE REVERSE WAVE IN RUSSIA

As always, Russia represents a paradox. Flying in the face of modernization theory, as its gross domestic product per capita increased under Putin, the quality of Russia's already fragile democracy eroded steadily. What are the internal factors that explain this reverse wave? What distinguishes these factors from the internal dynamics in Serbia, Ukraine, and Georgia, where electoral revolutions and democratic revivals took place at precisely the same time as Russia moved decidedly off the democratic path?

For the most part, the main ingredients of the color revolutions have been absent from Russia from 2000 onward. First, there was no electoral result that the mass public was willing to protest. The Duma (1999, 2003, and 2007) and presidential elections (2000, 2004, and 2008) became more tightly managed with each successive electoral cycle. Nonetheless, the results of each were widely accepted despite some evidence of coercion, fraud, and occasional ballot rigging. State-preferred candidates enjoyed special access to the media, so the elections were not exactly fair, but given the lack of viable political alternatives, and other factors pushing in favor of the status quo, there was little need, ability, or incentive on the part of Russian voters to protest these transgressions. Nor, given the gradual erosion of freedoms within civil society, were there mechanisms by which to organize mass protests.

How did this happen? In terms of internal factors that might explain Russia's authoritarian reversal, to be sure, the extent to which Russians actually freely choose their leaders has become highly circumscribed. When Vladimir Putin assumed the Russian presidency in 2000, he steadily clamped down on the freedom of the mass media to report critically on the government and the abilities of civil society organizations to protest state policies. He also created a strong ruling party in United Russia, as explained further below. In the face of high economic growth that began in 1998 and that continued in the face of high world oil prices (until their precipitous decline during the world financial crisis that began in earnest in the autumn of 2008), Putin enjoyed steadily increasing public approval ratings. Beyond economic growth, though, this public support was supported in no small part by the gradual state takeover of television, in particular, which bombarded the Russian public with Putin and positive economic news, while shielding them from anything off the regime's official message. Finally, Putin certainly learned from the color revolutions and deftly created institutions – such as Nashi and Young Guard – to prevent the rise of any unsanctioned youth or protest movements that might attempt to replicate the oppositional successes of Otpor or Pora.

In terms of external inducements to increase political freedom in Russia, the activities of international media, as well as international aid and non-governmental organizations within Russia, also became highly circumscribed. Finally, the United States has lost much of its moral authority to urge Russia to democratize at the same time that the EU has grown increasingly dependent on Russian oil and gas, and evidently therefore less inclined to criticize the erosion of Russian democracy.[1] In sum, we probably should not be surprised that Russia avoided an Orange-style electoral or popular revolution. In what follows, I

---

[1] Marshall Goldman, *Petro State: Putin, Power and the New Russia* (New York: Oxford University Press, 2008), pp. 7–8.

discuss the relative presence or absence in Russia of six characteristics enabling democratic revolutions in other parts of Eastern Europe and the former Soviet Union.

It is always harder to explain a nonevent, something that never happened, than to find factors that explain something that actually did take place. In a very real sense, the factors for there not being an electoral revolution in Russia are overdetermined. After all, throughout post-Soviet space, electoral revolutions have been more the exception than the rule. Why, then, should we have expected that Russia would defy this tendency? Although it may have been unrealistic to think that by 2008 and the rise of Russia's third post-Soviet president, the country would be a fully consolidated democracy, it is reasonable to examine why it actually took determined steps away from democracy at the same time that some of its neighbors to the West strode boldly toward it. If we look systematically at the constellation of factors that precipitated electoral revolutions elsewhere, we can see that most of the six main components are missing in the Russian context. The interesting question is how this came to be.[2]

1. A Semiautocratic Regime

As some of the preceding chapters in this volume demonstrate, in Serbia, Georgia and Ukraine, electoral revolutions took place against the backdrop of a semiautocratic regime. This is one of the few common starting points between the color revolutions and Russian politics since the year 2000. From 2000 onward, Russia clearly became a less open society than in the preceding eight years, although it still remained far freer than the Soviet system. In contrast to the Soviet period, Russians living post-Putin are not tightly controlled by the state in every aspect of their political and economic lives as under communism. Nonetheless, by about 2005, Russia was generally acknowledged to be "semi-autocratic," so in this sense, the broad political backdrop for a democratic revolution was present at about the same time that the Orange Revolution, for example, occurred in Ukraine.[3]

The checks and balances of an already fragile electoral democracy were carefully emasculated following Putin's ascension to the Russian presidency. This process included the effective fusion of the executive and legislative branches, the dominance of a new ruling party, state domination of the media, and decreased scope for political opposition and independent civil society. All of these are discussed below.

The dominance, and indeed, for practical purposes, fusion of executive and legislative authority in Russia began in 1999 with the parliamentary victory of

---

[2] I draw the six main components of the causes of the Colored Revolutions from earlier chapters in this book and from Michael McFaul, "Transitions from Post-communism." *Journal of Democracy*, 16, No. 3 (2005), pp. 5–19.

[3] 2005 was the first year that independent assessments such as that of Freedom House characterized Russia as "not free" on their ranking scales of relative freedom in the world. Prior to this, it had been characterized as "partly free."

a new "party of power," then called Unity, but known since 2003 as United Russia. Although neither President Yeltsin nor Putin was officially a member of any particular party (it remains to be seen whether President Medvedev will change this), both created parties of power in their respective tenures in office. All but United Russia have risen and fallen with electoral cycles. By the parliamentary elections of 2007, Putin (still president then, and not prime minister) was featured as the moral leader of the party on United Russia's official website, but did not run as a candidate of the party in either of the two elections that made him president.[4] Eschewing formal party membership did not hurt Putin's electoral prospects as president. In the March 2004 presidential elections, running as an independent, Putin was reelected to his second term with slightly more than 70 percent of the vote. His closest competitor, Communist Nikolai Kharitonov, garnered 13.7 percent. Similarly, in March 2008, President Medvedev recorded almost exactly the same percentage of the popular vote, also without a formal connection to a political party.

To be sure, parties have not been completely absent in presidential elections – indeed, all other candidates *except the winner* in the elections of 1991, 1996, 2000, 2004, and 2008 carried party affiliations, as Table 10.1 indicates. This, combined with the fact that such a large percentage of votes was claimed by candidates without party affiliations in each election, seriously damages the degree of influence political parties have had so far in actually governing Russia.

Despite never actually joining a political party himself, President Putin was far more systematic in creating a party of power that became a real electoral machine in the Duma. In part this was due to preferred access to the mass media for United Russia, but was also a result of the general failure of opposition politics in Russia to coalesce (discussed more later in this chapter), and finally, perhaps most importantly, the adroit manipulation of candidate and party registration laws in Russia since 2006 in particular. Until the December 2007 parliamentary elections, when the system became completely proportional representation (the implications of which are discussed below), after 1993 Russia had a mixed electoral system for national legislative elections. This meant that 225 of the 450 seats in the Duma were elected through proportional representation (PR) party lists, whereas the other 225 seats were elected through single mandate elections.

Table 10.2 indicates that between the first elections to the state Duma in December 1993 through December 1999, three parties (the Communist Party of the Russian Federation (KPRF), Yabloko, and the Liberal Democratic Party of Russia under Vladimir Zhirinovsky (LDPR))[5] consistently cleared the five-percent barrier that parties had to cross at the time in order to gain

---

[4] See "Edinii Rossii Ofitsialnii Sait Partii," available at http://www.edinros.ru/; accessed June 2, 2007.

[5] Note that in the 1999 Duma elections, the LDPR initially failed some registration requirements and Zhirinovsky reregistered the party under the name "Zhirinovsky's Bloc," although Zhirinovsky referred to the bloc as the LDPR throughout the election and its candidate list was virtually identical to the LDPR's originally submitted list. The Bloc should therefore be considered to be the LDPR in form if not in name.

TABLE 10.1. *Party Affiliations of Presidential Candidates in Russia 1991–2004*

Candidate	Party Affiliation	Percentage of Popular Vote
1991		
Bakatin	KPRF (Communist)	4
Makashov	KPRF	4
Ryzhkov	KPRF	17
Tuleev	KPRF	7
Yeltsin	None	57
Zhirinovsky	LDPR (Liberal Democratic Party)	8
1996		
Lebed	Honor and Motherland	15
Yavlinsky	Yabloko	7
Yeltsin	None	35
Zhirinovsky	LDPR	6
Zyuganov	KPRF	32
2000		
Pamfilova	For Civic Dignity	1
Putin	None	53
Titov	SPS (Union of Right Forces)	1
Tuleev	Communist	3
Yavlinsky	Yabloko	6
Zhirinovsky	LDPR	3
Zyuganov	KPRF	29
2004		
Glaziev	Motherland	4
Khakamada	SPS	4
Kharitonov	KPRF	14
Malyshkin	LDPR	2
Mironov	Party of Life	<1
Putin	None	71
2008		
Medvedev	None	70
Zyuganov	KPRF	17
Zhirinovsky	LDPR	9
Bogdanov	Democratic Party of Russia?	1

Source: Henry Hale, *Why No Parties in Russia? Democracy Federalism and the State*, p. 108 (New York: Cambridge University Press, 2006) and Central Electoral Commission of the Russian Federation. Results are from the first round of voting.

representation in the national legislature through party list voting. In addition to these three parties, a fourth, more fluid grouping (the name and membership of which has changed between electoral periods) consistently represented the government at the time of the election – a party of power. In 1993 this was Russia's Choice, in 1995 it was Our Home Is Russia (NDR), and in 1999 Unity. By 2003 Unity had morphed into United Russia and controlled a staggering two-thirds of the seats in parliament. In 2007, with Putin running as the only

TABLE 10.2. *Proportion of National Vote of Leading Parties (Those Having Cleared the Five Percent PR Barrier at Least Once) in Elections to the State Duma in 1993, 1995, 1999, 2003, and 2007*

	Electoral Year				
	1993	1995	1999	2003	2007
Yabloko					
PR percent	7.86	6.89	5.93	<5.0	<7.0
Total seats	23	45	22	4	0
LDPR					
PR percent	22.9	11.2	5.98	11.5	8.1
Total seats	64	51	17	36	40
KPRF					
PR percent	12.4	22.3	24.29	12.6	11.6
Total seats	48	157	113	52	57
Unity/United Russia					
PR percent	N/A	N/A	23.32	37.6	64.3
Total seats	N/A	N/A	72	122	315
Just Russia					
PR percent	N/A	N/A	N/A	N/A	7.7
Total seats	N/A	N/A	N/A	N/A	38
Motherland					
PR percent	N/A	N/A	N/A	9.0	N/A
Total seats	N/A	N/A	N/A	37	N/A
Agrarians					
PR percent	7.9	<5.0	<5.0	<5.0	<7.0
Total seats	33	20	0	2	0
Women of Russia					
PR percent	7.86	<5.0	<5.0	N/A	N/A
Total seats	23	3	0	N/A	N/A
Party of Unity and Concord					
PR percent	6.76	<5.0	<5.0	N/A	N/A
Total seats	19	1	0	N/A	N/A
Russia's (Democratic) Choice					
PR percent	15.5	<5.0	<5.0	N/A	N/A
Total seats	70	9	0	N/A	N/A
NDR					
PR percent	N/A	10.1	<5.0	N/A	N/A
Total seats	N/A	55	7	N/A	N/A
Union of Right Forces					
PR percent	N/A	N/A	8.6	<5.0	<7.0
Total seats	N/A	N/A	29	3	0
Fatherland/All-Russia					
PR percent	N/A	N/A	13.1	N/A	N/A
Total seats	N/A	N/A	65	N/A	N/A
Number of deputies elected as independents	141	78	119	68	0
Total number of parties running	13	43	26	23	11

Note: Total seats denotes total number of seats won in both proportional representation and single mandate contests between 1993 and 2003. In 2007, there were no longer any single mandate contests. Seats were apportioned purely on the basis of proportional representation to those parties receiving 7.0 percent or greater of the popular vote. N/A indicates that the electoral organization in question did not exist, or did not meet registration requirements in time for the election.

Source: Central Electoral Commission of the Russian Federation.

name on United Russia's national party list, it increased its dominance by winning sixty-four percent of the popular vote and a corresponding 315 of 450 seats in the Duma.

Putin did not actually take a seat in the legislature, because he was still president at the time, but this obviously completed his total domination over both the executive and legislative branches of the Russian political system. As his successor, Dmitri Medvedev (one of United Russia's original founders), became president in 2008, Putin deftly moved to the office of prime minister. This meant a high degree of staff retention in the president's office (because Medvedev had previously been first deputy prime minister and Putin's protégé).

By 2003, as Table 10.2 indicates, most of the other parties dominant in 1993 had either disappeared completely or failed to gain any substantial representation in the Duma. Only four (the KPRF, LDPR, Motherland, and United Russia) gained more than the (then) required 5 percent of the popular vote to gain representation by PR voting. Significantly, the reigning party of power, United Russia, dominated parliamentary elections in 2003 by winning thirty-seven percent of the popular vote, effectively replacing the Communist Party of the Russian Federation (KPRF) in short order as the most dominant party in parliament. By 2007, United Russia's control of parliament was complete and there was no longer any effective opposition to it.

But does the fact that the president's preferred party has control of the legislature mean that parties have finally found a foothold in actually governing Russia? The answer to this is not entirely clear, but seems to be more likely no than yes. One reason is the striking imbalance between executive and legislative authority in Russia. Throughout the presidencies of Yeltsin and Putin, the president was the undisputed ruler of the country and, as noted above, carried no formal party affiliation. This is a clear signal that personalities and personal loyalty mattered more than political parties as formal institutions important in governing Russia. This has continued to be the case during Medvedev's term as Russian President, given that he too maintains no formal party affiliation, and his personal ties to Putin appear far more important in determining who is in the presidential administration and government than any formal party affiliation. It is, however, difficult to disentangle these personal relationships from the formation and now functioning of United Russia, given that Medvedev was one of the initial founders of the party and the personnel of his presidency and Putin's are, at the time of writing, so overlapping.

A second issue is the fact that the Russian cabinet is not drawn from parliament, and so cabinet members do not have to actually carry a party affiliation or follow a particular party program while holding their cabinet posts.[6] Their

---

[6] On the relative lack of cohesiveness of party platforms in several postcommunist countries, see Herbert Kitschelt and Regina Smyth, "Programmatic Party Cohesion in Emerging Postcommunist Democracies: Russia in Comparative Context." *Comparative Political Studies*, 35 (2002), pp. 1228–56.

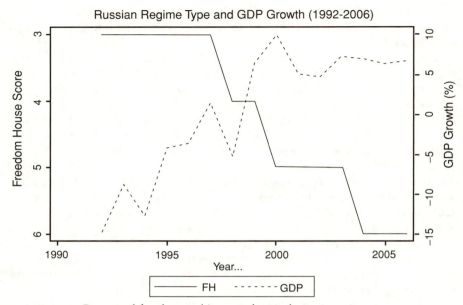

FIGURE 10.1. Decreased freedom and increased growth.

loyalty historically has been to the president of Russia rather than to any broader political institution such as a party. The president can appoint them and remove them virtually at his whim, although in some cases they require parliamentary approval for their initial appointment. This severely limits the effect that parties have in practice on the actual business of government in Russia as well as the force of any formal institutional checks on the personal rule of the president.

2. A Popular Incumbent

Although the primary background condition of semiauthoritarian /authoritarian rule is met in Russia, most other key components of the color revolutions, such as an unpopular incumbent, were not. On the contrary, at the same time that Russia became less free, its economy expanded and President Putin's popularity increased. The correlation between decreasing freedom, as measured by Freedom House, and increase in GDP per capita is shown in Figure 10.1. (Freedom House evaluates relative freedom in a country on a scale of 0 to 7, with 0 being most free and 7 being least free. For more information on Freedom House and its system of evaluating relative freedom in a variety of political systems, go to www.freedomhouse.org.)

I have argued elsewhere (with Michael McFaul) that the correlation between growth in Russia since 1999 and decreased freedom is spurious – that is, increasing autocracy did not cause growth, just as democracy in the 1990s did not cause recession.[7] But the belief that Mr. Putin in particular is responsible for Russia's resurgent economy is widely shared among the Russian populace and this has no doubt helped to fuel his popularity.

The Freedom House scale, although at best only a rough sketch, reflects an undeniable and now widely accepted view that Russia has become less free since the election of Vladimir Putin as president of Russia in 2000, with a precipitous drop following the color revolutions in Georgia and Ukraine in 2003 and 2004, respectively. (At the time of writing, this trend has continued under President Medvedev, with Putin as his prime minister.) Although elections have continued more or less unabated since 1993, and both President Yeltsin and President Putin avoided egregious transgressions of the Russian Constitution (although some would dispute this),[8] the institutions that constitute the main democratic bulwarks of the Russian political system have become seriously jeopardized. Power became increasingly concentrated in the presidency, backed up in no small part by the increased presence of the security apparatus in the business of governing.

Putin's persistent popularity among Russian voters helps to distinguish internal dynamics in Russia from that in Serbia, Ukraine, and Georgia. Although they were semiautocratic (not dissimilar to Putin's Russia), they all shared the fact that the incumbent president was unpopular. During his eight years in office, however, Putin managed to maintain popularity ratings pretty consistently over sixty percent. There are several factors that may explain this. First, Putin represented a marked contrast to Boris Yeltsin. He was young, fit, and a nondrinker. He stated clearly what he thought troubled Russia, and what he proposed to do about it. Second, as explained later in this chapter, Putin carefully backed a state takeover of the Russian television media, enabling him to better shape popular perceptions of his regime. Third, critics became less tolerated. Fourth, Russia's economy began a period of dramatic growth, in part on the back of high world oil prices and Russia's oil-exporting position in the global economy.

Because the two processes – increased authoritarianism and increased growth – occurred simultaneously, many average Russians do attribute economic recovery to Putin's more authoritarian ways. In a poll published at the end of Putin's tenure in office in March 2008, the Levada Center (one of Russia's few remaining non–state run polling agencies) reported that seventy percent of those polled credited Putin with success in establishing rising living standards, and fifty-five percent would have liked to see him run again for the presidency. Based on these results, Levada pollster Leontii Byzov concluded that

[7] Michael McFaul and Kathryn Stoner-Weiss, "The Myth of the Authoritarian Model: How Putin's Crackdown Holds Russia Back," *Foreign Affairs*, 87, No. 1 (January/February 2008), pp. 68–84.

[8] See, for example, Boris Nemtsov and Vladimir Mironov's critical assessment of Putin's rule in "Putin: Results," *Novaya Gazeta* (March 2008). Nemtsov was First Deputy Prime Minister of Russia from 1997 to 1998, and Mironov was Deputy Minister of Energy of the Russian Government in 2002.

Putin "embodies supreme power without accountability, so he is not blamed for policy failures in many areas, and they do not affect his overall support rating."[9] This is despite the fact that most Russians (fifty-three percent in the same poll) also reportedly notice the gap between rich and poor growing ever wider, and that one-third of those polled by the Levada Center acknowledge that Putin failed to curb corruption.

Indeed, the economy began to grow for the first time since the collapse of the Soviet Union in 1999 – a year before Putin assumed the presidency. It is important to note, however, that although the economy grew on average about six percent per year in the ensuing eight years, this occurred largely as a result of unusually high world oil prices, as opposed to any Putin-engineered systematic restructuring of the Russian economic system. To be sure, there have been important changes to the Russian financial and economic system in recent years – including the introduction of a thirteen percent flat personal income tax rate and a general tightening up of tax revenue collection – but a systematic restructuring of Russian industry that might make Russian manufactured goods competitive on world markets has yet to take place. Indeed, the global financial and economic crises that began in the fall of 2008 and the accompanying drop in world oil prices brought this fact into sharp focus.

It is possible that the pathology of a resource curse – where oil revenues keep taxation rates low, while public goods are provided at low cost and the state becomes ever less accountable to the public – helps to sustain levers of authoritarian control.

3. A Cohesive Political Elite and a Weakened and Divided Opposition

Other important factors in bringing about the color revolutions elsewhere in postcommunist countries were a split within the political elite and the presence of a united opposition capable of mobilizing supporters to protest a disputed electoral outcome. Both of these necessary conditions, however, provide an important contrast with the Russian political context since 2000.

Drawing on his extensive contacts with his former employer, Putin dramatically increased the role of the Federal Security Service (or FSB, which is the successor to the KGB) in governing Russia. He also resorted to arbitrary use of the courts (rule *by* law as opposed to rule *of* law) to punish political opponents (the Khodrokovsky case is a prime example of this), as well as using federal tax authorities and the police for political purposes. Finally, distinct from Ukraine in particular, the regime under Putin was clearly not fragmented – the president (and now evidently Prime Minister Putin) retains a tight grip in constitutional theory and in actual practice over the power ministries of the military and internal security services.

[9] As quoted in Elena Ivanova, "Corrupt but Stable: Most Russian Citizens Prefer Stability and Don't Blame Putin for Anything," *Vedemosti*, No. 52 (March 24, 2008); reprinted in *Johnson's Russia List 2008*, No. 61, item #3 (March 24, 2008).

TABLE 10.3. *Share of Occupied Duma Seats Held by Major-Party Fractions in the 1994–2004 Dumas*

Year	Party	Percentage of Seats
1994–5	Russia's Choice	16
	LDPR	14
	Agrarian Party	13
	KPRF	10
	PRES	7
	Yabloko	6
	Women of Russia	5
	Democratic Party of Russia	3
	TOTAL	74
1996–9	KPRF	33
	NDR	14
	LDPR	11
	Yabloko	10
	Agrarian Party	8
	TOTAL	76
2000–3	KPRF	18
	Unity	18
	Fatherland-All Russia	12
	Agro-Industrial	10
	SPS	7
	Yabloko	4
	LDPR	3
	TOTAL	72
2004–7	United Russia	68
	KPRF	11
	Motherland	9
	LDPR	8
	TOTAL	96

Source: From Hale, 2006, p. 132.

At the same time, effective political opposition melted away in Russia as Putin's favored United Russia party won strong electoral majorities (aided by renewed control over the media) in the Duma. There has been a marked decrease in the overall degree of pluralism of political ideas and programs within the Russian parliament since 1999 in particular. This is evidenced not only by the steady decrease in the overall number of parties in Russia, but also by the steady decrease in the number of functioning party fractions represented in the Duma. Henry Hale has calculated the share of seats occupied by major-party fractions in this period. This appears in Table 10.3.

In the first Duma session in 1994–5, there were eight registered fractions, claiming a total of seventy-four percent of deputies; the largest fraction had sixteen percent of deputies, and the smallest had three percent. The number of fractions dropped to five in the next session, from 1996 to 1999, with a total of seventy-six percent of deputies registered in them, the largest having thirty-three percent of deputies, and the smallest eight percent, and then increased to seven fractions in 2000–2003, with the largest having eighteen percent and the smallest having three percent of seats. But in the session that began in 2004 and ran through January 2008, there was a significant focusing of deputies into only four fractions, which are strongly imbalanced – United Russia, the largest party in parliament, had sixty-eight percent of deputies registered in its fraction, whereas the only three other significant parties (that is, those that jumped the five-percent barrier) had far fewer members – between eight and eleven percent.

Further, despite its enduring presence in parliament, the KPRF has effectively ceased being an opposition party. Since 2003 KPRF deputies have typically voted with United Russia, as have deputies elected through Vladimir Zhirinovsky's LDPR. This, combined with the fact that fewer deputies are entering parliament as independents (down steadily from an all-time high in 1993 of 141 to a historic low of 23 in 2003 under the formerly mixed single mandate/PR system to zero in 2007 under the now PR-only electoral system, as indicated in Table 10.2), and fewer parties are able to meet the increasingly high barriers for registration set by the Central Electoral Commission, has meant a decline in the number of parties running for office (again, lowest in 2007 – with eleven included on the final ballot). This is still an admittedly large number of parties running for the Duma compared with the number that run for the legislatures in more advanced electoral democracies such as the United States or United Kingdom, but only four cleared the new seven-percent barrier for entry into parliament in 2007, with United Russia gaining by far the largest share of seats (315).

The ascendancy of United Russia began initially in 1999 when it emerged as a completely new political party just prior to the December 1999 parliamentary elections. By 2003, it increased its share of Duma seats by winning the highest proportion of the popular vote of any single party in that electoral round – thirty-seven percent. The next electoral round, in December 2007, was the first legislative electoral cycle that eliminated the election of Duma representatives by single-mandate districts in favor of election of all deputies according to proportional representation according to party lists. This had the effect of disadvantaging more democratically oriented parties such as Yabloko and SPS, because they had always done better in single-mandate races than PR. With Putin as the only name on United Russia's national list of candidates, the party won a staggering sixty-four percent of the popular vote, completing its domination of parliamentary politics.

Beyond the elimination of any proportion of the Duma selected according to single-mandate elections, United Russia's electoral success was in no small part due to the uneven electoral playing field that was created by important revisions to the electoral law. Not only was the minimum requirement for party representation in the Duma raised from five to seven percent, but other revisions to the electoral law were introduced that further highly constricted the abilities of opposition political organizations to fairly contest elections, and thus limited the functional choices of Russia voters.

By January 2006, for example, the law required that each political party demonstrate that it had at least 50,000 citizens as members and branches with at least 500 members in more than forty-five of Russia's regions. This required money and organization that many of the smaller parties simply did not have. Candidates in local elections frequently were denied registration on questionable grounds, including accusations that they falsified signatures or improperly filed the necessary paperwork. In March 2007, for example, the opposition party Yabloko was barred from St. Petersburg's municipal elections after the local electoral commission ruled that over ten percent of its signatures were invalid.

In addition, the increase of the minimum threshold for representation in the party list voting for the Duma from five to seven percent had the effect of eliminating Yabloko and the Union of Right Forces from the electoral landscape, as neither proved able to surmount this barrier and gain representation in the Duma. The new electoral law also included restrictions on political parties' use of television air time to campaign against opponents, as well as eliminating the minimum turnout requirement for elections at the national, local, and regional levels, allowing even elections with scant voter participation to be accepted as valid.

As the Duma became increasingly dominated by United Russia, the upper house of the Russian parliament, the Federation Council, became yet another rubber stamp for Kremlin policies. Its members were not elected, but rather selected by regional executives and legislatures, and many are merely patronage appointees who may never have actually visited the regions they ostensibly represent. The Federation Council, then, was one more way for informal networks to help allies of the Kremlin gain power. Further, the liberally minded opposition in Russia (as represented by Grigori Yavlinsky, for example) has long been deeply divided and represented poor and unrealistic electoral choices for Russian voters, so it is perhaps not surprising that they have failed to do well electorally since 1991.

Presidential alternatives are also few and far between in Russia. Former Prime Minister Mikhail Kasyanov attempted to register to run as a candidate for president in 2008, but the Central Electoral Commission rejected his registration documents on the ground that many of the required signatures were faked. A small and relatively unorganized opposition group, the other Russia, was led in 2006–8 by former world chess champion Garry Kasparov, but it has not contested elections, nor does it play any meaningful formal political role at the time of writing. In sum, in Russia post-Putin, there is no opposition figure such as Yushchenko in Ukraine or Saakashvili in Georgia waiting in the wings as a viable opposition leader with a political organization actually capable of taking over the responsibilities of governing.

Finally, pluralism at the regional level – a seat of political opposition to the national government in the 1990s in Russia – was further circumscribed under Putin, and this remained the case under Medvedev. His first line of attack included the establishment of seven federal districts within his presidential administration, each encompassing approximately twelve subunits of the Russian Federation. This did not involve a redrawing of formal borders between provinces, but was an administrative change in that each of the seven districts would be headed by an appointed representative charged with coordinating the tasks of the federal bureaucracy in particular, as well as attempting to check the overt flouting of central authority on the part of elected regional governors and republican presidents. This was a controversial move in that the reform attempted to place appointed presidential representatives higher in the political–administrative hierarchy than elected governors and presidents of regions.

Second, in an effort to remove overly active governors from excessive regional involvement in national politics, Putin proposed, and the Duma accepted, a plan to reorganize the Federation Council, Russia's upper house of parliament, so that regional political leaders (governors, presidents, and heads of regional legislatures) would no longer automatically gain seats. Instead, each region is now represented in the upper house by two appointed representatives – one put forward by the governor or president of the region and the other by a vote of the regional parliament.

Moreover, the presidential election of Medvedev in 2008 reflected staggering consolidation of elites and the relative impotence of any form of political opposition.

4. Few Mechanisms of Mass Mobilization

The fusion of the executive and legislative, the power of a popular incumbent, and the disappearance of a real opposition in Russia were likely enough to prevent the rise of an electoral revolution in Russia, but there was also no opportunity to spark such a protest from below. An important contributing factor to the success of electoral revolutions in Georgia, Ukraine, and Serbia was the mass protests that occurred in the wake of disputed election results. Aside from the general acceptance of election results (no matter how overtly or covertly manipulated), it is difficult to see how such protests could have been organized in Russia given the marked demobilization of Russian civil society and the impotence of the past and present sources of political opposition.

Certainly, the adoption in 2006 of a new federal law on the activities of nongovernmental organizations (NGOs) that required the reregistration of NGOs as domestic Russian organizations has damaged the independence of Russian civil society (more about this below). But even before this, Russian society was not one of joiners. The mass demonstrations of the late 1990s demanding the end of the Communist Party of the Soviet Union long ago gave way to popular apathy and at times to powerful nostalgia for the communist era. This may have more to do with a desire for stability and predictability than with necessarily negative attitudes toward the concept of democracy and liberal rights and freedoms, because, in most public opinion polls, Russians appear to still value the latter.[10]

In January 2006, President Putin signed the controversial NGO law designed to bring foreign and domestic nongovernmental organizations under tighter state oversight. Putin defended the law as a necessary step to prevent foreign incursion into Russia's politics. Critics, however, interpreted the intent of the law as being to limit the previously vital civil society that had arisen in Russia following the collapse of the Soviet Union.

The law required the reregistration of all groups with the Russian Ministry of Justice by mid-October 2006. In practice, however, many groups failed to meet this deadline and fulfill the relatively onerous registration requirements as well as file an annual work plan beginning in 2007. As a result, they were forced to close until they were able to supply the required documentation. Some completely ceased to function in Russia. Notable among the international organizations forced to close their doors at least temporarily were Human Rights Watch, Amnesty International, the National Democratic Institute, the International Republican Institute, and Internews, in addition to approximately ninety other foreign NGOs.

Most of these groups eventually reregistered with the Ministry of Justice, but virtually all reported the process to be cumbersome, and most remain fearful of further bureaucratic interference in their activities in Russia stemming from required semiannual reports on daily activities and funding for these activities for all civil society organizations. The concern is that the law gives the Russian government unprecedented authority to regulate NGO activities and to decide what projects are permitted and which are not.

There is also good evidence that the regime in Russia learned from the Orange Revolution and actively sought to prevent any such event in Russia. First, some analysts claim a direct relationship between the Orange Revolution in 2005 in Ukraine and the passage of the Russian law in 2006 that restricted NGO activity.[11] Second, one could point also to the founding of the Kremlin-sponsored youth groups Nashi (Ours) and Young Guard as counterweights to any spontaneous youth group formation that might be antiregime, as were Otpor and Pora in their countries' respective color revolutions.

5. State-Controlled Mass Media

The fact that the media were kept on a tight leash under Putin also distinguishes internal dynamics in Russia from those in Georgia, Ukraine, and Serbia. Where B-52 in Serbia helped spread the message of change, for example, few

---

[10] Nemtsov and Mironov, "Putin: Results."

[11] Anders Åslund, *Russia's Capitalist Revolution: Why Market Reform Succeeded and Democracy Failed* (Washington, DC: Peterson Institute for International Economics, 2007), p. 248.

independent media programs exist in Russia. In part in response to a demand to increase order and stability in the wake of the unruly 1990s, and a declaration of a dictatorship of law, one of Putin's first acts in office in 2000 was to introduce tighter control over the print and television media. This was done by restricting access to broadcast licensing, raiding offices of media outlets, and helping to run independent newspapers out of business.

The media remain tightly controlled by the presidential administration, and Russia continues to be one of the three most dangerous places in the world to be a journalist (after Iraq and Colombia). Since Putin assumed the presidency in 2000, thirteen journalists have been killed in contract-style murders. In none of these cases has anyone been convicted.[12] The murder of forty-eight-year-old Anna Politkovskaya in her apartment building on October 7, 2006 was among the most notable of these deaths. Politkovskaya was a special correspondent for the Russian newspaper *Novaya Gazeta*. For seven years she had fought to bring the story of the Chechen conflict to light despite the dangers involved and the irritation it caused among Russian military and political officials. Politkovskaya had been threatened and detained for writing stories about human rights abuses against Chechen civilians by the Russian military and Chechen forces. Days after her murder, Putin described Politkovskaya as an insignificant figure and dismissed the notion that there was any official involvement in her killing (and indeed, at the time of writing there is no clear evidence that the state was involved). Other developments with the Russian media in recent years have also been troubling. In 2006, the Duma passed a bill, signed by President Putin, that broadened the definition of extremism to include criticism of public officials in the media. Several reporters were subsequently charged under this law, according to the Committee to Protect Journalists, including one journalist who allegedly defamed the governor of Vladimirov region in an Internet chat room.

The Russian government and Kremlin-allied businessmen have steadily consolidated their control of Russian print and television outlets since 2000. As of 2008, the main sources of Russian news – all of the major national television channels (Channel One, RTS, and NTV) – were state-controlled and effectively censored. The International Research and Exchanges Board (IREX) Media Sustainability Index has noted a steady decrease in freedom of the press since 2001. There is also little transparency in broadcasting regulation, although politics clearly plays a role, as evidenced by the decision in 2007 to prohibit rebroadcasting of Radio Free Europe/Radio Liberty in Russia.[13]

---

[12] For the ranking of Russia as third most dangerous for a journalist after Iraq and Colombia, as well as the number of journalists murdered since 2000, see Committee to Protect Journalists, "Attacks on the Press in 2006, Europe and Central Asia: Russia," available at www.cpj.org/attacks06/europe06/rus06.html.

[13] This section appears also in Kathryn Stoner-Weiss, "Russia," In *Countries at the Cross Roads* (Washington, DC: Freedom House, 2007), pp. 7–8. See also Christopher Walker, "Muzzling the Media: The Return of Censorship in the Commonwealth of Independent States," Freedom House, 2007, available at http://www.freedomhouse.org/specialreports.

6. Weak Independent Election-Monitoring Capabilities

The weakness of the media, an organized opposition, and mobilized civil society contributed to a sixth restraint on electoral revolution in Russia – the lack of independent election-monitoring capabilities. The Council of Europe and the Organization for Security and Cooperation in Europe (OSCE) had previously monitored the 2003 Duma elections in which United Russia won its first major parliamentary victory. They declared the elections free but not fair, in that election results were not significantly falsified, but access to the media and television in particular was biased in favor of United Russia in particular, and against the Communists, SPS (the Russian acronym for the Union of Right Forces), and Yabloko, the opposition parties.[14] In 2007, the OSCE ultimately refused to send election monitors to Russia during the December Duma elections of that year, indicating that the Russian government had imposed restrictions that would make it impossible to verify the veracity of the election. The same was true for the presidential election of March 2008 when the OSCE canceled plans to send a mission to Russia. Officials at the OSCE's Office for Democratic Institutions and Human Rights (ODIHR) complained that the Russian government would not allow observers into the country soon enough or in large enough numbers to actually monitor whether electoral laws were being observed adequately.

Russia has only one independent election-monitoring NGO, Golos, which operates in slightly less than half the regions of the country. It operates a hotline for reporting of electoral violations and has successfully brought some notable cases to light, but its activities are not capable at this point of sparking an electoral revolution given the other controls the current regime has been able to impose on the media, civil society, and the opposition.[15]

In the face of all these missing ingredients in Russia for a democratic revolution à la Serbia, Ukraine, or Georgia, do external forces have any role in encouraging democratic turnaround in Russia?

II. EXTERNAL FACTORS IN EXPLAINING THE REVERSE WAVE IN RUSSIA

Although the waves of democratic change may indeed be flowing eastward from Europe toward Ukraine and Georgia, they have apparently crashed on Russia's shores. Indeed, the Orange Revolution evidently had the opposite effect on Russia – it appears to have hardened the resolve of Vladimir Putin and now his successor, Dmitri Medvedev, to defend Russia from any sort of popular revolution against their authority.

If Russia is a bulwark against the tide of electoral revolutions, then what international factors might affect Russian politics to reverse the trend? Evidently, the events of September 11, 2001 had an important effect on internal

---

[14] See Anders Åslund, *Russia's Capitalist Revolution*, p. 242.
[15] Information on GOLOS and its activities can be found at http://www.golos.org/a18.html.

politics as well as helping President Putin's standing with President Bush as a reliable and caring partner. That Putin was among the first foreign leaders to call Bush and express his condolences is well known. But the events of September 11 allowed Putin to argue to Bush and the international community that Russia also had a domestic terrorism problem in the form of Chechen rebels within its own borders. This gave him a pretext to crack down further on Chechnya, although the rebels themselves certainly encouraged this by their own actions in Moscow and Beslan.

Allowing the United States access to key airbases in Central Asia was by far the biggest service that Putin performed for the United States and Europe to date, however. In other areas (most notably the invasion of Iraq), Putin was less cooperative with the United States in particular. The Russian government has also been a thorn in the side of the international community (not just the United States) in dealing with Iran's nuclear ambitions. Moreover, as Russia has become less democratic, as noted above, and more of a natural resource–based economy, it has reasserted itself as an independent force in international politics. The dependence of Europe and China on Russian oil and natural gas supplies makes them more vulnerable to Russian international ambitions and has given Russia increased clout in the international community relative to the United States in particular, because consumers of natural gas are often dependent on a single supplier. The United States and Europe have also lost a great deal of leverage over the Russian government. Since about 2003, Russia has reclaimed its status as a superpower – but an energy, and not a nuclear superpower. As Marshall Goldman notes regarding international politics and their relationship to oil and gas prices, "Concessions made at a time when Russia is weak and prices are low are invariably invalidated once prices rise again and Russia regains its strength. Put simply, higher prices increase Russia's bargaining power."[16] The global financial crisis, then, along with other points of vulnerability, might turn the tide in Russia back toward democracy.

III. CAN THE TIDE BE TURNED?

As I conclude this rather pessimistic overview of Russia's response to the waves of democratization in postcommunist countries, I want to be cautious about what might reasonably be expected in what is still a short period of time. The task of transition was especially difficult in Russia. It was, after all, the seat of Sovietism, the largest country on earth geographically (spanning eleven time zones), and was replete with inherited economic difficulties and gifts. Further, it is (of course) a sovereign state and former nuclear (and now energy) superpower. Although the West "won" the cold war, the United States and Europeans were not occupiers and were never capable of transforming Russia into a Western image – the task of transformation is ultimately up to Russians themselves. It is still too early to write Russia off – we may see it digressing now

---

[16] Goldman, *Petro State*, p. 49.

politically while it progresses economically, only to make a giant leap toward democracy in a few more years, especially if its economy continues the decline initiated in the fourth quarter of 2008.

Some cracks in the authoritarian façade may already be visible. Putin cited his desire to impose order and enhance the governing capacity of the Russian state in the wake of the wild 1990s as one of the main reasons that he circumscribed critical components of Russian democracy. Despite real and remarkable economic growth under his leadership, however, there is reason to believe that renewed authoritarianism has not actually resolved lingering governance problems.[17] The proliferation of institutions aimed at social and political control rather than public service and goods provision has merely made the Russian state bigger, but not more effective at the task of actually governing. In fact, there is good evidence that autocracy has done no better than even the disorderly, unconsolidated democracy of the 1990s, (even in good economic times), in promoting public safety, health, or a secure legal and property-owning environment.

The Russian state under Putin is certainly bigger than it was before. The number of state employees has doubled to nearly 1.5 million. The Russian military has more capacity to fight the war in Chechnya today, and the coercive branches of the government – the police, the tax authorities, the intelligence services – have bigger budgets than they did a decade ago. In some spheres, such as paying pensions and government officials on time, road building, or educational spending, the state is performing better now than during the 1990s. Yet, given the growth in its size and resources, what is more striking is how poorly the Russia state still performs. In terms of public safety, health, corruption, and the security of property rights, Russians are worse off than they were ten years ago.

Security, the most basic public good a state provides its population, is a central element in the myth of Putinism. But in fact, the frequency of terrorist attacks in Russia increased under Putin. The two biggest terrorist attacks in Russia's history – the Nord Ost incident at a theater in Moscow in 2002, in which an estimated 300 Russians died, and the Beslan school hostage crisis, in which as many as 500 died – occurred under Putin's autocracy, not Yeltsin's democracy. The number of deaths of both military personnel and civilians in the second Chechen war is substantially higher than that during the first Chechen war in 1994–6, and although conflict inside Chechnya appears to be subsiding, conflict in the region is spreading. The murder rate also has increased under Putin, according to the Russian State Committee on Statistics' data. In the "anarchic" years of 1995–9, the average annual number of murders was 30,200; in the "orderly" years of 2000–2004 the number was 32,200. The death rate from fires is about forty a day in Russia, roughly ten times the average rate in Western Europe.

[17] Kathryn Stoner-Weiss, "Russian Federalism and Democracy," *Journal of Democracy*, 17, No. 1 (2006), pp. 104–18.

Nor has public health improved in the last eight years. Despite all the money in the Kremlin's coffers, health spending averaged 6 percent of GDP from 2000 to 2005, compared to 6.4 percent from 1996 to 1999. (The figure for the United States is 15.4 percent). Russia's population has been shrinking since 1990, thanks to decreasing fertility and increasing mortality rates, but the rate of decrease has gotten worse since 1998. Noncommunicable diseases have become the leading cause of death (cardiovascular diseases account for 52 percent of deaths, three times the figure for the United States), whereas alcoholism now accounts for 18 percent of deaths of men between the ages of 25 and 54. At the end of the 1990s, annual alcohol consumption per adult was 10.7 liters (compared with 8.6 liters in the United States and 9.7 in the United Kingdom); in 2004, this figure had increased to 14.5 liters. An estimated 0.9 percent of the Russian population is now infected with HIV (1.0 percent is considered the threshold for an epidemic by the World Health Organization), and rates of infection in Russia now are now the highest of any country outside Africa, at least partly as a result of inadequate or harmful legal and policy responses and a decrepit health care system. Life expectancy in Russia rose between 1995 and 1998. Since 1999, however, it has declined steadily – to 59 for Russian men and 72 for Russian women.

At the same time that Russian society has become less secure and less healthy, Russia's rankings on economic competitiveness, business friendliness, and transparency and corruption all fell under Putin. According to the Russian think tank INDEM, in 2001 an estimated $31 billion was lost to corruption; in 2004, that figure was $319 billion. In 2006, Transparency International ranked Russia at an all-time low of 121st out of 163 countries on corruption, putting it between the Philippines and Rwanda. Russia ranked 62nd out of 125 on the World Economic Forum's Growth Competitive Index in 2006, a fall of nine places in a year. On the World Bank's 2006 "Doing Business" Index, Russia ranked 96th out of 175, also an all-time low.

Property rights also have been undermined. Putin and his Kremlin associates have used their unconstrained political powers to redistribute some of Russia's most valuable properties. The seizure and then reselling of Yukos assets to state-owned Rosneft was the most egregious, not only destroying value in Russia's most profitable oil company but also slowing investment (both foreign and domestic) and sparking capital flight. State pressure also compelled the owners of the private Russian oil company, Sibneft, to sell their stakes to the state-owned Gazprom, and Royal Dutch Shell to sell a majority share in its Sakhalin-2 project in Siberia to Gazprom. Such transfers have transformed a once private and thriving energy sector into a state-dominated and less efficient part of the Russian economy. The remaining three private oil producers – LUKoil, TNK-BP, and Surgut – all faced varying degrees of pressure to sell out to Putin loyalists. Under the banner of a program called "national champions," Putin's regime has done the same in the aerospace, automobile, and heavy machinery industries. The state further discouraged investment by arbitrarily enforcing environmental regulations against foreign oil investors, shutting out foreign partners in the development of the Shtokman gas field, and denying a visa to the largest portfolio investor in Russia, British citizen William Browder.

Most World Bank governance indicators, on things such as rule of law and control of corruption, were flat or negative under Putin. Those on which Russia has shown some improvement in the last decade, especially regulatory quality and government effectiveness, were started on a positive trajectory well before the Putin era began.

In short, the popular notion that by erecting autocracy, Putin has built an orderly and highly capable state that is addressing and overcoming Russia's rather formidable development problems is not supported by the evidence.[18]

This has left President Medvedev with considerable policy challenges. To his credit, he has acknowledged that Russia needs to build institutions, infrastructure, and investment and encourage innovation – what he has termed "the four I's."[19] These include institutions to administer greater rule of law and to combat corruption (a theme President Putin also hit when he assumed the presidency in 2000, but with little effect by 2008), as well as improving Russia's housing and health infrastructure. He has previously overseen and claims to want to make greater progress on national projects in education, health, agriculture, and housing.[20] To accomplish these tasks, however, will require greater private sector investment at a time when money is scarce as a global recession looms, and this may create an increased demand for the rule of law and security of property and investor rights.

Others have noted that Russia may well already be suffering from "Dutch Disease" (in that its economy has become focused on revenues derived from oil and gas exports, whereas it lacks the ability to manufacture anything else of value on world markets, and its export prices have increased) and other pathologies of oil-cursed states, which will doom it for some time to authoritarian rule. Should oil prices stay below $50 a barrel for six months or more (as they did in the global recession that began in the fall of 2008), however, Russia's economy will be exposed for all of its inherent weaknesses. Weak authoritarianism will be shown to have provided less to the Russian people than did weak democracy, and this might be the moment at which Russia tilts back toward a democratic path.

---

[18] The preceding section and data are drawn from McFaul and Stoner-Weiss, "The Myth of the Authoritarian Model."

[19] See Medvedev's first major policy speech prior to his election in 2008, the highlights of which appear in "Medvedev Says Four I's are Key to Russian Economic Program – 2," available at http://en.rian.ru/russia/20080215/99286756.html.

[20] *"Stavim Na Lederov! Vstrecha Dmitri Medvedeva s Liderami Politicheskikh Organizatsii,"* (Moscow: Evropa, 2008).

Contagion Deterred

*Preemptive Authoritarianism in the Former
Soviet Union (the Case of Belarus)*

Vitali Silitski
Belarusian Institute for Strategic Studies, Vilnius-Minsk

INTRODUCTION

The wave of democratic electoral revolutions in Eastern Europe and postcommunist Eurasia revived one of the most disputable but nonetheless appealing arguments in the theory of democratization: that is, successful democratic breakthroughs in one or several places help to shape the timing and dynamic of transformation in others. This interconnectivity of transitions in time (and space) is described in terms such as "contagion," "diffusion," or a "demonstration effect." Indeed, although hardly a decisive factor, the evidence that contagion played an important role in transmitting the spirit of democracy and techniques for achieving it from Serbia in 2000 to Georgia in 2003, Ukraine in 2004, and Kyrgyzstan in 2005 is evident.[1]

There is more than enough evidence that a large community of activists, policy advisors, local and international NGOs, and media were purposefully involved in translating the experience, strategy, and tactics of successful revolutions to new territories. This likely led to a repeated feeling of déjà vu among the international community, as the world read and watched television scenes replayed over and over of yet another autocrat being ousted and a new democratic leader being installed by "people power."

Why is contagion so important and vivid in this wave of democratic revolutions? First, as Valerie Bunce asserts,[2] there is a unique fellowship of democratic activists in the entire postcommunist world (that is, spreading from Prague to the far east in Russia) who share a common experience of the past and on this basis have developed a sense of responsibility for helping their thus far less

---

[1] For more discussion about the role of diffusion in recent electoral revolutions, see Chap. 2 by Valerie Bunce and Sharon Wolchik in this volume.

[2] Valerie Bunce's keynote address at the Fisher Forum on Color Revolutions at the University of Illinois, available at Urbana-Champaign, http://atlas-real.atlas.uiuc.edu:8080/ramgen/reec/reec-v-2005–1/smil/reec20050912_Valerie_Bunce.smil.

fortunate neighbors and comrades to achieve their dreams and goals of democracy and freedom. In the broader sense, the contagion is definitely facilitated by the proximity of historical experiences and present-day concerns and dilemmas that most societies in the region face. In other words, as far as the countries face similar problems, their audiences throughout the postcommunist world may have an immediate understanding of what sorts of solutions are suggested to them by the roaming revolutionaries.

Second, contagion is applicable because there is a generational profile of new democracy-builders in the region: most of them are relatively young and relatively idealistic, and many are well traveled and proficient in foreign languages. These intellectual democracy-builders combine a sense of purpose with the strong sentimental motivation of adventurism. With these powerful ideologies, personalities, and able bodies, the transition is infinitely more contagious.

Third, the dramatic proliferation of the democracy promotion community and international civil society over the last decade and a half has contributed to this contagion theory. Much of it initially settled in the region with the more humble task of assisting in democratic transformation in the early 1990s, and at that point it benefited from the initial benevolence and the readiness of incumbents who took the reins of power after the collapse of the Soviet system to play democratic games.

Fourth and last, the democratic contagion has greatly benefited from the advance of computer technology, international electronic media, and mobile communication. These advances made recent revolutions truly the first high-tech political transitions in history. New technologies allowed inspirational images of so-called people power as well as knowledge and political know-how to spread. And although off limits for many in the impoverished societies of Eurasia, the technologies of computers, mobile phones, and satellite dishes are definitely in use by activists in the region. Needless to say, these new technological capabilities assisted enormously in the mobilization and coordination of both electoral efforts and street protests.

But democrats and revolutionaries are not the only ones who can learn from the past and apply new knowledge to fulfill their political goals. Indeed, their antagonists appear to have mastered the science and craft of democratic transitions in order to stop the contagion at their borders. What is more, they are becoming increasingly aware, paraphrasing George W. Bush's second inaugural address, that the "survival of autocracy at home increasingly depends upon the failure of democracy abroad." The first trend, learning to combat the democratic contagion, is an essential element of the new political trend in postcommunist Eurasia, defined by the author as *preemptive authoritarianism*. The second trend, joining efforts to combat the democratic contagion, is reflected in the rise of an *authoritarian international*, which is rapidly emerging in the post-Soviet void.

This chapter consists of three parts. The first explains the concept of preemptive authoritarianism. The second gives an overview of preemption, drawing

upon Belarus, a country where such actions have been used the most extensively and proficiently. The third section highlights the international dimension
of preemptive authoritarianism, focusing on the example of Belarus–Russia
cooperation, which has increasingly taken on the responsibilities of combating
democracy. A brief conclusion addresses some implications of preemption and
the authoritarian international for scholars and democracy builders.

CONCEPTUALIZING AND EXPLAINING PREEMPTION

Preemption is a strategy of combating democratic contagion by anticipating the
political challenge, even when there is no immediate danger of regime change.
Preemption thus aims at opposition parties and players that are still weak. It
removes from the political arena even those opposition leaders who are unlikely
to pose a serious challenge in the next election. It attacks the independent press
even if it reaches only small segments of the population, destroys civil society
organizations even when these are concentrated in a relatively circumscribed
urban subculture, and last but not least, violates the electoral rules even when
the incumbent would be likely to win in a fair balloting.

This type of preemption, involving attacking the opponents and the infrastructure of the opposition and civil society, can be named *tactical preemption,*
and it does not exhaust the repertoire of available means of combating democratic contagion. Another more profound instrument is *institutional preemption,* consisting of tightening the fundamental rules defining the political game,
often in a repeated manner, before the opposition becomes strong enough to
compete. Examples of institutional preemption include rewriting the constitutions to strengthen presidential powers at the expense of parliamentary powers
and local legislatures; amending electoral rules to ensure stable majorities of
loyalists in the parliaments; adopting tougher media and libel regulations; and
restricting, delegalizing, and even criminalizing certain types of civil society
activities. A final and crucial instrument is *cultural preemption*: the manipulation of public consciousness and collective memory to spread stereotypes and
myths about the domestic opposition, the West, former communist countries
that shifted to the democratic track, and democracy in general – but especially democratic promotion. These cultural assaults instigate public fear of
and aversion to the very ideas surrounding and supporting regime change.

Before further analysis, three specifications concerning the concept of preemption must be clarified. First, preemption is not purely voluntaristic, but is
pursued on already well-nurtured ground, enhancing an already existing incumbent capacity to combat political challenges.[3] For example, twisting institutions
to ensure advantage for the incumbent is easier, and in many cases only possible, when imbalances in favor of presidential authority are already in place

---

[3] Lucan Way, "Authoritarian State-Building and the Sources of Regime Competitiveness in the
Fourth Wave: The Cases of Belarus, Moldova, Russia and Ukraine." *World Politics*, 57 (January
2005), pp. 231–61.

and existing regulations concerning freedom of expression and association are insufficiently democratic and transparent. Likewise, cultural stereotypes are more persuasive when they strengthen and amplify already existing collective memories, myths, fears, and prejudices. Moreover, already weak and fragmented oppositions are much easier to manipulate and weaken by repression than opposition groups that are professionally organized and politically efficient. Preemptive strikes against democratization, therefore, gain strength from contexts where authoritarians have already weakened the forces that support a more liberal order.

Second, the autocratic incumbents' capabilities to learn and hence to use preemption effectively are also affected by their structural and institutional advantages, as well as time. Thus, it is logical that the preconditions for electoral revolutions first matured in unconsolidated semiauthoritarian regimes that were prone to regime change by the very flaws in their construction. With no experience in sight, soft authoritarians were more likely to fall into complacency and arrogance of power (in contrast with the knowledge acquired by the opposition through contagion and diffusion); both of these characteristics were important agency-related factors that allowed the regime change to happen. For example, one reason that Milošević's regime fell in 2000 was that he was the first autocrat in the region to be taken down by electoral revolution. Although his regime was growing increasingly hard-line in 1998–2000, Milošević still did not have advance warning of the danger that lay ahead. In contrast, the opposition, civil society, and the democracy promotion community learned from the experiences of the Philippines in 1986, Chile in 1988, and even elections in Romania, Croatia, and Slovakia. Although those were not electoral revolutions, many of the instruments, such as voter mobilization, were fine-tuned in these locales before they were applied by the Serbian opposition.[4] Kuchma or Shevardnadze might have learned something from Milošević's downfall, but Serbia seemed to be far afield, and both the leaders and their subordinates chose instead to focus on why Georgia or Ukraine "was not Serbia."

Once the wave of democratization wiped out these semiautocratic regimes, however, more resilient and consolidated autocratic replacements remained in place. Thus, the autocrats enjoyed another asset, in addition to structural advantages: knowledge of the techniques most likely to be applied to oust them and, in more general terms, awareness of the danger of democratic contagion. The Orange Revolution in Ukraine was the true watershed in the political development of the region, due to that country's size and geopolitical

---

[4] Ironically, although the 1996–7 protests in Serbia following the annulled local elections won by the opposition should have sent Milošević a warning, they did not. After all, he ended up as a winner, successfully surviving the challenge by playing his usual game of dividing the opposition from within. His opponents, however, not only learned bitter lessons from self-defeating internal strife, but also drew positive lessons about what a united opposition can achieve both in elections and on the streets.

importance. The possibility of contagion could no longer be discounted once an electoral revolution had occurred so deep in post-Soviet territory and in the country previously thought to be secure for authoritarians. And although democrats found themselves agitated and hopeful as a result of the Orange Revolution, their thinking was often locked in what has become a standard model of regime change. Meanwhile, the incumbents immediately began using their structural advantages to further consolidate their regimes and make technologies of electoral revolution obsolete.[5] Ironically, the advance warning from recent revolutions not only enlarged the list of targets but also enhanced the repertoire of positive games played by incumbents to buttress their domestic legitimacy. They founded and promoted youth movements with "antirevolutionary" agendas and coopted artists and singers just as democratic revolutionaries did; in essence, they camouflaged antirevolutionary efforts by making them look like revolutions externally. Kazakh president Nursultan Nazarbaev went so far as to run a "color-coded" campaign for his reelection in December 2005. Belarus's Alexander Lukashenka used similar pop-culture tactics to combat contagion, although without a color code, in the run-up to the March 2006 presidential elections.

There was a self-limiting character of democratic diffusion; through the use of newly acquired knowledge to gain the advantage over potential opposition challengers, the authoritarians buttressed their surviving structural and institutional strengths. The process began in countries with the strongest domestic prerequisites for political change, and spread, by virtue of the demonstration effect, to those countries where "local structural support for change"[6] was considerably weaker. When revolutions began to be driven more by contagion than by the domestic conditions, they were increasingly characterized by "declining mass participation, more violence and less powerful democratic consequences."[7] As a result, later revolutionary cases (particularly Kyrgyzstan, but, to some extent, Georgia as well) were less suitable to serve as transmitters of democratic enthusiasm and hope to new territories in the region. Worse than not helping, these transitions may have even been hurtful: the increasingly violent transitions in these countries, and the political instability that followed

---

[5] Examples of preemptive attacks against democratic movements following Ukraine's electoral revolution are ubiquitous. The Belarusian president has strengthened his security forces and introduced a new law that allows the police to shoot street protesters when the president deems it necessary. In Kazakhstan, a major opposition party has been outlawed. Moldova, something of a post-Soviet oddity but still a semiauthoritarian country, blocked the entrance of Russian and Belarusian observers (mobilized by the Moldovan opposition) to its parliamentary elections last March. In Tajikistan, the government issued new regulations restricting contact between foreign diplomats and local civil society groups. And in Russia, President Putin announced a ban on democracy assistance from abroad. Almost all surviving Eurasian autocrats have issued public statements vowing not to admit another colored revolution on their home territories, referring to what has happened elsewhere mostly as terrorism and banditry.

[6] Valerie Bunce and Sharon Wolchik, "International Diffusion and Postcommunist Electoral Revolutions," *Communist and Postcommunist Studies*, (2006).

[7] Ibid.

them, endowed the surviving autocratic regimes with powerful propaganda resources. Thus, these regimes were able to scare the public away from the idea of regime change and favorably contrast the stability of their consolidated regimes with the chaos in newly transformed ones.

Third, preemption is not necessarily pursued to substitute for a lack of electoral legitimacy. Ironically, it may help to enhance it. In fact, one of the main purposes of advance strikes against proponents of democracy is removing visible and credible democratic alternatives from the public horizons. In this way, the regime can strengthen popular perceptions that the incumbent is the only available and realistic choice. Even when the election is rigged, the public may be left convinced that an incumbent would have won even in a clean ballot.

This last implication of preemption may be particularly counterintuitive for external observers of the region. Having access to independent information and various reports produced by the opposition and international monitors, outside observers often fail to realize that the domestic audiences may not be exposed to the same data and sources, and that the governments do thorough advance work to discredit the opposition (including its voting monitoring efforts). Likewise, political repression, when compartmentalized (i.e., applied to a fairly limited segment of the society), is perhaps more visible from abroad than from inside undemocratic countries. The same applies to vote fraud, especially once techniques for its administration become more sophisticated and are not limited to primitive ballot stuffing and multiple voting. It should be noted that authoritarian regimes have the instruments at their disposal to block attempts to produce any credible alternative information about voting outcomes – for example, by disorganizing or altogether banning exit polls and removing "unreliable" election observers. One more important factor is the general apathy and lack of interest in politics among vast layers of the population in repressive systems. This aids repression and helps preemption continue to go unnoticed.

In these conditions, when repression is compartmentalized and political alternatives are not only weakened but also invisible to the domestic audience, it is easy for incumbents to sell their message, arguing that the opponents cannot defeat them because they are incompetent, unrepresentative, and unprofessional. Thus, they imply that the opponents have failed the test of democratic contestation. Needless to say, another common message is that the failed opposition can only exist as mercenaries of external forces; this is often accepted as a foregone conclusion.

THE CASE OF BELARUS: LUKASHENKA'S LEARNING CURVE AND LANDMARKS IN PERFECTING THE POLICY OF PREEMPTION

Belarus is the focus of analysis in this chapter, mainly because as a post-Soviet country in particular, it has brought the policy of preemption to perfection – and to some extent became a model for other autocrats. President Alyaksandr Lukashenka has made headlines frequently in the last decade for his relentless crackdowns on political opposition, and the country now ranks among the most oppressive regimes in postcommunist Eurasia. The Belarusian leader's authority is based not only on outright repression, however, but also on a fairly high level of popular backing. His flamboyant autocratic style finds favor with a vast constituency of rural and elderly voters still nostalgic for the communist era; his oratorical skills and ability to manipulate public opinion through mass media are hard to beat; and his policies produce reasonable economic performance and contribute to a fair degree of social cohesion. Moreover, the weakness of a "widely popular national identity that can be framed in anti-incumbent terms" severely disadvantages the nationally minded opposition.[8]

Nevertheless, Belarusians do not seem to lag hopelessly behind their neighbors in terms of appreciation for democracy and reform: rather, some international opinion surveys rank them as the most committed democrats in the former Soviet Union.[9] Moreover, Lukashenka's approval ratings rarely exceeded 50 percent in the last decade, and sense of Belarusian identity has gradually strengthened over a decade and a half of independence. Considering these circumstances, it becomes clear that Lukashenka's policy of preemption, perfected since his accession to power more than a decade ago, is the reason political change in Belarus in the foreseeable future is rather unlikely.

Lukashenka's initial expertise in preemption had nothing to do with the contagion theory, but was rather a logical necessity during his drive to accumulate and preserve power. He launched his political career as a maverick parliamentary deputy and head of a collective farm. Then he captured public sympathy in 1993 as chairman of the parliamentary anticorruption commission, a position he used to promote his stature among potential voters in advance of the 1994 presidential election. Capitalizing on public outrage during the worst period of economic decline and collapsing living standards, Lukashenka used corruption charges to back up his claim that the country was being robbed by the elites, and also attacked the government for allowing the dissolution of the Soviet Union in 1991, which he insisted served no purpose but to facilitate the robbery of the state.

The June 1994 presidential elections ended in a huge upset. Still a political outsider, Lukashenka triumphed with eighty percent of the vote in the second round against Prime Minister Viachaslau Kebich.[10] Although he lacked the

---

[8] Lucan Way, "Authoritarian State Building and the Sources of Political Liberalization in the Western Former Soviet Union, 1992–2004," p. 233.

[9] Christian Haerpfer, "Electoral Politics in Belarus Compared," in *Contemporary Belarus: Between Democracy and Dictatorship*, Elena Korosteleva, Colin Lawson, and Rosalind Marsh, eds. (New York: Routledge Curzon, 2003), pp. 85–99.

[10] For more details on Lukashenka's road to power, see Vitali Silitski, "Explaining Post-Communist Authoritarianism in Belarus," in *Contemporary Belarus: Between Democracy and Dictatorship*, Elena Korosteleva, Colin Lawson, and Rosalind Marsh, eds. The best Russian-language source is Alexander Feduta, *Lukashenka: Politicheskaya Biografiya* [Lukashenka: Political Biography] (Moscow: Referendum, 2005).

support of a political organization and was ostracized by the entire political spectrum – from Kebich's conservative government to the nationalist opposition Belarusian Popular Front (BPF) – Lukashenka managed to take advantage of the public confusion and disorientation that prevailed in the postindependence era. His success also was made possible by the fair degree of political openness that had followed the demise of communism. Belarus had been the last former Soviet republic to establish the institution of the presidency; this had prevented the concentration of power and left room for a certain level of political and social pluralism (although the former party *nomenklatura* was never displaced). In 1994, the electoral process was relatively free and fair, in part because the incumbents had not yet discovered the finer points of manipulation and rigging. Finally, although major media outlets were controlled by the state, they respected freedom of speech and provided fair campaign opportunities for all contestants.

Lukashenka's convincing victory in a clean election made a strong impression on the public consciousness: for years to come, it remained the foundation for popular perceptions of his invincibility at the polls. But experience also made Lukashenka realize the potential threat of people power to an incumbent who experimented too much with democracy. As Lukashenka came to power virtually out of nowhere, he did not have a support base within the state machinery; all he could rely on initially was his sky-high approval rating. Within months of his July 1994 inauguration, however, his popularity began deteriorating due to persisting economic decline. As a result, he faced two tasks in his quest for unlimited power: trounce the existing opposition and consolidate his gains, so that the opposition would never have a chance to rise again.

Cultural Preemption: The Defeat of Nationalism and the Promotion of an Incumbent-Friendly Identity

The first task – the defeat of nationalism – was achieved by carrying out, in May 1995, a constitutional referendum on giving Russian the status of official language and changing state symbols to remodeled Soviet-era ones; to take it to the final level, voters needed to approve integration with Russia. The referendum ended up in a resounding victory for Lukashenka, as all the questions passed with huge majorities. This act of cultural preemption had a profound effect on future political developments in Belarus. By uprooting the feeble results of the new regime's national revival in the early 1990s, it firmly linked Lukashenka to a Sovietized political outlook – thus aligning him with the majority of Belarusians.

Essentially, the Communist-era "Soviet Belarusian" patriotism that the referendum revived as the de facto official ideology of the new regime was an important basis for blocking the creation of an anti-incumbent identity. This identity would have enabled mass mobilization by the opposition, but after the referendum it was adequately dismantled. The opposition itself was deprived of moral ground as long as it was associated with descendants of Nazi collaborators during World War II (in particular, the selling point of the official propaganda was that the independence-era national symbols, the white-red-white flag and the "Chase" coat of arms, were used by the pro-German nationalists during the war). Insofar as Lukashenka confirmed his pro-Russian orientation through this plebiscite, he would win much sympathy and support inside Russia; at this point, Russia began to view him as its only faithful ally in the international community. As a result, political and economic support for Lukashenka's regime was quick to arrive and remained substantial thereafter.

Institutional Preemption: The Legalization of Presidential Absolutism and Its Aftermath

The second task, obtaining an incumbent-friendly identity, was fulfilled in November 1996 by conducting a constitutional referendum that amended the Basic Law so that all formal power and control over all branches of the government, including the judiciary and legislature, was transferred into the hands of the president. Once again, this was an act of political necessity: the parliament, elected in May 1995 elections and in December 1995 by-elections, had only a weak democratic opposition, and not a single representative of the main opposition party, the Belarusian Popular Front, which had been trounced by the referendum results. Nevertheless, the new legislature proved to be of little help to Lukashenka, as the Communists and the Agrarians eventually joined the democrats in opposing his power grab. Moreover, the Constitutional Court continued to show remarkable independence by striking down nearly twenty presidential decrees in 1995–6. In November 1996, opposition MPs initiated impeachment proceedings. This attempt failed, however, due to the government's blackmailing of parliamentary deputies and Constitutional Court justices.

Lukashenka responded to this resistance by calling for a second referendum in November 1996. On the ballot was an amended version of the constitution, which extended Lukashenka's first term in office by two years, concentrated power in the hands of the presidency, and replaced the unicameral Supreme Council with a much weaker bicameral legislature consisting of a 64-seat Council of the Republic and a 110-seat House of Representatives.[11] Presidential decrees were given the status of law, meaning that they would supersede acts

---

[11] To attract more public interest in the referendum and support for the change to the constitution, Lukashenka proposed three additional questions. Two of them were completely populist: Voters were asked to reject the abolition of the death penalty and disallow private ownership of land. The last question aimed at further destruction of Belarusian nationalism: Lukashenka suggested abolishing the independence day celebrated on July 27 commemorating the adoption of the declaration of sovereignty in 1990, and proposed shifting the official holiday to July 3, the day Minsk was liberated by the Soviet army from the Nazis. The Supreme Council asked in response for voters to approve its own draft of the constitution that eliminated the presidency altogether; to authorize direct election of provincial governors; and to ban uncontrolled presidential funds.

adopted by the legislature. Furthermore, the prerogative of appointing members of the Constitutional Court and the Central Election Commission (CEC) was transferred from parliament to the presidency.

The official tally eventually reported that seventy percent of the electorate had voted in favor of Lukashenka's amended constitution, and even independent postelection polls challenged the referendum results on the constitution by only a few percentage points.[12] As a result, the referendum results, in spite of substantial evidence of power abuse, caused no large public protests. The referendum was carried not only by manipulation but also by substantial public support for Lukashenka, who effectively turned the ballot into a plebiscite on his own authority. The referendum's only negative effect for the government was that the House of Representatives[13] was boycotted by European parliamentary institutions and Belarus's observer status in the Council of Europe was suspended.

With the 1996 referendum, the institutionalization of personalistic authoritarian rule in Belarus was complete. The referendum eliminated all meaningful political competition and evicted the opposition from the decision-making process. Endowed with tyrannical, consolidated powers, Lukashenka had little problem ensuring his authority. First, control over all branches of the government meant almost unlimited ability to manipulate elections and turned them into meaningless exercises. Indeed, their irrelevance to political choice was firmly institutionalized: the electoral code enacted in 2000 contained no guarantees for an opposition presence in electoral commissions, severely restricted the work of election observers, and failed to provide all candidates with equal campaign opportunities.

Second, Lukashenka single-handedly restructured the security forces and the repressive apparatus of the regime to ensure their absolute loyalty. They were prepared to perform whatever task was necessary to ensure his enduring presence in office. More specifically, he reorganized the security forces and boosted riot special operations units that had been formed with each power ministry of Belarus (that is, the Interior Ministry, the Defense Ministry, and the KGB). All these units were conveniently located in or around the capital and were capable of acting quickly. According to unconfirmed reports, secret squads that carried out "particular" secret tasks were also organized on the basis of special operations units. Allegedly, their first acts were eliminating prominent mobsters, and then they shifted to more specific political tasks.[14]

---

[12] Andrei Jekadumau, "Aficyjnuja Vyniki Referendumu 1996 Hody i Dadzenyja Sacyjalahichnyh Dasledvanniau [Official Results of the 1996 Referendum and Sociological Survey Data]," in *Belaruskaja Palitychnaja Systema i Prezydenckija Vybary 2001* [Belarusian Political System and 2001 Presidential Elections] (Warsaw: IDEE, 2001), p. 65.

[13] Whose first composition was handpicked by Lukashenka himself out of 198 members of the old Supreme Council.

[14] Information of these units can be found in Feduta, *Lukashenko: Politicheskaya Biografiya*, (Moscow: Referendum, 2005); Pavel Sheremet and Svetlana Kalinkina, *Sluchainyi Prezident* (Moscow, 2004).

Tactical Preemption: Decapitating the Opposition

In 1999, some of the opposition leaders who had been considered potential contenders for the September 2001 presidential contest either died or disappeared. First to go missing was Lukashenka's former minister of the interior, Yury Zacharanka. In 1995, he had lost his job after refusing to evict opposition deputies from parliament and to forcefully disperse a strike in the Minsk metro. Zacharanka had become a leader of the United Civil Party, and just weeks before his May 1999 disappearance, he had announced the creation of a new opposition group, the Union of Officers. In September of that same year, former MP and chairman of the Central Election Commission Viktar Hanchar also disappeared, together with his financial backer.[15]

This final disappearance of Hanchar eliminated the most active, charismatic, and controversial opposition figure. After entering the political scene in 1990 as a newly elected member of the Supreme Council, he had quickly become popular thanks to his photogenic looks, oratorical skills, and legal expertise. Hanchar backed Lukashenka in 1994, but soon began to oppose the president's authoritarian style. He distinguished himself as an energetic and risk-taking opposition leader, whose unorthodox style inspired rank-and-file activists and attracted media coverage. Still claiming to be the legitimate head of the CEC, he organized a "shadow election" in the spring of 1999 to mark the expiration of Lukashenka's term according to the pre-1996 constitution. Although his planned "balloting" ended in embarrassment, Hanchar gained popularity among democratic activists.[16] By the time of his disappearance, he was emerging as a key figure in the opposition, but was still far from becoming its undisputed commander. But apparently Hanchar's commitment to fight openly against Lukashenka was more than the regime could tolerate.

Investigations of these disappearances carried out by the prosecutor-general's office allegedly cast suspicion on a special police unit overseen by then national security adviser Viktar Sheiman.[17] Dzmitry Paulichenka, an alleged

---

[15] This was not the only loss by the opposition in 1999. Henadz Karpenka, deputy leader of the United Civil Party, died on April 8 in under mysterious circumstances, ostensibly from a brain hemorrhage at the age of 50. Although no credible evidence of the authorities' involvement emerged, Karpenka's abrupt death could not have arrived at a more convenient time for Lukashenka.

[16] The logistics of the balloting were as follows: opposition activists carried ballot boxes from door to door, asking the residents to cast votes for one of the two candidates who joined the race. Hanchar declared that fifty-three percent of the electorate took part in the vote, whereas independent opinion polls discovered that only five percent did so. Moreover, of two "contestants" in the elections, one was in exile (the leader of BPF Zianon Pazniak) and the other was in prison on corruption charges (the former prime minister Mikhail Chyhir).

[17] According to media reports, the evidence produced by former security officers who defected to the West, and the findings of international investigators, the unit was created out of several security agencies and special operations forces in 1996. See Cristos Pourgourides, *Disappeared Persons in Belarus*, Report to the Parliamentary Assembly of the Council of Europe, 24 February 2004. Available at http://assembly.coe.int/Main.asp?link=http://assembly.coe.int percent 2FDocuments percent 2FWorkingDocs percent 2FDoc04 percent 2FEDOC10062.htm.

commander of the unit, was arrested in November 2000 in connection with the disappearances, but Lukashenka ordered him out of jail and fired the KGB chief and the prosecutor-general who had pressed charges. Sheiman was then appointed as the new prosecutor-general, which conveniently placed the investigation under his direct control.

An Early Acquaintance with Revolutionary Scenarios: Learning from Milošević's Downfall

Demonstration effects then entered into the calculus of Lukashenka's power. Taking note of the October 2000 overthrow of Serbian dictator Slobodan Milošević, he more readily learned that even a semblance of competitive elections can be a threat to an authoritarian regime. The reason for Lukashenka's watchful attitude toward Serbia under Milošević – and his modeling of the first electoral revolution in the postcommunist world – partly had to do with the special bond that developed between the two leaders. Milošević and Lukashenka had much in common, especially during the final years of Milošević's rule, a time when they shared the dubious reputation of being the last dictators in Europe.

Moreover, Lukashenka had been reading the signals: opposition leaders and international NGOs made no attempt to conceal the fact that Belarus would be the first place where the Serbian scenario of regime change would be attempted. Although his earlier strikes against the opposition had essentially equipped him to avoid his colleague's fate, Lukashenka remained perceivably anxious. As the presidential balloting approached, he grew highly suspicious of his own inner circle, in contrast to the regime-controlled media; they had began to frame public opinion about the "Serbian scenario" as first, an external plot that had nothing to do with domestic politics and, second, a coup that was achieved through the spin created by the opposition and media rather than by a genuine incumbent defeat. In the course of the election campaign through voting day on 9 September 2001, Lukashenka's regime created and applied many successful techniques to combat the electoral revolution scenario. He derailed the work of independent observers, disorganized exit polls, turned off mobile and Internet communications on election night, and sabotaged the opposition's mass mobilization for protest by blocking democratic activists' travel to the capital.

Lukashenka's reelection, with an official result of seventy-five percent of the votes cast, was a demoralizing loss for the opposition.[18] The opposition's failed attempt to mimic Serbia's electoral revolution had been easily and successfully

---

[18] The opposition questioned the official returns, and independent polls hinted that at least twenty-five percent of the votes were rigged in favor of the incumbent. Still, even these alternative data suggested a huge margin between Lukashenka and his main challenger, Uladzimir Hancharyk, who gained only fifteen percent in the official count and twenty-one percent according to alternative estimates. See "25 percent Dorisovano," [25 percent rigged], *Belorusskaya Gazeta* (November 12, 2001).

prevented by the regime, and the polls showed that Lukashenka would have won even a clean election. The defeat also led to a search for scapegoats within the opposition, and journalists and disaffected activists made public the squandering of democracy-assistance funds. Thus, an ever more degrading publicity disaster was added to the already defeated opposition.

Nonetheless, Lukashenka himself did not feel as though long-term political survival was ensured, for a number of reasons. First, following reelection, his popularity witnessed a slump, apparently due to his failure to deliver immediately on his overly generous campaign promises. Second, he felt he had yet to fully institutionalize his unlimited rule: he still needed to remove term limits for the presidency, which he had allowed to remain in the 1996 Constitution. And last, although the Belarusian opposition was in tatters and civil society still existed in only an embryonic state, it had become clear to Lukashenka during the 2001 election that both were gradually expanding and becoming capable of launching nationwide – perhaps eventually successful – campaigns.

Lukashenka had a long-term perspective. In contrast to Milošević's ultimately fatal habit of ignored warning signals, he wisely operated from an assumption of insecurity, rather than omnipotence. Lukashenka chose not to hold a referendum on removing term limits immediately, but rather took a more extended road, unleashing along the way familiar forces of institutional, cultural, and tactical preemption. He began taking many actions to cement his sovereignty, and although he easily survived the attempt to oust him in a Serbian-style revolution, he chose to eliminate those elements in uncontrolled political and social life that could serve as bases for a repeat performance: and, unlike Milošević, he did not wait until the last moment.

Thus, regulations punishing unauthorized street protests were hardened. Protesters at unsanctioned rallies (sanctioned rallies could be held only in one location on the outskirts of Minsk) faced not only physical beatings and imprisonment, but also prohibitive fines of up to US\$2,500 – a yearly income for an average family. The regime also forced almost 100 NGOs to close down or self-liquidate in 2003–4.[19] Because many of these organizations were prominent human rights groups or regional umbrella NGOs that assisted in the development of grassroots initiatives, the infrastructure of civil society was deeply damaged. Creating new organizations with agendas running counter to official policy became practically impossible, and the media faced severe penalties for reporting on the work of deregistered NGOs.

The independent press was also effectively silenced. Dozens of regional papers were closed down or suspended between 2001 and 2004. Some papers did survive the crackdown, however: after receiving official warnings that they would be closed down, most independent newspapers resorted to self-censorship. The government tightened its grip on electronic media by

---

[19] Alexander Dautin, "Kniga ne dla Shirokogo Chtenia," [Book Not for Common Audience], *Belorusskaya Delovaya Gazeta* (September 14, 2004).

replacing Russian television and radio broadcasts with homemade substitutes. This curtailment meant that the regime became the sole source of information for most of the population, and it was thus able to filter out harmful ideas.

The cost of disobedience, or even basic intellectual freedom, for the general public was also drastically raised. The regime stepped up its control over the educational system and closed down several independent institutions of secondary and higher learning. New regulations forbade institutions to grant students and professors leaves of absence to travel abroad, prohibited contacts with Western universities, and even prescribed "measures to prevent access of strange elements on campuses."[20] In January 2004, the permanent-employment system at state-owned enterprises was replaced with mandatory one-year contracts extended at the discretion of the management. As a result, any form of protest (even passive protest, such as refusing to take part in falsification of election results) could carry a very high price for state employees.

Tactical preemption continued with removing prominent opponents from the political scene, although this was done in a relatively soft manner. In April 2004, Lukashenka ordered the arrest of Mikhail Marynich, a former government minister. Marynich had defected to the opposition during the 2001 presidential election and had begun to emerge as one of the strongest potential contenders for the 2006 presidential election. Marynich was sentenced to five years in jail for allegedly stealing computers from his own NGO. His sentence was eventually reduced to two and one-half years, and he was conveniently released in April 2006, just weeks after Lukashenka was reelected.

Last but not least, Lukashenka managed to reinforce the moral ground for his authority with patriotism. Between 2001 and 2004, he effectively helped his cause by crafting and proliferating his own version of "Soviet Belarusian" propaganda. Lukashenka felt that his earlier version of practical ideology proved to be insufficiently reliable to validate his position of unlimited ruler of the country. Because pro-Russian rhetoric made the status of Belarus as an independent state ambiguous (and hence, Lukashenka's claim to absolute power in this state), Lukashenka was vulnerable to possible attacks from Kremlin authority. This was especially true in the absence of a method for rallying the public in support of his regime, and it became particularly visible during the 2002 brawl between Lukashenka and Putin. The tension started in June 2002, after the Russian leader announced his unwillingness to further subsidize Belarus in exchange for political union, and Putin soon demanded full unification in a form that would have turned the country into seven provinces of Russia.

Although Putin voiced his intentions regarding unification, the popularity of this relationship with Russia fell dramatically within Belarus under Lukashenka's rule due to the gradual strengthening of Belarusian identity. In response to the public's growing apprehension, Lukashenka had to boost pro-independence rhetoric and even went so far as to accuse his Eastern

[20] "Shutki v Storony" [No Jokes], *Belorusskaya Gazeta* (April 19, 2004).

neighbor of imperial ambitions. Lukashenka's pursued strategy was not a retreat to nationalism, but rather a boosting of the earlier version of Soviet Belarusian patriotism; it was somewhat reinforced with anti-Russian overtones, but it also evoked memories of the Soviet past encroachments and World War II. Encroachers on independence were identified primarily as Russia's oligarchs and remnants of its liberal establishment. Lukashenka also reinforced this ideological cocktail with regime patriotism by personalizing his independence rhetoric: in the public discourse on the survival of independence, he linked his own imposed political and economic model, as well as more generally his own survival in power.[21] It was a discretely sublime link, so that eventually, the campaign to support Lukashenka in the constitutional referendum that removed term limits did not even mention his name: instead, it was carried out under the slogan "For Belarus!"

The results of this extensive series of preemptive strikes became visible in 2004. In October, Lukashenka finally decided to carry out the referendum in conjunction with the parliamentary elections. No meaningful resistance was organized, in spite of the opinion polls, which had for several years shown that a majority of Belarusians would have voted against the proposition. Any attempts to organize a resistance were immediately blocked by the authorities,[22] and the referendum's passage highlighted the success of his preemptive activities.

According to the official CEC report, 79 percent of all voters supported allowing Lukashenka to run again for president. The official results were immediately attacked for their lack of credibility based on Gallup's extensive exit poll, which indicated that no more than 49 percent had supported the referendum.[23] There was plenty of evidence to support allegations of massive vote rigging,[24] but Belarusian society at large remained uninformed about these electoral abuses and alternative results. This lack of knowledge, along with fear of punishment, ensured that there was no large-scale resistance against the fraud. Street protests drew no more than 5,000 demonstrators on the day of the vote, and they were brutally dispersed. A postreferendum survey found

---

[21] In his most characteristic remark, he warned that if he was defeated in the upcoming presidential elections, "we will lose the country." Lukashenka's address to the Third All-Belarusian People's Assembly, 2 March 2006, *Sovetskaya Belorussiya* (March 3, 2006).

[22] The announcement of the referendum came on September 7, the day of mourning for victims of the Beslan massacre in Russia. A crowd of youngsters assembled in Minsk for a memorial rally had to watch Lukashenka's announcement instead. Only one man in the crowd publicly expressed disapproval: he was immediately arrested and sentenced to ten days in prison for petty hooliganism.

[23] Don Hill, "Belarus: Election Officials Say Voters Back Lukashenka," *Radio Free Europe/Radio Liberty* (October 18, 2004). Available at www.rferl.org/featuresarticle/2004/10/80d71056–54eb-42cd-9313–084f9aeceb17.html.

[24] Independent observers and opposition activists unearthed stuffed ballot boxes, premarked ballots distributed to voters, and vote-count protocols that had been signed before election day. On presigned protocols, see www.charter97.org/bel/news/2004/10/14/elections; on staffed ballot boxes, see www.oscepa.org/index.aspx?articleid=+367+367&newsid=255; on premarked ballot papers, see www.charter97.org/bel/news/2004/10/17/lebedka.

that forty-eight percent of respondents agreed that the referendum had been conducted in a free and fair manner, and only thirty-five percent disagreed.[25] Most important, the overall perception that Lukashenka could win any ballot, even a clean one, remained unchallenged.

Resisting the Orange Threat: The Tool Kit of Preemption Enhanced

The Orange revolution in Ukraine was a political landmark for the entire former Soviet Union, and, as mentioned above, galvanized the use and perfection of preemptive techniques by surviving authoritarians across the region. Conveniently for Lukashenka, it happened just after he carried out a constitutional referendum in October 2004 that removed term limits for the presidency (and technically provided for his infinite rule), and in advance of his planned March 2006 reelection campaign. Lukashenka's reaction to the Ukraine events proved that resistance to the democratic contagion had turned into the primary task for his entire regime – regardless of how likely a similar scenario in Belarus might be. The KGB was explicitly directed by Lukashenka to resist the export of democracy to Belarus. Anti-Orange propaganda intensified in the state media, which shared countless controlled reports, documentaries, propaganda broadcasts, and newspaper articles to explain the official position and opinion on the revolutions to the Belarus population.

Security forces began publishing special analytical reports and even manuals unmasking the efforts to organize regime change in Belarus, and these forces gave the officials advance instructions on how to combat the efforts of the opposition.[26] Through the use of new police tactics to disperse a few small demonstrations in early 2005, the Lukashenka regime made it clear that the country's security forces had been specifically trained to stop street protests immediately. Overall, it appeared that the regime was overreacting, perceiving the threat as much greater than it really was at the time. This possibly occurred in part because it fell hostage to its own propaganda: that is, it came to believe that colored revolutions were indeed externally manipulated events, rather than home-grown uprisings against acts of manipulation such as vote rigging.

In the run-up to the March 2006 presidential elections, the regime explicitly criminalized most of the opposition-related activities and established a direct legal basis for repression. Before this point, opposition organizations, civil society activists, newspapers, and journalists were simply harassed and arrested on bogus charges such as hooliganism, failure to comply with housing regulations, or corruption. The regime began to crack down heavily on activist activity, as

---

[25] Vitali Silitski, "They Knew Too Much: Leading Independent Thinktank Faces Attacks," *RFE/RL Belarus and Ukraine Report*, 6, No. 48 (December 29, 2004). Available at www.rferl .org/reports/pbureport/2004/12/48–291204.asp.

[26] A review of the most notorious such report, "Colored Revolutions on Post-Soviet Space: Scenarios for Belarus," can be read in Russian at http://www.belgazeta.by/20051212.49/010030141/.

the passage of Article 193–1 of the Criminal Code established punishment of up to a two-year prison term for participation in the activities of a deregistered NGO and up to three years for organizing such an NGO. Article 293 was amended so that teaching or other training of persons involved in organizing "mass upheaval" could also be punished by up to three years in jail. Additionally, anyone appealing to the international community in regard to "the external security of Belarus" could be punished with up to five years in prison. There was then a new article, "Defamation of the Republic of Belarus," which established a punishment of up to two years in prison for international organizations with data – deemed by the government to be deliberately falsified – on the political, economic, social, military, or international situation in Belarus.

Tactical preemption received a new focus: the main target of attack became not prospective presidential challengers but rather street organizers and grassroots activists who were capable of mobilizing the masses. Two of them, Mikalaj Statkievich, former chairman of the Belarusian Social Democratic Party, and Paval Seviarynec, leader of the unregistered Young Front movement, were both sentenced to two years of forced labor in May 2005 for organizing antireferendum protests. Another veteran politician, former member of Parliament (MP) and political prisoner Andrej Klimau, was also sentenced to two years of forced labor the same month; he was charged with staging unsanctioned rallies that had been advertised as the beginning of the democratic revolution in Belarus. Then, immediately after the amendments to the criminal code, the police arrested and charged several activists of the Young Front and Zubr movements – both known to be unregistered groups that united young, radical, and more revolution-minded opposition activists.

Beyond street activism, another target of repression was election observation. Thus, the regime would persecute any organization or institution that could or intended to systematically question the official election data. As such, the leaders of the largest election-monitoring group, Partnership, were rounded up in February 2006 on charges of terrorism and organizing an unregistered NGO. The Independent Institute for Socio-economic and Political Studies, the leading independent polling agency that questioned the official election and referenda data in the past, was closed down by court order in April 2005, and even conducting public opinion surveys without a license began to be considered a crime.

The regime, in addition to systematic legal and executive repression of the opposition, used a well-organized propaganda campaign: official propaganda was reinforced with new techniques and overtones. Much of it consisted of a traditional repertoire, but was specifically tailored to discredit and demonize the revolutionary aspirations of the opposition. It reached dramatic proportions when each of four official television channels (and a few Russian ones that were routinely overlapped with Belarusian broadcasts) repeatedly showed state-authorized documentaries and propaganda shows – even sometimes repeating and thus reinforcing the content several times a day. Some of that propaganda was typical for Lukashenka's media: for example, the work of director Jury Azaronak (now deputy head of the State TV and Radio Company), a man instrumental in the success of Lukashenka's first referendum in 1995.[27] His new cycles of propaganda, called Spiritual War and Conspirology, pictured the battle between Lukashenka and the opposition, and, by extension, the West, as one between the adherents of Christ and the Pharisees (i.e., Jews, Americans, and Europeans).[28] This type of propaganda, however, was apparently intended to consolidate the base of Lukashenka's traditional supporters.

More subtle productions targeted uncommitted citizens, working to scare them away from political alternatives and thus toward Lukashenka. These more subtle forms included a series of shows titled "Belarus: The View From Outside," in which prominent politicians, singers, artists, and sportsmen from abroad praised Lukashenka. There was also "Fifteen," a series of documentaries that emphasized day-to-day problems, social hardships, economic decay, civil wars, and so forth in every former Soviet republic, except for Belarus; the most horrific reports were produced on the Baltic countries, Ukraine and Georgia. Finally, the media attack targeted the groups where support for the regime was lowest: the younger and urbanized constituency. This audience was targeted with a different series of TV shows, concerts, and discos that were initially able to appear as apolitical entertainment; however, by the time of the elections, they had clearly turned into propaganda exercises, with pop singers from Belarus and all over the former USSR campaigning, once again, "For Belarus," and, now more specifically, "For the Daddy" (a popular nickname for Lukashenka). This style of message apparently was meant to clear the organizers of accusations of illegal campaigning, and there was one particularly interesting thing about this pop propaganda: it was organized and presented in the form of mass rallies of flag-waving crowds. Colors and messages aside, it was somewhat reminiscent of the political music shows that occurred during the Orange Revolution in Ukraine. However, the "show business" campaign in Belarus carried an antirevolutionary message instead.

During Lukashenka's reelection campaign, the official media perfected themselves in information dramaturgy and media spin by creating virtual conflicts and threats that justified the extremely repressive actions of the regime.[29] Because he had run for reelection only once before, and because parliamentary and local elections never presented voters with real choice or drama,

---

[27] His production "Hatred: Children of Lies" scared the viewers by alternating pictures of Nazi atrocities with pictures of opposition politicians and rallies, and definitely helped both to pass the questions on symbols and the Russian language and to create long-lasting hostility of the population to the BPF opposition.

[28] At this time, however, Azaronak's production caused some outrage among Orthodox believers, and the Belarusian Orthodox Church even withdrew his works from the church film festival in Minsk in April.

[29] Andrew Wilson, *Virtual Politics: Faking Democracy in the Post-Soviet World*, (New Haven, CT: Yale University Press, 2005).

the Lukashenka regime had little use for election-related information dramaturgy, except on rare occasions, before the 2006 campaign. But by this
time the regime felt it necessary to employ spin in full swing. One remarkable
technique was an advance warning to the society of the possible techniques
that could be applied by the opposition while campaigning. These warnings
creatively and efficiently attached information on the opposition's vile secret
agenda; the official newspapers, for example, would publish extensive excerpts
of classic books on democratization (including Samuel Huntington's *The Third
Wave*, especially his manuals on regime change, and Gene Sharp's *Techniques
for Non-violent Action*), or the newspapers would give particular interpreta-
tions to flash mobs and exit polls. The papers would advise the population
against using these sources, warning that peaceful techniques of regime change
and nonviolent actions were simply a cover-up. These peaceful protest activities were, the regime cautioned, secretly destructive and potentially bloody
efforts that the opposition was planning to execute in order to take over the
government and gain political power.[30] The purpose of these publications was
clear: to make the public dislike and fear the opposition. Another tool of information dramaturgy was preemptive revelations publicized by the state security
agencies and the official press. For example, arrests of Partnership activists, as
mentioned above, were accompanied by the "revelations" of the KGB, which
claimed to unmask a plot by election monitors attempting to overthrow the
government. Their plan, the KGB claimed, was to take place through organized
explosions in the center of Minsk on election day, and they stated that the opposition had planned to use the victims as a justification for violent actions against
the authorities. This particular attack was poorly executed, however, as KGB
head Sciapan Sukharenka ended up telling the audience overly exaggerated and
unbelievable stories: he insisted, for instance, that the opposition was planning
to poison running water in Minsk using – of all things – rotten rats.

Yet the attempts were not totally ineffective. Spin worked much better in
some cases, such as when the government dealt with the protesters filling the
central square in Minsk, who had occupied it for several days after the voting results were announced. The official media distributed bogus images of
prostitution rings, drug addicts, and even the spread of contagious diseases by
these allegedly disreputable oppositionists on the central square of Minsk. The
media images on the eve of a crackdown on the protest helped reduce the size
of the dissenting crowds. Additionally, the propaganda succeeded in helping
to secure overall approval for police actions immediately following it. Overall,
by associating violence and immorality with the opposition, the government
propaganda thus prepared public opinion for whatever measures the regime
would take against the opposition. The spin even continued after the crackdown had commenced: for example, after the brutal dispersal of the protests in
Minsk on March 25, 2006, the official media broadcast pictures of a reversed

---

[30] See, for example, "Tekhnologii destabilizacii" [Technologies of Demobilization], *Vo Slavu
Rodiny*, available at http://www.vsr.mil.by/index/nobrev.html.

scenario, with riot policemen and official TV crews beaten up by opposition supporters.[31]

This new round of preemptive attacks helped Lukashenka in his reelection, regardless of some recent speculation. On one hand, March 19, 2006 produced no surprise: the incumbent claimed victory with eighty-three percent of the vote, and it appeared that the society overall judged his message of stability positively. And he was fairly safe from the opposition, because even while managing to consolidate the prodemocracy electorate, they nevertheless failed to make a great impression on larger audiences. But the preemptive attacks were helpful when, less predictably, the official announcement provoked a wave of mass protests. This uprising started on election night in Minsk, when at least 20,000 persons assembled on the main square; they were defiantly retaliating against the KGB's illegitimate threats a few days before the vote to prosecute protesters on charges of terrorism – even pressing for death sentences.

This spontaneous outburst was partly caused by unrealistic official returns, but was also the result of the overall effort of the opposition during the election campaign. The opposition thus displayed its ability to establish credibility with the core anti-Lukashenka constituency. The efforts of two opposition candidates, the leader of the united opposition, Alyaksandr Milinkevich, and the former rector of the Belarusian State University, Alyaksandr Kazulin, were also consequential, and they both managed to campaign energetically in spite of restrictions and repression. The protest continued for several days with a tent camp set up on October Square, emulating the Orange Revolution in Ukraine in 2004.

The postelection protest must be regarded in the context of a highly repressive state that has a fine-tuned and well-trained security apparatus, and thus its size and persistence confirmed many important things. First, it showed that increasing political repression had inadvertently radicalized the democratic electorate in Belarus. It had done this especially to the core of opposition activists, who proved in the postelection to be ready to engage in seemingly hopeless and illogical protest actions. Second, it showed that civil society, when committed to democracy-building in spite of the serious consequences of criminalization, can spontaneously self-organize. This materialization of protest could occur even when the political leaders and street organizers were effectively wiped out by arrests – such as the arrests of dozens of opposition activists who were rounded up and sentenced to brief terms in jail days before the vote. Last, the protests revealed a final remarkable factor: the emergence of the Internet as an important alternative medium of information. During the peak political events – such as the beating of Kazulin by riot police, the election day, and the protests in the aftermath – the number of visits to the principal independent sites, in spite of the attempts to block them, was several times higher

---

[31] Dozens of opposition supporters were badly beaten on that day; three disappeared and were feared dead. The official television reported that only one protester, but eight riot policemen, were injured.

than usual. Likewise, spontaneous protest actions were mostly coordinated online. This upheaval also revealed how much the Internet had become a tool of campaigning for the traditional NGO sector, even if this was a consequence of essentially placing the sector's activity outside the legal realm. Although the regime can still block the Internet relatively easily, it cannot restrict access forever and for all; this reality was enough to create ample opportunities to inform and organize.

However, the Belarusian opposition did not even try to declare victory for its candidate. Due to complete elimination of opportunities to verify the election outcomes and the actual defeat in the elections, it merely argued for a fairer margin separating Lukashenka and his challengers. So, with no actual political breakthrough in sight, the opposition could not count on sustained public support. Moreover, the security forces remained totally loyal to Lukashenka and blocked off the square, arresting those trying to enter or leave. As a result, the protest quickly dwindled to just a few hundred activists and was ended early on March 24, when riot police destroyed the camp and arrested the protesters. The lack of initial or sustained levels of high defiance and activism also highlighted the gap that separated this democratic subculture in Belarus from the rest of society. The opposition was kept very small, due to a combination of fear imposed by the government on some parts of society and acceptance of the regime by others: the opposition's appeal and following appear to have thus been curtailed by these psychological facts, caused by the insurmountable restrictions put in place by the regime.

As a result of the limited opposition, the streets and squares of Minsk (in sharp contrast to Kiev in November–December 2004) witnessed indifference from passers-by, and there was also marked loathing of the protesters from the regime's supporters. But most importantly, the regime confirmed that it remained capable of efficiently rebuffing any challenge put forward by the opposition through the ease with which the protest was dispersed. This competent harshness sent a message to society that the personal price for disobedience had been increased. In response to escalating crackdowns, the political and social protests in Belarus took increasingly desperate forms by the end of 2006: there were a series of hunger strikes declared by harassed private businessmen, jailed opposition leaders, and parishioners of a Protestant church in Minsk whose community was delegalized by the government.

AUTHORITARIAN INTERNATIONAL

As mentioned above, cooperation between nondemocratic regimes is an important external dimension of preemptive authoritarianism. This importance is defined, first, by the increasingly internationalized character of the democratic movement and civil society that transcends national borders and restrictions. Second, democratic breakthroughs in close proximity usually create new opportunities for aspiring opposition movements in the remaining authoritarian states. This occurs, for example, in terms of informational and organizational resources provided by sympathetic elites in new democracies, opportunities for legal registration, publication, and training of activists abroad nearby. Third, and most importantly, smaller authoritarian regimes often need backing and cover-up from larger ones that possess more resources and influence in the international arena. It is from this vantage point that Russia in particular seems to play a role in the newly emerging authoritarian international, after its own recent retreat from democratic experiments at home.

It should be noted that the politics of Russia's former president Vladimir Putin are increasingly reminiscent of those that Lukashenka perfected and characterized by a similar logic of preemption. One difference, however, is that although Putin's initial ascension to the presidency occurred through dynastic succession rather than victory in a fair electoral contest, his popularity is still genuine and unmatchable for those who attempt to challenge him. Nevertheless, he chose to destroy the independent television channels that attempted to derail his rise to power in 1999. Similarly, he expelled regional governors from the upper house of parliament in 2000 and replaced them with appointed representatives in 2004 – even though most of those expelled fully supported his administration. And in 2005, he pushed through new electoral rules that make it nearly impossible for parties uncontrolled by the contemporary Kremlin to pass the threshold in order to enter parliament, even though Putin's brand of managed democracy had already succeeded in keeping them out of the State Duma in the 2003 elections.[32]

For Russia's elite, strengthening the authoritarian international in Europe and abroad nearby is clearly dictated by the perception that the advance of democracy would reduce the Russian sphere of influence in the region. The degree to which this perception dictates Russian foreign policy became visible with the failed attempt to promote Viktor Yanukovych's candidacy in the 2004 presidential elections in Ukraine. When the Orange Revolution was not prevented, the commitment of the Russian elites to fending off democratic elsewhere in the Commonwealth of Independent States (CIS) only grew. The most vivid and controversial example of Russia's new role in the CIS is perhaps the Kremlin's full backing of the Uzbek president Islam Karimov after the May 2005 massacre in Andijon, and the extradition of Uzbek opposition activists who sought asylum in Russia. Another example is the economic attacks against newly democratized states in the former USSR. These included the gas attack against Ukraine, Georgia, and the Baltic states in December 2005, as well as numerous bans on the export of products from Georgia and Moldova in 2006.

The economic attacks were presented by the Kremlin-controlled media as acts of punishment for colored revolutions and for the fact that the governments of these countries had attempted to leave Russia's orbit of power. In another development, the Russian parliament established in 2005, for the first time, its own funding program for civil society groups both in Russia and abroad, as well as officially private foundations cloned from Western democracy promotion

---

[32] See Chap. 10 of this volume, by Kathryn Stoner-Weiss for more on Putin's tactics.

institutions. These groups increasingly engage in founding media, recruiting politicians, and even establishing political parties abroad nearby.[33] As the most far-reaching integration project in the post-Soviet platform, the Russia–Belarus alliance logically became a cornerstone of this authoritarian international; this has developed even in spite of the fact that the relations between Russia and Lukashenka's regime are at times uneasy.

A prime example of the developing Russian authoritarian international presence is displayed in efforts at boosting the international legitimacy of the post-Soviet autocratic regime in Belarus. This has occurred even though Belarus is the only CIS autocracy located in Europe, and thus the most severely scrutinized and criticized by its observers. The team of CIS election observers, usually led by Russia's former national security head, Vladimir Rushailo, rubber stamps approving reports on any elections in CIS countries – except for Ukraine and Georgia. Moreover, Russia actively lobbies to undermine international election monitors that it cannot control – most notably the OSCE observers' missions. For the last two years, the Kremlin actively lobbied to downsize this dimension of the OSCE activities, threatening to block financing of the organization along the way. Recently, when it failed to block these international efforts, officials in Moscow began to engage in diplomatic counterattacks. Thus, after the OSCE issued a harsh statement of nonrecognition of the 19 March presidential election in Belarus, Russia's foreign minister Sergei Lavrov accused the observers of instigating mass disorder in Minsk.[34]

The second example of Russia's role in authoritarian international efforts is its extension of cultural preemption beyond its geographical borders. Much of the democracy-bashing in the former Soviet Union (with the help of the Russian language, Kremlin-controlled media have had a huge impact in forming public attitudes outside Russia's borders) occurs under the false pretense of combating international terrorism (IT). This message is still credible with audiences in the former Soviet Union, and IT is often not interpreted as a vehicle of anti-Western propaganda because Russia had joined the tactical alliance with the West in 2001 under this slogan. Although the abuse of antiterrorist rhetoric for the sake of covering up antidemocratic politics in Russia itself is well known, Russian security agencies began to help other regimes in establishing a link in the public consciousness between democracy and terrorism. Thus, almost a year before the Belarusian KGB declared false plans on behalf of the opposition (such as the above described explosions during the elections and poisoning the water supplies with rotten rats), Russia's FSB director Nikolai Patrushev "unmasked" an IT issue. In May 2005, Patrushev announced a plot

[33] See: Ivan Krastev, "Democracy's 'Doubles.'" *Journal of Democracy*, 17 No. 2 (2006), pp. 56–62; Karl Gershman and Michael Allen, "The Assault on Democracy Assistance." *Journal of Democracy*, 17, No. 2 (2006), pp. 36–51.

[34] "Russian Foreign Minister Accuses OSCE of Instigating Protests," *Belapan News Line* (March 24, 2006), available at http://elections.belapan.com/president2006/eng/show.php?show=49325.

by the West to use unspecified terrorist organizations to finance the Belarusian opposition in the run-up to presidential elections.[35] Similar allegations of terrorism have been issued against the opposition in other post-Soviet countries as well, and, more generally, Russian official media spare no effort in discrediting the newly democratized states of Eurasia – not only for their domestic Russian audience, but also for a broader CIS audience. Russian spin doctors provided cultural preemption assistance in various other internal propaganda campaigns, but notoriously failed during the Orange Revolution in Ukraine. It is not surprising, for example, that the services of the Kremlin's principal spin doctor, Gleb Pavlovsky, who currently hosts a propaganda program on one of Russia's nationwide TV networks, were offered to the official propaganda network in Belarus during the run-up to the 2006 elections.[36] During the March presidential election campaigns, the Russian media replicated the claims of official Belarusian TV networks: in the aftermath of the vote, they described the failed protest effort in Minsk as an action driven by a horde of extremists.[37]

A third way in which Russia involved itself internationally was in its tactical preemption assistance. The most notorious case in this respect was arresting and deporting Uzbek opposition activists from Russia after the Andijon events; however, a similar pattern – although with less grave consequences – began to emerge in Russian–Belarusian relations as well. Thus, in the run-up to March 2006 presidential elections, Russian printing houses located in Smolensk refused publication of the Belarusian independent press before the election, forcing some of the independent journalists to suspend publication altogether. Another interesting, but telling, fact is that the Russian embassy in Belarus made little effort to assist in the release of Russian citizens arrested in Minsk following the postelection protests.

A fourth and final example of Russian authoritarian international assistance is the "fraternal" economic support it provided to help allies survive the political storms. Thus, before the March 2006 presidential elections, Russia froze natural gas prices for Belarus at only a fraction of the price paid by Ukraine. This subsidy for Lukashenka's "economic miracle" helped him to maintain impressive rates of economic growth in general and wage hikes in particular. Lukashenka was then able to utilize this to make the claim of stability a main theme of his official election campaign. At the same time, such benevolence was meant to send a signal to the less compliant regimes – particularly those in Ukraine, Moldova, and Georgia.

---

[35] Information of the Belarus news agencies, available at http://www.pravo.by/showtext.asp?1115912591081.

[36] See brief transcript of the interview at http://www.afn.by/news/view.asp?newsid=71486. Official Belarus media welcomed and praised Pavlovsky's work. See, for example, http://www.sb.by/article.php?articleID=49872.

[37] Russia is currently the largest shareholder in Belarus. The Euronews Russian version coverage and great discrepancies between this and other language version were pointed to by several Internet blogs.

Moreover, the authoritarian international is not restricted to Russia and Belarus, but is expanding in the region – and even beyond. Anticontagion measures have been prominent since 2005 on the agendas of groups such as the CIS Collective Security Treaty Organization and the Shanghai Cooperation Organization. The latter group recently reaffirmed its opposition to "negative" developments, claiming that its "meddling" in the internal affairs of member states has been on behalf of human rights protection;[38] it has also adopted peculiar "antiterrorist" policies that in fact facilitate extradition of political opponents from one member of the alliance to another.[39] There are also signs of increased cooperation between like-minded regimes from inside and outside of the former Soviet Union on the watch against democracy. This is evident in an intensification of political and economic contacts of several former Soviet republics with Venezuela and Iran, as well as by the high-profile show of solidarity at the Non-Aligned Movement summit in Havana in August 2006.

CONCLUSION

The analysis in this chapter adds a sober note to the discussion of further prospects for democratization in postcommunist Eurasia. Lukashenka might be a champion and front-runner in preemption, but his example shows how far it can go and how profoundly it may affect society. Political change can indeed be blocked for a very long time. Moreover, other incumbents in the region are definitely catching up. Recent attacks on NGOs in Russia, mysterious killings of opposition leaders in Kazakhstan, and televised revelations of coup attempts just before the 2005 parliamentary elections in Azerbaijan are all examples of preemption being used extensively and even perfected around the region.

Likewise, preemptive authoritarianism seems to be well endowed not only with repressive capabilities and financial means, but also with intellectual resources. Autocrats can be and often are very intelligent and intuitive, and they possess the advantage of observation: examples and systematic studies of democratization present them with manuals of how to avoid democracy at home, at least for a substantial period of time. They are also not homebound any more, and demonstrate a remarkable capacity to organize internationally and establish some sort of self-defense and even group antidemocratic defense.

Last but not least, autocrats are capable of making preemption legitimate and even appreciated by domestic audiences. As of now, it is hard to predict when and where preemptive authoritarianism will eventually meet its demise – as the potentially insurmountable obstacles are still unknown. Given the generally disheartening tone of this paper, it may seen counterintuitive

---

[38] "Authoritarian Internationale Leads Anti-Democratic Backlash." *Democracy Digest*, 3, No. 1 (March 2006). Available at http://www.civnet.org/journals/democracy_digest_3_1.html.
[39] Available at http://ru.iras.ir/rendermodule.aspx?SelectedSingleViewItemID=1175&ModuleID=348&rendertype=print.

to suggest that surprisingly optimistic circumstances were revealed during the failed postelection protests in Belarus. Indeed, three points of optimism emerged from the experience: first, the radicalization of the opposition; second, the increasingly sophisticated underground democratic forces, capable of eschewing repression; and third, the limitations on the regime's ability to restrict access to information – especially through Internet technology. With luck and additional improvements, these may be considered essential factors that can potentially reverse and even defeat the forces of authoritarian preemption. On the international front, regime preemption may eventually stumble over decaying financial capabilities, and, by extension, political influence of the core petrostates that seem to be taking the lead in the authoritarian international. For the foreseeable future, however, rational expectations are discouraging: a slowdown, and even reversal, of the recent wave of democratization is likely.

A Horse of a Different Color

Revolution and Regression in Kyrgyzstan

Scott Radnitz

University of Washington

If Ukraine was destined to have a democratic breakthrough because of the dream of a "return to Europe," and Georgia, a Christian, historically Russo-phobe country, maintained the possibility of joining NATO and perhaps one day the European Union, then Kyrgyzstan, a small, mostly Muslim country in Central Asia surrounded by repressive authoritarian countries, had few external incentives for a democratic revolution.[1] Neither were the internal conditions especially propitious: Kyrgyzstan is a poor country with a weak civil society that, prior to 1991, had no history as an independent state. President Askar Akaev, once known as a liberalizer, in later years backtracked on his early reforms and pushed Kyrgyzstan in a more autocratic direction. Nevertheless, to the surprise of many, Akaev was overthrown in 2005 following fraudulent parliamentary elections, leading to only the second transfer of power in Central Asia since independence. Kyrgyzstan thus appeared to join the wave of popular uprisings that began in Eastern Europe, traveled east through former Soviet, but still ostensibly European, nations, and finally ended up in the heart of Asia.

How are we to make sense of this case, which, on one hand, lacked most of the structural prerequisites for democracy – a middle class, a high level of development, a tradition of nationalism, and some prior experience with democracy or independent statehood – but on the other hand showed some promising signs of pluralism?[2] It is a natural first step to ask whether the gamut of putative revolutionary preconditions applied to Kyrgyzstan, by analyzing

---

[1] Stephen E. Hanson, "The Uncertain Future of Russia's Weak State Authoritarianism." *East European Politics & Societies*, 21 (2007), pp. 67–81; Oleksandr Svyetlov, "Ukraine's 'Return to Europe': Path Dependence as a Source of Mutual Elite Misunderstanding." *Perspectives on European Politics and Society*, 8 (December 2007), pp. 528–43.

[2] Kyrgyzstan was a classic "competitive authoritarian" system. Such regimes usually allow opposition parties, some independent media and civil society, and a legislature that is at least somewhat independent, while carefully controlling political competition. See Steven Levitsky and Lucan Way, "The Rise of Competitive Authoritarianism." *Journal of Democracy*, 13 (April 2002), pp. 51–65.

the popularity of the incumbent, examining public opinion, and assessing the strength of opposition parties, civil society, and the media prior to elections. It is also reasonable to investigate the role played by external forces, in particular Western democratic assistance and the diffusion of ideas and repertoires from earlier "revolutionary" states.

Yet this will only get us so far. In order to make sense of the "Kyrgyz Spring," it is critical to look inside Kyrgyzstan's political system to understand how power was distributed, which actors were influential, and how mass mobilization was organized. The peculiarities of Kyrgyzstan's social and political structure vis-à-vis Georgia and Ukraine make the revolutionary template less applicable. The catalyst for the Tulip Revolution was an assortment of losing candidates for parliament, each of whom sought separately to rouse protests after the February 2005 elections. Once the leaders of these isolated protests coalesced, they brought their grievances to the capital and overthrew Akaev, but fragmented into disunity shortly thereafter. Most of the protagonists had not previously organized as a party, advocated no ideology, and did not initially intend to overthrow Akaev.

To call Kyrgyzstan's change of government a "revolution" is misleading at best.[3] It is also premature to label it a "democratic breakthrough" – a term applied to Serbia, Georgia, and Ukraine[4] – because most post-2005 developments have pushed the country in the opposite direction. In fact, the event would more appropriately be labeled a coup that led to the replacement by one set of elites by another – an occurrence that had important implications for Kyrgyzstan's political development since 2005.

As students of democratization recognize, the mode of transition goes a long way toward shaping political developments after regime change[5] – and Kyrgyzstan is no different. The improvised nature of mobilization, Akaev's unexpectedly abrupt downfall, and the country's underlying social and political forces, which these events reflected, bequeathed a poison pill to would-be democratic reformers in the post-Akaev era. Since the change in power, there has been little to divert the system from the course that Akaev had set it on, in terms of either the effectiveness of political institutions or people's everyday interaction with the state. Whereas Georgia has made significant reforms and reduced corruption and Ukraine has made intermittent progress toward consolidating its democracy, Kyrgyzstan under President Kurmanbek Bakiev

---

[3] A revolution is "an effort to transform the political institutions and the justifications for political authority in a society, accompanied by formal or informal mass mobilization and noninstitutionalized actions that undermine existing authorities." Jack A. Goldstone, "Toward a Fourth Generation of Revolutionary Theory." *Annual Review of Political Science*, 4 (2001), 139–87, esp. 142.

[4] Michael McFaul, "Transitions from Postcommunism." *Journal of Democracy*, 16 (July 2005), pp. 5–19.

[5] Geraldo L. Munck and Carol Skalnik Leff, "Modes of Transition and Democratization: South America and Eastern Europe in Comparative Perspective." *Comparative Politics*, 29 (April 1997), pp. 343–62.

has become less democratic without showing noticeable improvements in the quality of governance.[6]

The forces that developed under Akaev's fifteen-year rule and underlay the Tulip Revolution – pervasive corruption, independent business interests, and intense localism – continue to remain strong. This fact helps explain why the years following the change in power have been notable more for continuity than for change, with old patterns reproducing themselves and hindering efforts at real reform on major issues such as strengthening the state and improving the economy. Sadly, the March events appear to have been little more than a bump in the road that shook the political system only enough for a new set of elites to gain power, rather than pushing it in a new direction.

This chapter analyzes the Tulip Revolution and its aftermath in an attempt to draw lessons about political change in Kyrgyzstan and postcommunist countries in general. Section I provides an overview of the political situation on the eve of the 2005 elections and then traces the process by which mass mobilization developed. It details how a number of relatively obscure rural elites protested against their election losses and then confederated to create a national mobilization that challenged and then overthrew the regime. Section II looks at the political trajectory of Kyrgyzstan since the "revolution," focusing on the difficulties encountered by the new leadership in creating a stable political order, building state capacity, reducing corruption, and facilitating economic growth. Section III links the pre- and postrevolutionary eras by examining the persistence of localism and clientelism, which are deeply rooted in society and have underlain many of the recent political struggles. Section IV assesses the role of external factors, in particular Western aid and diffusion processes, in facilitating Kyrgyzstan's change of government. Finally, the Conclusion suggests what the forces at play in post-Akaev Kyrgyzstan augur for the country's future.

I. UNEXPECTED UPHEAVAL

Reform and Backsliding

Askar Akaev was once the darling of the West. Alone among the leaders of Central Asia's presidents, Akaev was not the first secretary of his republic's Communist Party or even a professional bureaucrat. A renowned physicist who became the head of the Kyrgyz branch of the Academy of Sciences, Akaev instead seemed a paragon of enlightened rule. Immediately upon becoming president, he set about weakening the power of the presidency in favor of parliament, empowered local elites at the expense of the center, and loosened

---

[6] This is not to imply that either of these transitions has been smooth or without contention. See Salome Asatiani, "Colored Revolutions: High Hopes and Broken Promises," *Radio Free Europe/Radio Liberty (RFE/RL)* (November 21, 2007), available at http://www.eurasianet. org/departments/insight/articles/pp112307.shtml. June 21, 2009.

restrictions on association and participation. He adopted an IMF stabilization program and pushed through laws breaking up collective farms and privatizing enterprises. Like other rapid reforms, these policies led to dramatic declines in personal income and social services that severely debilitated an already impoverished citizenry, but this did not prevent Kyrgyzstan from earning accolades in the international community. Kyrgyzstan became one of the first newly independent states to join the World Trade Organization and was dubbed, perhaps hyperbolically, Central Asia's "island of democracy."[7]

Kyrgyzstan's experiment with democracy ended prematurely when Akaev tried to regain some of the power that he had given away. After clashing with Communists in parliament in 1994, he worked to undermine the legislature and used a referendum to change the constitution to increase presidential power. He cracked down on the opposition and the media, closing down critical newspapers and arresting journalists. Akaev's family and close associates also came to own an increasing share of the country's assets.[8] The corruption that now pervaded most state institutions hampered the business climate and prevented Kyrgyzstan from paying down a public debt larger than the country's gross domestic product.[9]

As Akaev continued to take measures entrenching his power, he alienated some of his closest allies, who slowly eroded his ruling coalition. His former vice president, Felix Kulov, defected and threatened to run for president in 2000. He was subsequently arrested and imprisoned. Danyar Usenov, a parliamentarian and wealthy businessman, also declared his intention to run against Akaev, and likewise found himself the target of arbitrary prosecution. The 2000 elections saw the formation of a mostly Akaev-friendly parliament, but only after the substantial use of state resources to assist favored candidates. Even after 2000, Akaev's increasingly autocratic style of rule continued to alienate those close to him, leading to several more prominent defections.[10]

As later became clear, Akaev failed to recognize that his early reforms had led to broad pluralism in society, which could be managed through skillful politicking, but was also irreversible. Even at the height of his power, he was never able to rule unopposed. Early economic reforms yielded unprecedented opportunities for well-connected and enterprising actors to acquire privatized

---

[7] John Anderson, "Kyrgyzstan: Central Asia's Island of Democracy?" (Amsterdam: Harwood, 1999).

[8] After Akaev's ouster, authorities alleged that Akaev's family had at least partial control over Kyrgyzstan's largest mobile phone operator, a supermarket chain, a cement factory, a jet fuel supplier, and an ad agency, in addition to resort hotels, restaurants, casinos, gas stations, and liquor stores. Daniel Kimmage, "Kyrgyzstan: How Wealthy Is the Ousted Kyrgyz Leader's Family?" *RFE/RL* (April 18, 2005), available at http://www.rferl.org/content/article/1058559.html. June 21, 2009.

[9] Richard Pomfret, *The Central Asian Economies since Independence*, p. 13 (Princeton, NJ: Princeton University Press, 2006).

[10] See *Political Transition in Kyrgyzstan: Problems and Prospects* (Osh/Brussels: International Crisis Group (ICG), August 11, 2004).

enterprises or open businesses and accumulate wealth. This process led to a dispersal of resources to actors autonomous from the state and residing in diverse regions of the country. Many new businessmen parlayed their wealth into political influence by running for parliament. Holding seats in parliament allowed wealthy elites to protect their assets and advance their personal interests while enjoying immunity from prosecution. Parliament also became a forum for members to seek out common interests with each other and, when advantageous, to form tactical coalitions to block Akaev's initiatives. Some of the relationships that developed in parliament would later turn out to be consequential as the basis for future opposition alliances.

Kyrgyzstan from the early independence period saw the appearance of political parties, which, on paper, advocated various platforms such as nationalism and social democracy, but did not perform the functions that they do in consolidated democracies. Instead, parties were personalistic in nature, acting as vehicles to promote the political fortunes of the founders. They were usually confined to the regions associated with the founding politicians, with little organizational capacity and few links with the general population.[11] Most members of parliament, who were self-financing, ran as independents rather than as members of a party. This natural fragmentation of the political system worked against the formation of united, ideologically based parties, making it easy for Akaev to keep the opposition divided and weak.

From the early 1990s, Kyrgyzstan also saw the emergence and proliferation of nongovernmental organizations (NGOs), which were devoted to advocating a host of social, economic, and political issues. Yet although the statistics on registered NGOs were impressive on paper,[12] their overall impact on society was minimal. Their effectiveness was limited by dependence on the state and the demands of foreign donor organizations, but more importantly, they failed to establish links with their putative clientele.[13] Kyrgyzstan is a poor and predominantly rural society, and citizens' deficits of time, mobility, and access to information presented high barriers to NGOs, reaching out and making contact with the majority of citizens.

By the time of the 2005 elections, Akaev had a tenuous grip on the political system, but few expected that he would be overthrown. Although he was increasingly unpopular, he still had considerable leverage to stack election commissions and offer incentives to wavering candidates to support the presidential party, *Alga*, which he created solely for the occasion. Akaev had pledged to leave office in October 2005, and it appeared that he could at least hang on six

---

[11] Gregory Koldys, "Constraining Democratic Development: Institutions and Party System Formation in Kyrgyzstan," *Demokratizatsiya*, 5 (Summer 1997), pp. 351–75.

[12] According to official statistics, as of 2002 Kyrgyzstan had 1,001 NGOs, compared with 669 in Kazakhstan and 595 in Tajikistan, its next closest competitors. Lola Abdusalyamova, "NGOs in Central Asia." *Alliance*, 7 (March 2002), available at http://www.globalpolicy. org/ngos/role/globalact/state/2002/0302asia.htm. June 21, 2009.

[13] Kelly M. McMann, "The Civic Realm in Kyrgyzstan," In Pauline Jones Luong, *The Transformation of Central Asia*, p. 240 (Ithaca: Cornell University Press, 2004).

more months. Yet the rapidly approaching end of his tenure provided incentives for political aspirants to sort themselves out. Because the election could reveal the likely successor, aspiring politicians recognized the need to form alliances that could effectively compete for power.[14]

Although Kyrgyzstan may have lacked an organized or united opposition, it did witness a flurry of coalition-building in the months leading up to the parliamentary elections of early 2005. The single most important group to emerge was the People's Movement of Kyrgyzstan (PMK), an alliance of nine small parties that formed in September 2004 and elected Kurmanbek Bakiev – a former prime minister who had gone into opposition to the president – as its leader. In December, Roza Otunbaeva, a former member of the *nomenklatura* and foreign minister, created a new party, Ata-Jurt (fatherland), and immediately allied with the PMK. This move was significant because it united two influential opposition figures and transcended the main north–south rift in the country, with Otunbaeva's support coming from Osh and Bishkek and Bakiev's from Jalalabad. They attempted without success to ally with Kyrgyzstan's most popular politician at the time, Felix Kulov. The PMK had little in the way of a common platform – only to conduct fair elections and secure Akaev's resignation by October 2005 – and was unable to unite around a single charismatic figure (who would have been Kulov). Yet the PMK brought together several influential politicians who shared the goal of weakening Akaev.

All Roads Lead to Bishkek

Although the opposition appeared to fare badly in the spring 2005 parliamentary elections, it did not accept the results silently. Of the 32 races in which one candidate won a majority in the first round (out of 75 contests), only two went to opposition candidates, whereas the majority went to progovernment candidates.[15] Yet some candidates who had been disqualified due to technicalities or who had performed below expectations were vocally unhappy. The week after first-round voting on February 27 saw people across the country gather in protest on behalf of individual candidates. The protests were initially manifestations of local grievances, rather than part of a wider opposition strategy. Later, however, they increased in size and scope and became a vehicle for a hastily organized opposition to challenge the regime.

The first large-scale demonstration began building in a village in the southern province of Jalalabad shortly after first-round election results were announced. Several candidates, having lost or underperformed, gathered hundreds of

---

[14] Hale has argued that a president's "lame duck" status acts as an impetus for elites to coalesce around a successor. Henry Hale, "Regime Cycles: Democracy, Autocracy, and Revolution in Post-Soviet Eurasia." *World Politics*, 58 (October 2005), pp. 133–65.

[15] Michael A. Weinstein, "Kyrgyzstan's Chronic Complications," Eurasianet.org (March 18, 2005) available at http://www.eurasianet.org/departments/insight/articles/pp031805.shtml. June 21, 2009.

supporters – mostly staffers, relatives, and friends – to demonstrate in front of the local election commission headquarters and allege fraud. When their complaints fell on deaf ears, the protesters moved to Jalalabad city's central square, where they demanded to speak to the governor. They were joined there by several hundred other people pressing similar grievances on behalf of losing Jalalabad-area candidates. One of these was Jusupbek Bakiev, the younger brother of the head of the PMK. Most of the crowd consisted of jobless or retired older men from outlying villages, with smaller numbers of older women and unemployed middle-aged men. Though some city residents and students passed by or observed, few took part.

On March 4, the protestors managed to seize the regional-administration headquarters, where the governor and his staff ordinarily worked. (Most had already left the building.) For the next two weeks, protestors would occupy and guard the building, drawing media attention and support from previously unassociated oppositionists from around the region. By March 7, as many as 2,000 protestors had come to occupy the square in downtown Jalalabad, and an informal coordinating committee of protest leaders emerged to guide them. The protestors did not represent a cross section of villages in the region, but came overwhelmingly from areas where losing candidates were challenging the results.

A week after it was created, Jalalabad's committee was absorbed into a nationwide mobilization being improvised from Bishkek under PMK leadership, which began demanding not only new elections but also Akaev's resignation. As the first town to have its government headquarters occupied, Jalalabad found itself at the leading edge of an incipient national movement, with similar demonstrations breaking out in other regional capitals. As Akaev appeared indecisive and increasingly beleaguered, politicians who had earlier disapproved of street protests or feared challenging the government now jumped onto the bandwagon, swelling the opposition's ranks. On March 20, a worried Akaev made the fateful decision to reassert control: he ordered soldiers to clear Jalalabad's administrative building of occupiers and arrest the leaders. After a scuffle that caused several injuries, the news worked its way around the region by mobile phone, radio, and taxicab, replete with wild rumors (e.g., that drunken soldiers had thrown unarmed people from third-story windows). Outraged – or dragged out by incensed neighbors – many previously passive people began converging on Jalalabad. After overrunning a barricade of soldiers, the mob ran amok, burned down the district Interior Ministry, reoccupied the administration building, seized the airport, and installed a new government. Leaders in Jalalabad then began sending out emissaries to "export the revolution" to other towns.

Whereas the Rose and Orange Revolutions took place almost entirely in the capitals of Georgia and Ukraine, Kyrgyzstan's far northern capital city of Bishkek became the focus of mobilization only after the country's leading second-tier cities had fallen to the opposition. The southern town of Osh, the second largest city, saw smaller and less dramatic protests than Jalalabad did, yet proved a more important stepping stone to the capital. In Osh, as elsewhere, mobilization began as the complaints of losing candidates, but gathered steam over time. As in Jalalabad, protests were initially organized and supervised by a committee of the rural intelligentsia – teachers, lawyers, and engineers – who had been working for the candidates. Yet once it became clear that Osh was one of many sources of resistance in a larger struggle, leadership passed to more experienced oppositionists in Bishkek, who provoked confrontation with the government. Following Jalalabad, the crowd occupied Osh's government headquarters on March 18. Two days later, special forces troops raided the building and dislodged its occupants. On March 21, having increased its numbers, the opposition bloodlessly took back control of Osh.

Only after the Akaev government's fate was sealed in the south did the PMK and other oppositionists mount protests in Bishkek. There, a temporary alliance had emerged consisting of PMK leaders and unaffiliated politicians, mobilization leaders from other regions, local businessmen, and NGO activists. The first demonstration incorporating these diverse elements took place when losing candidates and several hundred of their supporters assembled on March 23. After police dispersed the crowd, the organizers regrouped and planned a massive march for the following day, in which the opposition would divide in two and converge on the government headquarters in the center of Bishkek for a massive demonstration.

The clash that ended up toppling the government the next day was unexpected, but probably hastened what was already inevitable. The opposition controlled half the country and had managed to gather more than 10,000 protestors in the capital. Akaev had lost the confidence of most of Kyrgyzstan's citizens and appeared irresolute, whereas the security forces had little interest in harming their fellow citizens and subjecting themselves to future prosecution to protect a lame duck president. The OSCE had urged all parties to act reasonably and was trying to arrange negotiations, whereas Russia criticized the opposition but was unwilling to intervene physically.[16] Akaev was on his own, with little political capital and uncertain ability (and desire) to order the use of force.

Perhaps fortunately for Akaev, the swift denouement spared him the agonizing decision. When the first group of demonstrators arrived at the square, they were met by a cordon of police and soldiers. After a scuffle, the protesters broke through and surged toward the presidential administrative building (locally referred to as the White House), whereupon several hundred men in civilian clothes and white hats, carrying clubs and shields – Akaev's last line of defense – appeared on the scene and began pushing the crowd back. After more clashes that left several people on both sides injured, protesters climbed over the gates of the complex and flooded into the building, sealing the fate of the government.

---

[16] Gulnoza Saidazimova, "Police Quash Bishkek Protest, Hint at Tougher Measures," *RFE/RL* (March 23, 2005); Maral Madi, "A Tulip Revolution Develops in Kyrgyzstan," *Central Asia/Caucasus Analyst* (March 23, 2005).

Akaev, who had earlier evacuated, fled the country for Russia, submitting his official resignation ten days later and clearing the way for Bakiev, as the head of the PMK, to become interim president. The clash had ended abruptly, but a new struggle was about to begin.

II. AFTER AKAEV

A Short Honeymoon

Kyrgyzstan's revolutionary euphoria was fated not to last long, as the new government was immediately faced with a number of serious challenges, culminating in a new semiauthoritarian regime. During his brief interim presidency, Bakiev gave the impression of being a committed and responsible leader. He stabilized the country and pledged to combat corruption and improve the investment climate, winning a decisive victory in a presidential election deemed free and fair by international observers. After that time, however, he alienated reformist members of the government, secured government posts for his relatives and close supporters, and passed a constitutional referendum that allowed him to exercise concentrated power though a ruling party along the lines of Russian president Vladimir Putin's creation of the dominant United Russia Party.

Following the sudden implosion of authority on March 24, 2005, Kyrgyzstan's new leadership quickly came to grips with the new situation and began to deal with the immediate problems of uncertainty and instability through pragmatic politics and tactical collaboration. Kulov, who had been released from prison moments after the government's collapse, proved instrumental in restoring order by instructing the police to patrol the streets and protect businesses. Bakiev, who was named acting president by a hastily convened session of the outgoing parliament's lower house, chose a cabinet and agreed to schedule new elections for July. In the meantime, the interim government coaxed Akaev to send his formal resignation from Moscow to ensure a constitutional transition, and took up the question of whether the parliament chosen in the dubious February–March 2005 elections should be allowed to serve.

To have any hope of governing, the new leadership had to play a precarious game of balancing regional interests.[17] Bakiev and Kulov, at the time the country's two most popular politicians, agreed not to compete against each other in the July 2005 presidential election. Instead, they crafted a deal under which the former would run for the presidency whereas the latter agreed to accept the post of prime minister. With Kulov's support coming primarily from the north and Bakiev's from the south, the certainty of their combined victory averted a contest that would likely have exacerbated regional tensions.

---

[17] Kyrgyz politics since the Soviet period has revolved around a north–south division of the country. See Pauline Jones Luong, *Institutional Change and Political Continuity in Post-Soviet Central Asia*, Chap. 3 (New York: Cambridge University Press, 2002), pp. 51–101.

Initially, Bakiev's pragmatic style of leadership averted some possible crises. For example, after Akaev had fled, a dangerous standoff persisted for several days while both the incoming and outgoing legislatures met. After OSCE mediation, Bakiev decided to recognize the dubiously elected and predominantly pro-Akaev parliament in exchange for the new parliament's formal recognition of his interim presidency. This decision, in spite of calls from radical protestors and NGO leaders to hold new elections, probably prevented greater instability. Bakiev then prudently selected a cabinet that reflected both a balance of regional representation and a mix of Akaev holdovers and new "revolutionaries."

The government's honeymoon ended abruptly in July 2005 when the new parliament began to oppose Bakiev after his presidential victory. For example, it rejected several popular cabinet appointments, including Otunbaeva. It also favored changing the constitution to increase its own power vis-à-vis the president. In April, a constitutional assembly consisting of parliamentarians, NGO activists, and members of the new government had been created to propose a new draft constitution. Parliament, as expected, endorsed a draft that would weaken presidential (that is to say, Bakiev's) power, but the president, contrary to his preelection pledge, resisted these changes.

Over the next several months, Bakiev demonstrated his prowess as a shrewd politician by outmaneuvering parliament and appealing to the public to win tactical victories. After first equivocating, Bakiev publicly accepted proposed constitutional changes in response to street protests, but then reneged and persuaded a majority in parliament to pass amendments restoring his powers. When the Constitutional Court annulled both versions for procedural reasons, Bakiev introduced another constitution and overwhelmingly won a popular referendum on it in October 2007. The new constitution introduced a system in which parliament would be elected by proportional representation (PR) and the winning party would nominate a prime minister, as the opposition desired, while also increasing the president's powers of appointment, oversight, and dismissal.

The new constitution appeared to satisfy both sides, but the design of the system ended up heavily favoring parties with a strong organizational apparatus, at the expense of smaller and weaker parties.[18] Taking advantage of his institutional leverage, Bakiev immediately dissolved parliament and called snap elections for December 2007. He set about creating a new party, Ak Zhol ("bright path"), which would promote his policies and enjoy the benefit of state resources for the campaign. Unsurprisingly, the party won overwhelmingly, taking 71 of 90 seats in parliament, effectively concentrating the power of all three branches of government in Bakiev's hands.[19] Following his party's

---

[18] In particular, it required that a party win at least 5 percent of the vote nationwide and 0.5 percent of registered voters nationwide (13,500 votes) in each of Kyrgyzstan's seven provinces and two largest cities.

[19] The judiciary is highly politicized and mostly subservient to the executive. See *Country Report: Kyrgyzstan 2007*. Available at www.freedomhouse.org. June 21, 2009.

victory, with parliamentary resistance finally neutralized, Bakiev laid out several new initiatives to reform the economy and improve growth.[20]

From the beginning of Bakiev's tenure, a "counterrevolutionary" opposition coalesced both inside and outside of parliament. Consisting predominantly of parliamentary deputies, the new alliance both worked to challenge Bakiev's legislative initiatives in parliament and acted outside official channels, employing the newly fashionable tactic of organizing street protests to signal its displeasure. Its most prominent figures were Omurbek Tekebaev, a longtime rival of Bakiev who also hailed from Jalalabad province; several northern businessmen who had not previously been prominent in politics, such as Temir Sariev and Kubatbek Baibolov; and members of the government alienated by Bakiev's domineering style of rule, including the rabidly anti-Akaev populist Azimbek Beknazarov.[21] In December 2006, Felix Kulov, half of the tandem that had ensured Kyrgyzstan's smooth transition, broke with Bakiev and joined the opposition. He later created his own movement and led street protests demanding Bakiev's resignation for over a week, but without success. Public demonstrations became the favored tactic for pressuring the government when institutional channels were blocked, but declined in effectiveness over time. Media crackdowns limited the opportunities for anyone other than the president to get his or her message out.[22]

State Weakness

Although Bakiev was successful at consolidating power, he was not able to strengthen state capacity, which was already weak under Akaev. The weakness of the state was both a cause and an effect of the Tulip Revolution. The sharp decline in public services and decay of infrastructure that characterized post-Soviet Kyrgyzstan had contributed to people's disillusionment at Akaev's rule. The police are notorious for soliciting bribes from the populace, and, given their low salaries, it is not surprising that they stood aside to let demonstrators storm the government headquarters in several cities. The power vacuum that occurred after the government's collapse in Jalalabad and Osh was filled by organized criminal groups and young thugs. These vigilante groups managed

---

[20] Irina Ermakova, "Kyrgyzstan: Kurmanbek Bakiev Addressed the Government and Parliament," www.fergana.ru (January 10, 2008), available at http://enews.ferghana.ru/article.

[21] Beknazarov created a "revolutionary committee" in early 2008 to oppose Bakiev after the latter won a parliamentary majority. The first two points of the committee's manifesto chastise Bakiev for rewarding his family with plum state posts, as his predecessor had done, and demand that the government return to the state the wealth "stolen" by Akaev. "Revolution Committee of Azimbek Beknazarov Reminds President about His Promises," akipress.com (January 24, 2008), available at http://www.akipress.com/_en_arc.php?find=ratify. June 21, 2009.

[22] Tyntchtykbek Tchoroev, "Kyrgyz Audiences Demand End to Radio Silence," *RFE/RL* (December 15, 2008), available at http://www.rferl.org/content/Kyrgyz_Audiences_Demand_End_To_Radio_Silence/1360047.html. June 21, 2009.

to restore order, but at the expense of official law enforcement, which had momentarily lost its monopoly on violence.[23]

Property changed hands with unusual frequency in the year following the change in government, as criminal groups took advantage of weak law enforcement to gain control of resources. Most of these grabs took place peacefully, as when a claimant enjoyed the protection of local bosses, newly installed officials, or even Bakiev himself. Some claims were contested and involved intimidation by hired thugs or ordinary citizens who were mobilized by local elites from their villages. In some cases, struggles over property took place between criminal groups and became violent. In the first five months after Akaev's ouster, three parliamentary deputies, each rumored to have links to organized crime, were assassinated. Most notably, Bayaman Erkinbaev, the owner of much of Kara-su Bazaar – the largest in Central Asia – was killed in September 2005. In May 2006, Rysbek Akmatbaev, the head of a major criminal network in Issyk Kul, became the fourth criminal/businessman to be assassinated. Following both murders – still unsolved – struggles ensued as rival groups sought to gain control of the property and networks of business dealings of the deceased.[24]

For some time, low-level violence of this sort was frequent and disrupted people's daily routines, but it eventually settled down after the contenders reached informal understandings on the division of spoils. Yet the state was not able to reassert control. One analyst recently estimated that there were 22 criminal groups operating in Kyrgyzstan.[25] The police remain underpaid and unreformed. It is widely suspected that law enforcement officials are complicit in drug trafficking, and customs officials and tax inspectors regularly take part in the illicit economy.[26] The low level of professionalism in the bureaucracy is compounded by the fact that the government awards state jobs as an outlet to keep young men employed but is not able to pay them a living wage.

As people's attention was consumed by the political machinations in Bishkek and the violent struggle for property on the streets, few noticed the less dramatic but nonetheless consequential political struggles going on in localities throughout the country. Following the collapse of central authority, the victorious forces in the regions installed themselves as the new provincial and

---

[23] See "The Unsung Role of Kung Fu in the Kyrgyz Revolution." Agence France-Presse (March 28, 2005), available at http://news.yahoo.com/news?tmpl=story&u,=/afp/20050328/ lf_afp/ kyrgyzstan politics_050328194347. June 21, 2009.

[24] On the changing ownership of bazaars after the change of power, see Regine A. Spector, "Securing Property in Contemporary Kyrgyzstan." *Post-Soviet Affairs*, 24, No. 2 (2008), pp. 149–76. On the complicity of state officials with smuggling networks in the Bakiev era, see Alexander Kupatadze, "Smuggling and Organized Crime in Kyrgyzstan." Unpublished manuscript. American University of Central Asia, 2007.

[25] Erica Marat, "Criminal State at Play: An Examination of State–Crime Relations in Post-Soviet Union Kyrgyzstan and Tajikistan." *Jane's Intelligence Review* (March 1, 2007).

[26] Alexander Kupatadze, "Political–Criminal–Business Nexus in Georgia and Kyrgyzstan." Unpublished manuscript. American University of Central Asia, 2007.

district-level administration. Local elites moved to secure control of city and district governments before power could be restored at the national level and projected to the regions. Some of these pretenders came from criminal and mafia circles. Others were local elites who entered into alliances of convenience with criminal groups, agreeing to defend their interests in exchange for protection or a share of profits. Bakiev initially recognized newly installed local officials out of necessity, but managed to replace several governors with loyal ones after restoring authority in Bishkek. In some cases the dismissed official, having established a political base, would mobilize supporters to protest his removal in order to increase his bargaining leverage in the future – for example, to receive a better future posting.[27]

Another struggle unleashed by the fall of Akaev revolved around land. Mountainous Kyrgyzstan has relatively little arable land and a work force dominated by farmers. Although a 1999 law nominally entitles every Kyrgyz citizen to a personal plot for farming, land scarcity has been a major contributor to poverty, especially in the south. The land problem was brought into the open when, shortly after Akaev's overthrow, several thousand squatters took advantage of the power vacuum to move onto the undeveloped terrain – much of it owned by wealthy city dwellers – that lies around Bishkek. Authorities used a combination of coaxing and coercion in their efforts to remove the squatters, who in turn organized, demonstrated, and demanded that officials meet with them to address their complaints.[28] The stalemate revealed a weak, temporizing government that was painfully aware that either side of the dispute could mobilize enough supporters to make any decision hard to enforce. It left the issue unresolved, and an unknown number of squatters continued to occupy land on the outskirts of Bishkek.

As time passed and the postrevolutionary situation stabilized, ordinary people still remained concerned about the state's ability to maintain order. In a November 2007 survey of Kyrgyzstan by the International Republican Institute (IRI) and the Gallup Organization, when asked what they feared most, a majority referred to disorder/instability, followed by the troubled state of education, economic crisis, and poverty. Respondents also betrayed some fatigue over the unsettled nature of the political system, appearing more likely to give Bakiev the benefit of the doubt than they would have previously: Asked whether it was healthy for Kyrgyzstan to have an "active opposition," sixty percent answered in the affirmative, as against seventy-nine percent in April 2005.[29] However,

---

[27] "Kyrgyz Governor's Dismissal Sparks Angry Protests," *RFE/RL* (January 23, 2006), available at http://www.rferl.org/content/article/1064984.html. June 21, 2009.

[28] "D. Usenov: Ne Odin Kvartel'nii Mitr Zemli v Gorode Vydavat'sya ne Budet, Vydannie Ranyee v Chastnuyu Sobstvennost' Zemli Pereraspredelyat'sya ne Budet," [D. Usenov: Not One Square Meter of Land in the City Will Be Given Out, and No Previously Awarded Land Will Be Redistributed], www.akipress.org (October 28, 2005).

[29] International Republican Institute, "Kyrgyzstan National Poll," International Republican Institute (November 1–13, 2007), available at http://www.iri.org/eurasia/kyrgyzstan.asp. June 21, 2009.

on questions of what the government's highest priorities should be, bread-and-butter issues such as unemployment topped the list.

Eliminating or Entrenching Corruption?

Of all the grievances that contributed to disaffection with Akaev, the most salient was high-level corruption. A small number of officials in the Akaev regime controlled an inordinate amount of resources and showed no sign of relinquishing their control even as the opposition intensified. Akaev, his son, and his wife's family were the most direct beneficiaries of official corruption – one economist estimated the Akaev family's net worth at $500 million–$1 billion[30] – but other regime loyalists also benefited from the protection (*krysha*) that Akaev provided.[31]

When Bakiev took over, he pledged to make the fight against corruption a priority. Initially, he took several bold steps in this direction. He appointed Danyar Usenov to investigate businesses reputedly acquired illicitly by Akaev's family, and retained a Viennese law firm to investigate leads outside Kyrgyzstan. Bakiev also appointed Azimbek Beknazarov, who had a reputation for honesty and independence, as prosecutor general to pursue those suspected of abusing their powers under the old head of state. Yet the anticorruption campaign had pragmatic limits. Measures such as purging Akaev-era cadres from the government or holding public trials would have risked provoking the accused to resort to extralegal means to protect their interests. Thus, after sensing resistance from those still in the government, Bakiev dismissed Beknazarov for pursuing his targets too enthusiastically, braving the inevitable protests from the fired official's home region. After Usenov's commission had identified 178 companies with reputed ties to Akaev,[32] parliament promptly rejected his appointment as first deputy prime minister. Investigations into Akaev-era corruption subsequently stalled.

Additional barriers to battling corruption persist thanks to the shady Akaev-era histories of current government officials, including Bakiev himself, in a society where blood ties and cronyism remain strong. Bakiev is reputed to be one of Kyrgyzstan's hundred richest people.[33] He has appointed members of his family to potentially lucrative government posts[34] and is reputed to have

---

[30] Aram Roston, "A Crooked Alliance in the War on Terror?" NBC News (October 30, 2006), available at http://www.msnbc.msn.com/id/15448018 June 21, 2009.

[31] See *Political Transition in Kyrgyzstan*.

[32] Daniel Kimmage, "Kyrgyzstan: Follow the Money – The Akaev Investigation," *RFE/RL* (May 5, 2005), available at http://www.eurasianet.org/departments/business/articles/pp050505.shtml. June 21, 2009.

[33] Akyl Stamov, "Fergana: 100 Samykh Bogatykh Lyudei Kyrgyzstana 2004 Goda," [Fergana: The 100 Richest People in Kyrgyzstan). Available at www.akipress.org. June 21, 2009.

[34] Gulnoza Saidazimova, "Three Years on, Kyrgyz President Taken to Task for Rampant Nepotism," *RFE/RL* (July 10, 2008), available at http://www.rferl.org/content/Three_Years_On_Kyrgyz_President_Taken_To_Task_For_Nepotism_/1182894.html. June 21, 2009.

made several "deals with the devil," including one with the late mafia kingpin Rysbek Akmatbaev, in order to shore up his base of support in the north.[35] The president was also accused of framing his rival, Omurbek Tekebaev, who was caught in the Warsaw airport with heroin in his luggage. Tekebaev convinced the Polish authorities of his innocence and accused Kyrgyzstan's National Security Services and its deputy minister, Bakiev's brother Janysh, of planting the drugs.[36] A parliamentary commission later determined that Janysh Bakiev was complicit, and he resigned over the scandal.

At the societal level, corruption has persisted in the face of feeble attempts to reduce it. According to the November 2007 IRI survey, forty-seven percent of respondents said that corruption was at the same level as one year before, whereas thirty-eight percent said it had worsened.[37] These figures are echoed by Kyrgyzstan's decline on the Corruption Perceptions Index from 2.3 (world rank: 130) in 2005 to 1.8 (world rank: 166) in 2008.[38] Thus, old habits die hard.

Economic Stagnation

Bakiev made strengthening Kyrgyzstan's economy a priority when he took office, yet he found himself constrained by forces beyond his control. As in other former Soviet republics, a vast share of the nation's wealth belonged to a small number of individuals. Although there were demands to retrieve and redistribute resources more equitably, Bakiev tended to support the status quo rather than risk greater instability. The restoration of order after the chaos of March 2005 was sufficient to bring foreign direct investment in 2006 back to its (prerevolutionary) 2004 level, after a steep drop in 2005.[39] However, it did not signal fundamental changes that would improve the investment climate.

For the longer term, the odds are stacked against a major boost in economic growth or foreign investment. Bakiev inherited a foreign debt of almost US$2 billion and a level of per capita GDP that places Kyrgyzstan only slightly higher than most of Sub-Saharan Africa. The government's inability to protect property rights – as seen in the squatter standoff, for instance – did not helped to lure investors back. While he was prime minister, Kulov lent some confidence by introducing reforms that streamlined the process for registering businesses,

[35] Erica Marat, *The State–Crime Nexus in Central Asia: State Weakness, Organized Crime, and Corruption in Kyrgyzstan and Tajikistan* (Central Asia–Caucasus Institute & Silk Road Studies Program, 2006), Washington, DC, p. 91.

[36] "Kyrgyz Lawmakers Say Security Officers Framed Opposition Leader," *RFE/RL* (September 21, 2006), available at http://www.rferl.org/content/Article/1071529.html.

[37] "Kyrgyzstan National Poll," See fn 29.

[38] "2008 Corruption Perceptions Index," www.transparency.org, available at http://www.transparency.org/policy_research/surveys_indices/cpi/2008. June 21, 2009.

[39] *World Investment Report 2007*, United Nations Conference on Trade and Development (New York: United Nations, 2007).

lowering the tax rate, and redirecting government investment to stimulate the private sector. Yet the intermittent street protests and Kulov's own defection to the opposition still left investors wary. On the bright side, GDP growth rose from 3.1 percent in 2006 to 8.2 percent in 2007, though the low 2006 growth rate came in large part as a result of an accident at the Kumtor Goldmine, the source of Kyrgyzstan's largest export.[40] Kyrgyzstan was initially not hit as hard by the fall 2008 financial crisis as internationally integrated economies such as Kazakhstan's, but it soon began to suffer from the combined effects of high food prices, falling commodity prices, and reduced remittances from labor migrants in Russia.[41]

In the meantime, Kyrgyzstan remains largely dependent on external sources of income. Kyrgyzstan had a chance to reduce or eliminate its debt with the invitation to join the IMF's program for heavily indebted poor countries (HIPC). However, after the government initially favored joining the initiative, anti-HIPC street protests organized by a coalition of NGOs caused it to reject the offer. Instead, the Bakiev government has relied on rents, such as the reported $150 million and $207 million extracted from the United States in 2005 and 2006 for continued leasing rights to a U.S. air base outside of Bishkek.[42] External rents of this nature tend to increase corruption and impede, rather than promote, the reforms necessary for sustainable economic growth.[43]

One bit of positive news comes from the IRI survey, which interviewed respondents about changes in their personal economic situation. Of those surveyed, forty-one percent said that the financial situation of their households had improved "a lot" or "somewhat" compared to one year earlier, whereas forty-two percent said it remained the same. The positive responses appeared to be a result of increased wages and pensions and their timely payment, which reflect the country's overall economic growth.[44] However, respondents also overwhelmingly blame the government for high inflation, and particularly for the rise in food prices that buffeted the entire region at the end of 2007.[45]

---

[40] "Kyrgyz GDP Growth Quickens to 8.2 Pct in 2007," Reuters (January 15, 2008), available at http://in.reuters.com/article/asiaCompanyAndMarkets/idINL1544587420080115. June 21, 2009.

[41] "After the Boom," *The Economist* (October 30, 2008); Deirdre Tynan, "Central Asia: Kyrgyzstan, Tajikistan, and Uzbekistan Confront a Financial Disaster," eurasianet.org (November 10, 2008), available at http://eurasianet.org/departments/insightb/articles/eav111008.shtml. June 21, 2009.

[42] "Kyrgyz President Sees No Clash with PM," *Kommersant* (February 15, 2006).

[43] Jakob Svensson, "Foreign Aid and Rent-Seeking," *Journal of International Economics*, 51, No. 2 (August 2000), pp. 437–61; Elissaios Papyrakis and Reyer Gerlagh, "The Resource Curse Hypothesis and Its Transmission Channels," *Journal of Comparative Economics*, 32, No. 1 (March 2004), 181–93.

[44] "Kyrgyzstan National Poll," See fn 29.

[45] Parvina Hamidova, "Central Asia's Poorest States in Crisis," *Institute of War and Peace Reporting* (February 15, 2008), available at http://www.iwpr.net/?p=rca&s=f&o=342698&apc_state=henh. June 21, 2009.

III. CONTINUITIES FROM THE REVOLUTION TO ITS AFTERMATH: LOCALISM AND CLIENTELISM

It is no coincidence that the problems that Kyrgyzstan faced before and after the Tulip Revolution were so similar. The reason that mass mobilization took the form that it did, and that the pre- and post-Akaev periods show such continuity, is that the fundamental basis of Kyrgyz politics has not changed. Two elements – localism and clientelism – have long been central in Kyrgyz social life and continue to afflict the country to this day, keeping state capacity weak and thwarting meaningful reform. They are also, unfortunately, difficult to eradicate, short of sustained economic development or a generational replacement of elites.

Scholars of Central Asian politics have written much about "clans" to explain political competition at the elite level and account for the unique dynamics of regime development in the region.[46] However, clans do little to explain why people participated in mobilization at the village level. The activity of ordinary citizens in their own communities can be better understood with reference to the bonds of localism. Localism refers to the salience of ties among those in frequent contact within a community, and allegiance to elites from that community. People who work and socialize together on an everyday basis in normal times can also activate those networks to participate in and recruit others for mobilization in extraordinary times. Respondents in every area of my research indicated that such person-to-person interaction was a vital source of recruitment.[47]

Localism also explains the ease with which losing candidates were able to mobilize members of their communities. In any given district, the first protestors to rise up were the close associates of the disaffected candidates, acting not out of principle or anger at Akaev, but for reasons of personal interest – having their chosen candidate elected to parliament. These first movers then recruited their neighbors, who joined out of solidarity. In the interviews I conducted with protest veterans, I rarely met anyone who expressed affection for a regional, much less a national, political figure. Instead, people would voice support for "their" (local) candidate. Only once these rural mobilizing groups were absorbed into a broader struggle did protest leaders begin framing their demands in terms of democracy and freedom, and direct those demands to a national audience.

Informal local ties, which motivated a defeated candidate's close acquaintances, neighbors, and extended family to lend him support, are only part of the explanation. The other part is clientelism. Competitive candidates were

---

[46] See Edward Schatz, *Modern Clan Politics: The Power of "Blood" in Kazakhstan and Beyond*, (Seattle: University of Washington Press, 2004); Gulnoza Saidazimova, "Uzbekistan: Islam Karimov vs. the Clans," Eurasianet.org (April 23, 2005); Kathleen Collins, *Clan Politics and Regime Transition in Central Asia* (New York: Cambridge University Press, 2006).

[47] I conducted research on the Tulip Revolution in Jalalabad, Osh, and Bishkek in April–May 2005 and June–July 2006.

typically either wealthy or already in parliament, and they used their assets to deliver charity to their communities – in the form of communal buildings (sport complexes, mosques), repair of infrastructure (roads, sanitation), and cash handouts – to win support. These material contributions tied local bene-factors to (mostly rural) communities throughout Kyrgyzstan and gave their residents ample incentives to reciprocate when called upon to do so, whether by voting, demonstrating, or serving in other ways. Kyrgyzstan thus offered a friendly climate for localized outbreaks of protest.

Together, localism and clienteles not only inhibited the formation of network ties that cross local and regional boundaries – making national mobilization difficult – but also prevented the formation of cross-cutting ties that could facilitate party formation, generalized trust, and effective governance.[48] Elites rely on their local networks as a social support base, whereas impoverished communities demand assistance from the newly wealthy or powerful. Those who enter the legislature use it as a means of tapping the state to divert pri-vate goods to their constituencies (and line their own pockets), rather than to provide public goods (legislation) that benefit the national constituency.[49] Parliamentary deputies may enter into ad hoc friendships with each other, but their political incentives rarely align with the creation of supralocal organiza-tions, and any ideology they profess tends to be subordinate to satisfying their short-term material interest and the needs of their constituents/clients. Thus, even national parties hastily created to compete under the new PR system were marriages of convenience between elites sharing a personal affinity and having bases in different regions of the country, rather than blocs advocating coherent and distinct ideologies or policies.

The cross-regional network that overcame localism and brought about the Tulip Revolution was a temporary and strategic alliance of political and busi-ness elites. The PMK, by forging new ties and strengthening older ones, pro-vided a vehicle for mobilizing candidates to coordinate and coalesce into a coherent national network of anti-Akaev protesters. The PMK bridged Kyr-gyzstan's geographic fragmentation and resisted the government's attempts to neutralize the demonstrations individually. Its leaders helped to mediate between unacquainted candidates, finance transportation and provisions for demonstrators, and coordinate protest activities by mobile phone. This alliance held together just long enough to topple the government and then dissolved as rapidly as it had coalesced, yielding the fragmented social configuration that Bakiev has struggled to master.

---

48 Robert D. Putnam, *Making Democracy Work: Civic Traditions in Modern Italy*, (Princeton, NJ: Princeton University Press, 1993); Deepa Narayan, *Bonds and Bridges: Social Capital and Poverty*, Policy Research Working Paper Series, No. 2167 (Washington, DC: World Bank, 1999).

49 Herbert Kitschelt and Steven I. Wilkinson, "Citizen–Politician Linkages: An Introduction," in *Patrons, Clients, and Policies*, Herbert Kitschelt and Steven I. Wilkinson, eds. (New York: Cambridge University Press, 2007).

The forces that toppled the Akaev regime – politicians mobilizing their local followings – continued to bedevil Bakiev after the collapse. It took only two days for new groups of demonstrators to appear in Bishkek with fresh demands. The first were Akaev supporters who marched in from his home-town and clashed in the streets with revolutionaries who were still in Bishkek. In early April, a group of protestors from three cities stormed the Supreme Court building to lobby for five losing parliamentary candidates.[50] With the precedent established, "people power" became a tool wielded by influential actors eager to assert their demands while circumventing the flawed legal pro-cess. Street protests had the benefit of allowing those excluded by the new leadership to signal their displeasure, but the single-minded pursuit of power by scattered elites, of which mobilization is just a symptom, exacerbated many of the country's ills. It threatened the stability of Kyrgyzstan and deterred for-eign investors, prevented law enforcement from pursuing criminals who could hide behind the veil of populism, complicated the government's efforts to dis-tribute the country's resources more equitably, hindered efforts to rebuild a weak state, and sapped the government's legitimacy in favor of independent, local, and often criminal providers of public goods.

Rather than work with the boisterous opposition to seek solutions to com-mon problems, Bakiev decided to emasculate it. With his party nearly unop-posed in the legislature and the opposition fragmented, the president centralized power without addressing the underlying causes of opposition. By reducing the scope for the opposition to act through institutional channels and suppressing protests by force, Bakiev created the appearance of stability while increasing frustration with his rule. Kyrgyzstan's path to democracy, so promising in the early 1990s, remains blocked, while the chances for a new upheaval grow by the day, especially in the throes of an economic crisis and energy shortages.[51]

IV. THE ROLE OF EXTERNAL FACTORS

This essay has already assessed several factors thought to have contributed to the Tulip Revolution. The usual suspects, such as parties, civil society, and (in Central Asia) "clans," played little part either in providing a basis for mobilization or in toppling Akaev. But what about external influences? Bunce, McFaul, Stoner-Weiss, and Wolchik argue in this volume that externally driven factors – in particular, international assistance to build civil society and the diffusion of protest repertoires – should be considered in explaining the demo-cratic transitions included in this volume. They argue that post-Soviet states

---

[50] "Verkhovnii Sud Okazal'sya v Rukakh Storonnikov Proigravshikh Vybory Kandidatov," [The Supreme Court Ended Up in the Hands of Supporters of Losing Election Candidates]. www.akipress.org (April 25, 2005).

[51] "Kyrgyzstan: 1,500 Attend Anti-Government Rally," eurasianet.org (November 18, 2008), available at http://eurasianet.org/departments/insightb/articles/eav111808g.shtml. June 21, 2009.

shared certain structural features stemming from their common history, and that elite-level contacts and perceptions of commonality facilitated the diffusion of ideas across post-Soviet space.[52] Perhaps these influences compensated for Kyrgyzstan's wanting structural conditions.[53]

The crudest theory of external influence in revolutions – not endorsed by the authors in this volume, but worth addressing nonetheless – is the direct role of foreign governments. In Russia, it is presupposed that Western meddling, specifically a covert CIA plot to further U.S. interests, is behind the wave of regime change in the nearby abroad.[54] Like the accusations that focus on Ukraine and Georgia, the argument fails on its face and upon further scrutiny. Akaev was by no means anti-American (as such a theory would presume), as evidenced by his allowing the United States to open a base on Kyrgyz soil in 2001. As a small, resource-poor, and landlocked country, Kyrgyzstan's foreign policy is by necessity conciliatory toward all interested powers, including Russia, China, and the United States. There was no reason for the United States to believe that Kyrgyzstan's foreign policy under another president would serve American interests better.

The proof is in the pudding: Bakiev has been, if anything, more pro-Russian than Akaev was. Although he did not shut down the base, as Russia desired, he did leverage a higher rent from the U.S. government – twice. Furthermore, Kyrgyzstan under Bakiev has actively courted Russian investment, especially in the energy sector,[55] and the large number of Kyrgyz migrants in Russia has bound the two countries together. Kulov even went as far as to propose a confederation with Russia.[56]

A more plausible theory of Western influence asserts the importance of support from USAID and other countries' democracy promotion programs to civil society groups such as Freedom House, the National Democratic Institute, *Kmara*, and *Pora*.[57] Although it is true that the United States gave large amounts of democracy assistance to Kyrgyzstan because the country was more open and

---

[52] Valerie Bunce and Sharon Wolchik, "Favorable Conditions and Electoral Revolutions," *Journal of Democracy*, 17 (October 2006), pp. 5–18.

[53] Beissinger lists four structural factors as favorable for youth movements, if not revolution per se: "gross enrollment rates in tertiary education; infant mortality rates; oil exports; and political rights." Mark R. Beissinger, "Structure and Example in Modular Political Phenomena: The Diffusion of Bulldozer/Rose/Orange/Tulip Revolutions," *Perspectives on Politics*, 5 (June 2007), pp. 259–76.

[54] Typical is a Russian television documentary implicating the CIA, Western NGOs, and domestic opposition groups in installing pro-United States regimes. See Robert Coalson, "Why the Kremlin Likes the CIA," *RFE/RL* (October 1, 2007), available at http://www.rferl.org/content/article/1078841.html.

[55] "Kyrgyz–Russian Ties Could Affect US," *The Hill* (May 9, 2006).

[56] Venera Djumataeva, "Kyrgyzstan: Politicians Underline Pro-Russian Stances ahead of SCO Summit," *RFE/RL* (August 10, 2007), available at http://www.rferl.org/content/article/1078082.html. June 21, 2009.

[57] Mark R. Beissinger, "Promoting Democracy: Is Exporting Revolution a Constructive Strategy?" *Dissent* (Winter 2006), 84–9.

willing than its neighbors to receive it, NGOs never took root to the extent that they did in Ukraine and Georgia.[58] Despite a relatively high concentration of NGOs – by far the highest in Central Asia – Kyrgyzstan's civil society networks lacked the financial resources and organizational ability to reach outside of urban centers. They were mostly confined to Bishkek and regional capitals, where they were not able to serve the people who needed them most.

My fieldwork indicated that NGOs played a smaller role in the March events than it appeared at first glance. Although the preelection criticism of Akaev that appeared in the international press came from NGO leaders, they in fact played no part in mobilizing people in Jalalabad or Osh, and only an ancillary role in Bishkek, by helping to coordinate between mobilization leaders. In the south, most protestors were from rural areas and had little contact with NGOs. Only after these protestors began their sit-ins in the provincial centers did a small number of NGO activists arrive from Bishkek, whereupon they helped instruct leaders on protest tactics. NGOs reacted to events as they unfolded but were generally ill prepared to make a significant contribution.

Youth movements in particular were seen as a major component of previous revolutions.[59] An organization called Kel-kel ("Come on!") emerged in Kyrgyzstan shortly before the election and made itself known to the regime. It self-consciously modeled itself after the youth movements in previous "revolutions" but received no financial support or training from any of those groups, in large part because it had its eye on influencing the fall presidential election rather than the spring parliamentary contest.[60] Because Kel-kel attracted media attention in the period after the elections (in part because its members gave numerous interviews), it is worth recounting its activities, revealing the small impact it had on events. It attempted with limited success to organize students in Bishkek, held seminars about Akaev's political history, and handed out flags, banners, and lemons to generate publicity for its activities.[61] It organized one protest in Bishkek, in February, which received a dismal turnout,[62] and did not recruit outside the capital until after protests had already started, when it sent several activists to Jalalabad to organize students. Enthusiasm for a march around the southern city was low, and many strayed from the group after it

---

[58] Between 1992 and 2004, Kyrgyzstan received $94 million in democracy aid from the United States as part of the Freedom Support Act, including $12 million in 2004. See Curt Tarnoff, "US Assistance to the Former Soviet Union," *Congressional Research Service* (July 2005), p. 8; Craig S. Smith, "US Helped Prepare the Way for Kyrgyzstan's Uprising," *New York Times* (March 30, 2005).

[59] Julie A. Corwin, "Fledgling Youth Groups Worry Post-Soviet Authorities," eurasianet.org (April 11, 2005), available at http://www.eurasianet.org/departments/civilsociety/articles/pp041105.shtml; June 21, 2009. Valerie Bunce and Sharon Wolchik, "Youth and Electoral Revolutions in Slovakia, Serbia, and Georgia," *SAIS Review* 26 (Summer–Fall 2006), pp. 55–65.

[60] Author's interview with civil society activist, written correspondence.

[61] Lemons were intended to represent Kel-kel's choice of yellow to represent the opposition. It did not stick. Author's interview with Kel-kel activist, Bishkek.

[62] Author's interviews with Kel-kel leaders, Bishkek.

began. University students I spoke with reported being warned by administrators and teachers not to protest or risk being expelled. This threat, though empty, turned out to be effective, as students watched sympathetically from the sidelines as their older relatives and neighbors protested.[63] Youth groups, like the young generation of Kyrgyz, lacked the resources and the will to be "revolutionary."

One indirect influence from the West came in the form of "rights defenders" (*pravozashitniki*), a cohort of civil society activists that provided freelance advice on constitutional and civic matters. Rights defenders flourished in Kyrgyzstan's open and liberal climate in the 1990s and received generous funding from Western organizations. After mobilization began in 2005, they advised leaders in several cities about civil disobedience, which they had learned from their Western counterparts. After the fall of the south, several rights defenders acted as liaisons between the PMK and other leaders in Bishkek and marched together with the leaders of the rallies on March 23 and 24. Their knowledge was thus useful for the opposition in choosing protest tactics and acting in accordance with the law. However, as rights defenders came overwhelmingly from the urban intelligentsia, they did not always enjoy good relations with the rural politicians and the ex-*nomenklatura* elites who roused protests and exercised real power, and they were mostly sidelined in the aftermath of the revolution.[64]

Was there a demonstration effect from the earlier revolutionary successes in Serbia, Georgia, and Ukraine? Although this seems plausible on its face, the impact of this effect is also weaker than it appears. First, whereas activists from the earlier cases had passed on advice about monitoring elections and building opposition movements, there was much less contact with the smaller NGO sector in Kyrgyzstan, due to fewer existing connections and the lower expectations for Central Asia. A small number of cosmopolitan and activist politicians, such as Roza Otunbaeva, did communicate with activists in Georgia, and Otunbaeva had many contacts with the West as a former ambassador to the United Kingdom. Otunbaeva spoke openly of her wish for a color revolution in Kyrgyzstan.[65] However, as an urban intellectual without a political base, she played a primarily managerial role in the revolution. With the help of some NGOs, she led protests in Bishkek in January 2005 after being disqualified from running due to having been out of the country as an ambassador, but they faded away before the election and had little greater resonance. Otunbaeva eventually played an important role as a mediator between opposition factions and subleaders of the PMK.[66]

---

[63] Author's interviews with students, Jalalabad.

[64] Author's interviews with rights defenders, Bishkek, Jalalabad, Osh.

[65] "Kyrgyz President, Opposition Comment on Political Situation," eurasianet.org (February 3, 2005), available at http://www.eurasianet.org/resource/kyrgyzstan/hypermail/200502/0005.shtml.

[66] See "Kyrgyzstan's Tulip Revolution: Interview with Roza Otunbayeva," *Demokratizatsiya*, 13 (Fall 2005), pp. 483–9.

A second reason not to overestimate the influence of previous mass mobilizations is that Kyrgyzstan has a history of indigenous protest that predates the earliest post-Soviet revolution. Elite-led protests first broke out in 2000 in support of both Kulov and Usenov, who had been arrested after challenging Akaev for the presidency. In 2002, a massive protest movement emerged in a rural district of Jalalabad Province, also in defense of an imperiled parliamentarian, Azimbek Beknazarov, who was arrested after criticizing Akaev.[67] This event made the national news, especially after an incident in which six demonstrators were killed, and provided a training ground for some activists who would later participate in mobilization in 2005. Perhaps most important, it planted the idea in the minds of potential oppositionists that mobilization was an effective tactic for challenging the regime. If there was a demonstration effect, it came from a domestic, rather than international, source.

A third reason to doubt the effect of previous revolutions was the actions of the protest organizers themselves. Although it is difficult to get inside the minds of those leading mobilization, we can make some inferences based on their actions. Candidates did not know in advance who would lose in the first round, and many opposition candidates advanced to a runoff in the second round. The candidates who first mobilized, in early March – Jusupbek Jeenbekov in Jalalabad, Duishenkul Chotonov in Osh, Naken Kasiev in Naryn, and Ravshan Jeenbekov (no relation to Jusupbek) in Talas – were not part of a preexisting alliance or associated with the PMK. Their initial complaints were made to local election commissions regarding the votes in their districts; they were not about the president. For the first week, protests occurred in isolation, and their initial tentativeness and shifting tactics indicated that the protagonists were improvising.

The impact of previous revolutions was only felt later, as they indirectly influenced how mobilization was framed. After the failure of their initial claims, candidates joined with the PMK and let its leaders direct the movement. At that point – after second-round elections on March 13 – the PMK began to apply the color revolution template: unified goals and tactics, slogans employing lofty rhetoric, demands for the president's ouster, the adoption of tulips as the movement's symbol, broad recruitment to boost protest numbers, solicitation of coverage by the international media, and theatrics for television cameras and newspaper reporters, including burning a portrait of Akaev in the central square, deploying national symbols such as yurts and horses in public events, shouting slogans in unison, placing elders and women in prominent positions in the crowd, and confronting the police.[68]

The knowledge that the political turmoil in Kyrgyzstan would enjoy an international audience thanks to the Georgian and Ukrainian revolutions (rather than being dismissed as irrelevant, as events in Kyrgyzstan usually are) helped

[67] See Scott Radnitz, "Networks, Localism, and Mobilization in Aksy, Kyrgyzstan," *Central Asian Survey* 24 (December 2005), pp. 405–24.
[68] Author's interviews with protest participants, Jalalabad, Osh, and Bishkek.

embolden the opposition not to fear repression and may have aided in expanding the size of protests in Bishkek. The quick collapse of the government precluded any need to erect a "yurt city" in Bishkek's central square,[69] which would have been a dramatic sight; but by that time there was little doubt among the protesters that Kyrgyzstan should be accorded due respect for confounding the doubters who said that people power would never come to Central Asia. The dramatic final breakthrough in Bishkek showed how far the situation had evolved from the mobilization's obscure origins three weeks earlier.

CONCLUSION

Sadly, Kyrgyzstan may be no closer to consolidating democracy than it was in 2005, but neither is the situation as bad as it could have been. Unlike its Central Asian neighbors, pluralism is the order of the day in Kyrgyzstan. Even Bakiev's de jure concentration of power may be deceptive, and will likely hold only as long as he can persuade the public that he is making meaningful and positive changes.

Although street clashes between police and opposition protesters alarmed many observers, some of whom warned that Kyrgyzstan stood on the brink of civil war,[70] cooler heads have prevailed time and again. Protesters, including those who are bused into town and paid by self-serving (or criminal) elites, are often pensioners and poor farmers. They rarely have a personal stake in the outcome and are not prone to precipitate violence. The organizers themselves are loath to discredit their cause by contributing to the outbreak of violence.

The greatest factor preventing greater instability in Kyrgyzstan is the fluidity of political coalitions among the elite. Opportunism is the overriding consideration. For example, Kulov defected from the government to the opposition, whereas Almaz Atambaev, once an opposition leader, briefly agreed to work as Bakiev's prime minister. It is also worth noting that political factions do not overlap with other cleavages, such as the north–south divide. Although it is true that Bakiev is a southerner, four of his five prime ministers have been northerners, and one was an ethnic Russian. Likewise, Tekebaev, a leader of the opposition and a longtime personal rival of Bakiev, comes from Bakiev's own Jalalabad province and collaborates with northern elites to oppose him.

Although it will probably avoid the worst-case scenario, Kyrgyzstan is still afflicted by deeply rooted social realities that will continue to impede real movement toward democracy. One lesson common to "fourth wave" transitions is that progress requires a concerted effort by a large group of people – ideally, a national consensus – but the concentration of power can also be

---

[69] Author's interview, politician, Jalalabad.

[70] See, for example, Anatoly Medetsky, "Threat of a Kyrgyz Civil War Looms," *Moscow Times* (March 23, 2005); Jeremy Page, "Civil War Grows Closer as Kyrgyz Leaders Fall Out over Parliament," *Times Online* (March 28, 2005); ICG, "Kyrgyzstan on the Edge." ICG (November 9, 2006).

used for authoritarian purposes.[71] On the other hand, a lack of agreement among political elites can lead to gridlock and instability. The new leaderships of Georgia and Ukraine, which came to power riding a wave of optimism and inherited fairly propitious starting conditions, have laid bare the setbacks that can put an end to postrevolutionary euphoria: Georgia's leadership has sought to stifle pluralism and Ukraine, though more democratic, has been plagued by factional infighting.[72] The "honeymoon" for Kyrgyzstan's leadership was the shortest of all and the barriers to reform remain the most formidable. It is possible, now that Bakiev faces limited opposition, that he will finally begin to tackle Kyrgyzstan's chronic problems and use his preponderance of power to implement changes to improve the lives of ordinary people, but past experience makes this unlikely. Kyrgyzstan, like many other states, has long lingered in the gray zone between democracy and dictatorship and, "revolution" aside, has demonstrated a remarkable ability in its short history as an independent state to simply muddle through.

[71] Michael McFaul, "The Fourth Wave of Democracy *and* Dictatorship." *World Politics*, 54, No. 2 (2002), pp. 212–44.
[72] Henry E. Hale, "Democracy or Autocracy on the March? The Colored Revolutions as Normal Dynamics of Paternal Presidential," *Communist and Post-communist Studies*, 39, No. 3 (September 2006), pp. 305–29; Asatiani, "Colored Revolutions."

Epilogue

The Changing Character of the Global Struggle for Democracy

Valerie Bunce, Michael McFaul, and Kathryn Stoner-Weiss

THREE PUZZLES

The purpose of this volume has been to bring together a group of scholars with diverse areas of topical and geographical expertise to analyze variations over time and across country in regime trajectories in postcommunist Europe and Eurasia since the collapse of communism two decades ago. Our interest in this subject was motivated by our collective desire to address three puzzles posed not just by the postcommunist experience, but also, more generally, by regime transitions around the globe.

First, what explains the wide range of regime-types that formed after communism – a dynamic that is particularly surprising in view of a shared communist past and the extraordinarily invasive nature of the communist experiment? Although some new regimes in the region were fully democratic and some fully authoritarian, the dominant tendency in the early years after communism was the rise of hybrid regimes that straddled democracy and dictatorship and that reflected a compromise between authoritarians and democrats, with neither player able to dictate their preferred version of the rules of the political game.[1] This is precisely the pattern, moreover, that we have seen in other countries that experienced transitions from authoritarian rule at the same time or later in the third wave of democratization.[2]

---

[1] Valerie Bunce, "The Political Economy of Postsocialism," *Slavic Review*, 58, No. 4 (Winter, 1999), pp. 756–93; Michael McFaul, "The Fourth Wave of Democracy and Dictatorship: Non-cooperative Transitions in the Postcommunist World." *World Politics*, 54, No. 2 (January 2002), pp. 212–44.

[2] Steven Levitsky and Lucan Way, "Competitive Authoritarianism: The Origins and Evolution of Hybrid Regimes in the Post–Cold War Era," Unpublished book manuscript (2007); "Thinking about Hybrid Regimes." *Journal of Democracy*, 13, No. 2 (2002); Axel Hadenius and Jan Teorell, "Pathways from Authoritarianism." *Journal of Democracy*, 18, No. 1 (2007), p. 143.

Second, to borrow from Marx's evocative characterization of capitalism, these hybrid regimes showed themselves to be unusually "restless" over time. Although some became more democratic, with Bulgaria (though starting relatively democratic), Romania, Slovakia, and Ukraine providing examples, albeit through different pathways (as our chapters by Petrova, Vachudova, Mungiu-Pippidi, Bunce and Wolchik, and McFaul discuss), others became more authoritarian. Here, the case of Russia under Putin and Medvedev looms large, though this description would also fit what happened in Serbia, Slovakia, and Ukraine in the years leading up to the pivotal elections that brought democratic oppositions to power (see, especially, Bunce and Wolchik, McFaul and Stoner-Weiss in this volume).[3] At the same time, these hybrid regimes, like hybrid regimes more generally, exhibited other forms of political instability.[4] They were often located in weak states, where, for example, secessionist regions challenged existing borders and interactions between majorities and minorities were often tense and sometimes violent. The relationship between weak states and hybrid regimes, of course, is far from accidental. Just as deficits in state capacity contributed to the inability of either democracy or authoritarianism to triumph, the mixed character of the regime undermined the ability of governments to define and defend borders and to establish coercive and administrative hegemony within those borders. The Serbian experience under Milošević and Georgia under Shevardnadze are two cases in point (and see the chapters by Bunce and Wolchik and by Welt in this volume).

A final puzzle that motivated our analyses was the wavelike character of democratic change in the postcommunist region – a dynamic of democratic change that has been shown to be characteristic, more generally, of the spread of democracy during the Third Wave.[5] Democratic changes in this region have tended to "bunch" in terms of both time and space, with clusters of countries (but far from all the countries in the region) exhibiting not just democratic progress within a limited period of time, but also the use of surprisingly similar methods of countering authoritarian rule. What is nonetheless distinctive to the postcommunist region and a pattern that provides an unusual comparative opportunity, however, is that there have been in fact *three* waves of democratic change in this region over the past twenty years. The first wave, which was tied to the collapse of communism and communist states, was characterized by

---

[3] Also see Michael McFaul and Kathryn Stoner-Weiss, "The Myth of the Authoritarian Model: How Putin's Crackdown Holds Russia Back," *Foreign Affairs*, 87 (January–February 2008).

[4] David L. Epstein, Robert Bates, Jack Goldstone, Ida Kristensen, and Sharyn O'Halloran, "Democratic Transitions." *American Journal of Political Science*, 50, No. 3 (2006), pp. 551–69; Philip Roessler and Marc M. Howard, "Post-Cold-War Political Regimes: When Do Elections Matter/" In *Democratization by Elections: A New Mode of Transition?* Staffan Lindberg, ed. (Johns Hopkins University Press, 2009); Jan Teorell and Axel Hadenius, "Elections as Levers of Democracy? A Global Inquiry," Lindberg, ed *Democratization by Elections*.

[5] Brinks, Daniel and Michael Coppedge, "Diffusion Is No Illusion: Neighbor Emulation in the Third Wave of Democracy." *Comparative Political Studies*, 39, No. 4 (May 2006), pp. 463–89.

the cross-national spread of mass protests and the use in some cases of pacts between communists and the liberal opposition to break with communism and to build a liberal political and economic order (see McFaul and Bunce and Wolchik chapters in Part I). By contrast, in the next wave we see a rather different dynamic: European Union (EU) expansion and conditionality associated with membership in that body and the ability of the EU to strengthen democratic forces within the countries of Eastern and Central Europe that became members of the EU in 2004 and 2007 (with the Baltic states, Poland, Hungary, the Czech Republic, Slovakia, and Slovenia entering in the first wave and Bulgaria and Romania in the second). Here, the chapters in Section II by Vachudova and Mungiu-Pippidi assess this wave, though differing somewhat in their assessment of the impact of the EU on democratic development.

What is fascinating about these waves of democratic change is not just their differences from one another, but also their similarities. All three waves nudged a number of countries in a democratic direction and sometimes produced veritable leaps from dictatorship to democracy. Moreover, they did not always produce democratic improvements, with the chapters on Georgia and Kyrgyzstan by Corey Welt and Scott Radnitz respectively providing cases in point. Finally, there were holdouts against each wave, with regimes that resisted joining the trend responding to the democratic threat by becoming more authoritarian (see the essays in this volume by Stoner-Weiss, Silitski, and Way). Of course, this is one reason that there were three waves, instead of one, with the successive waves in effect picking up some of the region's laggards in democratization. However, the question remains of why some countries participated in these waves of democratic change, why others did not, and, finally, why the waves themselves had different local consequences.

MAJOR CONCLUSIONS: THE SOURCES OF REGIME CHANGE

It is these three puzzles, therefore, that provided the starting point for this volume. The question then becomes the following: Once we pooled our insights and analyzed postcommunist pathways over the past twenty years, what did we learn about regime formation, stability, and change? Although each chapter is rich in insights about these questions, we would highlight in particular six conclusions that speak not just to patterns in the postcommunist region, but also to the global project of regime transitions.

First, regime transitions take place because of the confluence of three main factors. The first is domestic struggle between authoritarians and democrats. This is a dynamic that served as the sole focus in early studies of transitions from authoritarian rule and one that is best understood, in contrast to those studies, as a matter not just of short-term developments, but also of the lessons learned and the resources distributed and redistributed as a result of long-term interactions between these two sets of players that shaped the ability of both sides to bargain more or less effectively on behalf of their regime preferences and, what is more, to take advantage of shifting opportunities for political change (see the two chapters by Bunce and Wolchik and by McFaul, along with Way).

However, this struggle does not take place in a vacuum. Here, we discovered that we need to bring into the equation two other factors that were downplayed in earlier studies of regime transitions, but that proved to be critical not just in the postcommunist region and other later participants in the Third Wave, but also in fact in Latin America and Southern Europe – the very regions that informed analyses of the early studies of democratic change. The first of these add-on influences is short-term changes in the international system, which fill in some of the blanks provided by the phrase we used above: "shifting opportunities for political change." In particular, one can hardly understand the region-wide collapse of communism and the expanding window of opportunity for democratization without understanding the structure of the Soviet bloc, Gorbachev's ambitious program of domestic and international reforms in the Soviet Union, and the region-wide consequences, planned and unanticipated, of the Soviet reform dynamic. We also cannot make sense of the second round of democratic change without referring to the resources and incentives provided by the EU and NATO. Finally, although struggles on the ground were decisive in the third wave of democratic change in this region, these struggles, including the mechanisms used to counter authoritarian power and the resources enjoyed by those challenging authoritarian rule, cannot be understood in the absence of the contributions to free, fair, and increasingly competitive elections provided by Western democracy assistance and by transnational democracy promotion networks that brought together local, regional, and Western democracy activists in a common mission.[6]

The importance of the international environment in regime transitions, therefore, is at once considerable, yet variable in its forms – ranging from reduced external support for authoritarian governments, the cross-national spread of new democratic models, and an expansion of major incentives for regime change to the influx of new resources for democratic development and demonstration effects that encourage neighboring countries to emulate precedents set in other countries. However, when all this is recognized, it is important to add two amendments to this observation. One is that international events, political opportunities, technical and financial resources, models, and political precedents were influential in the regime game only insofar as they had direct consequences for the preferences and resources of players on the ground, including those who defended the regime and those who challenged it. The other is that international influences should not be reduced to short-term effects. For example, as the chapters by McFaul and Bunce and Wolchik in Section I and by Petrova, Welt, McFaul, and Bunce and Wolchik in Section III argue in concert, long-term changes in international influences also mattered – for

---

[6] This is elaborated by Valerie Bunce and Sharon Wolchik in *American Democracy Promotion and Electoral Change in Postcommunist Europe and Eurasia*, forthcoming Cambridge University Press.

instance, the loosening over time of Soviet control over Eastern Europe during the cold war and, after the cold war, long-term investments by the United States and other international actors in civil society development.

This leads to the final major factor shaping regime change: changes in the behavior of citizens. It is obvious that such shifts played a key role in the first and the third waves of democratic change, given their willingness in the first case to take to the streets in large numbers and in the second their willingness to support the opposition in elections and, where necessary, to defend their choice in the streets when authoritarian leaders or their anointed successors refused to admit to defeat. However, citizens also played a critical role in EU expansion. For example, it was in the electoral interest of politicians in most of these countries to support membership in both the EU and NATO, precisely because such membership was widely viewed as politically popular. As Alina Mungiu-Pippidi has argued in this volume though, such support was in some ways transitory.

TRANSITION OUTCOMES

If regime transitions are best understood as a product of the balance of power between authoritarians and democrats, changes in international opportunities and resources, and shifts in the preferences and political actions of citizens, then how can we link this constellation of factors to variations in regime formation? Here, we would argue that democracy seems to require three developments: strong (or at least strengthening) democrats and weakening authoritarians, expanded international opportunities for and support of democratic change, and citizens willing and able to express visible support for the democratic opposition over authoritarian forces. Meeting all three requirements is a tall order. At the same time, however, authoritarian outcomes materialize when all three factors work against democratic change. For example, in the Russian case since 2000, we see strong authoritarians, divided democrats, and limited international pressures for democratic change combined with substantial external resources supporting the regime as a result of oil and gas prices, and publics that are largely demobilized, except for some "pocket protests" that focus more on public policy than on the right of the regime to rule (see Stoner-Weiss in this volume).[7] Finally, it is in the case of mixed regimes where we see, not surprisingly, a "mixed" picture. For example, in contemporary Ukraine, we find a balance among citizens that somewhat favors democrats, but also publics divided with respect to the advisability of closer ties with the West versus Russia – a division that translates easily into high levels of political competition and governmental instability (see McFaul's Chap. 8 in this volume).[8]

[7] Jay Lyall, "Pocket Protests: Rhetorical Coercion and the Micropolitics of Collective Action in Semiauthoritarian Regimes." *World Politics*, 58, No. 3 (April 2006), pp. 378–412.
[8] Stephen White and Ian McAllister, "Belarus, Ukraine (and Russia): East or West?" Paper presented at the 39th Annual Convention of the AAASS, New Orleans, November 15–18, 2007.

REGIME FLUCTUATIONS

As the essays in this volume made clear, regime formation in many cases is just the beginning of the postcommunist regime transition story. Once we view the region from the vantage of twenty years, we make three discoveries. One is that the countries that began the transition by forming full-scale democratic or dictatorial orders (with the latter including Turkmenistan, Uzbekistan, and Tajikistan) have remained in these two categories – though Slovakia was in danger of becoming the exception to the democratic rule until Mečiar was defeated in 1998 and Bulgaria also faced the same possibility until its 1997 election (see Petrova in this volume).[9] Thus, both dictatorship and democracy have been very "sticky" since the beginning of the postcommunist era – a conclusion that is far from surprising, given, for example, Robert Dahl's analysis of the durability of democracy more than three and one-half decades ago and the pronounced tendency of transitions from authoritarian rule to lead to the formation of new authoritarian systems.[10]

Second, change has occurred largely in hybrid regimes – which is also not surprising in view of the global characteristics of these systems.[11] In these contexts, any number of developments have materialized, ranging from leaps into the democratic category (as with Serbia and Croatia after 2000) to what are more accurately characterized as strolls (as with Albania); a shift in political dynamics favoring democratic over authoritarian politics (Macedonia and, distinctive in the post-Soviet region, Ukraine since 2004); a steady state, though one demonstrating some and sometimes significant political turnovers (with Georgia and Kyrgzstan a case of the "some" category and Moldova an example of repeated turnovers);[12] and decided shifts in an authoritarian direction (as with Kyrgyzstan under Akayev and Armenia, Azerbaijan, Belarus, Kazakhstan, and Russia).

The question then becomes why hybrid regimes are so unstable over time and why they shift in different political directions. The essays in this volume provide several answers. First and most generally: hybrid regimes, precisely because they result from fragile compromises between democrats and authoritarians and because they tend to be located in weak states, are prone to political shifts. Second, most of the hybrid regimes that moved in a democratic direction benefited from participation in the waves of democratic change of interest in this volume – participation that reflected democratizing influences in their

---

[9] Venelin I. Ganev, *Preying on the State: The Transformation of Bulgaria after 1989*, (Ithaca: Cornell University Press, 2007).

[10] Robert Dahl, *Polyarchy: Participation and Opposition*, (New Haven, CT: Yale University Press) and Hadenius and Teorell, "Pathways from Authoritarianism."

[11] Philip G. Roessler and Marc M. Howard, "Post-Cold-War Political Regimes: When Do Elections Matter?" In Lindberg, *Democratization by Elections*.

[12] For an especially illuminating analysis of the Moldovan case, see Alina Mungiu-Pippidi, "Disputed Identity as Inescapable Pluralism: Moldova's Ambiguous Transition," Paper presented at the Project on Democratic Transitions, Foreign Policy Research Institute, February 8, 2007.

immediate neighborhood, the failure of authoritarian leaders to institutionalize their powers, and the formation of durable coalitions between external democracy promoters and local oppositions that facilitated, in turn, mobilization of citizens in support of democratic change (see, especially, Way in this volume and Bunce and Wolchik and McFaul on Ukraine in Chap. 8).[13]

Third, the ability of leaders to prolong their rule played a key role in strengthening authoritarian features of hybrid regimes. Long periods in office reflect in part control over elections, the media, and public spaces and the ability of leaders to carry out self-serving amendments to the constitution (as we are seeing in Russia today and as we saw in Belarus under Lukashenka and Azerbaijan under the Aliyev family). However, another reason was the design of political institutions early in the transition, with strong presidents and weak legislatures and courts supporting authoritarian development (as Kathryn Stoner-Weiss argues in her chapter).[14]

Finally, dependence on rents from natural resource exports contributes to the consolidation of authoritarian rule. This is especially the case if the regime already has authoritarian features in place; if world energy prices are rising; and if the regime has full control over the money earned from sale of energy products abroad.[15] This factor helps explain (although does not fully explain), for example, the shift toward authoritarianism in Russia, Kazakhstan, and Azerbaijan.

SIMILARITIES AND DIFFERENCES AMONG THE THREE WAVES

As we noted in our introductory essay, this book has been organized around three waves of democratic change, with the first associated with the collapse of communism and communist states; the second associated with accession to the EU; and the third involving electoral challenges to authoritarian rule. There is little doubt that all three waves were examples of the diffusion of democratic change, given their common focus on a project of breaking with authoritarian politics and empowering democratic oppositions and given, at the same time, the cross-national spread in each wave of similar drivers of

---

[13] Also see Lucan Way, "The Real Causes of the Color Revolutions." *Journal of Democracy*, 19, No. 3 (2008), versus Valerie Bunce and Sharon Wolchik, "Getting Real about Real Causes." *Journal of Democracy*, 20, No. 1 (2009).

[14] Valerie Bunce and Sharon Wolchik, "Mixed Regimes in Postcommunist Eurasia: Tipping Democratic and Tipping Authoritarian," Paper presented at the Workshop on "Democratization in European Former Soviet Republics: Limits, Obstacles and Perspectives," Florence, Italy, June 13–15, 2008.

[15] See, for example, Ben Smith, "Oil Wealth and Regime Survival in the Developing World, 1960 to 1999." *American Journal of Political Science*, 48, No. 2 (2004), pp. 234–46; Kevin Morrison, "Oil, Non-tax Revenue, and the Redistributive Foundations of Regime Stability," *International Organization* (forthcoming, 2009); Pauline Jones Luong and Erika Weinthal, "Rethinking the Resource Curse: Ownership Structure, Institutional Capacity and Domestic Constraints." *Annual Review of Political Science*, 9 (June 2006), pp. 241–63.

diffusion.[16] At the same time, we see a similar pattern in all three instances of less than full participation of all the countries composing the region (as noted by Way, Stoner-Weiss and Silitski) and diffusion moving from ideal circumstances, where democratic gains were considerable, to less ideal circumstances, where democratic progress was far more mixed – for example, the contrast in the first wave between Poland and Bulgaria (Bunce and Wolchik in Part 1 and Petrova Part III); in the second wave between countries that entered the EU in the first round and in the second (Vachudova); and in the third wave between Slovakia and Serbia, on the one hand, and Ukraine and especially Georgia and Kyrgyzstan, on the other (Bunce and Wolchik, McFaul, and Welt and Radnitz).

However, these similarities aside, it is important to recognize that these three waves were not identical. Most obviously, they varied in terms of country sites, though Bulgaria and Slovakia managed to straddle several waves. In addition, and not as obviously, the approach to democratic change varied. It ranged from protests and the lure of membership in the EU to elections. In addition, the drivers of diffusion were somewhat different, with demonstration effects paramount in the first wave and more conscious collaborations between local and international actors more important in the second and third. Finally, it is fair to say that, although the focus of the first wave was on ending dictatorships and the second wave on consolidating democracy, the final wave – that is, electoral defeats of authoritarian leaders – had more complex agendas, depending upon regime context. Thus, although the 2000 election in Serbia ended authoritarian rule and the 1998 Slovak election put an end to a dangerous episode of dedemocratization, the Bulgarian election of 1997 consolidated a largely democratic polity.

This brief comparison of our three waves contains two general lessons. One is that this region seems to be unusually prone to diffusion effects, with this tradition in fact going back to 1848. The other is that the use of the term "diffusion," although highlighting common patterns, can nonetheless obscure significant differences in goals, processes and outcomes.

MODES OF TRANSITION

Our discussion of the three waves of democratic change noted that, although international influences and mobilization of citizens were important in each, the modes of transition were nonetheless somewhat different. In particular, the third wave was distinctive in using elections (sometimes in combination with mass protests either before the election, as in Bulgaria, or after the election, as in Serbia, Georgia, Ukraine, and Kyrgyzstan) to break with authoritarianism

---

[16] For a more systematic analysis of why diffusion describes these waves of change, see Valerie Bunce and Sharon Wolchik, "Transnational Networks, Diffusion Dynamics, and Electoral Change in the Postcommunist World," Paper presented at the Institute for the Social Sciences seminar at Cornell University, March 25, 2008.

and to bring democratic oppositions to power. As a result, and especially in view of the role of elections more generally as important sites for democratic development in this region and around the world, we would draw the following implications.[17] First, elections should be added to the two other, more commonly cited modes of democratic transition: mass mobilizations through demonstrations and strikes and pacts about regime change crafted by authoritarians and democrats.[18] Second, like these two more familiar modes, elections carry no guarantees about subsequent democratic progress.[19] Even elections that led to the removal of dictators from office still had to confront sizeable constraints on democratic change. These included whether the victors were in fact democrats (which was a problem in Georgia and Kyrgyzstan), whether the victory of the opposition depended upon leaving the coercive apparatus supporting the dictator largely in place, whether electoral outcomes signaled decisive or more mixed support for regime change favoring democracy (which was problematic in Serbia, Ukraine, and Kyrgyzstan), and, finally, whether the elections served as a pretext for seizing power through extralegal means after parliamentary contests rather than winning power through presidential elections (as in Georgia and Kyrgyzstan).[20]

Thus, although important in providing opportunities for democratic change, electoral breakthroughs may not be, especially in the short-term, democratic breakthroughs. In some ways, this is not surprising. Hybrid regimes combine elements of democracy and dictatorship for a reason, and their costs with respect to political instability, weak states, and poor economic performance do not go away simply because of a change in government.

Finally, although distinctive, electoral modes of transition also remind us that the democratic project must always be flexible. In particular, it can be argued that the political context is the key to understanding why some modes are selected over others. Elections were out of the question in the first wave, because of the way communism worked; they became attractive vehicles for democratic change in the third wave, as a result of the political design of competitive authoritarian regimes (see Way in this volume).[21] However, as Russia and its authoritarian allies in the region remind us, the window of opportunity

---

[17] Teorell and Hadenius, "Elections as Levers of Democracy?" Valerie Bunce,"Global Patterns and Postcommunist Dynamics," *Orbis*, 50, No. 4 (2006), pp. 601–20.

[18] Lindberg, ed., *Democratization by Elections*.

[19] See, for example, Pauline Jones Luong, *Institutional Change and Political Continuity in Post-Soviet Central Asia: Power, Perception and Pacts*, (New York: Cambridge University Press, 2002).

[20] On the structural limitations on democratic progress after electoral breakthroughs, in part because of dynamics leading to these electoral shifts, see, for example, Henry Hale, "Regime Cycles, Democracy, Autocracy and Revolution in Post-Soviet Eurasia." *World Politics*, 58 (October, 2005), pp. 133–65 and Milos Vasic, *Attentat na Zorana*, (Belgrade: Politika/Vreme/B-92, 2005).

[21] Andreas, Schedler. *Electoral Authoritarianism: The Dynamics of Unfree Competition*, (Boulder, CO: Rienner, 2006).

for using elections can close very quickly (see Stoner-Weiss and Silitski in this volume). In that case, one often sees a reversion to earlier forms of challenges to authoritarian rule – for example, the recent interest by the Russian opposition in learning from the Solidarity experience in Poland during the communist era.[22] In this way, interestingly enough, the waves of democratization and the modes of transition they have embraced have turned full circle.

THE CHANGING NATURE OF STRUGGLES FOR DEMOCRACY

One decided benefit of looking at one region that shares a communist past, although with subsequent and frequent regime fluctuations over two decades, is that we are in a good position to reflect about the changing nature of democracy and authoritarianism more generally. Here, we can note, first, some continuities over time in how the struggle for democracy has been waged. These include the pivotal role of international influences, struggles between democrats and authoritarians, and mobilization and demobilization of publics, along with the stickiness of both dictatorship and democracy, the pronounced tendency of hybrid regimes to move between the poles represented by full-scale democracies and authoritarian orders, and the accumulation, as noted above, of alternative models for challenging authoritarian rule that can be recycled, depending upon domestic and international circumstances. That recognized, however, the essays in this volume reveal two important changes.

One is that we have seen a polarization of regime types – a dynamic that has also occurred in the larger world beyond the postcommunist region. Although much has been made in the last few years of resurgent authoritarianism, this must be combined with the other side of the story; that is, the resilience of fully free polities, to use the language of Freedom House. Thus, what we have seen in fact is an emptying out of the middle category, though somewhat in the favor of growing authoritarianism. In some ways, as already noted, this was predictable. Just as democrats have been emboldened by waves of democratic change, so these waves have advantaged authoritarians intent on consolidating their powers. They have been, in short, forewarned and forearmed in the face of waves of democratic change.

The other trend that we have discovered is that the role of the international system in democratization has changed. In the first wave, the spread of popular mobilizations against communist dictatorships occurred not just because of long struggles at home and the ways in which the structure of the communist bloc facilitated the cross-national movement of reform and protests, but also because of a loosening of the strictures on democratic change as a result of changes in East–West relations and Gorbachev's reforms. However, in the next two waves, a permissive international environment had ratcheted up to one

[22] Amy Knight, "The Truth about Putin and Medvedev," *New York Review of Books*, 55, No. 8 (May 15, 2008), pp. 11–14.

featuring much more activist interventions in favor of democratic change, with assistance from the EU, U.S. government–funded democracy promoters, and private foundations anchored in the West. However, these differences aside and recognizing at the same time that Western support of democratization was always uneven as a result of what Levitsky and Way term variations in linkage and leverage, the fact remains that in all three waves the international environment was skewed in the direction (in less or more active terms) of supporting democratic development. However, with the Orange Revolution in Ukraine in 2004, the international context of regime change shifted. As the chapters in this volume by Stoner-Weiss, Radnitz, and Silitski suggest, authoritarian leaders, such as Putin and Medvedev in Russia, began to combine their assaults on democracy at home with more concerted actions abroad to support authoritarian allies in their neighborhoods. Put simply, the international game of regime change expanded to include them, as well as the West. This leads us to close this book with an irony. The global march of democracy has stalled, in part because the international struggle for regime change, in collaboration with domestic struggles, has become a much more competitive process.

Index

Congressional Representation & Constituents

The U.S. House of Representatives has been frozen at 435 members for almost a century, and in that time the nation's population has grown by more than 200 percent. With the number of citizens represented by each House member now dramatically larger, is a major consequence of this historical disparity a diminished quality of representation?

Brian Frederick uses empirical data to scrutinize whether representation has been undermined by keeping a ceiling on the number of seats available in the House. He examines the influence of constituency size on several metrics of representation—including estimating the effects on electoral competition, policy responsiveness, and citizen contact with and approval of their representatives—and argues that now is the time for the House to be increased in order to better represent a rapidly growing country.

Brian Frederick is an assistant professor of political science at Bridgewater State College in Massachusetts.

Controversies in Electoral Democracy and Representation
Matthew J. Streb, Series Editor

The Routledge series *Controversies in Electoral Democracy and Representation* presents cutting edge scholarship and innovative thinking on a broad range of issues relating to democratic practice and theory. An electoral democracy, to be effective, must show a strong relationship between representation and a fair open election process. Designed to foster debate and challenge assumptions about how elections and democratic representation *should* work, titles in the series present a strong but fair argument on topics related to elections, voting behavior, party and media involvement, representation, and democratic theory.

Titles in the series:

Rethinking American Electoral Democracy
Matthew J. Streb

Redistricting and Representation: Why Competitive Elections Are Bad for America
Thomas L. Brunell

Fault Lines: Why the Republicans Lost Congress
Edited by Jeffery J. Mondak and Dona-Gene Mitchell

In Defense of Judicial Elections
Chris W. Bonneau and Melinda Gann Hall

Congressional Representation & Constituents: The Case for Increasing the U.S. House of Representatives
Brian Frederick

Forthcoming:
Can Presidential Primaries Be Reformed?
Barbara Norrander

Helping America Vote: The Limits of Election Reform
Martha E. Kropf and David C. Kimball